The Pina Bausch

Pina Bausch's work has had tremendous impact across the spectrum of late twentieth-century performance practice, helping to redefine the possibilities of what both dance and theater can be. This edited collection presents a compendium of source material and contextual essays that examine Pina Bausch's history, practice and legacy, and the development of Tanztheater as a new form, with sections including:

- Dance and theatre roots and connections.
- Bausch's developmental process.
- The creation of Tanztheater.
- Bausch's reception.
- Critical perspectives.

Interviews, reviews and major essays chart the evolution of Bausch's pioneering approach and explore this evocative new mode of performance. Edited by noted Bausch scholar, Royd Climenhaga, *The Pina Bausch Sourcebook* aims to open up Bausch's performative world for students, scholars, dance and theatre artists and audiences everywhere.

Royd Climenhaga is on the Arts Faculty at Eugene Lang College/The New School University in New York City. He writes on intersections between dance and theatre, including the book *Pina Bausch* in Routledge's Performance Practitioner series, and develops and produces new performance work as Co-Artistic Director of Human Company.

Figure 1 Café Müller (1978): Pina Bausch. © Ursula Kaufmann

The Pina Bausch Sourcebook

The Making of Tanztheater

Edited by Royd Climenhaga

Routledge
Taylor & Francis Group

LONDON AND NEW YORK

First published 2013
by Routledge
2 Park Square, Milton Park, Abingdon, Oxon OX14 4RN

Simultaneously published in the USA and Canada by Routledge
711 Third Avenue, New York, NY 10017

*Routledge is an imprint of the Taylor & Francis Group, an informa
business*

British Library Cataloguing in Publication Data
A catalogue record for this book is available from the British
Library

Library of Congress Cataloguing in Publication Data
The Pina Bausch sourcebook : the making of Tanztheater / edited
by Royd Climenhaga.
p. cm.
Includes bibliographical references and index.
1. Bausch, Pina. 2. Choreographers – Germany – Biography.
3. Tanztheater (Wuppertal, Germany) – History. 4. Modern
dance – Germany – Wuppertal – History. I. Climenhaga,
Royd, 1963-
GV1785.B349P5695 2012
792.8'2092 – dc23
[B]
2012007954

ISBN: 978-0-415-61801-4 (hbk)
ISBN: 978-0-415-61802-1 (pbk)
ISBN: 978-0-203-12524-3 (ebk)

Typeset in Times
by Taylor & Francis

Printed and bound by CPI Group (UK) Ltd, Croydon, CR0 4YY

This book is dedicated to the ongoing spirit of
Pina Bausch and the creative energy her work continues
to bring to the world

Contents

x *Contents*

Figures

All photographs © Ursula Kaufmann, Albrechtstraße 19, 45130 Essen/ Germany, www.ursulakaufmann.de

Acknowledgements

Pina Bausch and Tanztheater Wuppertal have provided me with nothing but warmth and support, and I am proud to help keep this important artist's legacy alive. Bausch's passing has been a blow to the artistic community around the world, and a loss for me personally as well. I feel fortunate to have met her, spoken with her and received her interest over the years. This book was helped along by support and interest from the Pina Bausch Foundation, and I want to thank Salomon Bausch and Marc Wagenbach particularly for their kindness and help. Sabine Hesseling and Felicitas Willems at Tanztheater Wuppertal were also both very helpful and I am indebted to them for their assistance.

Thanks also to the many authors I contacted to secure permission to publish their work. Many expressed their interest in helping to keep Bausch's legacy alive, and either waived or reduced their fees to help include a broader spectrum of voices in this book. Thanks to Mindy Aloff, head of the Dance Critics Association, who helped put me in touch with several American authors, and I especially want to thank Anna Kisselgoff, whose help in negotiating with the *New York Times* and personal generosity made it possible to include her important work on Bausch in this volume. Other specific credits are supplied with each essay.

Thanks to Ellen Cremer for her fluid and elegant translation work with me on the Raimund Hoghe essay, and to Mr Hoghe for his kindness and for allowing me to retranslate and include his seminal portrait of Bausch's rehearsal process in this book. At Routledge, Talia Rodgers has long shown an interest in my work and Ben Piggott was very helpful in preparing this manuscript.

Thanks to my colleagues and especially my students at Eugene Lang College, The New School for the Liberal Arts. They have all provided me with amazing support and encouragement that goes far beyond the classroom.

Finally, thanks to Marlowe for his patience, and to Ella, who only knows a daddy who works late into the night on this book. Most of all, thank you to my wife and partner Kelly Hanson, who was not only hugely helpful in assisting me in tracking down rights and permissions, but has encouraged and supported me through every endeavour I undertake. I will always try to live up to the love and belief she has in me.

Every effort has been made to trace and contact known copyright holders before publication. If any copyright holders have any queries they are invited to contact the publishers in the first instance.

Figure 2 Two Cigarettes in the Dark (1985): Julie Shanahan. © Ursula Kaufmann

Introduction

To discuss Pina Bausch's legacy is to talk about the impact of Tanztheater across the broader spectrum of performance practice, eroding the boundaries between disciplines and integrating visual, kinaesthetic, aural and dramatic impulses into a complete event. While she didn't invent Tanztheater (the roots of Tanztheater can be traced to Rudolf von Laban's choric dance presentations and Kurt Jooss's bringing together of choreographic form with dramatic intent), her work most fully redefined it for a new age and spread her particular developmental process and articulation around the globe.

Bausch's roots in German Expressionist Dance (Ausdruckstanz) have been well documented and her connection to historical theatrical practice speculated upon, but what is less well appreciated is the impact of her work on contemporary dance and theatre. Inter- or cross-disciplinary collage and process-based ensemble-generated new performance is the model for contemporary work, and while Bausch was not the only one to explore this terrain, she drew on historical precedents and played them out in a thorough overwriting of performance possibility. She rewrote the rules for how new work could be created in theatre and dance, and left it to others to discover their own pathway through the newly aligned performative universe.

Bausch has come to be considered among the game changers in dance, following in a line of innovation that extends from the work of early dance pioneers Isadora Duncan and Loie Fuller. Both created new possibilities for dance in Europe and America that were quickly picked up and carried through the first half of the twentieth century.

Following in their wake, Rudolf von Laban established a new dance paradigm in Germany, and his work was taken in new directions by his disciples Mary Wigman and Kurt Jooss. The promise of this thread of dance exploration ended rather abruptly with the impact of World War II, and lay dormant during the ballet boom in Germany immediately following the war. In America, Ruth St. Denis and Ted Shawn were the progenitors of new dance, with innovations in Modern Dance practice carried further by two members of the Denishawn Company, Doris Humphrey and Martha Graham. Graham in particular drew from the new artistic spirit in post-war America, and built upon her ground-breaking work of the 1930s to become the dominant force of new dance expression after the war and for years to follow. Vaslav Nijinsky provided a potential new path within the ballet tradition, though it was not ultimately followed, leaving George Balanchine to re-establish balletic form along new lines a bit later in the century.

Bausch follows in this succession of major innovators, resuscitating the latent German Expressionist tradition and working with others (Gerhard Bohner, Johannes Kresnik) to lead German dance in new directions. But Bausch also drew from her experiences in America in the early 1960s, incorporating some Modern Dance values from Graham, but also picking up the thread of a more emotive American tradition, established by Wigman's follower, Hanya Holm, and including the work of Anna Sokolow and José Limón. She also moved outside of Balanchine's overwhelming influence in ballet, dancing with the Metropolitan Ballet Theatre in 1961/62, directly connecting her to the psychologically structured work of Anthony Tudor.

As Bausch made her way back to Germany in 1962, American dance was just beginning to take a decidedly formalist turn, with the experimentalists of Judson Church inventing a new approach in Postmodern Dance based on the expressivity of movement for movement's sake, and solidified and carried forward by Merce Cunningham as the seminal influence of American Dance of the latter part of the twentieth century. Balanchine led the ballet world through its own formalist turn and both choreographers were highly influential throughout Europe as well. The German dance world was in a period of reconstruction after the war, with ballet eclipsing the former relevance of German Modern Dance. But Germany, like the rest of Europe, was in search of something new, and spurred on by student movements throughout the 1960s, sought an alternative to the abstractions of formalist practice coming from America. The experimental spirit of the time opened the door for a new theatrical and dance energy. Bausch passed through that door without really thinking that she was remaking any traditions; she simply drew on those influences that surrounded her.

Bausch's place within the European dance world is now secure, and she is often credited with introducing a new integration of forms to stage practice. Her early work drew from her dance roots and incorporated the legacy of experimental theatre, both from the pioneering work of

Bertolt Brecht (especially as it was connected to and derived out of a cabaret tradition), as well as the tradition of avant-garde theatre in Europe and America. Without any direct influence, she draws from a similar investigative experience to connect to a theatrical avant-garde tradition that passes from Antonin Artaud and Stanley Witkiewicz to post-war practitioners like Jerzy Grotowski, Tadeusz Kantor and Peter Brook, and is later picked up by Arianne Mnouchkine and Robert Wilson, among many others.

Again without any direct influence, she also echoes the essentialist influence of later Samuel Beckett, emphasizing the necessity of the stage and the primacy and impact of presence, supplanting Beckett's attention to the word as a marker for essential existence with a thorough investigation of the body as the primary expression of being. The modernist agenda in performance practice throughout the twentieth century increasingly moved away from presenting a world as a marker of another reality and towards the condition of being in time and space on the stage itself. As theatrical presence is emphasized, all of the other major innovators leave a concrete legacy: of technique in the dance world (Graham, Cunningham, etc.), and the lasting impact of words in an attempt to define a method in theatre (Stanislavsky, Brecht, Artaud). Bausch's legacy remains ephemeral. We see it around us in the work of contemporary theatre, dance and film artists, but the ability to document the growth and development of the work itself is vital to the long-standing influence of Bausch's work on the performance community.

The ability to catalogue an artist's work through video documentation (and the ability to distribute that video documentation through major research institutions) is of increasing importance as new pathways are carved through the performance world, but the lasting impact of words provide another cornerstone in keeping any artist's work alive, and none more so than Bausch, who leaves behind perhaps more critical response than any dance artist of the second half of the twentieth century. There is a breadcrumb trail of remnants to lead us towards a new consideration of performance practice: from Bausch herself in interviews, from others writing about the experience of preparing and building the work, from those who see its intersection with other forms, and from the overwhelming rush of reviews and criticism by those who have seen the work and try to create a structure of sense out of what they have experienced.

This sourcebook attempts to create a context for understanding and ultimately extending the influence of Bausch's work. It follows upon my own initial response to seeing Bausch's work, which was to try to understand where this came from, how it was created, what the implications of the work were within the world of performance, and how we can articulate a response to the feelings and images that are now such a vital part of our collective performance memory. I have broken the work into five connected sections that progress from the history of the work through the work itself, and end with its reception and critical explorations that can extend from there.

Section I begins with formative influences on Bausch's work, outlining her base and fleshing out the context of early German dance, and moving on to consider Bausch's work in the context of other theatre and dance artists of her time. Section II enters into Bausch's developmental process itself, both of individual works as well as what becomes a style of performance creation and presentation. The section begins with descriptions of Bausch's first attempts at a more exploratory theatrical developmental process and moves through to her commissions based on residencies in selected locales. The essays are arranged chronologically in this section to better understand the growth and evolution of Bausch's own process, and focus on first-hand experience, including interviews with Bausch herself and other essays from people who were in the room at the time of a piece's conception and development. Section III follows with a more thorough exploration of this integration of dance and theatre in the creation of a new form. Tanztheater stands apart from other approaches to performance, not just as a technique through which work might be presented, but as a developmental process.

Section IV considers Bausch's reception, and is again presented chronologically to follow the course of response as critics and audiences struggle to understand this new form, finally ending with a small sample among the wealth of appreciations that were published upon Bausch's untimely death. Section V shows the degree to which Bausch's challenges to worldviews and cultural norms provide a window for theoretical models, and help to advance dance studies towards greater arenas of complexity. An extensive bibliography follows, focusing on important works (primarily in English) directly connected to Bausch's output and legacy, and broken down by section to facilitate further investigation.

Each chapter could have easily offered enough material to create a book in itself, but I have tried to narrow each section towards a diverse and yet concentrated array of significant material. My selection criteria were to draw out those essays and works that have had the greatest impact on existing Bausch scholarship, to present a breadth of perspectives across a wide range of time, and to represent the major critics, journalists and scholars in the field without reproducing other material readily available through alternative sources. My further goal was to focus the selection to Bausch's earlier work and her initial impact across Europe, the UK and America.

The early formative period of Bausch's career was when she effectively challenged performance conventions in creating a new style, leading to a wealth of in-depth consideration from both dance and theatre critics and practitioners. More recent critique has been wideranging, but has not yet had the chance to settle into critical perspective to demonstrate its viability for scholarly research. Although Bausch's work has been widely influential around the world, from South American and Japanese tours to commissioned work from Turkey, Istanbul, India and Asia, I have chosen to limit selection here to primarily European, UK and American sources to focus the cultural discussion at play, to take best advantage of my own expertise, and to reduce the need for extensive translation services. This, unfortunately, leaves out material from Bausch's influence in South America or Asia due to lack of space and resources, but I leave that to someone with more international experience who would be better equipped to understand (and translate) the wealth of responses from those areas of the world.

Finally, my selections were derived in part by availability, leaving out much of the important foundational work by Norbert Servos, Jochen Schmidt and Suzanne Schlicher simply because it is available in published form already. Similarly, a wealth of reviews in publications such as the *New York Times* were left out because they are readily available online (and the New York Times Company, in particular, imposed hefty republication fees for all of their material). There are bound to be omissions, but I hope that the selections provide a connected narrative thread that will be helpful for students, scholars and the general public.

I hope this book will stand alongside many of the other available resources to more fully flesh out Bausch's career. These resources include my own introductory overview as part of Routledge's Performance Practioner series; Norbert Servos's excellent piece-by-piece analysis (*Pina Bausch: Tanztheater*) recently updated and published in English, and the numerous photographic studies of Bausch's work, including several volumes by Ursula Kaufmann, who contributes the photographs here. Together with the video documentation held at Tanztheater Wuppertal, the German Dance Archive in Köln and The Lincoln Center Library for the Performing Arts in New York City, I hope a sufficient base of materials will be left to carry Bausch's influence on to succeeding generations of dance and theatre artists, and to audiences in the future as well.

The company will continue to grow and move on, probably integrating new work into their efforts to continue to present original works from the repertoire. The Pina Bausch Foundation, established after Bausch's death, is creating a research centre to house Tanztheater Wuppertal's extensive video and print archives, as well as develop a space for active performance research and experimentation. Bausch's impact continues to expand, with Wim Wenders's documentary film capturing some of the work in a form that might be appreciated into the future, but perhaps the biggest legacy is the growth of integrated and interdisciplinary work around the world, and the importance of ensemble-generated developmental processes in both dance and theatre.

As Raimund Hoghe reports, Bausch claims no special abilities, but simply recognizes the significance of seeing the interactions of people around her. "What I do: I watch. Maybe that's it. I have simply looked at human relationships and tried to see them, tried to speak about them. That's what I am interested in. I don't know of anything more important." Perhaps it has never been more important, and if art can provide a catalyst and a model for cultural change, then we are prepared to take full advantage of the explorations Bausch has made.

Figure 3 *Áqua* (2001): Melanie Maurin. © Ursula Kaufmann

I
Dance and theatre roots and connections

Bausch's further development of Tanztheater comes from her base and training in German Expressionist dance, but is also linked to her interest in theatrical techniques. Without stopping to systematically apply any given theory, she incorporated ideas from her dance background and inherently drew on theatrical innovations, reinterpreting base operating principals for the stage as she erased boundaries between disciplines. Basuch's work founds a developmental process to explore ideas of performativity and consider the body as central to performance presence.

This section provides pivotal overviews that contextualize Bausch's work within the German Expressionist continuum. What is less well represented in the literature, probably because we lack any concrete referential data, is Bausch's connections to the experiments of the 1960s in both dance and theatre. Although her work is not as clearly aligned with the American formalist stance in Modern dance developed at Judson Church, it does reflect the revolutionary spirit that buoyed the theatrical experiments of that era and led to reconsiderations of dance and theatre in Europe and America. Bausch was in New York City in 1961/62, and supposedly was aware of, if not witness to, the work of the Living Theatre. Her early work upon her return to Germany is not particularly theatrically engaged, however, beyond the influence of Jooss's theatrical brand of dance, and the impact of her work in America with the more psychologically inflected ballet of Anthony Tudor and her connections to the expressive continuum within the Modern dance tradition. Her collaborators in the early years of her work with Tanztheater Wuppertal may have had more contact with that spirit, however, particularly her designer and partner Rolf Borzik. His approach to working within a charged environment that highlights real presence on stage echoes the 1960s experimental theatre derived out of the seminal ideas of Antonin Artaud. In piece after piece before his early death in 1980, he moved Tanztheater Wuppertal towards an essentialist confrontation with the stage.

Also often overlooked is the shaping influence of Jan Minarik, one of the only carry-overs from the original Wuppertaler Ballet when Bausch took over in 1973 and renamed the company Tanztheater Wuppertal. Minarik participates in the first few dance operas Bausch creates at Wuppertal (based on Gluck operas, *Iphigenie auf Tauris* and *Orpheus und Eurydice*), but his influence really shines through as the company confronts the growing crises within its ranks and moves away from more dance centred pieces to create more theatrically developed work, specifically *Blaubart*, *Kontakthof*, etc., in the incredibly fertile period between 1977 and 1980. Minarik continued to develop his role within the company, standing alongside Dominique Mercy as one of the longest-standing and most inspiring company members, and established himself as a consistent theatrical component of the work, often playing the role of the outsider or master of ceremonies, calling up an odd assortment of presentational images in each succeeding piece rather than more developed "dance" sections.

Borzik and Minarik provide a connecting link to the German theatrical tradition of Bertolt Brecht, and other more current theatrical experimentation, incorporating ideas from Artaud to Grotowski and Peter Brook. They help to place Bausch's work in this early period, and continuing on throughout her career, within the spectrum of the Theatre of Images. But Bausch brings together theatrical and dance influences in a wholly original way, re-inventing the idea of performance presence. She begins with a process of exploration rather than interpreting a given text, constructs her theatrical images from questions she poses to her performers in rehearsal, and weaves together the results in narratives of association built on a metaphoric ground of dream logic. The result is a developmental process that moves away from dance based structures built on movement values and echoes the ensemble generated work of her contemporary theatre artists, Tadeusz Kantor and Arianne Mnouchkine, and utilizes the same interdisciplinary building blocks as Meredith Monk and Robert Wilson.

A full cataloguing of Bausch's influence within and across the dance and theatrical spectrum would include statements from the many artists who have acknowledged their debt to her work, including William Forsythe, Anne Theresa de Keersmaeker and Bill T. Jones (among many others) in dance, and Wilson, Anne Bogart, Robert Lepage and others in the theatre world. Bausch's further influence has been incorporated throughout Asia as well, intersecting with Japanese traditions in the development of Butoh, and touching base with a resurgence and extension of classical Indian dance forms. Various Asian modes of performance have always integrated visual, physical and narrative forms to create a replete presentational style that Bausch picks up on and contributes back to. This section provides the basis for understanding Bausch's work within these contexts, but leaves much room for further exploration across disciplinary practice and within differing performance possibilities.

Dance Theatre from Rudloph Laban to Pina Bausch

Isa Partsch-Bergsohn

Originally published in *Dance Theatre Journal*, October, 1987

The Dance Theatre of Pina Bausch represents a new liaison between dance and theatre. First it is necessary to understand some of the historic developments of the German term "Tanztheater" (Dance Theatre) so that the reader might see Pina Bausch's version in the context of this historical background.

Laban

The term "dance theatre" goes back to the Twenties in Germany, when Rudolf Laban was a prominent figure. Laban directed some choral dance rituals at Monte Verita in 1917. In the early Twenties, Laban distanced himself from dancing as an expression of subjective feelings. He had systematised his thought about dance movement in a book entitled *Die Welt des Tänzers* (*The World of a Dancer*) published in 1920. His interest now turned to how to exemplify this new dance art with his newly established company, the Tanzbühne Hamburg. Dance was shown as an independent art form based on laws of harmonious spatial forms. Laban made it possible to analyse these dance forms according to the specific rhythms that the moving body described in space. Also, one of the fundamental laws of human movement is the principle of sequence: each movement radiates away from the centre of gravity and has then to return to it. The Tanzbühne Hamburg became an instrument for Laban to test his theories about dance in practice. The dances grew out of the combined efforts of the choreographer, the dance director and the dancers. The three main works were: *Die Schwingende Kathedrale* (*The Swinging Temple*), *Die Gebiendeten,* (*The Blinded*), *Gaukelei*, (*Trickery*).

Sylvia Bodmer, who was one of the original company members together with Kurt Jooss, described Laban's daily training for his company of 24 dancers to me in an interview. The technical workout consisted of a series of swings and studies in dynamic contrasts, and also group studies to build up ensemble awareness. "Dance was definitely an art form", said Sylvia Bodmer, "and Laban and the company worked with dedication to represent this new art form, modern dance, on stage." Laban made a clear distinction between movement choir and dance theatre. The movement choir served to give the laymen the dance experience, while the dance theatre professionally trained dancers presented the art form. He differentiated it according to its structure as orchestral, choric, or chamber dance including smaller forms such as sonata and song. Regarding the content of the dance theatre, Laban was not specific. The major pupils of his German period, Mary Wigman and Kurt Jooss, expressed their ideas of the relation between content and form in dance very clearly.

Wigman

Laban's first highly experimental period took place at Monte Verita and at his studio in Zurich from 1913–1917. During this time Mary Wigman became his close collaborator and his demonstrator. In his improvisation classes, she recognised his ability to free students and help them find their own roots. The students danced sometimes without any accompaniment in order to feel the rhythm of their own body. Wigman composed her first solo dances, *Witch Dance* and *Lento,* in 1914, under Laban's very critical eyes. She left him to pursue her own artistic way.

There were no traditions Wigman could relate to. "I knew that I had to find the form for dance out of the time in which we live," she said. Mary Wigman was more specific about her version of dance theatre than her mentor Laban. She called her dance art "dance absolute." She explained: "The contents of dance and dance art works are similar to those of other performing arts: the issue is man and his fate. Not the fate of man today, or yesterday or tomorrow, but the fate of man in his eternal change of appearances … humanity is the basic theme of an unlimited eternally meaningful sequence of variations." Wigman's solo dances spoke about man and his cosmic relationships. They were abstract, clear in form and expressionistic in the use of distortion, some of them performed in complete silence. Wigman's dances deserved without question Laban's term dance theatre. Besides her solo work, she choreographed also for groups, as in her *Scenes of a Dance Drama* and in *Dance Tale.* She used the larger, choric form for the first time in her *Totenmal* (*Monument to the Dead*), choreographed without music to the poem of Albert Talhoff. The work, the first of its kind, received a controversial reception. The question was raised: was this degree of abstraction still in the realm of dance? This experience forced Wigman to reevaluate her ideas of choric dance without music.

During the Fifties and Sixties Wigman created large scale master-works for the musical theatre. Her aim was a contemporary rebirth of the ancient Greek choric theatre. She was at her best creating spatial rhythms through simple unified motion of large choric group actions. She achieved the realization of this concept when she collaborated with leading German directors. In the program for the opera *Orpheus*, performed in Berlin in 1961, she wrote about choric dance: "The unyielding demand of the choric dance on its creator, the choreographer, is simplicity and one more simplicity in the organization of space, in its rhythmic content, in the dynamic shadings of the walk, body attitude and gesture. Wigman not only fulfilled Laban's definitions of dance theatre, she achieved an extraordinary balance of the different media, dance and music, as guest choreographer for the opera houses in Leipzig, Mannheim and Berlin."

Jooss

Another version of dance theatre was presented by Laban's other pupil, Kurt Jooss. He saw dance theatre as a dramatic group action. Jooss came to Laban in 1920, studied under him and became a member of the Tanzbühne Hamburg as his first performing experience. After a very brief period of solo work and experimentation together with Sigurd Leeder, Jooss became director of dance at the theatre in Münster, Germany, in 1925. Here he created his first choreography. In 1927 Kurt Jooss became co-founder and director of dance at the Folkwang Schule in Essen, Germany. The school followed Laban's ideals to combine music, dance and speech education. Jooss built up a training program on the basis of Laban's spatial and qualitative theories which consciously combined elements of classical ballet with the expressive dynamic range of the new dance. By 1928, he started to build a company. Dance theatre, as Jooss saw it, was dramatic, making its statement in movement terms. Jooss explained: "Our aim is always the dance theatre, understood as form and technique of dramatic choreography, concerned closely with libretto, music, and above all with the interpretative artists. In school and studio the new dance technique must be developed toward a non-personal objective tool for the dramatic dance, the technique of the traditional classical ballet to be gradually incorporated." (Jooss Archive, Wiesbaden).

In pedagogy and choreography Jooss pursued one aim: to develop dancers for the dance theatre as he understood it. His concepts were finally realized in his master work *The Green Table*. This work was an example of Laban's definition of the orchestral and dramatic structure. Jooss discussed the question of content thoroughly in an article entitled "The Language of the Dance Theatre." "A work of Art in order to have meaning needs a concrete subject. There are two ways of representing a theme in the theatre – by way of realism or through fantasy. Realism dominates Western drama; the way of fantasy is used in all forms of stylized theatre, as in oriental theatre, in Western opera, and even more in dance theatre. The choreographer conceives the theme of the dance work and he translates and structures it into harmoniously composed rhythmic movement, into dance." Jooss also considered drama in its relation to words. He argued that if in dance speech is eliminated then the art of gesture has to be intensified to a universally understandable language. He combined the intensified language of gesture with an integrated classical modern technique.

In 1933 Jooss moved his company to England. He established a school together with Sigurd Leeder, the Jooss/Leeder School of Dance at Dartington Hall. The Jooss company found a very strong response in England, Holland and Sweden. During the Thirties the company toured extensively throughout Europe under the name Les Ballets Jooss. The public saw the Jooss style as a modernized form of ballet.

Dance in the UK and USA

Ballet was still young in England and America in the Thirties. The Sadlers Wells Ballet under the direction of Ninette de Valois was traditionally oriented, whereas Marie Rambert aimed for a more experimental approach with the Ballet Rambert. Anthony Tudor was one of the early choreographers of British ballet. He created his characters by showing their psychological motivations through expressive gestures. Tudor's refinement of gestures and Jooss's use of gesture were similar in that they composed the dance phrase rhythmically, independent from the musical form. Familiar with Freud and Jung's theories, Tudor put the classical vocabulary into a twentieth century context. He brought his approach to America when he joined American Ballet Theatre in 1940.

The most influential choreographers in America were Antony Tudor and George Balanchine during the Forties and Fifties. Jerome Robbins was also an artist of great influence, presenting contemporary issues generally only voiced by the American modern dancers, such as Anna

Sokolow's social criticism expressed in her work *Rooms*. Jerome Robbins concerned himself with contemporary dramatic themes in works like *The Cage* and *Age of Anxiety*. He also showed the acute problems of American society on the stage of the musical *West Side Story*. The tours of New York City Ballet, American Ballet Theatre, and shortly after the American modern dance companies of Martha Graham, José Limón, Paul Taylor, Alvin Ailey and Merce Cunningham expanded the view of European audiences. It altered the concepts of theatre. Directors and administrators became more willing to recognize dance and to provide a place far experimentation.

Kurt Jooss experienced this change in mentality towards dance in post-war Germany when he returned to Essen in 1949 and started a new company, the Folkwang-Tanztheater. Lack of funds forced him to disband this ensemble in spite of a very successful start. Ten years later he received some funding for the establishment of an institute of advanced studies in choreography and performing skills, which led to the Folkwang-Ballet ensemble. Antony Tudor as guest choreographer revived *Le Jardin Aux Lilas* for this group. Lucas Hoving choreographed *Sequence*. The culmination of Jooss's efforts became visible in two young artists who grew out of this studio: Jean Cebron and Pina Bausch. Cebron had studied with Jooss in Chile and also with Sigurd Leeder and Simone Michelle in London. He is presently the main teacher for modern dance technique at the Dance Department of the Folkwang-Hochschule directed by Pina Bausch in Essen.

Bausch

Pina Bausch (born 1940) is from the first postwar generation and graduated from the Folkwang-Hochschule in 1958. After graduation she received a grant for further studies at the Juilliard School, New York. She studied with Antony Tudor and familiarized herself with the American modern dance techniques of Martha Graham and José Limón. It was precisely the time when a strong reaction against these formal techniques of modern dance arose and an avant-garde movement searched for alternative dance experiences and performing styles. After one year of intense study at Juilliard, she danced with the Metropolitan Opera Ballet during the 1961/62 season. Simultaneously, she was a partner to Paul Taylor in a program for the Spoleto Festival. She liked his choreographic style very much. Paul Taylor did not state his subject matter, but implied the meaning in his choreography. Bausch was very sensitive to what was happening around her in America. Issues of environment, civil rights, women, minorities and anti-nuclear concerns

were voiced in all the arts of the Sixties and led to new ways of conveying meaning. Collage techniques were used instead of plots. Artists
from the visual arts, music and dance shared their experimentation in
happenings, crossing freely the boundaries between the media. Turning
away from the idea of subject, patterns of sounds or movement were
used in repetition to create hypnotic effects. This period was tired of
heroic theatrical gestures, and choreographers now focused on pedestrian
movements, observing basic human relations of ordinary people.

Bausch returned with all these impressions from New York to the
Folkwang-Hochschule in 1962. Kurt Jooss offered her the position of
leading soloist with the newly formed Folkwangballett. She also taught
modern dance technique at the school. Pina Bausch and Jean Cebron
formed a partnership and choreographed for each other. They worked
very intensely under Kurt Jooss in these years from 1962–68. Kurt
Jooss retired from his work at the Folkwang-Hochschule, Essen in
1968 and Bausch took over the Folkwang Dance Studio, which gave
her the chance to experiment choreographically with the group for five
years. She accepted the directorship of the dance ensemble at Wuppertal
in 1973. This was the beginning of the Wuppertaler Tanztheater.

It is not surprising that Pina Bausch's work contains as many
American elements as European. Contemporary issues now appeared
on European stages as well, in the works of Rudolf van Dantzig and
Glen Tetley at Netherlands Dance Theatre, and in Britain in the
remodeled Ballet Rambert, which incorporated American modern
dance techniques. What distinguishes Pina Bausch's version of dance
theatre from Dutch and British forms is the way she blends American
trends with European traditions.

Elements of European theatre traditions found in Pina Bausch's
Tanztheater include the arrangement of her dance theatre works into
dance numbers, a choreographic form she adopted from the operetta
popular in Germany during the first half of this century. She commented on the frivolity of this form of entertainment that personified
to her the shallow forms of amusement of the nineteenth century
bourgeoisie. As part of her European training, Bausch is conscious of
the dynamics of space (Laban–Jooss tradition). Studies with Antony
Tudor sensitized her to the refinement of gestures and phrasing. Kurt
Jooss sharpened her observation and taught her articulation of dance
movements and orchestral use of the dance ensemble, so that she was
able to use these skills for her own purposes. It might be said that Jooss
and Tudor were the strongest influences in building up her choreographic
craft. Kurt Jooss's dance theatre was based on the belief of a counter-
balance of vital forces. She saw dramatic action as a struggle of

energies that found harmony in the realm of fantasy. As a post-war choreographer, Bausch based her dance theatre on realism. She revolted against the false feeling of security of the Adenauer era and showed men destroying themselves and their environment. Bausch had no direct contact with Mary Wigman, but she responded strongly to two of her ideas: man and his relation to the universe and Wigman's belief in fate. Bausch reflects on how the theme of men and women in conflict affects a single life. She is not a feminist, but like Wigman, believes in fate. Bausch sees woman as the eternal victim.

Pina Bausch's dance theatre is largely autobiographical; its strength is in the intensity of the experience and its expression. Its limitation is its subjectivity. It offers no solutions, but articulates the problems. Pina Bausch intrudes uncompromisingly into the private sphere and observes the seemingly unimportant with clinical eyes. She brings out people's motivations. Her dancers address the audience directly and speak about themselves (a common practice during the Sixties in off-Broadway theatre).

According to Jooss's belief, all those practices are breaking the illusion of theatre. For Bausch, it is more important to make a statement about the human condition. This is what she said in an interview for the yearbook *Ballett*, 1986: "I only know that the time in which we live, the time with all its anxieties is very much with me. This is the source of my pieces."

Expressionism?

"Ausdruckstanz" and the New Dance Theatre in Germany

Hedwig Müller

Originally published in Festival International de Nouvelle Danse,
Montreal, Souvenir Program, Fall, 1986. Translated by Michael
Vensky-Stalling

Expressionism? The term is bound to mislead, since it covers two historically related phenomena – the German *Ausdruckstanz* from 1910
onwards and during the 1920s, and today's German dance theatre.
What do Pina Bausch, Reinhild Hoffman, Susanne Linke, Gerhard
Bohner and Hans Kresnik have in common with their predecessors
Mary Wigman or Rudolf von Laban, with Gret Palucca or Kurt Jooss?
If one compares the pieces of the contemporary dance theatre with
those of the *Ausdrucks*-dancers there are no obvious parallels. We neither have the conditions that gave an impetus to choreographers at the
beginning of the century – the cultural and political upheaval in
Europe up to the Second World War – nor do the young choreographers of today seem interested in the themes of their elders. A fateful
"ecce homo" pathos or eurhythmically directed moving choruses could
hardly grasp and express the social problems of today. Those subjects
which engaged the attention of artists at the turn of the century and
during the Weimar Republic, and in part united them (the phenomenon of the metropolis, the hostile rejection of modern technology)
could justify the use of a global term like expressionism. Yet those
subjects have also been superseded by events, have become anathema
or *themselves* subjects of a rebellion.

Nonetheless, connections can be made.

If, for example, the dance theatre of Pina Bausch, freed from the
rules of the *Danse d'ecole* and even modern dance, developed as it did, then
this was only possible after the *Ausdruckstanz* movement had smoothed
the way with its rejection of the classical academic style. If today
"everyday" themes and "everyday" experiences are acceptable subjects
for a theatre of dance oriented towards reality, then this is so only
because dance in the Twenties took the first steps in this direction by

including "everyday" movements in its choreography. At that time, it was tried for the first time to use observation of everyday social life for the purpose of dancing. It was then that a liberated "technique" was developed, which made it possible to express (hence *"Ausdruck"*) personal experience – or what was taken for personal experience. Therefore we have the term *Ausdruckstanz*, called respectfully though irritatingly *German Dance* or *German Expressionist Dance* by the Americans, or even *Central European Dance* by the British. In view of such confusion, it is best to preserve the phenomenon of *Ausdruckstanz* by leaving it untranslated. It also shows how little the general term of expressionism applies to the new and old avant-garde of dance in Germany. What joins both – the transmission of experience and freedom gained over a period spanning two world wars – can only be explained by a detailed description. It may be proof of the indirect, continuing influence of *Ausdruckstanz* that Pina Bausch, Reinhild Hoffmann and Susanne Linke all trained at the Folkwang-School in Essen, a school whose curriculum and company were rebuilt by Kurt Jooss in 1949 after his return to Germany.

Ausdruckstanz

Fascism in Germany created a gap, which separated dance after 1945 from its revolutionary heritage. Joining up or continuing with the old impulses and innovations was almost impossible, except in the cases of individual choreographers or dancers, who began working again in Germany after the war – such as Jooss, Wigman and Palucca.

German dance after 1945 means, in the first instance, a return to supposedly timeless classical values, means a restoration in the political and artistic sense. One sought shelter under the umbrella of a supposedly unpolitical classical academic tradition that ruled the opera houses during the fifties and into the sixties almost without exception. After the Third Reich, Germans feared contact with anything political and this also led to an estrangement from the artistic innovations of pre-fascist days. Exploration of new possibilities was something unfamiliar to the generation that had supported fascism to a considerable extent. It was time for rebuilding and this initially meant restoration of old principles. Dance sheltered under the classicism and romanticism of the nineteenth century and rarely ventured outside this area.

Only with the sixties did a time arrive – with the Easter marches and the student movement – which opened up new spaces for

Figure 4 Iphigenie auf Tauris (1973): Tanztheater Wuppertal. © Ursula Kaufmann

dance. These were exploited mainly during the seventies, particularly in Darmstadt and Bremen; also in Cologne, where the
Tanz-Forum 1970 was founded, the first modern-trained company
without separation of ensemble and soloists; later in Wuppertal
under Pina Bausch, who took over directorship of the dance theatre
for the 1973/74 season. But this movement differed from the old
Ausdruckstanz.

The history of German dance from the turn of the century to the
present day seems contradictory – at least on the surface. On the one hand
as something broken up by the Hitler era; on the other as something
hidden, with an almost "subterranean" continuity. One could say that
the new theatre of dance reflects a good deal of the rebellious energy
of its predecessors. However, a considerable part of the spirit of
Ausdruckstanz, rising towards new horizons, blended in quite neatly
with fascist ideology.

The rise of the youth movement

The background to *Ausdruckstanz* was a general, body-oriented mood
of renewal. Its origins can be found in the youth and hiking
movements of the 1890s.

Then we have the time from the doom-laden *fin de siècle* to the
First World War. The youth movement and its protests were based on
the everyday experience of youths who saw themselves cheated out of
their future. It was a mixture of a taste for adventure, stemming from
childhood, and a rejection of the narrow world of their elders.
The cultural criticism at the turn of the century provided the blueprint
for the intellectual discussion that was at the root of the youth protest.
The youth movement itself was actually far from being motivated by
intellectual or culture-critical reasons. The alternative it suggested – an
intimacy with nature achieved by hiking and camping under the open
skies – was an attempt to break out of metropolitan culture and isolation. The leading images were taken from the past: from the time of
romanticism, the minstrels of the Middle Ages and the educational
ideals of antiquity. This was the first combination of these elements that
would be expressed visually and sensually by the classical movements
of an *art nouveau* personality like Isadora Duncan. At the same time,
the rebellious spirit was flawed; a fact that was also to influence
Ausdruckstanz irrevocably. The vagueness of the rebellious purpose, its
rejection of actual social conditions were all too easily appropriated by
the political force, which pretended to be giving clear content to
vague ideas.

The dance farm on Monte Verità

On Monte Verità, near the Swiss town of Ascona on Lago Maggiore, all those representing counter-culture between the turn of the century and the First World War, got together. Here, too, began an important chapter of the history of German Dance and of two of its protagonists.

In 1913, Rudolf von Laban opened a summer school in Ascona, as an offshoot of his Munich school for free dance. After the beginning of the war, the school moved to Zürich altogether. Mary Wigman soon joined him. Both were making a late debut: Laban was 34 years old, Wigman – not yet profiled as a dancer – was 27. Their practically accidental meeting (Wigman originally planned to take a summer course only) developed into a collaboration that created two of the leading exponents of *Ausdruckstanz*: Laban, the definitive theoretician – Wigman, the practical demonstrator; Laban, director of masses – Wigman the soloist of individual themes.

In 1914, Wigman choreographed the first version of *Hexentanz* (Witches Dance). This was a short study with ascetic movements that would make her famous throughout Europe and the USA. The specialty of this piece – which is danced barefoot – is that it begins with the dancer in a crouching position and then develops along the vertical and horizontal axes from the centre of the body. It contains the essential elements of the new dance: the inclusion of the floor, against the traditions of classical ballet, the development of the principle of contraction and release (long before Martha Graham's concept of "contraction and release" became a stylistic principle of Modern Dance) and the creation of expressive gesture (*Ausdrucksbewegnung*), based on the emotions of the dancer, involving her in the action for the first time and giving her the role of *auteur*.

A particular idea, which greatly occupied the period even before the arrival of fascism, and which eventually led to mass formations, was expressed by Laban's "choral games" (*Chorische Spiele*). This insouciant preoccupation with mythical–archaic rituals in the middle of a world war is bound to irritate and anticipates those later celebrations of summer solstices by the Nazis as a way of claiming their "German heritage". But this return to mythical images does disqualify itself. It represents a playful naiveté, teamed with complete political ignorance – a situation by no means uncommon.

The mass choreography of Fascism

The susceptibility of *Ausdruckstanz*, both from a technical as well as a philosophical point of view, to external ideological influences was provided under the well-organized attack of National Socialism (*Nationalsozialismus*).

Mary Wigman was able to continue her work with relative ease, even after the Nazis seized power. Her essentially soloist-oriented presentation of general human themes did not go against the new political system. In fact, integration was possible without major problems. Kurt Jooss, whose pieces *Grosstadt* (Big City) and *Grüner Tisch* (The Green Table) are representative of a more politically committed and enlightened attitude, emigrated in 1933 and continued working abroad. The case of Rudolf von Laban was quite different again. Although he followed Jooss to England in 1938, his eurhythmic concept of mass dancing (*Massentanz*) fit in with the fascist idea of mass organization.

In 1920 Laban already felt drawn to the idea of "the great aim of healing our race, its new flowering and thus the ultimate flowering of all mankind."[1] His idea of a festive group, moving eurhythmically, united by a common ecstasy, his choreosophical, totalitarian concept of a harmonious *Gesamtkunstwerk* far exceeded the general self-understanding of the *Ausdruckstanz* rebellion.

By rhythmicizing the individual and by integrating it into a whole, Laban wanted to change society. By revolutionizing dance, he hoped to gain access to everyday human life. But although this link with a social utopia revalued dance, the concept itself was unable to eliminate irrational elements and develop into true emancipation. These "irrational influences" and the specific emphasis on individual self-realization outside any social reality sapped the revolutionary energy of *Ausdruckstanz* and caused it to founder. The rebellion, created through dance and aiming at revolutionizing all of society, was finally caught in an ideological trap. Nonetheless one must not underestimate the influence of *Ausdruckstanz* on the development of free dance up to Modern Dance and the contemporary theatre of dance. And this in spite of those mythical–mystical elements that were all too easily appropriated by others.

Tanztheater

The term Tanztheater (theatre of dance) goes back to the time of *Ausdruckstanz*. During that period, essential elements of the new "free" dance, as it was called, were already predefined. The joining of theatre and dance announces the desired integration of genuinely theatrical and balletic means. Although "free" dance was based on "pure" movement, thereby emancipating dance for the first time from reworking music, it also attempted to explore and integrate ordinary, everyday movements. *Ausdruckstanz* shifted the emphasis to a theatrical, dramatic *Ausdrucksgebärde* (*Ausdrucks*-gesture) that was intended to speak for itself. This emphasis on the independence of dance differed fundamentally from the dramatizations of Jean-Georges Noverre for instance, at the end of the 18th century. Now dance no longer needed a story to tell, creating sense and significance out of the movement itself.

On this emancipated basis, the new theatre of dance of the sixties and seventies was able to develop. This was the time during which the student revolt also exerted its influence on the theatre. Dance emerged from the shadows of the visual image and reacted to the political controversies of the times. Choreographers no longer considered themselves executors of the classical estate, needing merely the odd innovation here or there. Instead, they became the emancipated authors of their own pieces. The traditional range of movements no longer sufficed to express the Vietnam discussions and social analyses initiated by the Frankfurt school.

The dance theatre of Bremen and Darmstadt

In the season of 1968/69, the Austrian Hans Kresnik took over as director of the dance theatre in Bremen. In his pieces, actual history began to replace the old ballet classics which now only lent an ironic title, such as *Schwanensee AG* (Swan Lake AG) (1971), to a work, or else were quoted like relics from a museum. In his confrontations with actual political events, set against a critical social analysis – as in *PIGasUS, America under Nixon* – Kresnik established the choreographer as a radical. His pieces, often interspaced with effective jazz dance elements, are a confrontation with contemporary trends and therefore he uses modern writers, popular music and contemporary composers.

With his provocative political *revues* Kresnik appropriated dance for the first time for making concrete social statements. Dance no longer repeats the historical situation in an "unconscious" way, but gains awareness by means of reflecting on its origins and its relationship with reality.

Gerhard Bohner, engaged in 1972/73 as director of the dance theatre in Darmstadt, tried to construct his pieces with the company on the basis of group processes. His choreographies, closer to Modern Dance than those of Kresnik, sometimes with acrobatic elements, seek to create strong, impressive subject-related images.

Bohner's choreographic development is marked by his involvement with the dance concept of the Bauhaus. In 1977, Bohner reconstructed

Oskar Schlemmer's *Triadisches Ballett* for the opening of the *Berliner Festwochen*. Schlemmer's abstract mathematics in space, his reduction of character to type, which makes the dancer vanish behind his costume, turning him into a representation of a sculptural idea of motion, affect Bohner's later works. With Schlemmer we have the realization of a moving sculpture rather than dance – with Bohner this is condensed into a tableau of high visual intensity. Against the tendency of the Bauhaus towards schematic composition, Bohner sets a spatial concept and characterization leavened by many refractions. His style has changed increasingly towards an eclecticism of forms that combines the aesthetics of the Bauhaus, Modern Dance, a parody of classical dancing, everyday movement and abstraction.

The Wuppertal Dance Theatre

Unlike Kresnik's political revues, the Tanztheater of Pina Bausch, who became director of the Wuppertal company in the 1973/74 season, seeks a poetical link with reality. For Pina Bausch, it is not political awareness which is the choreographer's prime mover, but observation, everyday perception, which come together little by little to form pieces or scenes. With the openness of her work and her ability to include contradiction and withstand it, Pina Bausch has probably achieved the most radical break with conventional ballet and sharpened the resources of dance with and for reality in an unprecedented fashion.

Pina Bausch's Tanztheater is best described as a theatre of experience. By overcoming the limitations of categorized theatre through inclusion of musical elements, mime as well as cinematic effects, the choreographer is increasingly able to work in her subjective fears, desires and needs. The spectator is included in the action on stage, as a fellow player also concerned, by this method of subjective representation. The theatre of experience aims at an emotional involvement with the problems raised – not with the characters.

Conventional dramatic structure with a beginning, a turning point and an ending is completely abandoned in favor of a form that appropriates reality by means of excerpted individual situations. Pina Bausch's method of "work in progress," allowing changes and revisions of a work even after the première, explodes the usual closed loop. Beginning and ending no longer represent the temporal frame for the development of characters. Using the principle of *Nummern-dramaturgie* (sequence of dramatic numbers), separate scenes are joined in a loosely associative sequence. The aim is no longer a logical, accurate development of plot and character, but an unfolding of groups of motifs, along the lines of free association with images and actions. Instead of representing human characters, the problematical aspects of a subject become the focus of interest. Since the usual distinction between principal and supporting cast is no longer made, the spectator is unable to identify with the protagonists of a story. Tension, in these works, is created through the combination of diverse means and scenic contents, through changes from quick to slow, loud and quiet, light and dark, moving and stationary.

Because the *Bewegnungstheatre* (theatre of movement) does not use a story-line for communicating information, its aim becomes communication of bodily experienced reality. Direct involvement is more important than rational enlightenment, physical experience of the necessity for change more essential than intellectual insight. In this way, the *Tanztheater* opens up a hitherto neglected dimension: that "conditions" are always manifest in (physical) "behavior." The body is not merely a medium that carries a message, but is itself the subject of the representation. As in the war between the sexes, where the female body is used as an instrument of power, the body in general here becomes a means of exerting power. From within the limits of conventions the afflicted body tells its own story.

This is also the purpose of alienation through comic effects. Slow motion or slapstick-type acceleration of events reveals real desires and needs, hidden by the drudgery of daily living. As in the early Chaplin slapstick films, comedy may soon turn into tragedy. The representation of conventional limitations is not a way of laughing at a character. On the contrary, the self-evident nature of daily gestures and rituals is suspended and the seemingly irrevocable logic of conventions broken. Laughter provoked in this way leads to awareness in the spectators when they recognize on stage their own restricted behavioral reality.

The same method of contrasting elements is used for dealing with the mass media. Increasingly, Pina Bausch picks up the trivial dreams created by Hollywood films, comic strips, pop songs or associated media (operetta revue). The patterns of human relationships propagated by these media and the resulting stereotypes of beauty, love and happiness, are comically alienated by setting them against reality, thus demonstrating their uselessness and ludicrousness. The *Tanztheater* seizes on the social function of media stereotypes and unmasks their emotional conformity by showing them as clockwork mannerisms – as for instance the impracticality of a tight Hollywood embrace when seen in a realistic context: the studied gestures go awry. The logic of cheap myths is overcome by a conscious demonstration, by a comical–serious rehearsal of cinematic conventions. The subject of women is particularly important here. Their reduction to goods-for-men with a price tag, their fixation in the roles of the man-eating vamp or the naïve girl-woman are themes that are treated again and again in the form of grotesque exaggerations.

Pina Bausch's poetical theatre of experience introduces the body to the theatre by choosing as its subject the body in its corset of bourgeois conventions; it emancipates dance and creates its own means of expression. In the *Tanztheater* of Wuppertal the body speaks for itself about itself – as was the goal of *Ausdruckstanz*, but now without the irrational fatefulness of that form of dance.

Folkwang, Reinhild Hoffmann and Susanne Linke

The idea of the autonomy of a purely physical expression derived from *Ausdruckstanz* connects the protagonists of the new theatre of dance with the dance traditions of the twenties. For Gerhard Bohner, Pina Bausch, Reinhild Hoffmann and Susanne Linke this connection is established through their training at the Folkwang-Schule in Essen and their work for it, as well as, in some cases, direct studies under Mary Wigman.

The Folkwang-School was founded in 1928 as a school for the performing arts. Kurt Jooss became head of the department of dance a year later and assembled a company of dancers, the *Folkwang-Tanzbuhne*, which performed his works. When Jooss returned to Germany in 1949, he began again at Folkwang, working with its small company. He remained head of the department of dance and director of the company until 1968. During the fifties and sixties, when in the course of political and artistic reaction classical ballet ruled the German stage and memories of the revolutionary innovations of *Ausdruckstanz* were receding, the Folkwang-School, through the work of Kurt Jooss and his collaborators, maintained the link with the twenties. Together with the private schools of the few *Ausdrucks*-dancers still active – especially the Mary Wigman Studio in Berlin – the Folkwang-*Tanztheater* became one of the centers of the *Ausdruckstanz* heritage in Germany.

Reinhild Hoffmann came to Essen after training in physical education and studied under Kurt Jooss, Hans Züllig and Pina Bausch. In 1971 she moved to Bremen and Hans Kresnik, then returned to the Folkwang-School and became a dancer in the school's company. Pina Bausch had already moved to Wuppertal when Reinhild Hoffmann conceived her first choreography during the mid-seventies. Her breakthrough came in 1977 with *Solo mit Sofa* with music by John Cage and subsequent performances of the work, after taking over the Bremen company, together with Gerhard Bohner. Her work, too, is characterized by the stylistic effects of the Tanztheater – i.e. the alienation effects, the special use of "everyday" movements and the dissolution of conventional storytelling in favor of individually assembled *tableaux*. Her work is different from Pina Bausch, however, since dance remains the fundamental means of expression. Hoffmann's theatrically inspired tableaux are constantly interspersed with choreographed solo and group formations. Unlike the Wuppertal Tanztheater, Hoffmann keeps the focus on dance as the decisive means of expression – not on theatre and acting means. Unlike Hans Kresnik, too, Reinhild Hoffmann is not concerned with current politics and criticism of society. Her main interest is not in the social but in the personal, individual conflict. This introspective view of the psychological and emotional experiences of the individual represents a continuation of the preoccupations of *Ausdruckstanz*.

However, she transcends these preoccupations by showing the psychological structures as socially determined – determined in the main by the power struggle of the sexes. Reinhild Hoffmann looks at everyday types of relationships from a specifically feminist point of view. Her work is dominated by a singular factor – the systematic restrictions imposed on the independent, feminine expression of free will. Because of psychological symbolism of her images, Reinhild Hoffmann remains somewhat closer than Pina Bausch to the body language of *Ausdruckstanz*. This, of course, exposes her to the danger of ingesting fragments of *Ausdruckstanz* ideology.

Susanne Linke is considerably closer to Pina Bausch's criticisms of conventional behavior than to Hoffmann's symbolism. Her training as a dancer reveals the influential heritage of *Ausdruckstanz*. Together with Gerhard Bohner she studied in Berlin with Mary Wigman, then went to the Folkwang-School, where she remained as a dancer at the Folkwang dance studio under Pina Bausch until 1973. The exposure of everyday forms of behavior and the criticism of society determine her work just as strongly as psychological developments. Linke names her principal subjects as "meaninglessness, emptiness, boredom."[2] She, too, assumes a feminist point of view in her work, although her stance is less committed than that of Reinhild Hoffmann. The 50 minute *Frauenballett*, performed for the first time last year, shows women toiling senselessly and monotonously with yards of cloth, to the point of exhaustion. Among them two men are seated, discussing a chair in a scientific manner. They, too, work – think – and the distribution of roles is evident. As for Hans Kresnik, Gerhard Bohner, Pina Bausch and Reinhild Hoffmann, the resources of the *Tanztheater* form the basis of Susanne Linke's work. Body action, functional use of props, choreographically structured scenes constitute the complete work. The *Tanztheater* is not merely the result of the social awareness of the late sixties. It is also a consequence of the memory of the body-oriented rebellion of *Ausdruckstanz* seeking new horizons. This synthesis determines the new German *Tanztheater* and reveals its direction. In the words of Susanne Linke: "I hope that the rhythm and 'swinging' of modern dance, as well as *Ausdruck*, which we have always insisted upon in Germany, will be preserved."

Notes

1 Rudolf von Laban, *Die Welt des Tänzers.* Fünf Gedankenreigen Stuttgart 1922, p. 198.
2 "Es ist schon bitter, dass unsers Stärke zugleich unsere Schwäche ist" Susanne Linke in conversation with Ulric Tegeder. In: *Ballet-Info*, March 1981, p. 17.

An American perspective on Tanztheater

Susan Allene Manning

Originally published in *TDR*, Spring, 1986

At a symposium of German and American modern dance held last fall at Goethe House New York, Anna Kisselgoff, chief dance critic for *The New York Times,* turned to Reinhild Hoffmann, director of the Tanztheater Bremen, and asked in exasperation, "But why aren't you more interested in dance vocabularies?" Hoffmann did not answer but instead turned to Nina Weiner, a New York choreographer, and asked, "But why aren't you more interested in the social problems seen in a city like New York?" Weiner did not answer.

This incomplete exchange – two questions that received no answers – summarizes the divergence between German and American modern dance today. While American choreographers generally emphasize the inherent expressivity of pure movement and consider narrative or representational subject matter beside the point, new German choreographers reverse these priorities and consider subject matter far more important than the formal display of movement values. In other words, the new German choreographers are no more interested in exploring "dance vocabularies" than their American counterparts are in engaging "social problems." With few exceptions, critics follow the inclinations of their national choreographers. Hence the New York critics by and large dismissed the *Tanztheater* (literally "dance theatre") featured as part of the Brooklyn Academy of Music's Next Wave Festival last fall. The same critics who praised American postmodern choreographers for challenging received definitions of "dance" criticized Pina Bausch, Reinhild Hoffmann, and Mechthild Grossmann because their works were not "dance." And even though critics conceded that the works of Susanne Linke exhibit dance interest, they still criticized her solos' overt content. (Gerhard Bohner, whose *Triadic Ballet*, 1977, received its American premiere at the Joyce Theatre, generally escaped the critical polemics that embroiled his female colleagues, perhaps because his work was not burdened with the "Next Wave" label.)

The German critics are no less chauvinistic than the Americans. They too defend their own modern dance tradition by criticizing the dominant style on the other side of the Atlantic. Jochen Schmidt, dance critic for the *Frankfurter Allgemeine Zeitung* and a participant in the Goethe House symposium, once compared the "depth" of tanz-theater with the "lightness" of American postmodern dance and concluded that "the American art of lightness [may] all too quickly [become] an art of insignificance" (1982: 13).

Although German and American modern dance have always defined independent traditions, the divergence between the two traditions has not always been as great as it is today. Although choreographers like Isadora Duncan, Mary Wigman, Kurt Jooss, and Martha Graham developed distinctly different styles of modern dance, they were united in their refusal to separate the formal values of movement from the social import of dance. In fact, modern dance originated in Germany and America from the double impulse to not only establish movement as a self-sufficient means for expression but also to subvert and perhaps transform dominant social values. At first modern dancers connected the formal and social impulses in utopian terms. They believed that the experience of dance could free energies within the individual and within society, energies that could lead from personal to cultural renewal. Modern dancers later turned away from such utopian visions and staged their social critique through sympathetically portraying marginal social types or enacting agitprop parables. They believed that dance should confront the viewer with aspects of social life demanding reform. But whether utopian or confrontational, modern dance in Germany and America took its social mission as seriously as its formal mission.

After World War II modern dance lost this sense of its dual mission, for clear socio-political reasons. After 1933 National Socialism appropriated *ausdruckstanz,* (literally "dance of expression"), as modern dance was known in the '20s, and made it serve ideological ends, as in the opening-night spectacle for the 1936 Berlin Olympic Games staged by Wigman, Gret Palucca, Harald Kreutzberg, and others. After the war *ausdruckstanz* never regained its earlier stature, in part because of its Fascist ideological taint. To Germans it seemed unsuited to the new era of postwar recovery, an era that preferred the supposedly untainted classicism of ballet. Yet, in actuality, the Nazis had promoted ballet as requisite training for professional dancers and an appropriate public diversion. Even so, as West German cities vied to found ballet companies of international stature during the '50s and early '60s, they built on the foundation laid by National Socialism. Ironically enough, ballet at the time seemed a refuge of internationalism, classicism, and formalism.

While West German dance took refuge in ballet during the early post-war years, American dance adopted an increasingly formalist credo. Ballet choreographers followed the example of George Balanchine, and modern dancers that of Merce Cunningham, as both idioms enjoyed the security of America's newfound cultural and political dominance. Choreographers no longer struggled to fuse formal values with social import. Rather they gloried in technical virtuosity and formal experimentation and play. American critics responded by orienting their writing more toward description and less toward interpretation.

Beginning in the late '60s, stimulated by the youth upheavals of the 1968 period, young German choreographers reacted against the formalism of German ballet and of American dance. In fact, they associated the ballet boom with the postwar era's relentless Americanization, and they wanted to break its hold if only for that reason. So they reached back to the traditions of *ausdruckstanz* and intermingled influences drawn from experimental theatre and, surprisingly, from American modern dance. Indeed, tanztheater shows the simultaneous rejection and integration of American influences, a paradox that serves as an apt metaphor for cultural relations between West Germany and the United States in the '80s.

Perhaps even more surprising is the paradoxical relationship between tanztheater and German ballet. While tanztheater choreographers explicitly negate the principles of classical and neoclassical ballet, they generally work with ballet-trained dancers in companies within the municipal repertory system. Because tanztheater choreographers are dependent on the repertory system's patronage, they must accept its orientation toward ballet. They both resent this orientation and exploit the values of their dancers' daily discipline.

Pina Bausch has evolved the most distinctive and the most internationally known form of tanztheater. Directing the Tanztheater Wuppertal since 1973, she has evolved a large-scale, improvisational performance mode that long ago transcended its specific sources in her training with Kurt Jooss at the Folkwang School (1955–59) and her studies at Juilliard in New York (1960–61). Like her contemporaries in theatre, Bausch combines a visually rich production style with techniques drawn from Stanislavski and Brecht, and the result approaches Artaud's idea of a theatre of cruelty. Her performers employ Method principles, infusing their interactions with the intensity and pain of remembered experience. At the same time they employ alienation techniques, undercutting the spectator's sympathetic identification by presenting their role-playing as self-consciously theatrical. The result is a performance that simultaneously distances and engages the spectator. This push and pull leaves many spectators exhausted by the end of the evening, overwhelmed by the emotional complexity of the experience. Bausch's theatre of cruelty effects a peculiar catharsis, for the experience of the work leaves spectators drained, but with no sense of resolution.

Especially unresolved are the images of gender roles and sexual relations. Bausch shows men and women locked into power plays and obsessive patterns of physical and emotional violence. For instance, near the beginning of *Bluebeard* (1977), Beatrice Libonati lies on her back, clutching Jan Minarik's head on her stomach, and drags the two of them across the floor strewn with dead leaves. Near the end Minarik reverses the action and drags Libonati across the floor, her body rigidly bloated by layers of dresses. In *Gebirge* (1984) Josephine Anne Endicott repeatedly lies down before Jan Minarik, pulling her skirt up over her head so that he can draw a red X on her bare back. But even when he stops marking her back, she continues to prostrate herself before him. In Bausch's works moments of tenderness and humor only occasionally relieve the ugliness of male–female relations.

The women, often dressed in old-fashioned formals and high heels, become sex objects and sexual victims, while the men, often dressed in black tuxedoes, become sexual oppressors. At times the images reverse: men become the victims and women the victimizers, or the men dress in drag and become narcissists, competing with the women to become sex objects. The images of masculinity and femininity are never idealized, for Bausch presents no independent yet caring women, no strong yet sensitive men. Rather she frames the images of gender roles in the boundary zone between reality and fantasy. The men and women on stage suggest both the projections of unconscious desires and the real-life analogues of battered wives, numb whores, and sexually confused men. Hence Bausch's theatre functions both as psychological projection and as reflection of reality.

Bausch's distinctive mode of tanztheater emerged in the mid-'70s. Strikingly, its characteristic form evolved together with its characteristic subject matter. Although Bausch had shown choreographic daring from the time her first work premiered in 1968, she did not push her dance structures beyond the limits that traditionally define choreography until the mid-'70s. At that same time gender roles and sexual relations became her primary focus.

In earlier works Bausch respected the traditional limits of choreography by setting dance to a continuous musical score. Hence *Afterzero*

(1970) and *Actions for Dancers* (1971) were set to music by contemporary composers, Ivo Malec and Günter Decker respectively. A triumvirate of dances set to classical compositions followed: Wagner's "Bacchanale" from *Tannhäuser* (1972), Gluck's *Iphigenie on Tauris* (1974) and *Orpheus and Eurydice* (1975). During the same period other works, namely *Fritz* (1974) and *Ich bring dich urn die Ecke ...* (1974), moved toward a fusion of dance and theatre. Bausch's performers began to not only execute choreographed movement sequences but also to play theatre games, to sing and tell stories, and to project shifting character roles.

The Rite of Spring (1975) and *The Seven Deadly Sins* (1976) marked the transition to Bausch's mature mode. Although both used familiar scores, neither was limited to the score that titled the work as a whole: in *The Rite of Spring* Bausch set the titled score as the third part, following the first two parts set to other Stravinsky compositions, and in *The Seven Deadly Sins* she set the titled score as the first half, followed by a collection of other Weill songs under the subtitle "Don't Be Afraid." Thus both works sprawled beyond the duration and unity imposed by a continuous musical score. As Bausch developed her fusion of dance and theatre, she left behind live orchestral accompaniment and substituted a collage of recorded music, the dancers' own voices, the sounds of their moving bodies, and silence.

The Stravinsky and Weill works also introduced Bausch's characteristic subject matter. While earlier dances like *Afterzero* and *Actions for Dancers* had made little distinction between the sexes and instead focused on images of debilitated bodies – according to Jochen Schmidt, both men and women looked like "the leftovers from some war or atomic catastrophe. ... members of some deformed thalidomide society" (1984: 14) – *The Rite of Spring* and *The Seven Deadly Sins* presented clear distinctions and tensions between the sexes. While the Stravinsky work comprised three choreographic variations on the theme of antagonism between the sexes, the Weill work staged two alternate visions of male exploitation and female self-degradation, visions that challenged any simplistic interpretation by showing women dressed as men and men dressed as women. With *The Rite of Spring* and *The Seven Deadly Sins* Bausch had found her form and her subject matter.

The works that followed – including *Bluebeard*, *Kontakthof* (1978), *Arien* (1979), *1980* (1980), and *Gebirge* – charted the contours of Bausch's mature mode. Interestingly, this mode juxtaposes two extremes of scale – the monumental and the intimate. These dances comprise huge assemblages of fragments and push the performers' and

Figure 5 The Rite of Spring (1975): Tanztheater Wuppertal. © Ursula Kaufmann

spectators' endurance beyond the usual limit of a two- to three-hour performance broken by one or two intermissions. Everything about the works is monumental – their duration, the size of the theatre space opened to the back walls of the opera house, the 20 or more dancers always onstage, and the sprawling, multi-focused, chaotic quality of the stage action.

Yet at the same time a definite intimacy characterizes the works, an intimacy that results from the use of improvisation as part of both the choreographic process and the performance structure. Never alone on-stage, performers are always interacting and responding to one another and to the stage environment. They constantly shift from one role to another, and yet, paradoxically, each dancer projects a coherent identity. The performers seem more like people with widely varying body types, accents, and personalities than like dancers. Throughout Meryl Tankard seems clownlike, Monika Sagon demure, Sylvia Kesselheim shrill, Dominique Mercy sunny, Lutz Forster aloof. Especially when the performers break the proscenium, spectators feel an intimate connection with them as people. This sense of intimacy contradicts the works' monumental scale.

Each work creates an environment often defined through distinctive floor coverings – dead leaves in *Bluebeard*, water in *Arien*, grass in 1980, dirt in *Gebirge*. As each work progresses, the dancers mark and are marked by their environment. Their hair becomes entangled with dead leaves, their clothes become waterlogged, their skin becomes smeared with dirt. They bring on objects and then discard them – chairs, pieces of clothing, toys. Other objects appear of their own accord, like the miniature frigate and the hippopotamus in *Arien*, and add to the accumulation of things onstage. The environment is constant – remaining essentially the same at the end as at the beginning, except that it becomes worn, littered, used up.

Discarded costumes often appear among the stage debris. In fact, constant costume changes mark the performers' shifting roles, suggesting that the performers' roles are like costumes to be put on and taken off at will. The performers often dress and undress onstage, frequently assisted by one another. Even when they change offstage, they often reenter still adjusting their undergarments, zipping their last zipper, or buttoning their last button. At times the performers, usually the women, are forced into layers and layers of costumes. This happens to Libonati in *Bluebeard*, when Minarik dresses her in the Victorian gowns cast off by the other women; to a row of seated women in *Arien*, when the men doll them up with make-up and odd pieces of clothes; and to Keselheim in *Gebirge*, when Minarik wraps gauze around her, covering even her face. The women become paralyzed by the layers of clothes, paralyzed by the signals of gender identity.

Costume changes are only one of the motifs that recur from work to work. Indeed, Bausch's works are like miscellaneous assemblages of motifs that keep reappearing in transformed guises. There are children's games (duck-duck-goose in *1980*, musical chairs in *Arien*) and social rituals (the dinner party in *Arien*, the funeral and formal good-byes in *1980*). There are images of food and of eating. In *1980* performers enter with plates of jello, and Kyomi Ichida throws her piece into the air and catches it on her plate like a juggler, while Grossmann shakes her piece of jello and then her breasts; in *Gebirge*, Minarik makes a sandwich of his hand and offers it to a spectator. There are endless line-ups, processions, and take-offs on beauty contests. In *1980* one woman has a row of men drop their drawers, exposing their buttocks to the audience, while she walks in front of them inspecting their genitals; later the women line up, a man walks down the line inspecting the jiggle in their breasts, and ultimately a quarrel breaks out as to who has the best-looking leg; as *Kontakthof* begins, the performers one by one come downstage, show their various profiles, and bare their teeth. There are images of narcissism and self-display. In *Kontakthof,* Dominique Mercy and Anne Marie Benati sit across from one another and with adolescent self-consciousness strip to their undergarments; in *1980* the performers expose all varying patches of skin as they sunbathe.

The catalog continues: performers play word games, monologize, tell stories. In *1980* Benati tells the story of her father dressing her as a child and often forgetting her underpants; later the dancers shout out three-word associations with their country of national origin; in *Arien* performers play a game substituting the name of a body part for the blank in a sentence. Two men or two women perform a turn together, as in *Kontakthof* when Tankard and Endicott appear in party frocks and dance girlishly. In *Gebirge* Forster and Mercy dance a soft-shoe number. Authoritarian director/choreographer figures appear. In *1980* Minarik functions as a master of ceremonies; in *Kontakthof* he wanders around with a clip-board inspecting the technical equipment while Endicott and Sagon instruct the others like ballet mistresses.

Needless to say, the disparate images come together in different ways for different spectators. For me the parts of *Gebirge* remained fragments and never coalesced as a whole. Minarik as a monster man, Kaufmann wearing a red woman's bathing suit and heavy red lipstick, pine trees hauled onstage and then carted away – these incongruous juxtapositions seemed like a bad dream of a Bausch work, designed to confound and bore the spectator. Yet the various images of *1980* and *Kontakthof*, probably no less disparate than those in *Gebirge*, came together for me and resonated around an ineffable center. The theme of play seemed to anchor *1980* – the children's games, the physical self-display of the sunbathers, the magician's display of skill, the role-playing of Tankard as the dotty English tourist and Grossmann as the punk screaming "fantastic." The work seemed to equate theatrical play and social play: we play at roles in life, especially at gender roles, just as performers play at roles in the theatre. This same double reference to theatrical and social realities seemed to anchor *Kontakthof,* except that it cut sharper and deeper than in *1980:* just as performers take on roles vis-à-vis the audience, we take on roles vis-à-vis one another, and in both instances role-playing involves a mixture of pleasure, self-disgust, resentment, and desperation.

This is not to say that Bausch's work can be reduced to the theme of role-playing. Indeed, her works deliberately defy any single, reductive interpretation, even as they demand to be interpreted. This paradox of interpretation also appeared in the works of modern dancers between the wars – Wigman, Jooss, Graham, and others – and appears in the works of the generations of George Balanchine and Merce Cunningham. Bausch's fusion of dance and theatre, however antithetical to current modes of American dance, does not place her outside the tradition of modern dance, for she revitalizes its tension between the denial and the possibility of interpretation. Although Bausch, like her American contemporaries, breaks the essential connection the earlier generation effected between dance's formal values and its social import, she continues the tradition by recasting the paradox of interpretation. Violating one aspect of the tradition while reworking another, Bausch pushes the evolution of modern dance in a new direction.

Bausch exerts a pervasive influence on the second generation of tanztheater choreographers, especially on those who have worked directly with her, such as Reinhild Hoffmann and Mechthild Grossmann. Hoffmann studied at the Folkwang School with Jooss and Bausch from 1965 to 1970. She later directed the Folkwang Studio from 1974 to 1977 before she took over the Tanztheater Bremen in 1978, at first in tandem with Gerhard Bohner and since 1981 alone. Grossmann worked as an actress in Bremen, Stuttgart, and Bochum before joining Bausch's company in 1979, having first worked with her in 1976 on *Don't Be Afraid.* Grossmann has pursued independent theatre and film work while maintaining her affiliation with the company. In varied ways the works of Hoffmann and Grossmann echo Bausch. At the Goethe House symposium Hoffmann noted that the images of violence between men and women in tanztheater were often intended as symbols of violence between other oppositions such as ideologies or nations. But this level of reference was not apparent in the work she premiered at the Next Wave Festival. Curiously, *Callas* (1983) takes for granted the assumptions of tanztheater, yet the work subverts the mode by presenting only its form and not its content. The characteristic devices of tanztheater become Hoffmann's subject, rather than the world at large.

Set to a series of arias recorded by Maria Callas, *Callas* is more formalized and more self-referential than Bausch's work. Hoffmann displays her choreographic control by clearly structuring the work into eight titled sections, each built around the use of a specific set of props. Unlike Bausch's work, *Callas* does not show motifs overlapping and doubling back. Nor does it evidence the improvisational energy characteristic of Bausch's work. Hoffmann's dancers exhibit a more uniform body type and seem more anonymous than Bausch's dancers. Hence they appear less like individual personalities the spectator comes to know in the course of a performance. The dancers remain firmly behind the proscenium and do not intrude into the audience's space. The stage for *Callas*, curtained and carpeted, suggests a theatre foyer. Hence *Callas* refers to itself as theatre rather than to an environment half-fantastical, half-real. The title, the accompaniment, and the set suggest self-reflexive comment, though the comment's point of view escaped me.

The work echoes images from Bausch – the cross-dressing, the high heels and old-fashioned evening gowns, the violence between men and women. Although the images are original and not simply derivative, they seem hollow, for they refer only to their own theatricality. In the first section, "At the Opera," both male and female performers appear in long red evening dresses, carrying forms shaped like torsos dressed in formal attire. The dancers promenade these forms as if holding invisible partners. Later the forms become theatre seats, and a man and woman lose and find one another within the seated crowd. In "Two White Women" a woman paints her shoes red, and then the red paint smears her white dress and a runway of white paper, as her alter ego, also dressed in white, flits around her. In "Taming" the men crack whips at the women, and later the women respond by cracking whips at the men. Men carry a cut-out of a grand piano on their backs in "Grand Piano," and they hold cut-outs of dress forms and mirror the movements of the women in "Doll and Mirror." In "Table" a woman walks over a table created by a long length of cloth pulled taut by the other dancers, presumably guests at her dinner party. In "The Fat

Singer" men stuff balloons into the underclothes of a woman wearing only a fur coat, and in "Swing" a woman with a stool affixed under her dress sits in semi-darkness as a metronome ticks, and a young girl swings on and off stage. Whereas Bausch shows the process and struggle of creating tanztheater, Hoffmann takes its aesthetic for granted as the dominant mode.

In *Where My Sun Shines For Me* (1984) Grossmann also assumes the basic principles of Bausch's tanztheater, though she internalizes them in order to reveal an unexplored aspect of the mode. She reduces Bausch's revue format to a solo form by zeroing in on costume changes as the essential structure for her series of transformations from one role to another. Significantly, the highpoint of the series is her cross-dressing. In this way Grossmann explores an area that Bausch leaves relatively untouched, for male impersonators appear far less often than female impersonators in Bausch's work.

Grossmann impersonates a man the way a Japanese *onnagata* impersonates a woman – by seeming to embody the opposite sex not only physically but also spiritually, but without attempting to fool the spectators as a transvestite might. The high point of her performance comes when she impersonates a father reciting advice to a son while moving through a series of repeated gestures – hitching up his pants, scratching behind his ear, reaching into his vest pocket. Finally "he" strips to briefs, complete with a false penis, and assumes body-builder poses. Grossmann's male impersonation convinces even when she is nearly nude. Like an *onnagata* who seems feminine even offstage, Grossmann seems masculine even when impersonating women. Sitting on top of a piano and belting out a cabaret song in her low throaty voice, she exposes a generous length of shapely leg, yet something about her still reads as masculine. The overt unifying device for *Where My Sun Shines For Me* is the sun motif – as sung in the title song, as recited in a passage from *Antigone*, as drawn on the blackboard in the shape of a sun face. But the real interest of the piece lies in Grossmann's fusion and confusion of gender identity. Like Bausch, Grossmann uses her tanztheater to explore the fragility and complexity of our notions of masculinity and femininity.

Although Susanne Linke also studied with Bausch (1968–71), her work does not show as strong an influence as Hoffmann and Grossmann's. From 1973 to 1975 she directed the Folkwang Studio along with Hoffmann. Earlier (1964–67) she had studied with Wigman and saw Dore Hoyer, the last of the *ausdruckstanz* soloists, perform. When she first presented her solo evenings in 1981, the *ausdruckstanz* influence predominated.

Whereas Grossmann reduces Bausch's revue format to a solo form, Linke reaches back to the solo form characteristic of Wigman and Hoyer. This form extends one central dance idea to its fullest yet most economical realization. In *Orient-Occident* (1984) the core idea is the confusion of the dancer's costume with her body. The result is that she seems creaturelike rather than human as she crosses the stage in a horizontal shaft of light. The spectator cannot differentiate the creature's limbs from her gauzy costume from her loosely-flowing hair. In *Flood* (1981) the core idea is the dancer's play with a long length of blue cloth. The cloth becomes the flood engulfing Linke, and Linke in turn dissolves her body in the free flow of energy impulses, like rushing water. Unlike Bausch, Linke does not eschew the earlier generation's emphasis on the formal values of movement.

But Linke's solos are more than nostalgic evocations of the *ausdruckstanz* aesthetic. Like her female contemporaries, she cannot help but explore images of gender. *Swans Weigh* (1982) presents the image of a debilitated swan who becomes progressively weaker and ultimately collapses in a symbolic death. On one level, the work ironically comments on Petipa's *Swan Lake* and Fokine's *The Dying Swan,* suggesting that today's scene distorts the swans of earlier ballets. But on another level, the solo associates the swan's debilitation with the layering of masculinity over femininity, for Linke wears an oversized black tuxedo jacket with tails over a romantic-length tutu. Her distorted movement cannot be separated from the costume's distortion of her form, and her distorted form cannot be separated from its layering of the masculine tuxedo over the feminine tutu.

Bath Tubbing (1980) presents a woman interacting with an old-fashioned stand-up bathtub. On one level, the solo is a virtuosic play between the dancer's form and the bathtub's form, requiring Linke to precisely control her weight against the weight of the bathtub. But on another level, Linke seems like a housewife lost in fantasy as she performs her daily chore of cleaning the tub. However, she never fully realizes the fantasy of the lady of the house luxuriating in her bath, for when she completely disappears into the tub, it falls over with a clank and reveals her inert form inside. Like *Swans Weigh*, *Bath Tubbing* ends with a symbolic death. In this way the two solos uncannily connect to the *ausdruckstanz* tradition, for Wigman's solos often ended with a symbolic death. Without presuming to recreate Wigman's aesthetic, Linke manages to reinterpret its spirit in a manner attuned to the concerns of tanztheater.

Gerhard Bohner also connects his works to the *ausdruckstanz* tradition. Bohner trained as a ballet dancer and performed with the

Deutsche Oper in Berlin from 1961 to 1971; he also studied with Wigman in the mid-'60s. Since that time he has worked as a freelance choreographer, with longer stints in Darmstadt (1962–75) and Bremen (1978–81), where he shared the directorship with Hoffmann. But whereas Linke reinterprets the spirit of the earlier tradition, Bohner attempts to reconstruct a lost masterpiece – Oskar Schlemmer's *Triadic Ballet*, originally premiered in 1922. In contrast to Linke, Bohner presumes to recreate Schlemmer's aesthetic, but in the end he manages neither to do so nor to reinterpret Schlemmer's aesthetic in vital contemporary terms. His attempted reconstruction, set to a contemporary score composed by Hans-Joachim Hespos, involves a free improvisation on Schlemmer's costume designs. That Bohner's work fails to recreate the spirit of the original is evidenced by the divergence between the opening 12 sections and the closing "Wire Costume and Gold Balls," the only section notated sufficiently to allow for an "authentic" reconstruction. "Wire Costume and Gold Balls" shows how Schlemmer piled symmetry on top of symmetry – the geometries of the costumes against the grid of the choreography's spatial design against the measures of Handel's music – and in so doing dehumanized the dancers. In contrast, Bohner layers the asymmetries of modern music and modernist choreography on top of the symmetries of ballet technique and Schlemmer's costumes, and the result confuses the absurdity of dehumanization with the idiosyncrasy of contemporary style. Bohner's *Triadic Ballet* attempts to humanize a work that relied on dehumanization for its effect and ends up distorting both the prewar and postwar aesthetics of German modern dance.

Perhaps the most astounding aspect of last fall's appearances by the companies of Bausch, Hoffmann, Grossmann, Linke, and Bohner was the negative response by the New York dance community, critics and performers alike. It is puzzling why so many interested Americans – and Germans – feel compelled to take sides, why they cannot accept each other's aesthetic on its own terms. Obviously, if the American proponents of formalism and the German proponents of anti-formalism felt totally secure about their own positions, they would not react so defensively to one another. Their defensiveness suggests to me that the most vocal advocates fear that their positions are incomplete and inadequate. It is as if both the formalists and the anti-formalists sense the impoverishment of the postwar split between the social mission and formal mission of modern dance. On some level, the Americans realize that they have reneged on the early modern dancers' belief that their art could transform the dominant values of society. On some level, the Germans realize that they have reneged on the early modern dancers' belief that movement alone could become articulate.

It would be naive to predict a synthesis of the two aesthetics, even though certain trends in the American dance world point to the possibility of a reconciliation. But these trends, like the work of Meredith Monk and the engagement of postmodern choreographers with narrative and spectacle, are not new, and they have yet to make a significant dent in the prevailing formalist aesthetic. More likely is that American dance will absorb the influences from abroad – not only from tanztheater but also from Japanese butoh – and render them as additional possibilities within the compass of formal pluralism. If that happens, American modern dance will have missed a chance to assess itself critically through the mirror of its other. Such a self-assessment might well spur the recovery of its lost sense of social mission.

References

Schmidt, Jochen. 1982 "What moves them and how: on several trends and tendencies of the '81/82 Dance Season", *Ballett International*, 5(6/7), June–July.

——1984 "Pina Bausch: A Constant Annoyance", In Norbert Servos and Gert Weigelt, *Pina Bausch Wuppertal Dance Theatre*, Cologne: Ballett-Buhnen-Verlag.

The theatre of images

Pina Bausch and the expressionist temperament

Barbara Confino
Originally published in *Cityweek*, 18 July, 1988

An armless woman in a red dress stands alone on the stage, smiling fatuously at the audience. A man and a woman rush on, only to fling themselves to the ground. A second man enters, carefully arranges their now inert bodies, and then performs the marriage ceremony. A man on a hospital bed is wheeled onstage and left there by himself. Eventually he sits up, asks for something, is ignored. Increasingly agitated, he ends by having a temper tantrum and screaming. *Yo quiero café! Yo quiero café!* All these scenes take place at the bottom of a dirt pit. The pit is at the Brooklyn Academy of Music and the poor bedeviled creatures floundering in it are members of Pina Bausch's celebrated Wuppertal Tanztheater.

Ever since she took the New York dance world by surprise in 1984, Pina Bausch's Tanztheater has been eagerly awaited by audiences avid to see what new wonders this brilliant German choreographic *Kapellmeister* might bring to our relatively tame theatrical shores.

A dazzling exponent of the theatre of images and the direct inheritor of the German expressionist tradition, Pina Bausch has synthesized and brought to a high degree of theatrical perfection major trends in both 20th century dance and drama. Beginning, in a certain sense, with symbolist theatre and the fascination felt by the likes of W. B. Yeats and Ezra Pound for the intensely visual, gestural, and ritualistic Noh drama of Japan, a theatre of images has evolved that removes the emphasis from the spoken text and places it on other aspects of production, notably scenic design and physical gesture.

Classical Ballet, of course, had done this since the days of Caterina de Medici, but formal ballet with its *commedia dell'arte* mime tradition was too romantic, too ethereal to express a modern vision. Though it has proved itself surprisingly elastic and almost parasitically absorbent of other traditions, ballet is steeped in a formal esthetic that goes directly back to the Renaissance, particularly to the Florentine *quattrocentro* with its emphasis on line, symmetry, and mathematical relationships. To top this off, it embodied a quintessentially (if we are to believe Jung) Western desire to defy gravity and fly. Consequently, two things were all important in classical ballet: an elegant line and *ballon,* the mysterious ability possessed by every great jumper to float suspended in mid-air, hesitating a moment before descent. Ballet in fact had an undeniable aversion to the ground. Air was its element. Modern dance, on the other hand, has been earthbound from the start. Martha Graham, for example, has her dancers do most of their exercises on the floor. As far as form is concerned, however, her technique is built on an angular variation on the Renaissance line inherited from ballet. And so, despite the heroic struggles of its founders, modern dance, when seen side by side with ballet, constitutes a minor rebellion from the great European tradition, not a full-scale revolution. The kinship of the two styles is abundantly clear.

Enter post-modern dance. Chafing at the limitations of the still highly confined and stylized vocabulary of modern dance, in the late 1950s choreographers such as Merce Cunningham and Ann Halprin began to experiment with the expressive possibilities of everyday movement. The focus shifted from dance to gesture. Any kind of movement in conjunction with any other became the legitimate stuff of choreography.

As for drama, the avant-garde rejection of realism began early in the century. With his 1902 *A Dream Play,* Strindberg created the precedent for the revolutionary expressionist experiments soon to come. Episodic, non-linear, dream-like, using type characters ("the Father," "the Woman") and polyphonic dialogue in which the lines of one actor flowed into the lines of another, almost as if they were participants in a collective stream of consciousness, his play was considered virtually unproduceable until directors began to place the scenes in stark, simple settings. These located the actions in the realm of the imagination and helped to free the audience from the need to "make sense" of plays intended to be experienced like-rituals, not understood like textbooks.

From *A Dream Play,* it was only a short step to the full-blown expressionism of the German stage. Preferring rhythmic and staccato language or long, droning monologues, and – particularly in the work of the Russian director Meyerhold, whose biomechanics and *jeux de theatre* trained the actor's body acrobatically and gesturally – a non-realistic movement style, expressionist theatre made a definitive break with narrative structure in favor of a rhythmic, musical, non-rational conception of theatre.

If formally expressionism was musical, emotionally it was grim – often violent, almost always somber, its humor invariably bleak. Even when it appropriated, as Pina Bausch frequently does, pop culture elements full of *joie de vivre,* it did so wryly, as ironic touches of light on a black canvas. When dance moved away from the studied ballet style and drama broke with the naturalist tradition, it was inevitable that the two forms should start exploring some of the same territory. While dance, which had been highly artificial, was moving towards a kind of naturalism by incorporating everyday movements, avant-garde drama was rejecting realism in favor of various forms of abstraction as well as cultivating an increasingly physical style of acting. As each began adopting some of the prerogatives of the other, the boundaries between them broke down and a hybrid form emerged: a new theatre of images. Like music, this theatre does not tell a story; it conveys feelings via physical, vocal, and visual images treated symphonically. Depending on the director's orientation, the emphasis is varied. While Richard Foreman's theatre is more verbal, Robert Wilson's is more pictorial.

In Pina Bausch's Tanztheater the stress is on movement. And yet, her impulse is dramatic: it's just that the drama is broken into fragments. A sequence in which women are carried uncomfortably onstage by men is followed by one in which the men are carried onstage by the women; both are followed by an auction scene in which furniture is moved about in a similar manner. The analogy is clear.

In another image a woman in a loose-fitting coat runs onstage, throws down her coat, says good-evening to the audience, then glances at her watch and runs off in dismay. She does this again and again. We are left to fill in the details of the story. Is she a suburban housewife, eternally late? A harried professional with a back-breaking yuppie schedule? Instead of sketching in the moment before and the moment after, Bausch repeats this carefully chiseled image until we have memorized it.

Unlike Robert Wilson's use of repetition, Bausch's does not hypnotize, but awakens. Her images make you think as well as feel, establishing a rare balance. Intellectual as well as emotional associations come tumbling to mind. Though, again, unlike Robert Wilson, there are no concessions to beauty. Hers is a singularly unsensual theatre; instead of the almost languid gorgeousness of Wilson's work there is a gritty, coarse quality to Bausch's *mise-en-scène.* The gestures she employs are frequently awkward, even gawky, and the stage is dully illuminated by flat overall light. Yet what never fails to impress is the richness of her invention. One striking image, one mini drama after another takes the stage, unravels, and is gone.

Viktor, the new work presented at BAM, while not possessing the concentrated imaginative brilliance of earlier offerings, exhibits all the Bausch trademarks. The images flow into each other with the seamless quality of a film montage, coming and going rhythmically as in music; the choreography is made up of crisply modeled theatrical moments that often take ordinary words and movements as points of departure, the set is stark and evocative, juxtaposing monumentality with emptiness; the vision is bleak and Germanic; the laughter funereal.

Bausch's foxtrots and folksongs have the merriment of a wake, not the sunlit exuberance of an Italian fiesta. Here, even more than in her formal and technical aspects, Pina Bausch is the quintessential German expressionist, dark, brooding, uncompromising; someone for whom nothing escapes the taint of universal despair. An aura of Weimar decadence pervades her work; yet unlike her expressionist predecessors, she does not voice her social concerns in obvious polemics or long harangues; her images make her social vision clear. By placing her dancers at the bottom of a dirt ruin that is slowly being filled, we know without being told exactly what she thinks. In the Wuppertal Tanztheater of Pina Bausch, the expressionist sensibility and the theatre of images are a perfect match.

The mistrust of life – relations in dance

Connections between Butoh, *Ausdruckstanz* and Dance Theatre in contemporary experimental dance

Eva van Schaik

Originally published in *Ballett International*, May, 1990

Ger van Leeuwen has directed a small dance laboratory in Amsterdam called Danslab since 1981. Although his studio and modest theatre facilities in a former factory are primarily intended for young inexperienced dancers coming from Dutch dance schools, experimentalists in mixed media performance from all over the world work at the space showcasing a variety of extremely different approaches (and results), ranging from Japanese Butoh expertise to neo-expressionist melodrama, and from visionary surrealist images to biotechnical presentation. These experimentalists in contemporary dance range from ambitious youngsters with lofty aspirations to elder diehards with quieter approaches, presenting themselves as the respectable survivors of a hard struggle for life. Going to these performances, you should be prepared for everything: once I saw a girl swallowing a goldfish, a boy suffocating in clay and a naked couple screaming, biting and scratching their nails upon each other's breast(s). The cruelty of beauty, the tenderness in aggression: the realm of imagination by, in or through dance has no boundaries. Although all these performers searching for old roots are supposed to represent their original cultural identities, according to national differences and daily practice, they also have one and the same intention. Together they create an undercurrent of different streams in contemporary dance; that invisible but powerful force beneath the surface of experimental dance. They are the creation of style, with its various, personal signatures, but through which powerful forces, and under which directing influence is the creative process developed and set in motion? Many outlets of modern dance today that originated in different continents show remarkable similarities in form and vision. Should we ascribe this to pure coincidence – the simple result of certain trends and waves to which every style is subjected – or is this striking similarity in form the result of a coherent chain of socio-political powers at work? Are distances in time and space bridged today, and can we speak of an observable interaction between prewar Ausdruckstanz and postwar neo-expressionism and Butoh, or is the force that determines the movement of dance still a mystery? Simply stated: can we detect the undercurrent of experimental dance? Could there really be one unifying link between all these different outlets in one Amsterdam dancelab, ranging from the deformation of Japanese Butoh to the extreme realist expressionism of dance theatre? As dance belongs – more than any other art form – completely to the instant of its occurrence, it leaves us with nothing more than fixed, static traces and the remnants of remembrance. Supposing there exist intangible interrelations between these streams on the outer surface of modern dance: how, why and to what extent do they interfere and interrelate beneath the surface?

Intrigued by this theoretical question, put forward by the daily practice in his studio annex theatre, Ger van Leeuwen initiated the project "Relations," which took place in several Amsterdam theatres and institutes, from October 1989 to February 1990. The simple question, originated by curiosity, slowly but surely grew into an extensive state-subsidized project of several supporting institutes and foundations. It resulted in more than fifty performances, several workshops (by Rosalia Chladek and Kazuo Ohno), public discussions, extensive video programs and one exhibition, all intended to investigate the possible relations between Ausdruckstanz, Butoh and neo-expressionism. Performances by Kazuo Ohno, Carlotta Ikeda, Yoko Ashikawa and their European followers Pierre Paol Koss, Leonore Welzien and Theo Janssen were programmed next to Anna Sokolow ("Rooms") and Kurt Jooss ("The Green Table") by German Opera Berlin-West, Susanne Linke and Urs Dietrich, Barbara Passow, Michael Diekamp, Christine Brunel, Svea Staltmann, Karin Stefani and Sasha Waltz. Meanwhile, the Foundation V van Laban (five Dutch dancers) produced a historically relevant reconstruction program of solos and duets by Mary Wigman, Gertrud Leistikow, Yvonne Georgi, Harald Kreutzberg, Ruth Page and Roger George. The leading and linking motif was the question: how do these artistic creeds, rooted and developed in different cultural contexts, inspire, influence and shape one another? The supposed relations are indicated by some well known traceable facts: Japanese students followed lessons of Wigman in the 30s, becoming inspired by pictures of La Argentina and other Western dance soloists after 1945; Kreutzberg and Page toured, for instance, in Japan. At the start of the 80s the combined, forceful influences of Pina Bausch and Butoh could be seen in many European companies, differing from France (L'Esquisse, Maguy Marin, Carlyn Carlson, Compagnie Diverres/Montet, Karine Saporta) to England (DV8) to the Federal Republic (Raydiation, Ko Murobushi) and Holland (Shusaku & Dormu Theatre, Anneke Barger) to mention just a few. What do these performances from all over the world, concentrated in time and space, teach about the so-called undercurrents in the ocean of dance?

GER VAN LEEUWEN: Time automatically prompts form. In dance, alternative flows of abstract and expressionist forms follow one another. New dance was still dominated by postmodernism until the end of the 70s, which I define as dance that fulfills itself in abstract terms of space, body and patterns. Consequently, it's quite logical that the Essen-Werden movement (the Folkwang School), emerging in the 70s and with its orientation towards expressionism, struck us as eye opening due to its psychological motives. A transformation introduced itself, a break away from formalism to neo-expressionism. Coincidentally, this Federal German initiative corresponded in time with emancipatory dance movements in Japan, where Butoh dancers reacted against the tradition of formal theatre in which every bodily movement, from nail to nose, had its precise meaning. The Butoh dancers searched for the human being in their experiments. In this respect a striking similarity can be seen between Bausch and Butoh: both are forces of liberation. It sounds a bit dramatic, but in the emergence of the prewar "Absoluter Tanz" one can see an identical resistance towards classicism, formalism and rigid ballet traditions. In its search for emancipatory tools, European modern dance was fifty years ahead of the Japanese. Compared with occidental dance, oriental theatre traditions die more slowly, as they are more deeply rooted, more constricted and constraining. The modern dance of the 80s should be seen as a counter-reaction to formalism. The relation between Ausdruckstanz, Butoh, and dance theatre is their longing to be free from tradition and to be open to new creative pathways. Where academic ballet was often used as a tool for the liberation of the male (often homosexual) creator, modern dance functioned as a liberating force for female homosexuality. Heterosexual liberation in dance is now on its way, and the end of the 80s shows a certain sexual inclination where the battle of the sexes is guided by a remarkable increase of physical violence on stage.

In Butoh dance, however, the nucleus of the performer combines male and female elements; it is epicene in its expressiveness. Butoh always refers to soul, and soul is seen without sexual implications. So, in this respect, Butoh and Bausch differ in their expressions. Another striking resemblance between Federal German and Japanese postwar dance is the process of mourning. Resurrection, after a disastrous war, unmistakably had to lead to the reinvestigation of the fugitive: death is spying around every corner. Therefore, both cultures dance belongs to the domain of doom, destruction, deformation, defeatism, disbelief, and even denial, as a result of a general notion of individual impotence and the disability to deploy and develop one's own faculties and potential during one's life. Shoah and Hiroshima confronted the post-war dance generations in the FRG and in Japan with two undeniable facts: first, the irreversibility of life, and second that nobody can turn away from the realization that the shocking destruction put upon mankind is enacted by none other than mankind itself. Destruction must be recognized in each and every one of us, and 1933–45 proved that we all are capable of these acts of brutality.

Butoh in the Orient and Bausch in the Occident can be seen as second and third generation problems, but, based on my experience, the Federal German audience is not yet ready to cope. The Second World War is still regarded as a natural catastrophe, and moving away from this idea is not yet fully accepted. In this respect, Bausch has been a real breakthrough. Fascinated by her directness, many epigones have stolen her forms, not only in the Federal Republic, but also throughout Europe. Bausch's work spread when the War instigated by Germany and also the Peace, guaranteed by America, had finally been confronted.

The Butoh break away from tightening traditions, with its strong orientation towards dark forces underneath the polished surface, can also be explained as a visible side effect of Shintoism. When everything in life is unified and integrated into one whole, how can anyone discern individuality? Butoh essentially searches to unify or reconcile incompatible elements: so everything is Soul or inspired by Soul, as Soul exists within all natural manifestations. As an individual one has to subject one's manifestation to this unifying idea, producing images in which cruelty and beauty have merged. Bausch certainly emphasizes individuality on different terms: she reacts against predestination in its Calvanistic interpretation and emphasizes the harm people can do one another, both directly and indirectly.

After the performances and workshops of the "Relations" project, I'm convinced that any supposed ties between prewar Ausdruckstanz and postwar Japanese Butoh are purely hypothetical, if they exist at all. The ties are restricted to feelings of respect by some Japanese students toward some European teachers. In fact, this proved to be the weakest link in the chain of our project. To see connections is the result of thinking that such relations exist. Japanese dance-lib looked for emancipation from its own cultural corset and the restrictions of a Coca-Cola mindset as its alternative. Social engagement is much more evident in European dance-lib, even dominant, in its reaction against the superficial happiness of "have a Coke." American athleticism, vital energy, sensibility for movement is answered by a strong longing for more sensitivity. In Bausch and Butoh, performers try to free themselves from rigid role patterns, realizing their subjugation to social systems and the threatening danger of doom and destruction, when power is put in the hands of certain people. Anyhow, it never ends well on their stages ... the newest dance wave in Europe, as well as in Japan, never liberates anyone at the end. Humor and dance have never had a very good relationship, but there seems to be no desire or intention to relax even a little bit in these studios. This general absence shows a striking similarity between the Federal German and the Japanese approach to their shared mourning. Nevertheless, we now are confronted with a remarkable historical cycle, a strange paradox in the general process of time. Japan and Germany as the big losers of 1945 have become important winners – after less than fifty years – not only in terms of economics and politics, but, strangely enough, also in their breakthrough to new directions and explorations in dance.

Today, physical violence on stage collides with increased technical demands of the given dance training. Strange but true, one can observe the most brutal expressions of aggression on stage, but never is any real harm done! The French company L'Esquisse is a very good example: they illustrate strategies of survival. They tell us how to train the body. When you do this correctly the realistic violence we see on stage can do no harm. Once you accept the inevitability of death and the fleeting nature of life, every technique to reconcile the extremities of Eros and Thanatos is acceptable.

Our "Relations" project showed that Federal Germans and Japanese go very well together. Unfortunately, the history of our age has proven this once before. To my mind, this collision of artistically shared ideas is based upon pure coincidence, but their influence on other European dance scenes seems much more interesting. French dancers, for instance, stranded in formalism and the remnants of Petit, developed new approaches after their confrontation with Bausch and Butoh.

It says a lot about American dance since 1945 that this integration of Oriental and Occidental mourning and coping with feelings of impotence never took place, though it is unclear why. Lucas Hoving – one of the founding fathers of American modern dance and still very popular as a caretaker of the tradition and advisor of workshops etc. – once explained to me about the American greed toward physical qualities. This thinking in terms of achievement and prestige does not allow feelings of pessimism. Their last lost war gave the Federal Germans and Japanese graveyards and ruins, from which Butoh and Bausch could rise. Korea and Vietnam, on the other hand, gave the Americans their post-traumatic war invalids, for whom the arts of psychedelia and the escapist cult of drugs and disco could be a compensation during their hospitalization and return to reality.

The undercurrent of Ausdruckstanz, Butoh and dance theatre in the ocean of dance is expressed as a far-reaching tendency toward pessimism. However, the directing force is not a preoccupation with death, but the mistrust of life. The issue is more is there life before death? Sometimes this research leads to moving moments of tenderness, passionate lyricism and clear happiness. But alas, they are very rare and always destroyed after a short while. Melancholy dominates the undercurrent. Even when spring is coming, we feel autumn in its wake. Like Lucky Jim in Kingsley Amis's novel, the individual has many faces for the tidings of unhappiness, but once confronted with happiness itself, he is forced to realize that his face is a blank.

Hurts so good

Judith Mackrell

Originally published in *Guardian*, 23 January, 2002. © Guardian News &
Media Ltd 2002

In modern dance you can count on the fingers of one hand the choreographers who have changed the territory. Martha Graham is one,
Merce Cunningham is another, Pina Bausch is a third. But, while
Graham and Cunningham developed a style that could actually
be taught – that remodeled the training of dancers as well as opening
new windows for choreographers – the influence of Bausch is different.
There's no specific technique that can be labeled Bauschian – there are
no Bausch classes. Yet her influence on the dance profession has been
huge. It is impossible to enumerate the hundreds of works over the
past 20 years whose bleak *Weltanschauung*, skewed narratives and self-
consciously bizarre stagings have screamed their indebtedness to
Bausch.

In Britain, the operation of this influence is especially mysterious.
Over the past two decades Bausch's company, based in the German
town of Wuppertal, has performed only twice in London, and twice in
Edinburgh, showing a total of five works. Val Bourne, the power
behind London's Dance Umbrella festival, remembers the London
season of 1982 as "euphoric, ground-breaking. Everyone in the dance
community was there, and no one had seen anything like it." Bausch's
company did not return to London until 1999. Yet during the intervening years, most British-made dance theatre bore her imprint. Lloyd
Newson, Ian Spink, Mark Murphy and Yolande Snaith are among a
long list of choreographers who are Bausch's natural descendants;
either from having seen her work or from being exposed to its influence
though choreographers such as Anne Teresa de Keersmaeker.

Bausch's works are anything but modest. Most of them are created
on a huge scale, lasting for up to four hours and taking place on stages
that have been transformed into giant dreamscapes. In *Viktor*, 20ft-tall
walls of mud flank the dancers on three sides, so that they appear like
an exposed ant colony or a lost tribe unearthed in an archeological dig.

In *Nelken* the floor is carpeted with thousands of carnations and patrolled by Alsatians. In *Arien* the floor is covered in water. These magical places, simultaneously sinister and beguiling, are peopled by the dreamers themselves, men and women whose fantasies collide in controlled mayhem.

Bausch weaves together her productions from threads of dance, speech, theatrical effects and music, and she spends long months finding the special pattern of each. Often starting with no more than a feeling, she spends weeks with her designer, devising a way into the work's look. In rehearsal she is both catalyst and confessor, getting her company to play with movements and words, drawing out their personal secrets. The final, edited material is part therapy, part play, part fantasy. The characters on stage reveal their damaged psyches in brutally explicit verbal confessionals; they fight for love in bruising duets. Their imaginations flare in wild games and loopy jokes, their dreams concentrate in moments of great tenderness and beauty.

At her best, Bausch finds images of precise visual impact and inexplicably large resonance. In *Nur Du*, her recent piece about California, a pair of reckless lovers embrace on a chair with a stick of lighted dynamite fizzing beneath; in contrast to their heedless passion, lonely narcissists repeatedly tear off their clothes in order to gaze with obsessive desire or horror at their bodies. In *Viktor*, a man appears blinded by lust as he embraces his lover, seemingly unaware that his arms are around another woman, whose breasts he is inadvertently fondling. Bausch's vision of sexuality can be very funny – but it is usually pretty dark.

Bausch's main influence has been her blurring of theatrical boundaries and her peculiar brand of surrealism (as Bourne says, she spawned a lot of imitators in the mid-1980s "who thought all they had to do was talk on stage and improvise in a wild way"). But Bausch is in turn heir to the German expressionist Ausdruckstanz movement and her own first experiments in the mid-1970s have parallels in the work of New York choreographers such as Meredith Monk. A much easier way to source a second-hand Bausch is by looking for certain tics and devices in her work that have been copied the world over.

First on the checklist is the confessional. This has been favored by so many choreographers that it's no longer a surprise to have young men and women interrupt a dance show in order to tell us exactly who they would like to fuck, in what precise ways their parents have messed them up, or what their really weird ambition in life is.

Even more frequently copied has been Bausch's repertoire of sado-masochistic rituals, in which dancers (usually women) hurl themselves repeatedly at their indifferent partners, or submit to various punishing maneuvers, such as being pushed off chairs, tripped over or made to perform humiliating tricks. These fruitless displays of energy and devotion, these desperate acts of submission, have always been a crucial aspect of Bausch's take on power play between adults.

Bausch's fondness for dressing her performers in formal evening wear has become close to cliché, too. In her own shows these outfits frequently suggest that their wearers have been stranded at some long-terminated party, or have got lost in some dream of glamour. Sometimes her dancers look beautiful in their costumes, sometimes they look like travesties – women, in particular, may seem crippled by the height of their stiletto heels or sadly exposed by the cutaway sexiness of a neckline or skirt.

Proof, if any were required, that Bausch has become an institution, is the fact that she has entered the repertory of Les Ballets Trockaderos de Monte Carlo. Best known for their parodies of 19th-century ballet, the Trocks have admitted a few 20th-century classics to their hit list. In *I Wanted to Dance With You at the Café of Experience* (a barely veiled allusion to Bausch's *Café Muller*) their cast of dysfunctional women in saggy cocktail frocks do a wonderfully droll imitation of Bausch's most demented and downcast characters.

So widely imitated is Bausch that her work could start to seem like a parody of itself. Yet the real thing hits you like a force of nature. Not only is Bausch's imagination so much larger and more mysterious than those of her followers, but she also stage-manages it with ruthless skill. As Bourne says: "No one else has her rigor and her powers of editing." What you see in the theatre has the strangeness and the familiarity, the weirdness and the specificity of dreams. It's a very, very hard thing to achieve.

The *New Yorker* critic Arlene Croce once defined Bausch's work as the "pornography of pain" but the term is cheap and inaccurate. It fails to accommodate the glinting, bawdy comedy of which Bausch is capable. It also implies that her take on the world is general and dehumanized, when in fact her dancers always emerge as unique, volatile, funny and knowable. It's this mix of intimacy and off-the-scale weirdness that holds the key to Bausch's greatness. It's the reason queues for return tickets will stretch round the block for her run in London next week, and the reason her most devoted fans – like fanatical followers of Wagner's *Ring* – travel the world in order to catch her every show.

Figure 6 Viktor (1986): Tanztheater Wuppertal. © Ursula Kaufmann

II

Creating Bausch's world

In rehearsal, Bausch asks questions. Questions of elemental purpose, allowing her performers time to answer with words, with movement, with a performed moment. "How do you cry?" A simple question, but built on different means than one expects in theatrical improvisation. Not "Why do you cry?" with all of its attendant psychological motivation, but the more elusive "How?" She is looking for the way in which each individual contains his or her expression, how it lives in his or her body. Bausch uses tools of theatrical presentation to readdress the base assumptions from which interpretation arises, asking not only what moves us, but more specifically how we are related to the question at hand, both as performers and as people in the world. The means of presentation themselves are questioned, always viewing forms of presentation to reveal how we are involved in the process of performance.

The mode of questioning and exploration that the rehearsal process embodies draws on basic assumptions: a concentration on experience as the way we are connected to the world, and a prioritization of process over product and content over technique. The questions are posed to lead towards an uncovering of experience rather than the way that experience may be expressed, and that process is revealed in the performance. How do we exist on stage, and how do we use the stage to approach the way we are in the world?

Going to see Bausch's performances has been described as an archeological dig, unearthing images that are beguiling in themselves and that all connect to create a larger picture of what you know is down there somewhere. Each shard you uncover reveals a portion of a new civilization. The individual works are complete performance experiences, taking into account and utilizing every element of the performative environment to work towards their themes. The subtlety and density of her creative process produces richly layered pieces that adeptly draw on historical precedents and leave ample room for interpretation.

Bausch's developmental process works as an exploratory journey, shifting the focus from the experimental theatre (theatre that grows from a process of experimentation, testing different hypotheses on stage) to a model of exploration and discovery (performance that delves into a world and works to uncover previously hidden forms and expression). There is no method, no technique to follow; so what is left is a process, and to build from that ground becomes Bausch's greatest influence, moving in your own direction and taking advantage of the resources available to you. Most of us cannot match Bausch's resources (both in terms of money, time to develop new work, and the extensive training of her international ensemble of performers), and so we are forced to mine what we have in the room. Even for Bausch, beyond the time, money, and training of her ensemble, her greatest resource is people, the personalities of those with whom she works. She has famously said "I am not so much interested in how they move as in what moves them," in reference to her ensemble, and that statement could be used as a credo for a new theatrical approach. People are one thing we all share in our performance explorations, and to go through the process of exploration with a group of people, uncovering common interests, fears, joys and individual sadness, will put you closer to a collective expression of a more universal truth. For Bausch, "the pieces are about how much we want to be loved. We are all afraid of death." To successfully experiment often requires the right materials, but to explore requires a willingness of spirit and a vulnerability to let the process lead you rather than you leading it, and to have the courage to express what you find when you get there.

The focus of the essays in this section is on the people in the room, from Bausch herself in interviews, to a new translation of Raimund Hoghe's important consideration of his time as Bausch's dramaturg, and Renate Klett's similar role in developing *Kontakthof*. As the company moved to work through residencies and develop pieces based on their experiences in specific locations, we were given the opportunity to see more than just the piece itself, we were let in on the process. Bausch's trip to the American West provides a key into her work for American audiences, just as her work in South America, or Hong Kong, or India connect her to those locations so much more palpably than simply the tours and performances. This section draws on the wealth of work that came out of Bausch's American visit. We were given access to the questioning process of exploration, and encouraged to set off on our own journey.

As the Tanztheater Wuppertal moves on after Bausch's death, their first step has been to reflect back, with more and more company members discussing what it has been like to be in the room, including the testimonials that make up the bulk of the narrative of *Pina*, Wim Wenders's film portrait and remembrance. The material now exists to get a clearer picture of what Bausch's mode of creation was, moving a little closer to answering my initial question upon seeing Bausch's work: "How do they do that? Why does this work have such an impact and resonance for so many people?" I have included a large number of interviews, overviews, video documentations and personal memoirs in the bibliography for this section that provide a more full description of Bausch's process and, most importantly, offer the resources to travel our own path, whether in rehearsals or in watching the pieces themselves. The destination is less important than the getting there.

Into myself – a twig, a wall

An essay on Pina Bausch and her theatre

Raimund Hoghe

Originally published in *Pina Bausch: Tanztheatergeschichten*, 1986.
Another version of this essay first appeared in English in *The Drama Review*, 1980. New translation by Royd Climenhaga and Ellen Cremer

I am still in the foyer of the opera house after a performance of *Arien* when I randomly come across a poem by Else Lasker-Schuler that has a lot to say about the performance that evening and about Pina Bausch's particular brand of theatre, her themes and the people she works with.

> Let me go back into the limitless,
> Back to myself.
> The autumn crocus of my soul blossoms already,
> Maybe it's even too late to go back.
> Oh, I am dying with you!
> You suffocate me with yourself.
> I want to spin threads around me,
> End confusion,
> Misleading,
> Confusing you,
> To escape
> Into myself.

A rehearsal space in Lichtenberg, a former movie theatre now separated by a wall from a McDonald's that is settled into the front of the building, showcasing the usual Big Mac and Filet-o-Fish, polished tables and quick service. Pina Bausch and her ensemble are rehearsing just behind the wall in front of a large empty screen. I am sitting by the partition looking at unplastered masonry and fixating on a small twig that seems to be growing out of the wall high above me. Something just as improbable will appear later in *Arien*: a love story between a women and a hippo – but the hippo's not available yet and so is replaced here by a shy man in a grey suit. The hippo and the man merge to become a monster man, their roles interchangeable, and we see that at times the relationship between a man and a woman feels as impossible as one between a woman and a hippo. That impossibility is made comprehensible in *Arien* and other pieces by Pina Bausch, the impossible made possible in context, even if you try to resist it. Except the dancer dispels the impossible from the start, laughing loud and long when she first catches sight of the hippo after a glance in the mirror. Slowly and ponderously, the love-sick pachyderm retreats into the stage darkness. To test yourself, to look inward and perhaps find something. The author/choreographer/director starts that process of discovery and self-exploration with the ensemble and then stands back, rarely intervening. Pina Bausch gives her dancers/actors/co-authors time for this process. Even a week and a half before opening night (at this point the piece is still without a title) there is no rush, no attachment to the elements already in place, but a willingness to break up existing structures and an openness to new discoveries. Pina Bausch is very calm and focused observing her ensemble's search. "Everyone should have the freedom to do what they want, or create things for themselves," she says, capturing an attitude that extends beyond the rehearsal room. "What I do: I watch. Maybe that's it. I have simply looked at human relationships and tried to see them, tried to speak about them. That's what I am interested in. I don't know of anything more important." She watches rehearsals, sitting in a chair, her hands often resting on her forehead or chin, her legs pulled back. There are rarely any interruptions and only occasional breaks during longer rehearsal periods.

A little later, the dancers form groups. Pina Bausch mingles among the performers and very quietly speaks to them individually. Her comments are unnoticeable to outsiders, and are meant only for the person to whom she is speaking in his/her situation. She doesn't offer general suggestions, no grand theories. When a female dancer asks her if there can be spoken words in a scene or simply mood, she answers, "We have to try it. I can't say – theoretically."

Pina Bausch says words are not her thing. Sitting in an Italian restaurant a few hours after rehearsal, she talks about trying to script things. She tosses aside a bunch of written lines developed in rehearsal. Taken out of context, they aren't true anymore and sound too much like pearls of wisdom. "I don't pronounce life's wisdoms," she insists. She also resists a collection of tidy explanations for another reason. "Then it looks as if I decided on things, that I have determined how to do things. But that's not true," she says, "I'm searching too. I am floating just like everyone else."

Words that could keep you from floating, sentences that you can hold on to: Pina Bausch's theatre refuses such anchors. Even with those boundaries she has already crossed – between theatre and ballet, speaking, movement and music-theatre – she doesn't want to make any pronouncements or to explain. In her pieces, words are fleeting, fragmented, blurred, they rarely serve to communicate, and understanding, reaching another person, is a rare exception. In *Arien*, a women sitting in the water near the ramp recites a bit of Gretchen's monologue from Faust. "My rest is done, my heart is heavy; I find you never and nevermore." She is as hard to place as the loud couple laughing over a book about the love life of insects. At a certain point, their comments simply stop, as is often the case in this theatre of fragments. The excerpts refer to a present reality and illuminate small bits of experience, calling attention to them, expanding them into a palpable form. Jan Minarik brings out that momentary spotlight in a scene from *Kontakthof*. He walks down a line of men and women seated facing the audience and holds a microphone to their faces to catch bits of individual monologues about trivial and daily experiences of love. The little stories continue even as the microphone moves on, blending in with the cacophony of voices in the background. "You could keep playing a piece like *Kontakthof* all night long," Bausch says.

People try, again and again, to tackle the volatility of words, pictures, situations or experiences in Bausch's productions, attempting to assert themselves in an often fleeting reality. They create concrete moments in a search for safety in an uncertain environment. In *Kontakthof*, measurements are taken and carefully registered in a book – the distance between a dancing couple's faces – and several moments are photographed, documented for an unknown catalog somewhere. A woman in a short black dress and a nicely dressed man present themselves to the photographer, look earnestly into the Polaroid camera, and after a click and a flash, change partners and repeat the familiar ceremony. They insert themselves into each new scene with the expectation that they will look back and say, this was a beautiful and happy moment. Similar images appear in *Arien*, stand-ins that can never really replace a life unlived. At the very beginning, a nervous couple in vacation attire stops and breaks into a carefree pose, asking to be accepted, to be recognized. Their wish is granted and Jan Minarik takes a picture of them jumping for joy. Later, Minarik walks through scenes with his tripod and camera, focuses on individuals, groups, and finally himself, holding the self-timer. He joins unsuspecting groups, presses the timer and captures a "real" moment – a little bit of evidence that something did exist.

The attempt to hang onto some objective image or detail with the camera, the measuring tape, or the tape recorder isolates those trying to archive those moments from the exact thing they are trying to document. It's a feeling anyone trying to write about Pina Bausch's theatre knows all too well. Looking at the attempt to record those details on stage, I end up insecurely sitting in the auditorium, taking notes and trying to capture what I see. But the images slip from my grasp, and escape any attempt at objective or neutral description. The images on stage are always so much more than you can see. You connect them to your own experience and they expand to become something bigger than merely what's on stage, they are inextricably bound to your own life.

Watching Bausch's work, you become aware of your own perspective on people and relationships, you try out alternative views and are forced to acknowledge that the world is bigger than your own experience. When I saw *Arien* performed three times within a few weeks, it was like seeing three different productions – without being able to say if a scene had changed or if I was the one who had changed and saw the situation differently. For example, the piece is filled with moments derived from children's and parlor games. On first seeing "Going to Jerusalem" [a version of musical chairs, trans.] or "Now we sail across the lake" [a traditional German folk song with an accompanying game for children, trans.], the moments seem harsh and brutal, reminding me of the ruthless brawls that would accompany those odd man out games. In a different performance, those same games feel much less hostile, less hurtful and centered on competition, more like joint efforts to kill the time, and maybe recapture some lost piece of childhood.

"I've never meant: 'This is how it is,'" Bausch says, and her work is much more open than many people assume. "I often have something else in mind [than what people think], and mean something different, but not only that." She avoids direct interpretations and doesn't want even clear and recurring images placed in a particular drawer. If it appears women are being treated like puppets by men, that can be seen quite differently as well. "For example, in *Renate Wandert Aus*, there are men who place the women somewhere and hug them. That can mean many things – not only that a man simply takes a woman, carries her away and hugs her. You could think the men want a situation like this where the girl is so docile. You can see it one way or the other, though. It's your choice, but a one-sided approach simply isn't true." Or, as Bausch adds, "You can always see it the other way around."

The images and scenes are always open to the possibility of seeing them differently, with misunderstandings accepted and made a part of the piece. "That someone can see it this way and someone else see it so differently – I like that." Even after countless interpretations of her work, Bausch says "these have nothing to do with me." She accepts those strange views and conclusions, but still: "I find it dangerous when people attempt to insinuate a particular point of view, just because they want to see it that way." With her work, it's easy to see only what you want to see, and try to criticize an open theatre that provides so many escape routes, but the pieces give you a chance to pick from the images and stories the ones that best fit your own experience and world view.

The images aren't forced on you, and yet Bausch's pieces trigger reactions that would seem impossible in the theatre. Pina Bausch and her work have been the victim of strong attacks and criticism, even if people claim their views "weren't meant to be aggressive." Beginning with the head of the department of culture, who publicly asked what to do with a ballet director who doesn't keep the municipal orchestra busy enough and only sparsely fills the theatre, all the way to a bank teller who terrorized Bausch and her ensemble with anonymous insults and threatening phone calls for a year and a half. The current atmosphere of popular and political struggle is often felt in her performances as well. The premiere of *Macbeth* in Bochum was accompanied by tumultuous scenes and emotionally charged confrontations, while Bausch's productions back in the opera house in Wuppertal were regularly met with loud protests from angry subscribers. They resist any performance that refuses to provide the desired sense of completion. The disgruntled audience members leave what has become an unbearable theatre, slamming doors as they hurry out. "Without knowing, they suspect their life will become completely unbearable," Adorno writes in *Summary of the Culture Industry*, "as soon as they let go of what no longer gives them satisfaction."

Pina Bausch's theatre admits doubts and insecurities, and includes corners and edges that you can bump against to rip open old wounds and release repressed feelings. "I would never want to smooth out the edges," to make a singular point. "I couldn't even do that." Her pieces ask questions. Answers remain open. To provide answers, "that would be presumptuous. I can't say: this is the way things are," Bausch says, and repeatedly questions herself in conversation. She narrows down her statements, emphasizes a personal point of view, and phrases like "perhaps," "I don't know," or "I have a feeling" frequently appear in her sentences. At one point she says, "I find it important to affirm feelings, feelings that you can't necessarily place. But you need to say yes to a feeling you can't quite define. At most you circumscribe it, without ever saying, that's how it was."

To surrender. To feelings, experiences, circumstances. Pushed into unsafe areas without a plan. "I wanted it that way," Bausch commented while creating a scene, and then immediately corrected herself. "What does that mean, 'wanted' – it happened somehow." Her pieces are not planned out based on an overarching idea. "With the recent pieces, there was a starting point somewhere – and then where it goes – that is all developed in rehearsal. It's not planned, it just happens, from all of us together. It has a lot to do with the constellation of the group, what we've been through and what someone wants to try." The starting point changes, expands, circles around and gets called into question – like the starting point of "tenderness" for *Kontakthof.* "Tenderness." What is it? Where does it start? Where does it go? How far does tenderness go before it turns into something else? When is it no longer tenderness, or does tenderness persist?

So, *Kontakthof* – Exercises in tenderness, attempts at tenderness, a search for tenderness. An old record: "Pull me close, so we can dance the tango." Friendly, smiling couples stand across from each other and touch. A man takes a woman's hand and bends her finger backward. A woman approaches a man and bites his ear. Men and women pinch each other's armpits, push their eyes closed, pluck out a hair or pull a chair out from under them and then calmly walk away, arm in arm. Later on these little antagonisms continue. Tender gestures turn into punches. The transition is smooth; it is only on the other side that you realize the gestures of tenderness have turned into something else. At the end of the performance, all the men surround and touch a woman (Meryl Tankard). They cover her body with touches. Hands stroke her hair, eyes, forehead, mouth, nose, neck, arms, legs, chest, belly, back – until the woman slumps under the weight of what you might consider tenderness.

Tenderness only seems possible as something in the distance. One of the most tender scenes in *Kontakthof,* for me, shows a couple seated far apart. They hesitantly smile at their partner on the other side of the room and coyly remove a piece of clothing. They shyly glance at each other and remove another, undressing in front of each other until they are naked, vulnerable, and yet there is a delicate intimacy between them despite the outer distance. The approach is far less delicate in another moment that develops from a similar starting point. Again, women and men sit across from each other, but this time they are in a dance lesson type of situation. The men desperately gesture with invasive movements as they move their chairs forward across the space, and the women respond with equally frantic gestures. As the men meet the women against the far wall, they reach impatiently toward their partners without actually grabbing them, but their proximity triggers defensive reactions. Tenderness becomes violence as touch turns to assault.

People discover that their actions, desires or relationships often become something very different than what they initially thought of or dreamt in Bausch's work. Moments are perceived and judged differently from the outside, as in one of the main images from *Arien*. A row of chairs is set up at the front of the stage. With serious expressions, the women tiredly walk toward the chairs, looking like they are on their way to their own funerals. One after another, they sit down in the chairs, handing themselves over to the men who are stationed at each chair. With Mozart's "Eine Kleine Nachtmusik" playing, the men begin to transform them. The women are dressed in old clothes, colorful wraps and pastel children's dresses, while gaudy make-up is put on their faces, until – bizarrely outfitted, colored and masked – nothing resembles what it once was. The dress and make-up aria may seem to many like a distinct reference for Bausch to the condition of women being forced into a cliché by men, made into types and robbed of their own identities. The starting point for this image, Bausch remembers, was very different. "It actually started one day when all the women were very sad, and we thought they should put on make-up, maybe that would help cheer them up." At first it didn't have anything to do with the men treating the women like puppets, or with the oft cited feminist stance that has been associated with her work. Bausch says "That's been foisted on me over the years."

Images, situations, depictions in Bausch's theatre are quite different than the familiar, etched in stone creations and stories of men's lives. Two years earlier, when I first saw one of her productions, *Bluebeard* no less, I was impressed by this distinct difference. I couldn't identify it at first, but could only say that I knew I had experienced a fundamentally different view and attitude toward people and how to tell a story, one that could only come from a woman. There is an obvious difference in Bausch's work, a greater openness, an unconditional surrender to emotion and experience, and a setting aside of rational and safe insights and autocratic claims of absolute truth. You enter into the work and admit your own fear and desire, lust and grief, dreams, hopes, risks, complexes, hurts and vulnerabilities. A woman: "How could I follow other people's advice and make myself invulnerable, so that these spikes won't hit my innermost being any more and we could all walk next to each other on an undisturbed path. That would only lead to surface endurance," Marieluise Fleisser, a love letter, 1930.

Figure 7 Bandoneon (1981): Julie Shanahan, Dominique Mercy. © Ursula Kaufmann

"I can only do it this way," Pina Bausch answers when talking about her approach to theatre. "Of course it has something to do with who I am, but actually, I can't judge that and I don't have to." A theoretical debate about feminine aesthetics is not her thing. She admits, laughing, "I have never thought of that at all." A little later she adds, "Certainly there are different qualities in men and women, it's different for each person. Obviously there is a range of possible masculine or feminine qualities and areas where they blend. But ultimately, I've always thought more about the person."

She has always had difficulty with feminist arguments. "Feminism, maybe because it is so trendy, I have always retreated into my snail shell. Maybe because it feels like there is a strange separation that I don't actually like. It feels like there is more of an energy against rather than with each other." The pieces don't shy away from the difficulty of desperately trying to sustain a connection, and often show incompatible couples clinging together. Beatrice Libonati and Lutz Forster in *Arien*: a very tall man carries a very short woman across the stage, rigidly hanging from his chest. When he lifts her up to kiss his mouth, her feet dangle at his knees – she no longer has ground to stand on. When she is released, she slides down her partner and sinks into the water by his feet.

Set against each other, men and women face one another like rivals on a battlefield. They respond hurtfully to each other and try to assert themselves. Pina Bausch shows these battles without wanting to be an umpire, without wanting to judge. "Looking back, I notice that I am somehow always acting as a defender – I am always trying to justify things. When you would normally say that this is uncomfortable or not right or, what do I know? I'm actually trying to understand: Why? So, somehow I try to comprehend why this is so. And in that moment I am a defender: when I want to understand, how is it possible that people behave the way they do?"

A woman melodramatically collapses to the ground, but before she falls, she says, "I pretend that I want to be alone, but really I want someone to come." Later, a man drops a heavy stage weight on his chest. Another slams the piano cover on his fingers. A woman sets up four chairs, walks around them and knocks each one over with a thrust of her hip. Another woman in a pink cocktail dress pulls up her skirt and jumps against the wall, while the others reward her with polite applause. These are all moments performed in the community center set for *Kontakthof*; a piece that returns to one of Bausch's central themes: "the desire to be loved" – the lengths to which we will go to receive affection. *Kontakthof* shows us women who force themselves into tight dresses and painful shoes. *Bluebeard* includes men attempting to look masculine by adopting body-building postures in front of the women. *Arien* – characters perform tricks and show off accomplishments. Or the act of performance itself, risking your life under the circus tent – are they only trying to be loved, or are they compelled to do it, just for that bit of recognition?

"What is happening when someone performs? In the circus, for example, when someone walks on the tightrope up so high? Why do they do it? So that the audience below can experience fear?" Pina Bausch questioned their motives, but doesn't hide the fact that she admires their courage, the potential consequences, the control. "You need that as an artist. That's an incredible risk they take on the trapeze, much more than what we do. If something goes wrong, you don't just twist your ankle." Later she says she would like to spend a year at the circus, "but maybe I'm imagining something that's not really there."

"What comes to mind when you hear an aria?" Sylvia Kesselheim stands in front of a mirror and reads off the answers she received. "Cold rooms, nasty pink, elaborate artifice, empty stage." *Arien* refuses to indulge in these images. Designer Rolf Borzik strips the stage of the opera house down to its bare walls and covers the stage with ankle deep water to create a living space rather than a constructed world – a space that is not forced or imposed on people, but develops along with the performers and the stories they tell. "It's not like deciding on a set and thinking, O.K., this is where we perform the piece. The space evolves through the work," Bausch explains, and adds, "I think it is beautiful, real things on stage, dirt, leaves, water." Her work is also about the desire to deal with real things, to allow yourself to be somewhere and have a real experience – without being afraid to get wet.

For Bausch, theatre "has a lot to do with what children do. What we do in rehearsals and in performance you are usually only allowed to do as a child – splashing in the water, getting dirty, painting your face, playing. I think its great that we get to do that again, even bigger on stage." Bausch struggles to understand a critic who feels disgust at some of the scenes in *Arien*. "If I felt disgusted by the performance, I wouldn't be here. Even though it is sad, and there are many things that I am troubled by, I still think something important is going on. There is a possibility of working together, that you get to try things out and gauge others reactions. There is something about that. Of course, I often feel sad or desperate, or frustrated, or angry, but that is just like any human relationship. It has nothing to do with being disgusted by theatre. I love it – that's what makes it so difficult."

Dance. "At first it was only about myself." – "I wanted to express myself." – "At first, it was all about dancing." – "I wanted to do it because I had so much inside of me." – "I have always taken it very seriously." In the beginning: ballet classes as a child. "There was something I immediately liked about it. I don't know what. Maybe it had to do with creating a fantasy and being able to play." In school: "I began creating small dances because I was frustrated and wanted to dance more. I really just wanted to do it so I could dance more. I never thought I would be a choreographer. That wasn't my plan, or some idea I had. I only wanted to dance." Over the last few years, Bausch has only appeared as a dancer in the short piece *Café Müller*, but she has the desire to dance more. "I still have it, but that's a problem with so many in the group. They all want to dance." The desire to dance remains. "If you lose that desire, I think you can quit altogether."

The last few pieces created by Tanztheater Wuppertal have included very little dance. Bausch explains that she has not turned against dance, "but what I find so beautiful and important there – I need to leave it untouched for a bit, because it *is* so important." She adds, "I believe that you have to learn to dance anew, or you need to learn something different, then maybe you can dance again." A tentative attempt to dance makes its way into *Arien*: one after another, each of the dancers stands alone, eyes closed and performs a series of strange, careful little groping movements and gestures. They move with precision, performing the gestures tightly against their bodies, but it feels like they are removed or sealed off from themselves. Dance becomes a possibility, a chance to experience yourself in space – and not move away from yourself, but break through the boundary separating body and space to dance back into yourself. The movements stop suddenly, just like so many physical actions in *Arien* – a frantic race, or large undulating individual dance movements that often end with a fall into the water. A loud sound abruptly interrupts the peaceful dance – and self-discovery. The dancers open their eyes and peer out with a look of fear and insecurity before we see them retreat into a safe zone and re-establish the distance necessary to confront the unknown, or what we call reality.

"That's really nothing compared to reality," Pina Bausch comments about what she considers her feeble attempts to capture something real. "People often say that it is so unrealistic the way people behave in my pieces, how they laugh or whatever they do. But if you simply watch people in the street, if you had them walk across the stage like that – simple walking, nothing ridiculous – if you let that play out, people wouldn't believe it either. What happens is so unbelievable, and what we do is tiny compared to that." Simple walking. People are walking on stage like they would cross a street. These parades of human behaviour are often found in Bausch's pieces, tired and aggressive, embarrassed and arrogant, anxious and searching, tense and friendly, gestures are the visible reactions to invisible situations. The seemingly personal and yet universal gestures, not placed in a (theatre) story become the story itself, and reflect the traces of a lived and unlived life. "We really are quite transparent if we just look at each other. The way someone walks or how they carry themselves says something about the way they live, or about what happened to them." "Somewhere it's all visible, even if you try to hold back. You can even see it if feelings have been repressed. There are times when people don't think about how they normally control their behaviour." Bausch's work confronts the attempt at (self) control, making it transparent and unsafe, even if you'd rather retreat into that safety. For example, during the intermission at *Kontakthof*, the situations we just witnessed on stage are performed again; not knowing what to do with your hands, you're suddenly exposed, caught trying to hide behind a now brittle façade.

Pina Bausch sees and exposes people in all of their complexity and contradiction, with and without masks. Even at the end of *Arien*, Jan Minarik removes his make-up while couples walk across the stage. They stroke their partner's back or play with their hands while he releases himself from the white-wash, the painted on mask, to reveal a recognizable face, a person.

Two jokes, a story and a dream. "A man walks up to a circus director and asks if he needs a bird imitator. 'No,' the circus director answers, and so the man turns and flies out the window." Just like Minarik, Sylvia Kesselheim tells her Berlin joke twice, once at the beginning and again at the end of *Arien*. "Berlin – A passenger asks a taxi driver, 'do you know how to get to the philharmonic?' 'Of course,' the taxi driver responds, 'that's easy. Practice, practice, practice.'" A friend tells me after a performance of *Arien* "they practiced and were able to fly for two hours," which reminds me of another piece, the same dream. "How do you want to live?" Lady Macduff asks her son twice in Pina Bausch's *Macbeth* piece; "Like birds."

In rehearsal with Pina Bausch

Renate Klett

Originally published in English in *Heresies*, 1984

Pina Bausch is the director of the Wuppertaler Tanztheater, which has gained international fame for its unique blend of theatre and dance. It began about ten years ago as a ballet company attached to the opera house in Wuppertal, West Germany. At first Bausch choreographed ballets, but soon she began to work on modern operas like Bartok's *Bluebeard* and plays like *Macbeth*, adapting them for dancers. Then she started to create her own plays, loosely collecting improvised scenes around a given theme. Bausch's plays are nonlinear and deal with dreams and desires, associations and fantasies; the dancers/authors invent stories and actions that reveal their personal lives as well as a kind of collective unconscious.

What follow are excerpts from a report on rehearsals for *Kontakthof*, with which I assisted for four weeks.

The rehearsals take place in the "Lichtburg," a remodeled movie theatre with old-fashioned lamps; a narrow stage in front of the screen, a row of chairs before it, a piano in the corner; the floor covered with a dance rug. (The stage set will later have a similar structure.) There are twenty dancers: nine women in pink rehearsal dresses, eleven men in suits. As most of them are foreigners – from twelve different nations – English is spoken primarily.

This is the third week of rehearsal for a piece that does not yet exist. Instead, there are themes: "tenderness," "desire," "I show myself, introduce myself." And there is music – a large number of tapes with tangos from the '50s, Rudi Schuricke, music from Chaplin and Fellini films, "The Third Man," and some classics (Sibelius).

There is no piece, so anything is possible. This doesn't make decisions easier; rather, harder. Pina Bausch has never been limited by a piece, whether it was *Bluebeard*, *The Seven Deadly Sins*, or *Macbeth*, she always made something of her own out of it – something that distanced itself greatly from the original and yet, in spite of it or because of it, was very close to the original. Here everything must be fantasized without the provocative, but also helpful, friction of a story and its characters.

The rehearsals are relaxed and disciplined. They start with an hour of classical ballet training, followed by work on the piece, which means gathering material. Pina suggests movements, specifies themes for improvisation. "Let's do something with our complexes," she says. "We all have complexes, so let's demonstrate them. Everyone show what they don't like about their bodies." She puts on blaring circus music. The dancers cross the room; stop in the middle; hide double chins or wide hips, a nose too big or breasts too small. The tall ones make themselves shorter; the short ones, taller. They exit with the frozen gesture; return with it on the next go-round, adding a new "complex." This is repeated four times, until they can hardly move for all the contortions they must make to hide their faults.

Interestingly, what the individual finds unattractive, others find beautiful. It is striking that the women are much more composed and honest with this exercise than the men are – and therefore "better." (In the final piece, "The Complexes" will be performed as a circus number, the music loud and peppy, with commentary in Filipino by Luis P. Layag.)

The motif of presentation

The dancers leave their chairs against the back wall; one after the other, they cross the room to the director's table and present themselves as if before a jury. They show themselves from the front, the back, in profile; present their foreheads and teeth, their hands and the soles of their feet. Their seriousness and concentration, along with the slow, kitschy music, make this self-presentation look very sad. Associations: auditioning, offering oneself, being vulnerable on stage and in life, slave-shows, prostitution, sell-outs. Vivienne and Gary are a couple who show their naked bodies to each other. They sit far apart and undress slowly, shyly. They smile at each other and are ashamed. It is a very tender scene, touching ... like two children who are curious and afraid.

The "Parade of Complexes" is a form of presentation, too. As is an exercise that is later dropped: showing parts of oneself – the shoulder blade, the little finger, the navel. Presentation also means couples who give instruction on inflicting pain, demonstrating with the routine gestures of a tired vaudevillian how to best poke each other in the eye or twist an ear. The gentleman offers his arm, the lady takes it, and they return to their seats – elegant, polite married couples, accompanied by schmaltzy music and the applause of the ensemble. This exercise is called "Aggressive Tenderness." Then there is "The Museum": everyone stands around as if at a party, until someone falls down, throws up, smashes against the wall. The others watch, indifferent or interested, as if looking at a work of art instead of a person

Pina allows a lot of time to try things out. She doesn't interrupt the dancers, but allows everyone to live out the fantasy, even if something is all wrong. In this phase of rehearsal, the activity lies in the dancers' determining if, how, and with whom they want to carry through an improvisation. Sometimes they digress and lose themselves, thereby giving the stimulus for a new theme.

For me, this kind of work is more collective than what is usually called that. The mutual exchange and inspiration, the enjoyment and spontaneity remind me of rehearsals I saw at the Théatre du Soleil in Paris. Perhaps it is not a coincidence that the directors of both groups, Ariane Mnouchkine and Pina Bausch, are women.

With Pina Bausch, every scene has a bundle of meanings that complement and contradict each other. Nothing is narrow or unequivocally definable; even apparently obvious meanings are suffused by a lot of minor doubts. When I try to pin her down to interpretations, she says, "I don't know exactly." That is true and not true. Of course she knows: only she does not know exactly. "Can one know *exactly?*" she asks.

Hits from the '50s

> Oh dear Miss Crete, when you dance with me
> I feel so deeply that you belong to me
> You are the sweetest, the most lovely creature that I know
> Whoever meets you I am sure will never let you go.

or

> Blond Clair, being next to you
> makes me feel that my love is true
> Will you do me the honor
> And be my prima donna?

Men sing to women, never vice versa. The women Pina invents, however, are much more active, more conspicuous than the men. Jo-Ann Endicott's "Wild Animal Walk" for "Blond Clair": long strides on tiptoe, voluptuously swinging her hips, stroking her arms and hair; she feels good in her body. Jan Minarek sits behind a music stand and nervously leafs through papers. As Jo-Ann floats by he grabs for her, runs after her, grabs again – always coming up empty-handed.

She is so at one with herself that she remains "untouchable"; doesn't even perceive the grasping hands. A vamp straight out of the book and yet a parody of this cliché, invented by men who then added the epithet "man-killer."

> My lovely vis-à-vis
> As far as I can see
> You drink your wine here all alone
> I wonder what you'll say
> If I insist to stay
> To get the number of your phone

The social lie that women sitting alone – especially drinking wine – only wait for a man to take the situation in hand is fundamentally ridiculed: Pina Bausch's women are much too self-assured to hold themselves to such rules.

But she also shows, and with the same empathy, the men's side: their difficulties and frustrations, their helplessness and uncertainty. "Perhaps he's so unbearable because he is so desperate," she says. Or: "If you are brutal, it must be out of distress; otherwise it's just silly." Her sadness about the impossibility of being a couple is too existential to be satisfied by discussing the question of guilt.

With every day of rehearsal the material grows, and slowly the outline forms from which the piece can develop. A group of people in a closed space and what they do with/against each other. Couples – those who are and can't manage it, and those who will never be, although they dream constantly of it. Couples who seek, find, and immediately lose each other; or couples who can't separate and hate each other for it. An antipole: two boarding-school girls on a Sunday outing – a couple, too, with their pink dresses and expectations too great for a world too small They fall in love and are unhappy, cry together and comfort each other with a film on the life of ducks

Many stories emerge and disappear again – stories that tell of loneliness and desire, referring to each other in such a concealed way that their common point is sometimes hard to find. Pina doesn't want a continuous story, line; that is too smooth for her. She seeks a logic coming from intuition instead of intellect. That explains the many repetitions and the penetrating detail, to which much of the audience is unreceptive.

The improvisational material adds up to a catalog of gestures and behaviors according to the themes of the piece, such as "tenderness." "Tenderness toward oneself" is the title of an exercise in which the dancers fondle their own bodies to fulfill their emotional needs. They caress their faces and arms; play with their hair; touch their breasts, their bellies; tickle their knees and feet. When everyone practices these gestures on themselves, the effect is harmonious and relaxed; when couples try it on each other, a struggle develops – affection becomes burden.

This leads to an exercise in which all the women subject a man, and all the men a woman, to the gestures of tenderness. The small, playful gestures of the women have an unpleasant, pushy effect ("It's like ants on an apple," Pina comments), but the men's gestures appear to be really brutal, aggressive and possessive (the infamous slap on the ass). They command the woman, encircle her, lift her up, lay her down. Meryl bears it like a doll, her face expressionless. It is one of the strongest scenes in the play – a ceremony of submission, a desecration of the dead.

From collecting the material to performance

Pina has a pile of paper scraps with all the exercises written down. "Chairs Fighting" reads one; "Suicide with Laughter," "Men's Step," "Narrow Shoes," "Shaky Knees." Every night in the Spanish restaurant we rearrange the scraps in a new order. "Line them up," Pina says, and we try to order them according to themes or movements, music or dancers. This game of solitaire never ends, and sometimes we come up with a meaningful frame. The individual sequences change with the context in which they are placed, Jo-Ann's "Ow Aria" ("ow" in all pitches and moods) turns from funny to sad when it follows a tired waltz.

When I suggest solutions to this theatre puzzle, I do so according to traditional patterns of action. I try to show a couple in its different stages or a character in its development. Pina finds this boring ("Now the whole secret's out"). She wants a total impression, from which the audience can choose the events it wishes to follow. Therefore she doubles scenes, complicates their structure by intermixing them. Many scenes run parallel, commenting on and overlapping each other. Sometimes ten different actions occur at once, then again everything is concentrated on one single event.

It is a form of theatre that is too demanding for most of the spectators (and critics); they cannot handle the offer to assemble the piece themselves. It is a theatre without instructions for use, without an ostensible structure and interpretation – a subjective reality that can be encountered only subjectively. A similar thing happens in Robert Wilson's pieces, but with a decisive difference that perhaps derives from the difference between men's and women's art. Wilson's point of departure is abstract: a mathematical, precisely calculated pattern that is repeated and varied many times. Pina Bausch, however, starts with the personal, making her private sense of rhythm and association the coordinator of the piece.

The more the play develops a shape, the more it changes. Scenes that appeared harmless in rehearsal take on an unexpected aggressiveness through the order in which they are rearranged; it has become a malevolent piece, even if there is much to laugh at. "Maybe the saddest thing about it is that it's so cheerful," Pina says. The empty space has something oppressive about it – an elegant prison in which people are at their own mercy and very small. The women wear evening dresses in gaudy colors, changing them often; the men are in dark suits and use lots of hair oil. The elegant style only seems to underscore the wretchedness of the tricks everyone plays on everyone else. "I am standing on top of the piano and threaten to fall off," says Vivienne Newport in one scene. "But before I do, I scream very loudly so no one will miss it."

There is still no title. We search the rehearsal protocols and songbooks, make a long list of words and quotes that suit the piece. Finally Pina comes up with a title she had proposed in the beginning: *Kontakthof* (contact zone). Some like it, others – mostly men – don't. Kontakthof – this terrible word refers not only to brothels; prisons and juvenile institutions have their Kontakthof too. We test people, ask strangers and friends what they associate with the word. A lot of men emphasize that nothing occurs to them at all. That confirms it: a title that causes so much suppression must be good.

I cannot summarize the work of the Wuppertaler Tanztheater from the four weeks I spent with them. Too much defies description, especially if the work is extremely subjective as Pina Bausch's is. There are also the many long nights, the lack of sleep, too many cigarettes – an entire rhythm of life dictated by the work and reflecting back on it. This cannot be conveyed except in terms of voyeuristic theatre gossip.

The end

Anecdotes have something unserious about them, but I want to relate one nevertheless. When I ask Pina what kind of theatre she likes, she tells me a story. Two people are speaking about Robert Wilson's *Einstein on the Beach*. Says one: "The part I liked best was when the white horse slowly crossed the stage." Says the other: "But there was no white horse," Says the first: "But I saw it quite clearly." Pina Bausch: "Theatre where something like this is possible is theatre I like."

Pina Bausch: "You can always look at it the other way around"

Anne Cattaneo

Originally published in *The Village Voice*, 19 June, 1984

A dancer stands on an empty stage strewn with carnations. She listens to the music of *Swan Lake*. She doesn't dance.

On opposite sides of the stage a man and a woman sit and regard each other shyly. Slowly, tentatively, they begin to remove pieces of clothing. The intensity between them grows as they expose themselves, but they remain apart – the vast expanse of the stage between them.

On a large, bare proscenium stage open to the fire walls and covered ankle-deep in water, a man dressed as a hippopotamus gracefully pays court to a beautiful young woman. Surprised and yet intrigued, she goes off with him.

A group of men surround a woman and begin to caress her. She responds. The caresses grow stronger and more direct until they threaten to overwhelm her. She fights to get out of the circle of men.

A group of women surround a man and begin to caress him. He responds. The caresses grow stronger and more direct until they threaten to overwhelm him. He fights to get out of the circle of women.

A large blond man pulls a delicate black-haired woman up in his arms, kissing her slowly. Her feet barely reach to his knees. As he release's her, she sinks to the floor, sliding slowly into the pool of water at his feet.

A group of female dancers leave the stage and enter the audience laughing and joking. They offer ice cream and chocolate to members of the audience. They ask men to help them finish dressing, to zip up their clothes.

A line of sad and wistful women sit on chairs facing the audience. A group of men enter and begin to dress them and paint their faces until they appear garish and fantastical. They appear totally changed.

These are images from the dance/theatre of Pina Bausch, the 44-year-old German choreographer whose Wuppertaler-Tanztheater troupe is currently making its first visit to the United States. Having opened the ambitious Olympic Arts Festival in Los Angeles earlier this month, she is in New York offering a program of three evenings of dance at the Brooklyn Academy of Music from June 12 through 24.

For the last 10 years, Bausch has been one of the most influential figures in the German theatre – in the company of such brilliant directors as Peter Stein, Peter Zadek, Klaus-Michael Grüber and most recently America's own Robert Wilson. Her Tanztheater has grown to be recognized throughout Europe as perhaps the most exciting and imaginative company working anywhere in the world today.

Based in the industrial city of Wuppertal in the Ruhr Valley – one of the many small cities in Germany which actively support an opera, an orchestra, and both a theatre and a dance company – Bausch has been the director of the Wuppertaler-Tanztheater since 1973, creating approximately two works each year for her company of 26 dancers. She has generated her share of controversy over these 10 years. She was expected initially to use the Wuppertal opera orchestra to accompany her dances: her use of recorded music, often scratched and rewound during performances, along with her choice of music – kitsch ballads, tangos, and pop songs, interspersed with Stravinsky, Purcell, and Bartók-ruffled feathers in the sedate cultural bureaucracy of Wuppertal and enraged subscribers who had come to see the ballet evenings their parents and grandparents had seen for generations.

Bausch's first work outside Wuppertal – her meditation on *Macbeth* called *He Takes Her by the Hand and Leads Her into the Castle, the Others Follow* (the title is drawn from the stage directions at the end of Act 1, Scene 6, where Duncan enters Macbeth's castle with Lady Macbeth on his arm) – also caused a storm of controversy. Rather than presenting a production of *Macbeth,* Bausch organized her performance around fragments of text from the play, presenting images of female manipulation and male power and helplessness. The performance was disrupted and had to be stopped after the first half hour.

Bausch's visit to New York is in some sense a return to her roots, for she began her career as a dancer as an exchange student at Juilliard in the late '50s. She remained in the city until 1962, dancing with the New American Ballet, the Metropolitan Opera Ballet, and Paul Sanasardo and Donya Feuer's company. She returned to Germany as a soloist in Kurt Jooss's Folkwang Ballet company in Essen (New York audiences will remember Jooss's expressionistic ballet *The Green Table* from the Joffrey's repertory) where she had begun as a student at 15. As a choreographer, her first dances for Jooss's company appeared in 1968, and the following year, at the age of 29, she took over the direction of the group. In 1973 she moved on to become the director of the Wuppertal opera ballet – soon to be transformed into the Wuppertaler Tanztheater – and she has remained there ever since. (She recently made a foray into acting as well – she is the haunted, aristocratic grand duchess in Fellini's most recent film, *And the Ship Sails On*.)

The themes that continue to fascinate Bausch, and that have functioned as remarkably consistent leitmotifs in her work over these 10 years, were already apparent in her earliest dances for the Wuppertaler company. In her first ballet, an homage to Jooss about childhood, the title character Fritz was danced by a woman. She choreographed two baroque operas by Gluck and several works to the music of Stravinsky (one of which will be seen in the current BAM program) as a kind of farewell to her classical training. In 1976 she presented an evening of Brecht in which she broke with her past and began to define the style that would characterize her work to come. Bausch's *The Seven Deadly Sins* (in contrast to Balanchine's romantic 1933 version, which explored the glamour of the twin Annas' dream of fame and success) presented a vista of an endless line of women going up a road. Bausch looked beneath the glamour to the underside of the dream – to the sweat, the violence, the sex, and the sadness that accompany their quest. Bausch's characteristic imagery – actions and gestures that are held, repeated, and which then gradually transform themselves over a period of time – began to appear in this ballet. A woman is having her hair combed, for instance. The combing continues until she is being groomed like a horse. Finally the combing and twisting and cutting of hair take on the aspect of a kind of castration.

To accompany *The Seven Deadly Sins* Bausch's dramaturge prepared a revue of Brecht/Weill songs to be performed by a man. At the same time, the other men in the company dressed as women. It was a look at roles and role-playing – and like many of Bausch's later pieces, it looked at an astonishing number of sides of the question. Men manipulated women like dolls, women were more engrossed in shoes and mirrors and makeup than men. The Wuppertaler actors/singers/dancers portrayed a world too self-involved to take action. Bausch's concept – to present a revue with song and dance numbers that was at once a critique of the form and the society that created it – led the prestigious German theatre journal *Theatre Heute* to proudly declare that "Fürchtet Euch Nicht" ("Don't Be Afraid") was "Wuppertal's answer to Bob Fosse's film *Cabaret*."

Long before Peter Brook began the investigation that led to *Carmen*, Bausch was interested in working with actor/dancers and creating a form somewhere between theatre, dance, and performance art. By 1977 she had gathered together the remarkably fierce-spirited and devoted group of dancers who have come to personify her work. Part and parcel of any reaction to Bausch's theatre are the critics' and audiences' responses to this maenad-like troupe gathered from around the world, who literally throw themselves off the wall for Bausch in dance after dance. The sensitivity, combined with their energy, strength, and physicality, define a world of strong sensuality joined with a spirituality that for Bausch is the essence of the female sensibility. But for many, this mixture of passion, inwardness, sexuality and violent energy is disturbing. It portrays aspects of life with an openness that is unsettling – "controversial" in the best sense of the word.

Bluebeard (which will also be seen at BAM) is particularly representative of this brutally expressive side of Bausch's work. Organized, as are many of her performances, around a piece of music – in this case Bartok's dark hour-long opera about the woman killer and his victim – the play is set in a large, deserted mansion littered with leaves. The production was designed by Rolf Borzik – the Tanztheater's remarkable designer who was responsible for the environments of Bausch's pieces throughout the '70s. Borzik broke the boundary between the stage and the audience, allowing Bausch to take the dancers into the auditorium, to move among and address the audience. He created spaces which suggest rooms as seen through the eyes of a child, spaces which define a mysterious interior world that is littered with the real objects of Bausch's mythology. For the 1979 *Arias*, Borzik covered the entire floor of the Wuppertal opera house with water. He covered the stage floor with thousands of flowers for *Dance Evening: Carnations*, and in the *Macbeth* piece left a garden hose running onstage – a hose which the dancers used to wash and dissolve (literally and figuratively) images and forms that appeared on the stage. Borzik was also a dancer in the company, performing in the 1978 *Café Müller* (a dance that will also be featured at BAM) together with Bausch herself. Borzik, who was Bausch's companion throughout the '70s, died of cancer in 1980 at the age of 35. *Café Müller* is the only role Bausch has continued to dance.

In contrast to the dark and violent *Bluebeard,* pieces such as *Arias, Legends of Chastity*, and *Renate Emigrates* explored the dreamy, sexy, and humorous side of Bausch's sensibility. After *Bluebeard*, in her operetta *Renate Emigrates*, Bausch turned to the theme of love, fantasy, and the dream lover. To a score that began with "Some Enchanted Evening" and continued through Henry Mancini to Kurt Weill, Bausch and Borzik presented a bright, imaginary world of snow and flowers, of chocolate and ice cream, of kisses and birthday parties and giggling, of women who wake out of their dream of ideal love to a world of emptiness.

Where the spirit of Jacques Tati haunted the production of *Renate Emigrates,* with its nonlinear structure and its lovely and aimless charm, the 1979 *Legends of Chastity,* organized around a reading of Ovid's *Ars Amatoria,* was more frankly sexual. To the accompaniment of a score of waltzes and kitsch ballads, the evening was a meditation on childhood and the awakening to adult sexuality – of the pleasure of looking and being seen, of what it means to be chaste and unchaste. The central image of the production, alternately childish and sexual, funny and obscene, was a tongue sticking out. As usual with Bausch, this exploration included a look at the political and social background as well: beginning as a childish instinct, the urge to hide/to expose oneself was followed into the commercialization of that desire in the seamy, male-dominated world of pornography and striptease. But the pleasure and power of exposing oneself sexually is openly acknowledged. The childish instinct is not forgotten.

The creation of a Bausch piece has been documented by her dramaturge Raimund Hoghe in a series of articles and a short book describing the work on the 1982 *What All is a Tango Good For?* Bausch's non-goal-oriented dramaturgy is arrived at during a three-month rehearsal period of exploration, improvisation, free association, and personal discovery on the part of the company as whole. Perhaps it is the gentle, hands-off way in which Bausch guides the group that accounts for the highly personal yet oddly unspecific – one might say universal – nature of the work. Unlike a choreographer such as, say, Meredith Monk, whose work is more autobiographical, more psychological in nature, Bausch's visions remain collective.

Bausch begins work with her international and multilingual company (her plays use a mixture of French, Spanish, English, German, Portuguese, and other languages) around a piece of music or a text and slowly starts to investigate the emotions, thoughts, long-forgotten memories, and attitudes the members of the company associate with it. For the first month she will carefully ask questions and take note of the company's responses: stories, recollections, songs from many countries, improvised scenes, etc. In the *Tango* project, for instance, Hoghe reports, "Pina Bausch continues to ask questions. 'Something, a thing that you never knew before. Tell about something that you had never heard of, and then suddenly experienced – what it was like when you discovered something.' Mechthild Grossman [a company member]: 'Once I wanted to eat in a restaurant and there were some tulips in a vase on the table – and for fun I tore off one of the leaves and ate it. It tasted incredibly good and ever since then I really like eating tulip leaves – green ones.' Later, when she appears on the stage eating a single tulip, many audience members are sure the flower isn't real. Reality: how improbable it is, once again." Hoghe reports Bausch commenting gently in another rehearsal: "Something's funny here. So far this is only illustrating, it isn't speaking directly. It should have more to do with all of you, your lives, your concerns. Maybe you should do something at the same time, an activity – and then through that something will emerge."

At the end of about six weeks, Bausch chooses a hundred or so stories, images, gestures, and sentence fragments from her list (her "catchwords," as Hoghe calls them) and these form the spine of the work. The second half of the rehearsal period is devoted to discovering the form of the piece – how the images should be connected and ordered. Here Bausch may work purely visually – juxtaposing words and gestures, groups of dancers, etc. like a giant jigsaw puzzle to find the structure that supports the evening's theme. According to Hoghe, she is continually looking to clarify the pieces of the montage: "Pina Bausch in rehearsal: 'It will keep on being reduced – until only the small, simple things remain.' To reduce without diminishing. Language too. Many of the words and sentences have become superfluous. Images appear in their place." Crucial to this part of the work is Bausch's commitment to letting the form emerge organically from the material – not forcing it to conform to a pre-conceived shape. During the rehearsals for *Legends of Chastity*, Hoghe remarked to Bausch that it looked as though the results would be funny and optimistic – to which she responded, "You can never tell in advance how it will turn out. We laughed a lot and had fun with the other plays too, but then in the end it turned into something else."

At the crux of Bausch's art is her unwavering courage to follow the material "into something else" – to embrace the complexities and the contradictions as the material transforms itself without judgment or oversimplification. The energy and desire it takes to push out into what is mysterious, along with the intellectual acumen to acknowledge and wonder at the many sides of things, are for Bausch the essence of the female sensibility.

In *Arias*, when Bausch began the exercise that led to the row of wistful women being dressed by the men until they were unrecognizable, the goal of the group had been to cheer up the women, who had been feeling sad – to please them, to make them happy. It is the inevitability of this kind of misunderstanding that interests Bausch – how it comes about and how each side perceives the situation.

The world Bausch presents on stage is a world where everything is relative – there is always another side. "Man kann immer auch umge-kehrt gucken," Bausch has stated: "You can always look at it the other way around." The plays allow the audience to choose, to order the images according to their own way of perceiving. It may depend on what languages they understand, what images they choose to pick out of the multitude on stage, what emotions are called up at the sight of the dancer in the field of carnations, the man being smothered by the women's caresses. It is well known that seeing a Bausch piece for the second time is often a completely different experience. One brings other emotions, new experiences in one's personal or political life into the theatre – and one's perception of the work is changed as a result.

What gives Bausch's work its edge is this dizzying juxtaposition of personal secrets and objective insight. One's most private fantasies and fears are magnified and carried to their extreme conclusion in full public view. And, oddly, in this way one gets a glimpse of them in the light of a larger experience – in the context of society and the world. Of course events in one's personal life mysteriously shape what happens on the stage for Bausch as well. Bausch's work has continued to change (the most recent play being shown at BAM is *1980* – the first work she did after Borzik's death) and the Tanztheater's international touring has brought new material into their repertoire; the *Tango* project came partially as a result of their South American tour. Bausch's return to New York, 20 years after her professional debut, may well set in motion new ripples of change. But as always for her, the transformation will no doubt be mysterious and unexpected. Sitting in one of Pina Bausch's rehearsals, Hoghe was reminded of a quote from Federico Garcia Lorca: "If things are not carefully and very gently hidden, they will never be discovered at all."

"I pick my dancers as people"

Pina Bausch discusses her work with the Wuppertal Dance Theatre

Glenn Loney

Originally published in *On the Next Wave*, October, 1985

Pina Bausch is usually too busy, too preoccupied to talk about her work. Like many innovative artists, she prefers to let the choreography speak for itself. If it doesn't do that, she explains, then it's really not effective. Several journalists were initially impelled to make the point at an Edinburgh Festival press conference several years ago that they found the company lacking in beauty. They wanted to know if the choice was deliberate on Ms. Bausch's part.

Pina Bausch, her face wreathed in cigarette smoke, looked puzzled, annoyed, amused – all at the same time. This was a question she had heard too often in Germany. She shook her head: "I pick my dancers as people. I don't pick them for nice bodies, for having the same height, or things like that. I look for the *person*, the personality."

In a gesture of goodwill, a member of the press suggested that it's not easy for dancers to talk. The implication was that everyone would be sympathetic and understanding if Ms. Bausch and her young dancers couldn't find the words to describe what they do. Although English questions were being translated, the choreographer had no real difficulty in understanding – after all, she had studied and worked in New York – and in answering. Her dancers were even more voluble, some being Americans and Britons, and were precise about what they do, why they do it and how they feel about it – and Pina Bausch.

One of them, an American, told me: "You know, I love her and I hate her. She is remarkable, but she can drive you so hard. Sometimes she doesn't seem to care that you are only human, that you can do only so much. At other times, she has the most concern you can imagine. I went away, finally, but I had to come back. Nowhere else can I have this experience as a dancer."

In Germany, she is already a legend in her own time, not easy in a land where so many young talents are competing for attention.

She has transformed the Wuppertal Ballet, once a center of the classical–romantic ballet under such choreographers as Erie Walter, Alan Carter, and Ivan Serticias, eventually out of existence – replacing if with her Wuppertal Dance Theatre. Her dance-theatre works are so alien to the former tradition of balletic beauty and fairy-tale magic – which once made a pleasing contrast to the industrial ugliness of the city of Wuppertal in the heart of the Ruhr – that she has been called "the Wicked Fairy of German Ballet."

If anything, Pina Bausch is more a legend with those in Germany who have *not* seen her choreography. A legend and a scandal. Tales are still told of balletomanes who had to desert their subscription seats at the Wuppertal Opera once Bausch had banished *The Sleeping Beauty* and other fairy-tale ballets. For her daring version of Shakespeare's *Macbeth*, she had a shallow lake of water on the forestage. Members of the West German Shakespeare Society who had bought out the front, high-priced rows of seats had to retreat to a safer distance. Her dancer/actors, stressing the neurotic importance of washing out that "damned spot," managed to splash a lot of water into the orchestra area. They also, in the interest of cleansing themselves of the murder of Banquo, took showers in full evening dress in a portable showerbath.

When you see something like this on stage, in the context of a thoroughly conceptualized production – no matter how bizarre individual events may seem – it has an internal logic and does develop the central theme. But when you read about it in a strangely negative review, or hear a nearly hysterical account of it from someone who didn't bring an umbrella, then Bausch's ballet becomes somewhat a forbidding legend.

For anyone who did not see Ms. Bausch perform in *Cafe Mueller* as part of her June 1984 season at the Brooklyn Academy of Music, there is still a chance they have witnessed her in action. In Federico Fellini's most recent cinema epic, *And the Ship Sails On*, Ms. Bausch played the role of the blind Princess Lherimia. And she played it with a sinister, mysterious, smiling remoteness, creating a character that could easily haunt one of her curiously disturbing choreographies.

But who is this *enfant terrible* of German dance? Where did she come from? What was she doing in the United States in the 1960s – and why wasn't she noticed then?

She was born in 1940 in Solingen, West Germany. In 1955, she began dance studies at Kurt Jooss's well known Folkwang School in Essen. In 1959 she completed her studies – including preparation as a dance teacher – winning the Folkwang Achievement Prize. A scholarship brought her to New York in 1960, where she studied with leading choreographers and was a "special student" at Juilliard. She joined the Metropolitan Opera Ballet in 1961 and that summer was in Spoleto with the New American Ballet. The following year, Jooss called her to be a soloist in his newly founded Essen Folkwang Ballet, where, until 1968, she was kept busy dancing for Jooss in Germany and abroad, including many festival engagements. That year she did her first choreographing for the Folkwang Ballet, *Fragments* (Bartok) and *In the Wind of Time* (Mirko Dorner), for which she won first prize in a Cologne competition. Professor Jooss asked her to take over the Folkwang Dance Studios in 1969.

Her first connection with Wuppertal came in 1971, when the Ballet asked her to create a work for the ensemble, *Actions for Dancers* (Gunter Becker). In 1972, she choreographed the bacchanal for Wagner's *Tannhäuser*, also for the Wuppertal stage; in 1973, she was awarded another prize, this time the one given by the State of North Rhine-Westphalia to encourage young artists; and then assumed leadership of the Wuppertal theatre's dance work, offering a premiere of *Fritz*. In her first years in Wuppertal she created versions of two Gluck operas, *Iphegenia in Tauris* and *Orpheus and Eurydice*, rethinking these classics, using dancers to interpret what soloists were singing and the orchestra playing.

After creating a three-dance Stravinsky suite, *Spring Offering*, in 1975, the next year she premiered *The Seven Deadly Sins* and *Don't Be Afraid*, which will be seen this fall at BAM.

Of her stripped down *Seven Deadly Sins*, danced by Jo-Ann Endicott, an Australian, and sung by Ann Holing, the *Sud-Zeitung's* reviewer commented, "Everyone grabs and tears and tweaks Anna; lecherous men in dark suits and women dressed as men. Roughly treated, she submits to them, crying defenselessly." In the second work, *Don't Be Afraid*, which is a collage of songs from *Mahagonny, The Threepenny Opera*, and *Happy End*, abuse of women is even more explicit. A smarmy tenor makes crude sexual approaches to a girl, singing "Don't be Afraid," but wearing gloves so as not to dirty his hands. A year later Ms. Bausch created *Bluebeard – On Hearing a Tape Recording of Bela Bartok's Opera, "Duke Bluebeard's Castle,"* seen at BAM in 1984, which continued her exploration of the violence of male–female relationships.

One of the biggest Bausch legends – or scandals – has been her *Macbeth* theme and variation, which she has labeled: *He Takes Her By the Hand and Leads her into the Castle, the Others Will Follow*, with music by Peer Raben. This was done in 1978 as a co-production between Wuppertal and nearby Bochum. The title, German critics have been careful to explain, is taken from a stage direction at the end of the sixth scene of Act One. (In fact, the only stage direction there is "Exeunt," at least in the Oxford University edition. But Duncan at the close of the scene, does say: "Give me your hand; conduct me to mine host ... By your leave, hostess.")

A critic–admirer of Pina Bausch, Edmund Glede of the Hanover *Allgemeine*, points out that although there were strenuous protests when she first swept the Wuppertal stage clean of fairy-tale ballets, some of the people who demanded her immediate departure are now her strongest supporters. That may be, he suggests, because she has managed to make Wuppertal – heretofore something of a culture-joke, similar to citing Hackensack in the eastern U.S. or beautiful Burbank in the far west – a city of some consequence in Germany and even internationally. Critic Glede says the Wuppertal Opera's music directors used to play Tchaikovsky's crescendos extra loud to drown out the sound of an aerial tramway grinding and creaking away outside the theatre. But when Pina Bausch's troupe got up steam, with Jo-Anne Endicott uttering the most piercing shrieks from the stage, matters were reversed: "People outside stood still with fear, suspecting a road accident nearby."

Pina Bausch's work has little to do with conventional ballet – although she insists on having dancers do classical training. Even the more classical forms of modern dance have been left far behind. Her dancers not only dance, gesture, run, hop, and even seem to sleep on stage; they also talk and sing and hum and, like Ms. Endicott, scream. Supportive German critics understand that they are watching the creation of a new theatre aesthetic. As one says " ... a unique combination of Artaud's Theatre of Cruelty and Grotowski's Poor Theatre." Thus the operative work in her troupe's title may be *theatre*. Although the company was ten years old in 1983, some of Bausch's stage devices, such as having the dancers recall old memories or share their opinions with the audience, hark back to the turbulent 1960s and the theatre of Tom O'Horgan and Richard Schechner. To celebrate a decade of Dance Theatre Wuppertal, Bausch created *Premiere,* in which dancers told of their "first times," whether at six or sixteen. The stage was lined with 8,000 pink paper carnations; musical quotations were from Franz Lehar and Sophie Tucker; and Bausch even used some trained Alsatian dogs in this work.

Some of Pina Bausch's admirers used to be worried. They thought she had come very far very fast. But now after twelve years at Wuppertal, she has created a new ensemble, a new type of dance-theatre, and something of an ongoing scandal. Still some Bausch fans are afraid something might happen, that she might lose ground under feet.

But in an interview with Bausch, she gave the impression of intense dedication, absolute security in what she was doing, balanced by a sense of humor and a kind of calm which could be a controlled frenzy. Describing her situation at that time in Wuppertal, Ms. Bausch said, "We are 26 people and we work in an opera house. In Germany, in an opera house, there is always a ballet company to do the dances. So it must have been a shock for Wuppertal when the former Intendant – Arno Wustenhofer – asked me to head the company. They liked it ... and then they saw *my* work ... So the dance public changed a little. We didn't get so many of the regular subscribers anymore, the Wuppertal people who liked operetta. But the city is in the center of a large region of cities – Cologne, Essen, Dortmund, Dusseldorf – and our audiences come from this entire area."

That doesn't mean that Pina Bausch hates opera. But she does like to find new ways of doing it. For Gluck's *Orpheus and Eurydice*, she tried something new: "The first evening, I had singers in the loges. I was afraid of the singers – and the chorus of this big theatre. They don't *want* to move. They say: 'If I have to move like this, I can't sing!' They don't want to do this; they don't want to do that. They won't sit two meters higher. They say: 'I don't go to the mountains for my holidays, so why should I sit up there?' There are all kinds of excuses. Finally, we did it with dancers dancing the story, but with the main singers on stage and the chorus offstage."

Did her dancing at the Met influence her interest in opera? Pina Bausch thinks hard about this, then she says, "It was very long ago, but for me it was nice because Anthony Tudor was running the ballet. For me, the contact with the singers was good. Not just personally either. When I was growing up, in the town where I lived, I'd seen only two operas. And I didn't like them. They were so *ugly*. So I had no real idea about music, about opera. Oh, what I *heard* was ok – but what I *saw!* What was wonderful for me at the Met: when you are in your dressing room, you always have a speaker on so you can hear what is going on on the stage. I got so I could recognize different voices, and I enjoyed it. It was an experience to be able to tell the difference in voice qualities. And I'd think: 'Oh, that's him!' So I got interested in opera. I had to do *Aida* – of all things – in the old Met house."

Curiously, most of the advance publicity for the troupe's debut in the Edinburgh Festival stressed Pina Bausch's work with Kurt Jooss at Folkwang. There was hardly a hint of her American experience. So it wasn't entirely a surprise to read some reviews which purported to find

Figure 8 Viktor (1986): Tanztheater Wuppertal. © Ursula Kaufmann

wonderful Central European influences of Mary Wigman, *et al*, in the Bausch work, and thanks be, none of those tiresome American mannerisms of Graham, Cunningham, and Tharp, etc., etc. I found this amusing, for my first thought, on seeing Bausch's Stravinsky triad, was of Martha Graham. To me, American influences permeated the work – but with a difference. I asked Pina Bausch about this: *Are* the influences on her work solely from *Mittel Europa*?

She smiles. "Oh, *I* didn't write the program notes. I never saw Mary Wigman or Harold Kreutzberg. Never. Not even in films; pictures only. But I certainly saw Martha Graham, and I studied Graham Technique. Of course, because of the school where I studied and worked in Essen, the Folkwang, I had a long experience with Kurt Jooss, and he was wonderful to me as a teacher. Anthony Tudor too. It wasn't just the kind of work they did, but *how* they did it – remaining true to their art, even in the most difficult situations. That was a big influence on me.

"In rehearsals, when Kurt Jooss danced – he was an older man then – when he danced as a young girl, a mother, he was so much better than any woman dancer as a woman. He was so sensitive, so beautiful. He could do anything. And I have met and worked with a number of people like that. It doesn't have to do with their technique, but with their emotional responsiveness to the dancer. These people went their own ways, but they knew how to work with dancers."

And how does Pina Bausch work with her dancers?

"Sometimes they hate me, when I ask them to do something – but I like to think they do it because they want to do it. Of course the choreography is set. It must be, with music, unless there is a place where we can improvise on stage. But we aren't exactly a collective. Someone has to be in charge.

"I don't design dances around dancers, around 'stars,' because we don't have any stars. But when dances are developing, you see who can do this, who can do that."

In the powerful Bausch *Rite of Spring* choreography, for example, a male elder of the tribe picks out a young maiden from a group of excited girls. The program doesn't indicate who is to dance the elder or the girl. Since the chosen one must don a red sacrificial dress and dance herself to death, collapsing in the mounds of peat moss strewn around the stage, does that mean that each time this Rite is celebrated a different girl is the sacrifice? That the dancers themselves, as well as the audience, have no idea who will be chosen?

"The audience shouldn't know in advance who the girl will be, who will be chosen. Where is the suspense? Of course all the girls in the troupe know the dance the chosen one must do, but in terms of rehearsals, we can't choose a different girl each time." Pina Bausch is thoughtful: "That is a terrific idea, though!"

She says she toyed with telling the man just before performance who the girl would be.

"We work as a company, so how can you single out anyone in *Le Sacre* – you can only call them 'The Girl' and 'The Man Who Is Judging.' And some people have said the dancers are like actors who can move. It would be fantastic if only actors could move like these dancers! Most of them have had classical training, with widely varied kinds of modern dancing. Either in schools, or with the companies they belonged to before they came to Wuppertal. It's really an international company. We counted, there are thirteen different countries represented.

"Some of the dancers didn't get much classical training, so every day we have classes in classical ballet. If they didn't have it, they will get it.

"We put in an eight-hour day. From ten to two and from six to ten – classes and rehearsals. When there is a performance, the evening is reserved for that. When there is an opera which needs a Spanish ballet, we will do it, but we don't have to do that too often. If opera ballets can be cut, they tend to leave them out.

"I never really liked opera ballet music. And all the pieces I have done – with two exceptions: *Sacre* and *Seven Deadly Sins* – they have never used ballet music. All the others are made with other kinds of music, not ballet music."

Is the Bausch ballet music specially composed then?

"No. I listen to music. I pull it together myself. *Der zweite Fruhling*, or *The Second Spring*, is made with eight different short pieces."

That work, in which an old man and an old woman remember the days of their youthful courtship in rather different ways, is a wonderfully wry commentary on a man's sexual longings and a woman's desire for propriety, respect, and affection. Visualized in Art Nouveau style for the past and Art Deco style for the present, it is lively and funny, something Pina Bausch's reputation for seriousness seems to exclude.

"I always thought I had no sense of humor," she explains. "But I found out, when I did this, that that's not true. I never thought I could do something like *The Second Spring*. Now I'm doing many more different things."

And how does Pina Bausch develop new work?

"First of all I do a lot of the work myself. Concept and movement I have to do myself, on my own. I find the music I want to use, then I go to the studio and teach the material to the company. Now, choosing the music is really more in my stomach than in my head. Sometimes I find a piece and I say: 'This!' Because I was looking for something like it – but not knowing it in my head. At other times, the search for music is more conscious – but weak."

Do you choreograph on your own body as some do?

"Yes. I make the material and take it to the dancers. Then we start playing with it. But first I teach it. I see what they can do with it. I change tempos. Or I let them change. They do it; I do it; or it's mixed. Or I cut it. I play around with it. And I always bring a lot, lot, *lot* of material! Then, as we work something I feel STRONGLY – from all of the material you feel maybe *this* is right. This you should pick and keep. You keep what is right. Or *more* right.

"But there is another way to begin: to play with the music and the movement. I never start from a 'beginning.' I have a lot of things … I don't know what they will become yet. Then, gradually, I begin to see where a work should start. What we have been working on is usually a big mess of things – a big chaos of things, materials, in relation to the finished piece.

"For a while, I'm completely helpless. And I do more and more and more. Then suddenly, I have the beginning, and I can start building the piece. I ask myself: How should it develop from that beginning? I start organizing the material. I cut those things – even when I like them – which don't fit, since the piece is moving in a different direction. Or because I saw the dancers do something new, interesting, I move the pieces in that direction. Sometimes it takes off in a different direction entirely, and then I have to find new materials. In rehearsals, suddenly somebody is so beautiful, so right, I have to change the idea to use that.

"I don't know" – Pina Bausch shakes her head, smiling looking at her attractive, sensitive dancer Vivienne Newport for support or a better explanation. "It's so hard to describe how I work …

"After *Sacre* in Edinburgh, people came up to me and asked me to explain how it was conceived. And what it means!"

But the dance shows quite clearly what the meaning is, doesn't it?

"Yes, exactly. You saw that. When we have danced the *Sacre*, we have nothing more to say about it. We have said it in our dance."

She looks at a loss; what can one say to people who don't understand what she finds, if not obvious, at least subtly translucent.

"*Sacre*, as a work, just is!"

What about those critics who found, the spirit of Mary Wigman and Kurt Jooss in your *Sacre*?

"It has nothing to do with Jooss technique, nothing! I studied with Jooss, yes, but I had many teachers. You can say I'm eclectic, but what is eclectic? I don't like that description. And I don't like to call what I do a 'System.' And I don't use this, this, and this. Whatever I saw, whatever 1 learned, I have digested it all. Oh, I could have a System if I wanted to make up one. But I don't want to do that; every time, I want to try new things. For every production I want to try something different.

"When I did the opera, *Orpheus*, I thought how people in a room behave with one another. They try to hide their feelings, their real feelings. You walk here; you sit down there – but never show what you feel. Well, dancers show those feelings. And in *Orpheus*, I let the dancers be the feelings of the singers. That was good for the singers; they weren't exposed. Being safe, wanting to be safe, is very human. So I didn't do it as a baroque opera – stylized, but not baroque. I don't know how to describe it – I get stuck! I never know what is 'modern,' and what isn't. It's very difficult to say what a 'modern ballet' is. We don't really have a word for it … that's funny, isn't it."

Ms. Bausch's productions are known for their elaborate scenic effects. In the repertory seen at BAM in June of 1984, for example, *The Rite of Spring* covered the stage in peat; *1980* used live grass and *Bluebeard* required 400 pounds of dead leaves. In *Arien*, which opens the 1985 NEXT WAVE Festival, there are six inches of water covering the stage, while *Gebirge*, also to be seen this fall, features a mountain composed of two tons of dirt.

But do you need all that? Can't your people say what they have to say dancing on a bare stage, against black drapes?

Pina Bausch grins. "No. It has all changed. It sounds funny to say it, but our work is a mixture of elements. I don't now what it is. They dance; people talk; others sing. We use actors, too. And we use musicians in the works. It's theatre, really. For us, the stage – the settings – are important, too. We aren't just dancing in a room, in a space. Where it is, the location, the atmosphere where the movement happens, that matters in my works."

Because of the complexity of her productions, the life of the innovative, imaginative choreographer is not easy, especially when she and her troupe take to the road like gypsies. But the real problems may be closer to home. Pina Bausch's work and her ensemble may have brought some fame to Wuppertal, but there are still some powerful, wealthy traditionalists who would like a speedy return to *The Sleeping Beauty* and a swift farewell to the "Wicked Fairy" of what might be called – for want of a better term for Pina Bausch – The Poor Dance

Theatre of Cruelty. No, the Dance Theatre of Wuppertal is not the Royal Ballet. Not by a long shot. Nor is it the New York City Ballet either. No way. And, although Pina Bausch studied Graham technique, danced for Anthony Tudor at the Met, and matured as a dancer and choreographer under Kurt Jooss's benevolent guidance, she is a unique artistic spirit, with a very special vision of dance as theatre. She cannot be compared with anyone; she is virtually incomparable.

"Every day a discovery …"
Interview with Pina Bausch

Christopher Bowen

Originally published in this form in *Stagebill: Cal Performances*, October, 1999

Pina Bausch is perhaps the most influential creative force in world theatre today. Inspiration to an entire generation of choreographers and widely imitated by theatre and opera directors, her stylistic imprint can be seen in the stellar works of Robert Lepage, Peter Stein, William Forsythe, Luc Bondy, and Robert Wilson. For more than 25 years, she has directed her ensemble in Wuppertal, located in the Ruhrland of northern Germany. Bausch has made Wuppertal a place of pilgrimage for those who see dance as theatre of the mind as well as the body.

Her spectacles are presented in the manner of grandiose revues, melding dialogue and repeated patterns of movement into surreal dream-like sequences. Brutal, funny, chaotic, and performed with searing honesty by her multinational ensemble, Bausch's work can provoke strong reactions from her audience – though seldom indifference. Yet even her detractors are curious to know what makes her, and her pieces, tick.

Famously elusive, she seldom gives interviews. But her disinclination to define her work in words paradoxically attracts the attention it seems designed to repel. Christopher Bowen met Pina Bausch in Amsterdam during Tanztheater Wuppertal's season at the Holland Festival, and spoke to her about her work. What follows is an edited transcript of that conversation.

CB: *You never state what meanings lie in your works, only that they are open to interpretation. Are you sometimes surprised by those interpretations?*

PB: Yes. The feelings in my work are only there because what I do is so exact, not just something free. It is the same with music. Music says things that cannot be said with words, yet the notes are very precise: why do you cry when you hear a certain piece of music, or feel happy? This is something we don't know much about. I am also surprised when some people don't see what I do. For me, it is so clear.

CB: *It is often assumed your work comes out of improvisation. Is this true?*

PB: I don't think this at all, even though some of the dancers say we "improvise." There are always moments in rehearsal when something happens spontaneously. Usually I ask a question and they think about it, and when they are ready, then they show it. But they practice what they show, and everyone is asked to write what they have done. We collect all the material, and sometimes after weeks, I ask, "can you do that? Show me again." When they show me, they know what they are doing, so it is not really improvisation. Maybe a few of them let themselves go. Feelings you can trust; our head can say one thing, but our heart says another.

CB: *Are your pieces a battle between heart and head?*

PB: No, but the more you know, you also lose. Sometimes I feel I want to do what I really feel, but my head is in the way. I would love to do what I really feel, but that is very difficult, because we know so much, we are always thinking, checking. And it is necessary.

CB: *Is that not easier as time goes on – with experience and knowledge and confidence? Is it not easier now to run with your instincts?*

PB: It would be nice, but it isn't. I am not that wise. I think it gets more difficult. With knowledge also comes responsibility – there are problems around you; you don't want to hurt people; it is a very complicated thing. I don't just have a piece of paper where I can write what I feel; I deal with human beings and all their complications, frustrations. They have private problems, jealousies. There are many different individuals in my company, and they all want to be loved very much and they are very sensitive. And each day you have to keep it alive, to explore and find a harmony. Every day it is a discovery. Maybe I should relax a bit more.

CB: *Have your working practices changed over the years?*

PB: Yes. In the pieces like *Sacre*, or the Gluck operas, or *Bluebeard*, there is a framework that already exists. So you know what you are looking for. It is very different in the other work. There are no main characters – there is just a group of people on a stage. We are the heroes now – the dancers and the public. That changes the shape and therefore the construction of the work.

CB: *Do you think this is a movement in late 20th-century performance art – people talking about their problems, the human condition in a very direct way to the audience, rather than through fictional/historic characters?*

PB: I'm sure you see many more performances than I do. I don't see so much, so it is very difficult for me to answer that. What we are doing is still an abstraction. It is not a private thing; there are certain feelings that belong to all of us. If you are really honest, it is not private, because we all know these feelings. We all have the same desires; we all are scared. There are differences – the taste, the flavor is different. But we are all together and it is the richness – all our possibilities – that I celebrate in my pieces.

CB: *You have said you use 5% or less of what you gather for a work – how do you know when to stop in the rehearsal process?*

PB: Deadlines – the limit of my timetable. The process of gathering and working can overlap. I am free in that way; I don't have a system. But there is never enough time. Even if I feel I am not ready, I have to go with it.

CB: *In 1993, Tanztheater Wuppertal staged a 20th-anniversary retrospective of your work – 13 pieces in three weeks. Was it a revealing overview?*

PB: I saw two things: what a pity I can't have this view because I am too busy with all these details, and hoping everything works well. I was so busy that I couldn't relax and really look at it. And I also thought "so much work, and so little we have done." To be able to do 20 years work in three weeks – this is not very much, no? This is shocking. I feel we have to work more!

CB: *Have the works changed much in those details over the years?*

PB: We try to do it in a certain way, but of course they change slightly. But where I see something really works, I always want to keep it like that.

CB: *How much room is there for individual interpretation when a new company member takes over a role?*

PB: When we do a new piece, it is done, it is set. But when new people come in, they take it on like any role, and they should make it their own. It is the same as in *Hamlet.* They are very *exact* parts. Like music, you cannot improvise in the middle of a Beethoven sonata. They have to create the same each time, or better, of course.

CB: *I heard a story about Beethoven recently: he played a piece of his music, and when he finished he was asked what he wanted to say, and he played it again in reply to the question.*

PB: That is beautiful. I must remember that.

CB: *I remember you said in Budapest that if you say what the work means to you, then people will understand you, not your work. But does that mean you do not wish to be understood?*

PB: It is not wrong what you say; but if I tell what I feel or what I want in a piece of work, then the people in the audience try to look at it with my eyes. They try to follow what I think. But they should feel it themselves. That is why I do not talk about meanings. The audience is part of the creation.

CB: *Jann Parry in* The Observer *wrote that at the end of* Nelken, *the audience is in love. Is it like a love affair with the audience?*

PB: I think so. Yes.

CB: *Do you have an "ideal" audience in mind when you create a work, the way a writer may think of an ideal reader?*

PB: No. They are old and young, rich and poor. For what audience can I do it? I can just be as sincere as possible. I too am the audience, and I want to feel something, too. This is the only thing I can offer.

CB: *A lot of people focus on the male/female violence in your work and it has become quite a controversial issue.*

PB: I think somebody once wrote a piece about the brutality in my work and now people see it all the time, even when it is not there. I know this reputation precedes me. But how can you make clear on stage the feelings if we don't see why there is suffering, or anger? I only use moments of violence to make certain feelings clear. It is not *for* the brutality, it is always to show the opposite.

Many things we do on stage are real; people run, they fall, they smash themselves against the walls, or they are soaked in water. The grass on stage really smells. The contract between the public – it is all real. That is what I like. If we experience that moment together in the theatre, it is very realistic, and that for me is hope, because it is something real. It is optimistic. I am not a pessimist in that way. If you share feelings, there is something beautiful and that gives us strength.

CB: *Many visual motifs recur in your work: the chain-dances, the very beautiful, elegant women. I heard an audience member in London wonder if all of the women were meant to be you ...*

PB: Nice idea. But not only the women ...

CB: *So you do perform in all of your works.*

PB: Of course.

CB: *One of your famous quotes is that you are "less interested in the way people move, as in what moves them." What moves you?*

PB: I think Beethoven had the right answer to that.

Working with Pina Bausch
A conversation with Tanztheater Wuppertal

Faynia Williams

Originally published in *TheatreForum*, Winter/Spring, 1997

> The boles of seven gigantic redwood trees dominate the stage, dwarfing puny humans who picnic, parade, scream, sleepwalk and dance beneath them. The primeval forest is indifferent to their triumphs and terrors – though one of the tree trunks bears a gash some twenty feet above the ground. Nature is not inviolate: a man constructs a house for himself in the wounded tree, watching, then joining the surreal carryings-on down below.
>
> Jann Parry, *Observer*, London

During rehearsals of *Nur Du* (*Only You*) taking place in the north German industrial town of Wuppertal in the Spring of 1996, I talked with some of Pina Bausch's collaborators about their work. Australian dancer Julie Shanahan, one of the newest members of Bausch's company, told me, "We've still got a bit more time, but personally it's always a struggle every day not to lose faith in yourself. You've worked hours and then you feel afterwards 'Oh my God, there's nothing left.'" Dominique Mercy, a French born dancer who has been with the company since Bausch founded it in 1973, felt similarly: "I'm completely disoriented. I'm completely depressed. I don't know what's going to happen, because we start off at zero. There is nothing."

Working with Bausch requires extraordinary flexibility, bravery, and resilience. Bausch says, "Dancers ask me always 'What are we going to do, what will it be in the end?' I can never answer this, because the thing is I don't know too, what it's going to be. And somehow it happens. I just make the way that it happens." It is now five weeks before the first preview performance in May and designer Peter Pabst doesn't know what the set will be. Company manager Matthias Schmiegelt worries because the presenters "all want to know how big it will be, how many trucks are involved, how many people, and how much money it will cost. I can't say."

Jann Parry, dance critic for the London *Observer*, also came to Wuppertal to observe the process of making *Nur Du*. While she found it "fascinating to watch a Bausch work-in-progress, before her sure sense of theatrical timing has pulled it into shape," it requires a lot of trust on the part of everyone, not least the presenters, to believe that the work will be ready in time. Indeed, when the presenters arrived in Wuppertal for the May previews, they discovered that it was ready, but that those stunning redwood trees would not fit into the two containers budgeted for their shipment through the Panama Canal. Seven containers were now called for, doubling the already million-dollar-plus budget.

Bausch is notoriously reluctant to talk about her work and hates any explanations of it: "Don't try to understand me. Pay attention to the piece and then you'll know." She asks the audience to bring their own imaginations and feelings with them:

> Each person in the audience is part of the piece in a way; you bring your own experience, your own fantasies, your own feelings in response to what you see. There is something happening inside. You only understand if you let that happen, it's not something you can do with your intellect. So everybody, according to their experience, has a different feeling, a different impression. Also, on different days, what you feel is different.

Jann Parry, on her first encounter with the work of Bausch, described the process from her point of view:

> You started off on this adventure with her at the beginning of each piece – you had no idea where it was going to go and even trying to think half way through, if you had a spare brain cell available, what's behind this, what's linking it up, am I following this through? – there was no way of doing that. You just had to go with it, live in real time, the duration of each piece, and discover as you went along how the little bits connected, and then try to think of it retrospectively and make sense of it. I think nobody had been as daring as that – to leave something apparently unstructured, to put the onus back on the audience of finding out what it's about, where it's going.

I wondered if Bausch, in this first co-production outside of Europe, would be making any concessions to American sensibilities in the making of *Nur Du*. Matthias Schmiegelt told me:

Pina is not doing pieces for nations. She has never done pieces for Germans. That's probably why they're understood in Japan and in India as well as in America or wherever. And also I think it's a very strange thing to think about what's American. I mean what is America? The German Americans or the Native Indian Americans? I think that was one of the main reasons why we chose this experience with the people in Los Angeles, in Berkeley, in Texas, and in Arizona: that it involves so many Americans of different origins. This was the exciting thing about the multicultural situation of the West Coast society, much more than the national situation.

Dominique Mercy agreed, "it was not the thought of making a piece with or about America." In their co-productions there is never a question of making a literal response to the place, "it's more getting an impression and trying to give back what we felt about the place where we were."

If they didn't begin with images from their research in the United States, then where did they begin? Dominique said they started where they always start. "Pina comes in one day and she decides 'Okay we start' and that's the way we start. Each one of us makes a little bit of personal investigation about the theme, but, like every piece, we never discussed with Pina the subject, the story, whatever's going to happen. One day she asks a question and here we go." And what question did Pina ask that started this work? "I couldn't tell you now precisely what it was. I should look it up in my book."

In Wuppertal, preliminary work on the production had started by the end of December 1995. When the company went to California for the research trip in January and February 1996, they saw and heard as much as they could and, in addition, had classes in the dance and movement of the various cultural components of Los Angeles, including flamenco and martial arts. This was part of the three week workshop held at the University of California, Los Angeles campus. They had classes in the morning, then rehearsals, and then went out and about as much as they could. Dominique said they went to "different music and dance, to nightclubs, we went to see drag queens, to hear gospel singing, a lot of different things … The first impression you get is the surface of things, how they appear to be, as people. That for me was the start of a strong impression."

Upon returning to Wuppertal the research was naturally followed by a digestive period. Dominique told me,

Then Pina asks questions in relation to what she experienced, or she tried to find out how we received things … And sometimes you have a sort of reflection from what happened and then it brings you back to the old questions, the first questions Pina asked, and maybe now you have an answer because you went through these three weeks. Maybe the question was too early before, you couldn't answer, not in the way you think now.

As with all her other pieces, *Nur Du* (*Only You*) work begins in the Lichtburg rehearsal room, a large converted cinema, situated between a porn video shop and a McDonald's. When Bausch founded her Tanztheater in Wuppertal in 1973, the town was more famous as the birthplace of aspirin and Friedrich Engels than for any rich cultural life. To reach the theatre, Bausch used to ride the city's Schweberbahn, a creaky suspended monorail, hailed by Jean Cocteau as "the flying angel." Her memories of the rooms and glimpses of people as she passed by their upper story apartments informed much of her work.

The rehearsal room is huge, with costumes hanging on rails around the walls, a video camera set up, and a monitor behind a screen. There are tables and chairs, a telephone, and paper to write on.

PINA BAUSCH: These weeks now, what we did, is just like finding material, just material. From this material, I'm using five percent maybe, and reworking it and doing it differently. And then we start to work on a piece. But I first create something that I can work with.

DOMINIQUE MERCY: She starts to ask questions. For instance, in one piece she says: "Tell me what you ate last night," or something to do with Christmas, or six different ways to be sad or angry, and of course with time, because this lasts quite a while, the questions become more complicated. Each time it's always your own experience. Even if you take things from the outside, it's the way you see them. It's yourself which is on stage.

Julie Shanahan remembers that at the beginning of the *Nur Du* development process the question actually arrived at the rehearsal studio by telephone. Bausch was at the theatre rehearsing *Danzón* for its premiere (1995) while early work on *Nur Du* continued at the Lichtburg rehearsal studio. At an early rehearsal Shanahan told me that Bausch's telephone instructions to the group had been, "write *Liebe*."

We had to write the word love with our body. We worked that night from six o'clock till ten o'clock, and when we had our movement somebody took a video of it. Then the next day Pina wants to see it also live, she doesn't just want to watch the video. We had to show her what we had done the night before. And I was embarrassed. I knew it was really long. I knew it wasn't good. I didn't know where to go from there. So we looked at the video of what I had done and Pina said what movements she thought were the most important ones. So I took my piece of paper where I wrote down the movements. I didn't start again until today, because I needed to get some distance from it. What I did today was much less than what I had, and I thought the material was so much richer.

So, the work that Jann Parry feels appears unstructured is, in fact, meticulously composed, combining speech, movement, dance, high art, and popular culture, creating a world without formal boundaries. Bausch told me:

> I can't think without the time or without space. Everything belongs together. If it's together once, you can't take it apart. The feeling, the energy, all that you can hear, the music or the not-music, the space, all what is there, for me it's impossible [to separate them]. I can't think movement, only movement.

One of the hallmarks of a Bausch production is the use of real materials on stage – earth, water, grass, sand. While these can be headaches for a designer or a company manager, they create a brilliant if difficult sensual working environment for the dancers.

PINA BAUSCH: It's a big joy to dance in the earth. It's like we are lucky in the theatre. We can do so many things that it's impossible for other people to do. We can dance in the earth, we can get sweaty, we can have evening dresses get completely wet … If you walk on the grass it's silent, it's soft, or there are some mosquitoes around. It has a smell. It has a certain temperature … Or when you are in the water, when you run there is the noise of it, or if it's quiet it's like a mirror … Or the leaves when you walk … you can see where you walked. All this I like very much. It's joining with something. For me it's not a resistance. It's the opposite. It's touching.

JULIE SHANAHAN: You learn all of the movements and when you come on the set you have such a different relationship with those movements. I remember the first couple of times I danced on earth. I thought, "Oh my God, I can't dance." But you realize the more you let yourself go and feel the earth, the easier the movements become. You rely on the feeling of the earth and the music. And the smell, you know, is so important. You don't only dance, hear the music, feel the earth underneath your feet, you smell it. It gets in your mouth, you taste it, you feel it on your skin. I mean, it's wonderful.

Another key design element that has become a Bausch trademark is the clothes her dancers wear, usually created in collaboration with Marion Cito. The 1930s shifts, the stiletto heels, the suits, the cross-dressing, and in *Nur Du*, the live-mouse-bra, carry a textual influence. They often add to the humor of the piece, and one is inclined to forget how much humor there is in her work. What is particularly Bausch is the lurking reminder. In *Nur Du* it is voiced by Julie Shanahan's blonde vamp: "Did you know – beneath our clothes, we are all naked. I'm sorry."

Always when I have done the piece, I realize that I knew it before. My feeling knew. I know what I'm looking for. But not in my head. Certainly I know also when I find it. Yes – I know.

Pina Bausch

Sources

Personal interviews with Pina Bausch, Dominque Mercy, Julie Shanahan, Peter Pabst, Matthias Schmiegelt, and Jann Parry in Wuppertal during rehearsals for *Nur Du* (*Only You*), and at the Edinburgh International Festival in 1995 and 1996.

Nur Du (*Only You*): Pina Bausch, Tanztheater Wuppertal in a newly commissioned piece

Royd Climenhaga

Originally published in *TPQ*, July, 1997

Pina Bausch is often considered one of the most influential artists of the latter part of this century. Her non-linear, image based work is cited as a turning point in both Modern dance and contemporary theatrical practice, an open door into a more loosely structured dramaturgy through which many artists have now passed. These claims are in spite of the fact that very few people have actually seen her work, at least in America. In Europe her company has performed everywhere from festivals in Avignon to Zurich, with regular stops in Paris, Rome, Edinburgh, Amsterdam, dozens of individual performances along the way, residencies in Rome, Madrid, Palermo, and Vienna, and the premier of each new piece back in her home base of Wuppertal, a quiet little industrial town in the Ruhr valley of Germany that has become a Mecca for Europe's inquisitive dance and performance audience. But Americans outside of New York have had little opportunity to appreciate what she herself claims must be experienced first hand to have an impact. She notoriously refuses to talk about her work in detail and shuns interviews. "I can't explain anything. You have to hear it or you have to see it. But I do all this to not speak, you know" (Sublett D4[1]) she says. Besides an eye opening visit to Los Angeles for the Olympic Arts Festival in 1984, Bausch's only other American appearances had been at BAM, as part of the Next Wave Festival. Until now. Through a unique collaboration between several independent university presenting organizations, Bausch and her company, Tanztheater Wuppertal, were able to present a newly commissioned piece, *Nur Du* (*Only You*), at four locations in the American west.

Pebbles Wadsworth, Director of UT Austin's Performing Arts Center, commented that "it was important to bring Pina Bausch here. A lot of American artists have been influenced by her work, yet most of the American audience has never even seen it. ... I think so much of our work is influenced by her, people who aren't even aware of who she is" (Stagebill 25). This mini-tour of the West presented the opportunity for a completely new audience of artists and theatre-goers to finally witness what had only been hearsay. And yet, according to many, the power of that hearsay had influenced a new generation of dance and theatre artists. When I asked Bausch about the role of influence in her work, and whether she could point to any major influences on her own style, she responded that "of course there was the work I did with Kurt Jooss and Anthony Tudor, but more recently I don't have the time to see too many things, though I'd like to." But that doesn't mean she isn't influenced by others, she continues. "Its more of something that is in the very world around you, an absorption of ideas from the world around you. I did a piece based on some Brecht material, and although I did not make a conscious effort to study and employ his techniques, they come. You are in his world for a period of time and they come." When I returned the idea of influence back to her and asked how she feels about being such an influence on others, she said that she didn't know if she was. "I just do my own little thing, and if other people see it or hear about it and can now do something of their own, well that is good. But I think sometimes people see something we do and they think, well if Pina can do that, then I can do my thing. It is their work, and if something I did gave them the initiative to do it, fine, wonderful. Now show it to me so I can do maybe something else."

The commissioning and presentation

The idea for this commission and presentation of Tanztheater Wuppertal grew out of Wadsworth's simple desire to expose more people to Bausch's work. But simply booking the company to perform was not possible. The biggest problem has always been funding. European festivals often have the resources to bring in the best the world has to offer, even if that means travel and housing expenses for a company that ranges from twenty-six to thirty-four dancers, along with usually massive sets and a large team of technical support personnel. American presenters are constrained by quickly receding resources and government aid to bring in artists of Bausch's stature. And in this case they were further hindered by Bausch's desire to work on a newly commissioned piece, rather than simply being presented at new venues. Robert Cole, Director of Cal Performances, comments "Pina Bausch's name is always a fundamental part of any discussion involving dance and dance/theatre. Yet, until now, we've had to travel to Europe or occasionally New York, to see any of her work. Nearly a decade ago, my colleagues and I decided to make a difference in that inevitability and by pooling our resources, as well as the artistic interests of our audiences, we are now able to achieve this joint ambition" ("Creative commissioning ..." 16A). In the end it took an unprecedented alliance among four university cultural presenters – Cal Performances at UC Berkeley, UCLA Center for the Performing Arts with the James A. Doolittle Southern California Theatre Association and the Music Center of Los Angeles County, the Performing Arts Center at UT Austin, and Arizona State University Public Events – to raise the 1.2 million needed for the performances and to provide the resources for not only the company's fall tour, but also the exploratory visit they would make earlier in the year to gather material on which the new piece would be built. Bausch was interested in exploring the concept of the American West, and so the presentation developed into a commissioning of a new work to be based on her and her dancer's experiences visiting the four cities involved in the tour. The stated mission of the commission and presentation was to "provide a whole new context in which to view American dance and theatre of the past few decades" ("Creative commissioning ..." 25).

Bausch and German dance

German Dance was itself energized by two brief tours by American artists. One, by Isadora Duncan in the early part of this century, ignited a modern dance boom that was to coalesce into the work of Mary Wigman, Kurt Jooss and other Expressionist dance masters. Duncan showed the German dance world that dance could be centered on the individual.

And in the sixties, a visit by Merce Cunningham and dancers polarized the German Dance scene, with many following the lead Cunningham had set of formalist post-modern dance, while others, wanting to break from the dominant ballet tradition, returned to Germany's expressionist roots. Pina Bausch was among the latter group.

After an early grounding in traditional ballet, Bausch entered the Folkwang School in 1955, the center of expressionist dance training in Germany and one of the only schools that offered an alternative to the dominant ballet tradition. There she studied with Kurt Jooss, among others, who perhaps first showed her the value of combining dance structure and theatrical technique. She certainly gained at least a working awareness of dramatic gesture as a choreographic tool from Jooss's emotive style. After graduating from the Folkwang School she went to New York to study at the Juilliard School. Here she familiarized herself with the American modern dance techniques of Martha Graham and José Limón. Limón and Louis Horst were among her teachers, and she was undoubtedly influenced by her work with Paul Sanasardo, who had worked extensively with Anna Sokolow, and maintained the strongly dramatic work built on psychological gesture that Sokolow had begun. But perhaps the most vital influence on Bausch during this period was that of Anthony Tudor. Tudor was one of her instructors at Juilliard, and she danced with the Metropolitan Ballet Theatre during the 1961/62 season, then under his direction. Tudor's strongly psychological style, with its emphasis on character built upon emotive gesture, must have reawakened and reconfigured some of Bausch's earlier experiences with emotive gesture in the German dance tradition.

Bausch took this strong background in dramatic dance technique back to Germany in 1962, where Kurt Jooss offered her the position of leading soloist in his Folkwang Ballet. Her dancing with the Folkwang Ballet, under Jooss's direction, was riveting and enigmatic. Hörst Koegler recalls, perhaps with the added insight of subsequent experience, that "it was through no special will or effort, but just by her very nature that she stood apart from the rest of the dancers. She recalled the women Käthe Kollwitz has drawn; women carrying the burden of generations, who have been exploited through no fault of their own other than having had the misfortune of being born female in a male-dominated society" (51).

Bausch worked closely with Jooss for the next six years and formed a partnership with Jean Cebron to experiment with new choreography. Though tightly constructed, what stood out in these early efforts was Bausch's own emotionally charged attitude. Koegler reports, "There was something behind the movements, and if one couldn't say exactly what it was, it seemed to have to do with muted despair and mourning for a beautiful world in which man was inevitably going to seed" (52). Themes of gender construction and the opposition of the sexes were explored in Bausch's early choreography, setting the tone for the work of her mature period.

In 1968 Jooss retired and Bausch took over his position at the Folkwang Dance Studio where she began to work out a mixture of dance and theatrical technique. In 1972 she was asked to choreograph the dances for Hans Peter Lehman's production of *Tannhäuser* at the Wuppertal Opera Company. The success of her unconventional staging led to her being offered the position of director of the Wuppertal Ballet. She accepted the position on the condition that she could bring along many of the dancers with whom she was working at the Folk-wang Studio in Essen.

At Wuppertal she began to reconfigure the dramatic structure of her source material and apply collage techniques, the source of which has been attributed both to the experimental theatre she witnessed in New York and to cabaret and operetta traditions popular in Germany earlier in this century. The result was a dance form with some of the aims of *Ausdruckstanz* (Expressionist Dance, "*Ausdruckstanz* shifted the emphasis to a theatrical dramatic *ausdrucksgebarde* (emotive gesture) which was intended to speak for itself. ... Now dance no longer needed a story to tell, creating sense, significance out of movement itself" (Müller 12)) and some of the techniques of both American modern dance and experimental theatre. She drew on her own and her dancers' personal experiences to create presentational movement patterns formed from emotive gestures and derived from a response to, rather than in service of, formal story structures.

It is this open form of theatrical presentation, based on collages of images drawn from her and her dancers experience, that Bausch has continued to explore over the last twenty or so years. The dancers are asked questions and encouraged to find physical metaphors that engage the dancer's body as the site of meaning, not simply as an object to be arranged under the guidelines of an established technique, as in previous dance traditions, but as the locus of subjective presence, the means by which we are in the world and through which we establish a sense of ourselves as both individuals and part of a community. It is this method of working that Bausch and her company brought to their residency in Los Angeles and the experience gathering side trips that she and her set and costume designers made to the San Francisco area and Austin, TX.

The visit

Bausch arrived in Los Angeles in January without an agenda. After meeting with reporters for an opening press conference and being a little overwhelmed by the expectations many seemed to have, she responded, "I just want to say please don't forget that I'm just a little human being. We'll move around with open eyes, open ears and our feelings" (Kapitanoff 49). But moving around proves to be rather difficult, and Bausch is dismayed by the lack of urban street life. The company is constrained to two vans that shuttle them back and forth between their hotel and the UCLA dance center where they begin each day with a ballet class and then spend the afternoon in rehearsal. They spend the evenings exploring Los Angeles, visiting everything from a boxing gym to a UCLA basketball practice. They went on a whale watching trip and bowling at Hollywood Bowl. They even saw Florence Henderson receive her star on the Hollywood "Walk of Fame." Over fifty sites and events in all were visited. The company had hoped to wander the streets and mingle with the people, but the residents, spending most of their time in the world trapped in their cars, were not so easily observable.

After their stay, Rainer Behr, one of the members of the company, commented that, "Los Angeles seemed very poor to me, although not in a material but in a spiritual sense. So full of illusions ... These opinions, these mindsets, these lives – to be honest, it really blew me away. Right there, in your face, the situation of all those who can't make it, who can't function ... There, they've got the freedom to really live out their dumb things, their lost ideals. Everything is lived out, without limits" ("Thoughts ... " 30).

When asked how this wealth of experience would find its way into a dance, Bausch responded, "I am looking for something I felt, or touched, or saw, or somebody I met. It could be something very simple – what happens because of the people who are there and how they interact. I would like to see, to learn, to meet, and then see what happens" (Breslauer 3).

In rehearsals, the dancers try to mould their experiences into performed moments that Bausch will later recontextualize and rearrange until something coalesces into what will be the final piece. "She wants us," says Dominique Mercy, one of the longest running members of the company, "to be as sincere and simple as possible" (Daly 10). In response to a question on how all of the events the dancers participate in and watch will translate into a piece about America, Mercy continues, "the American commission should not be taken as literal or descriptive. The point is much larger than the occasional flash of American imagery. There is also something behind those specific experiences that speaks to larger issues of human relations" (Daly 20). When asked what the company members get from working with Bausch and how they contribute to the rehearsal process, Nazareth Panadero, another long-standing company member responds, "I was especially drawn in by Pina's great interest in people. That is the most important thing. There are so many of us, but it is still something very personal, there is room for everybody. Everybody works together, but you also work all by yourself – very focused on yourself. Also, the discoveries that one makes about oneself here – that's what working with Pina is like. She searches people for things as if she was searching for something foreign or new. She gives you the opportunity to search and find them" ("Thoughts ... " 30).

Nur Du differs from some of Bausch's other works in that, rather than her usual strategy of suggesting series of movements to her dancers, in this case she relied on the dancers own work, eliciting movements from them with more movement-oriented prompts than usual. Like: "a small phrase about the feeling of comfort," "a shape that encloses," "a pause in space."

A select group of students were allowed to witness the process, some from UCLA and others who traveled from UT Austin to partake in the experience. It is here that Bausch's influence might be at its strongest. All of the students leave with a sense of amazement at how hard each performer works, and how involved they are in developing the material, rather than simply trying to complete the choreography that is dictated to them. When the company returns for the performances, they continue their contact with the students in each locale they visit. Dominique Mercy offers a class for dancers at UC Berkeley. The class is fairly straightforward ballet technique coupling the usual extension of ballet with a purposeful fall. The work is simple and grounded in an established movement vocabulary, a common ground from which the students might all begin, and yet what is emphasized is not so much the mastering of physical positions as the place of fullness from which the movement begins. While correcting one of the students who was striving to reach a particular position, Mercy explains, "you need energy from the start. It's like going on a trip with an open suitcase, what you do." And then in perfect mime he picks up his imaginary suitcase, takes a few bold steps forward and immediately stops to pick up the scattered contents.

In response to a question on how the work on her pieces begins, and whether the experiences they collect find a home in the finished piece, Bausch answers, "I can only make something very open. I'm not pointing out a view. There are conflicts between people, but they can be looked at from each side, from different angles. I don't know from where the piece comes. Even there, already something is there. It's not a picture, not a structure, but it has something to do with where you are in life at that period, the wishes, what you find scary." The early stages of shaping a piece, she says, "are very naked, very sensitive. The dancers have to be patient with me, to try to follow me" (Hoffman 12). When asked how she thinks the American audience will respond to her work, Bausch explains:

What I try is to find the pictures, or the images that can best express the feelings I want to convey. And you have to find your own way to show these things. I am not telling a story in a normal way. Each person in the audience is part of the piece in a way; you bring your own experience, your own fantasy, your own feeling in response to what you see. There is something happening inside. You only understand if you let that happen, it's not something you can do with your intellect. So everybody, according to their experience, has a different feeling, a different impression.

(Meisner 15)

The piece

The lights come up to reveal an open stage with seven giant redwood trunks rising from the floor to above the sightlines at the top of the proscenium. One of the trees is cut off about halfway up, and another has a large gash taken out of the side some fifteen feet in the air. A woman (Regina Advento) enters from upstage, walks through the trees and down to the front of the stage. She sits facing the audience in the chair she has brought with her and slowly raises her skirt, revealing her crossed bare legs. She very quietly begins singing "The One I Love" in quite a good impression of Billie Holiday. The audience struggles to hear.

In *Kontakthof* (1978), the piece begins with each performer coming to the front of the stage and displaying him or herself to the audience, first front, then profile, back, and then front again. They bare their teeth as if they were a horse for sale, or show their leg. The impression is confrontational, an implied, you paid your money and you are going to sit there and look at me for the next three plus hours, so here I am, this is what you get. In this instance that same sense of display is taken to a different level. It is oddly more personal and yet more removed at the same time. You sense no reluctance on the part of the performer to display herself in this fashion, and yet no great willingness either. She is resigned to the fact. It is what one does. After she has completed the song, we see a group of men enter from stage left and move across the back of the stage. They lift one man up and he crawls, fly-like, across the surface of one of the great trees.

The piece continues through several small episodes. A theme of display begins to emerge as each performer moves about the space in isolated moments. Julie Shanahan falls to the ground, grabs her silk dress by the chest and brings herself back to standing. She says, "pick yourself up, and dust yourself off." She then pulls her jaw down and lets out a scream. Helena Pikon confidently walks to the front of the stage, lifts her skirt and empties her panties of hay, leaving a small pile on the stage. She turns with a smile and walks out. A man walks from stage left to right sending a feather in gentle arcs. He catches the feather and repeats the action, each time looking out to the audience with a subtle smile. A woman strides across stage, plucks at her dress and announces "Silk" as she continues out. Another man enters with a basketball, places it on the floor and then rolls on his back across it so that it ends up as a pillow to support his grinning face looking out at the audience. He repeats this several more times. A man enters with a shy grin standing behind a trashcan. He quickly removes his shoe and puts it into the trashcan, takes a few steps across the stage and removes the other shoe, all the time watching the audience with his demure look. He makes successive stops across the stage to remove his socks, his shirt, his pants, and finally his underwear, until he is naked, still hiding behind the trashcan now full of his clothes. After one last grin to the audience he quickly leaves. Andrei Berezine enters with a rocking chair. He calls for Jan, and looks around, but Jan is not to be found. He sits in the rocker and lights a cigarette, and then blowing smoke and looking supremely comfortable, he says "Help." His tone is playfully facetious. He continues, "If something happens to you, call 911. After, do something, jump, scream. When they come they can see you."

All of these moments are performed as if there is a need to be seen in order to exist, that only in calling attention to yourself do you become yourself. So far it has been a particularly fragmentary evening without as much connection or fluidity between elements as in some of the other pieces. Bausch's work has been described in the program as a theatre of isolated elements, and she seems to be living up to her billing. But I begin to wonder if that is a problem with the piece or a reflection of the isolation inherent in LA and America more generally. The same alienated couples that appear in many of Bausch's pieces take on a new twist as the energy is pushed out toward external markers of beauty and life rather than the more usual internal struggle.

In *Palermo, Palermo* (1989) Nazareth Panadero plays a woman who desperately holds a sheaf of pasta. She screams at the audience, "You see these pastas, they are mine, all mine. You see this one," and she removes one piece of pasta, "it is mine. And this one, mine. This one, mine." And as she continues removing pieces of pasta one by one, "Mine. Mine. Mine. Mine. They are all mine. You can't have any, they are mine." Here, she walks to the front of the stage with the same sense of prideful ownership and says to Andrei, "Andrrrrrei," deliberately overemphasizing the roll of the r. "Come on, Come on, Andrrrrrrei." Andrei stands in sheepish silence and then walks off, as Nazareth continues to the audience, "You see, I can do it, he can not. Andrrrrrei. You see. RRRRRRRegina, RRRRRainer, Ferrrrrrnando. You see, I can do it, he cannot. Berrrrrnd. Barrrrrbarrrra. I can do it, he can not." Self is determined by what you can show. The first act ends with the title song ("Only You") emerging from a bit of frantic activity on stage. Julie Shanahan has brought a small card table all the way downstage, and after sitting behind it, raises her skirt to use as a table cloth, revealing her crossed legs under the table as Regina Advento had done at the beginning. All of the women line up down stage and repeat the opening gesture, raising their skirts and looking directly into the audience. The song begins as Jan Minarik, who has been with the company since the early seventies, and in this piece adds to his growing repertoire of slightly off-kilter loners, enters from upstage wearing only high heels and two mink stoles, one around his crotch like a diaper and the other strung along his shoulder like a beauty pageant banner. He walks to the line of women and begins, one after the other, to arrange their hair in precisely the same fashion. The song plays out while he continues on. Andrei enters to inform us that it is time for intermission, but even with the house lights up and people starting to make their way to the lobby, Minarik continues his deliberate styling of the women's hair, making his way off stage only after each one has been given the same style. In this world, "Only You" is true only as you adopt the look of the moment, the currently fashionable way of representing yourself.

In *Bandoneon* (1980) the performers constantly itch, or try to scratch an itch just out of their reach on their backs. It is a little quirk that speaks volumes about need and necessity and lack of fulfillment. *Nur Du*'s quirk is a quick glance in the mirror. A woman enters from stage right holding a pocket mirror and some lipstick. She desperately attempts to apply the lipstick, and when her tries at a clean line seemingly fail, she throws herself on the ground screaming. Dominique Mercy sets up an elaborate image by spreading out a piece of plastic, stopping to check himself in a small mirror he takes from his pocket, smiling at the audience and then piling up a few stones. He checks himself in the mirror again, smiles at the audience and removes his shirt. He checks himself in the mirror once again and removes his pants to reveal a short gold lamé skirt. One more check in the mirror before he stands on the stones, assumes the position of a cherub in a Roman fountain, and spews water from a water bottle in an arc on to the plastic. One last check in the mirror before he gathers up his props and exits.

If they do not check themselves in a mirror, the performers will often check in with the audience for approval. Bausch's performers have often addressed the audience directly in prior pieces, but before it was more of a challenge. You want to see something, here, I will show you. Dominique Mercy is pressed into service in *Nelken* (1983). He begins clearing the stage and screams, "You want to see something? Well, I'll show you something. Get rid of those chairs," demanding that the others clear the stage. He moves to the rear of the stage and says "What do you want to see? You want to see turns?" Whereupon he does a series of *chaînés* turns across the carnation strewn floor. Although he executes the fundamentals of ballet with more desperation than precision, the audience applauds. He continues to ask what the audience wants to see, and offers them a series of ballet moves, double *tours en l'air, grand jetés,* and *entrechat six.* The audience responds to his desperate showcasing with awkward silence, until, finally, drenched in sweat and gasping he screams: "What else do you want to see? What else do I have to show you?" He begins to move off stage, utterly exhausted, and says, "I've had it, I'm tired." A man in a suit comes out, stops Mercy, and says "Your passport please." Though frustrated by the process, he uses his ballet training to do what it has always been meant for, to call attention to and define himself. He chastises the audience for our part in defining him by what he can do rather than by who he is.

Now the check to the audience seems to be a more deliberate attempt to gain approval and to claim some sense of being. It is still a knowing glance, but the frame is altered. That sense of display is always in evidence in *Nur Du.* And indeed that idea of auditioning for the part is taken to a new end. In direct contrast to Mercy's desperate attempts to show us what he can do, and his dissatisfaction for being forced to define himself in that way, Julie Shanahan begins the second act by walking to center stage and standing with her back to the audience. She wears simple black clothes in marked contrast to the dresses and heels worn by the women throughout the piece. She states, "I don't have anything to show. I don't have a costume. I don't have any high heels. I'm not even wearing any makeup," whereupon she bows her head and exclaims, "I'm sorry, oh god," and then, once again confronting her unseen interrogator, "But anyway, I'm here. I came." It's as if without anything to show, her very existence is in doubt, echoing Vladimir's response to the boy's question in *Waiting for Godot* of what is he to tell Mr. Godot. "Tell him … tell him you saw us. You did see us, didn't you?"

Each moment in *Nur Du* has individual value, but the real strength of the piece comes in accretion. We are left with a feeling of isolation and desperate showcasing. Of arrogance and resiliency. And a surface quality that is hardened and shined to mirror like quality, but that does not permit entry into any interior world. Although some of the California critics were reluctant to see this as a portrayal of the American West, the overall effect had just the quality of transcending the specific references that Mercy had claimed was the aim. And, as usual in Bausch's pieces, there was room to derive out of the evening whatever you were willing to put into it. If you came looking for some entertaining moments, they were there to be had, and if you invested more of your own place in the world, you might find a way to approach the surface values we all confront in our daily lives.

Nur Du is punctuated by several solos done in more of a traditional dance idiom. The men in particular shine through these isolated moments, all of which incorporate a certain degree of dramatic gesture pushed toward full body swoops and collapses to the floor. The piece ends with one final solo, done by Dominique Mercy. He hurls his graceful body into the space and flails his arms with abandon. This final dance seems to be a dance of death, where we witness the last gasps of a dying bird, the death of the swan in *Swan Lake*, done double time. I left feeling that after all the surface gloss we have been shown, and the many humorous moments, we are left with the fragility of one individual confronting death. A solitary man, seemingly out of context, going through his final attempts to hold on to life.

When asked about her reputation as someone who often portrays violence on stage, particularly in regard to relationships between men and women, Bausch responded:

> How can you make clear onstage the feelings if we don't see why there is suffering, or anger? I could just tell the audience, but I like them to feel it. Many things we do onstage are real: People run and smash themselves against walls, they fall, they get soaked in water and covered in soil. The contact between the public, it is real. If we experience that moment together in the theatre – that realism – together, then that for me is hope. I am not a pessimist in that way. If we share feelings, there is something beautiful, and that gives us strength.
>
> (Bowen 41)

The question remains, will this visit and the added exposure Bausch's work has gained increase her influence on American dance and theatre? The answer, of course, is yet to be seen. But as Bausch points out, part of the power her work provides is the freedom to do something new. The luxury of not actually having seen the work in many ways is a greater draw than the work itself. Artists gain from the expanded possibilities that Bausch's mere presence suggests, but are forced to draw on their own resources. The other large difference between Bausch's visit and other trend setting visits by performing artists in years past is that rather than providing a new technique that may be followed and adapted, Bausch's real innovation is simply the courage to push through with a process and the genius to move it beyond a personal expression and into a universal one. Part of what Bausch is able to do is contingent on the company she has formed, and the nearly six months of full day rehearsals that each piece takes to develop and perform. Those resources are not really a possibility in America. We are left to draw breath from the creative air Bausch engenders and then use the resources we have to develop our own material in our own ways. *Nur Du* itself forces you, as an audience member, to make your own connections to the open ended images presented on stage. It turns the attention from the performers' interpretation of the life they saw around them to your own struggles with life, love and death. These are hardly new themes, and ones that leave attempts to explain what Bausch means unnecessary. As she says: "If I tell you what it means to me, you will understand me, not the piece." With that thought in mind, I am left to recall one last image from the piece. After doing a bit of a vaudeville sketch, using one of the other performers as a ventriloquist's dummy, Jan Minarik says "one of the greatest gifts, is knowing when to leave." He stands, and walks off the stage.

Note

1　Many of the citations of Bausch's comments and those of her dancers, when not specifically stated as part of a personal interview, were drawn from various press conferences Bausch has given over the years, and are cited in other articles, reviews and program notes. In each instance I have given the specific source from which I am drawing the quote, though others may exist.

Sources

Beckett, Samuel. *Waiting for Godot,* New York: Grove Press, 1954.
Bowen, Christopher. "Pina Bausch", *Datebook: San Francisco Chronicle* (29 September–5 October, 1996), 40–41.

Breslauer, Jan. "Open-eyed in L.A", *Los Angeles Times* (17 March, 1996), 3–4.

"Creative commissioning and collaboration behind the scenes in *Nur Du (Only You)*, a piece by Pina Bausch", *Stagebill* (September, 1996), Berkeley/Cal Performances edn., 16A–25.

Daly, Ann. "Pina Bausch goes West to prospect for imagery", *New York Times* (22 September, 1996), 10–20.

Hoffman, Eva. "Pina Bausch: catching institutions on the wing", *New York Times* (11 September, 1994), H, Section 2, 12.

Kapitanoff, Nancy. "Pina goes West", *In* 2/96, 48–51.

Koegler, Hörst. "Pina Bausch Tanztheater Wuppertal", *Dance Magazine* (October, 1991), 88.

Meisner, Nadine. "Come dance with me", *Dance and Dancers* (September/ October, 1992), 12–16

Müller, Hedwig. "Expressionism? 'Ausdruckstanz' and the New Dance Theatre in Germany", *Festival International de Nouvelle Danse, Montreal, Souvenir Program*, trans. Michael Vensky-Stalling (1986), 10–15.

Perlmutter, Donna. "Pina Bausch comes to town", *Performing Arts: Music Center of Los Angeles County Program* (October, 1996). Pina Bausch Tanztheater Wuppertal. Dorothy Chandler Pavilion: 53–59.

Sublett, Scott. "Pina Bausch's take on American West", *San Francisco Chronicle* (20 February, 1996), D1–D4.

"Thoughts on the creation of *Nur Du* and Bausch's work", *The University of Texas College of Fine Arts Performing Arts Center Program* (22 October, 1996). Pina Bausch Tanztheater Wuppertal. Bass Concert Hall.

Dancing through the dark

Pina Bausch finds a ray of light

Rita Felciano

Originally published in *Dance Magazine*, October, 1996

> One day the sun entangled himself in a tree, and the earth plunged into darkness. A little squirrel lost its tail, had its fur burnt off and went blind, but gnawed at the tree's branches until the heavenly globe could rise again. As a reward, the sun changed the naked creature, who had always wanted to fly, into the first bat.
>
> "How the bat came to be", Anismanabe
> (Native American) myth

A would-be lover lowers himself on top of his partner until another man pulls her away from between his legs. A woman has her hair brushed with a broom. Two men embrace until it hurts. A man in a tutu walks around with a watering can; another reads a story about a faithful squirrel who becomes a bat. Two women draw hearts on a blackboard. Dancers chase each other with office chairs; others prefer skateboards. It's all in a day's work in Pina Bausch's 2002 *Für die Kinder von Gestern, Heute und Morgen (For the Children of Yesterday, Today and Tomorrow)*, which receives its American premiere on November 16 at the Brooklyn Academy of Music's Next Wave Festival.

For over thirty years, Bausch has peered into the darkness of the human heart, searching for love and tenderness and finding precious little. The world she put on stage has been full of fractured relationships, cracked identities, and soul-numbing loneliness. But she never gave up looking. Repetition, so integral to her work, reminds us of our inability to break the shackles of our imprisoned spirits, but, conversely, also of the Sisyphusian task of trying to do it again and again. While Bausch saw dignity, even humor in this persistence, we didn't laugh. It was too painful.

But since the mid-'90s, Bausch's tonal palette has changed. Her voice is less strident; her edges are rounder; her heart seems lighter, and some of her vignettes are devilishly funny. Maybe traveling the world, Bausch's version of the Grand Tour, has softened her perspective. In 1996 she created her first site-specific work outside Europe. In *Nur Du (Only You)*, Bausch's look at the American West, she seemed more bemused than troubled at the superficiality and self-infatuation she saw in the New World. A year later *Der Fensterputzer (The Window Washer)*, inspired by the hectic but orderly life in Hong Kong, was full of sudden delights. Then came *Masurca Fogo*, Bausch's love affair with life, love, and lust as observed in Portugal and its Cape Verde culture. The scene where the dancers build a little tropical hut and dance a joyous rumba inside it is still talked about. *Masurca* was followed by *Água*, her perspective on Brazil; it overflows with a similar kind of *joie de vivre*. Lee Yanor's film, *Coffee with Pina*, shows *Água's* battle of the sexes as kissing competitions, and men and women splashing each other with water bottles like kids on the beach.

So has Bausch mellowed? Is it possible to grow from *Café Müller's* loneliness to the fragile but real community of *Masurca Fogo*, as film director Pedro Almodovar, in his wondrous film *Talk to Her*, seems to imply? Almodovar has said he was struck by Masurca's "vitality and optimism, its bucolic air, and those unexpected images of painful beauty which made me cry from pure pleasure."

Recently Lutz Forster, a company member and guest artist since 1975, addressed the question about whether Bausch has become more hopeful about our capacity to create meaningful relationships. Speaking from Japan, where he was on tour with the company's newest work, *Ten-Chi*, he said he wasn't sure. "My feeling is not that she is more hopeful, but that she is convinced that what we need is hope. We need to see that there is something else besides what's going on in the world.

"I remember when we started *Für die Kinder* – it was the first production after 9/11 – she said to me, 'How can we do a piece today? What can we do?'"

Für die Kinder has an intergenerational cast of fourteen dancers, a music collage by Matthias Burkert and Andreas Eisenschneider, and set design by longtime collaborator Peter Pabst. In a May interview, Bausch explained her choice of the topic. "Children are a symbol of hope; they are our origin, and their fragility is ours. That's why it is important that we talk about them."

Bausch's interest in childhood, of course, is not new. Her perspective on it as a complex mix of innocence and misery wends its way through her work like an underground stream. Childhood interests her primarily for the residue it leaves in the adult. Her dancers often move, act and talk as if unaware of consequences, much the way children do.

Figure 9 Für die Kinder ... (2002): Jorge Puerta Armenta, Azusa Seyama.
© Ursula Kaufmann

With this newest work, Bausch hopes to throw another beam of light into an essentially chaotic world. Sounding almost Freudian, she said of the process: "We were looking at things that we had forgotten and thanks to which sometimes we can better understand the world that surrounds us."

As always, in *Children* Bausch worked, as she calls it, "from the inside out." She prepares a series of questions to which her dancers try to find answers – in actions, dance, language, images. They work alone or together until they are ready to show the results. Bausch then edits, layers, and combines the material into the incidents that pepper her landscape.

Cristiana Morganti, an ensemble member since 1993, describes the process as one of "mutual discovery," open and wide-ranging. Suggestions might be gestures which call up a mood; a movement which takes lots of space; a way to protect yourself from the rain; to show something which reflects longing; make visible a high violin sound. "As of late," Morganti observed, "she likes us to speak less and do more in actions and movement." For Morganti, developing a new piece is an adventure, one in which "we trust her, and she trusts us."

While the pieces from the late '90s are less abrasive, they also incorporate more pure dancing. A group of spectacularly trained movers from every continent – except Antarctica – has joined, and in part replaced, the older generation of actor/dancers. Wuppertal Tanztheater today is an intriguing mix that allows for dance and theatre to hold each other up more evenly. The gesture-derived choreography of earlier days, explained Forster, "was always developed by Pina. These days, she often lets dancers develop their own material, though she, of course, has the last word."

Is there a connection between Bausch's increased use of dance and what might be called her more hopeful prospect about the relationships we can have with each other? Forster demurred, pointing out that as an artist, Bausch wants, first of all, to evolve. But even if she were more hopeful, "it can be dangerous to talk about hope, or something like that on stage, I think that dance can do this more easily."

Longtime dancers Dominique Mercy and his wife Malou Airaudo left the company twice in order to return to sunny Marseille. Both times, they changed their mind. You can't live in Wuppertal, they have said. But you can't live without Pina either. Some artists carry the sun in their heart.

Figure 10 Rough Cut (2005): Julie Shanahan. © Ursula Kaufmann

III

Tanztheater

A new form

In dance, the world is made present through the dancer's body. The dancer's bodily presence is not simply re-presented so that it might be looked at as a marker of a created reality, but creates a world so that it might be seen; that is, engaged with as present. Within this created world of bodily presence is an underlying ethos that governs the dancer's bodily action on stage. Ballet works with the basic ideal of flight; a refutation of gravity, as the condition to which the dancer's body aspires in its portrayal of the world on stage. The specific techniques of ballet are developed with this underlying ethos as a constant source of inspiration. In reaction against this ideal, Modern dance ascribed to a base condition of groundedness; the dancer's body in touch with its tie to the earth.

The implications of these two different approaches are far reaching, both technically and metaphorically, but both reflect a view of the dancer's body as a material to be manipulated in order to achieve the desired condition of expression. This leads to an attitude of the dancer's body in motion as the ground from which dance is able to represent reality. It may employ other elements in the production, but these are basically additions to the base condition of the dancer's body in motion as the means of representation in dance. Postmodern dance worked hard to bracket out those (unnecessary) other elements, leaving the dancer's body in motion as the sole expressive element on the dance stage. But if we consider the body in motion more broadly as and engagement of performative action – the involvement of our bodies in experience and the subsequent subjectification of that event (in that our subjectivity is derived from the relation of our bodies to the world and expressed in experience) – then we arrive at a very different idea of dance, one that can account for the "other elements" of the production as part and parcel of our bodies' relationship to experience.

The representation of this aspect of experience is the goal of Tanztheater. It engages a human subject as present in her body rather than as a means to achieve an illusive quality of beauty through a developed technique. Tanztheater seeks a form of representation that embodies the contradictions and frustrations of life and presents them in living form. We are confronted not with the stabilizing form we usually look to art to affirm, but with a dynamic system that provides an entrance point for our engagement with the world, and that destabilizes our assumptions and causes us to look anew. The means of expression on stage are shifted away from the dynamic movement of the human form in dance towards the metaphorical expression of experience as a necessarily bodily phenomenon that is enmeshed within a more theatrical presentational structure. The way the piece unfolds reflects the conditions of its creation, and just as the dancers are shifted from objectified movers, choreography is re-oriented beyond the sequencing of steps to become the overall condition of the piece and the dancers' implicit bodily engagement in the event. The structural integrity comes out of dance principles and the individual moments come out of theatre. It is an inversion of the traditional structure of story ballets, for instance, that use a movement-centred language to tell a theatrical story. In this case, we take moments of theatrical presence, and put them together through dance construction principles.

Bausch's seminal role in the revitalization of Tanztheater is well documented, and the formal concerns and impact on performance modes are far-reaching. They place Bausch within the context of other innovators developing new possibilities in the world of dance and theatre. To reimagine possibility along a body centred axis of theatrical presentation reconfigures the roots of dance and theatre as performative practices. The result is a performance form that echoes the structure of dreams, and invades our conscious perception through metaphoric pathways of relationship and connection.

The essays in this section all begin with Bausch's work as a base in redefining performance potentials within the reinvention of Tanztheater. Extensive studies on German Tanztheater are available from Suzanne Schlicher and Jochen Schmidt, and I hope they are translated into English soon. Both place Bausch firmly at the centre of what has become, along with American Postmodern dance and Japanese Butoh, the most influential movements in dance of the second half of the twentieth century. Tanztheater's reach is potentially even broader, however, influencing a generation of theatre artists and performance artists coming from the world of visual art as well as a growing range of dance producers. It has had more impact on the gradual dissolution of boundaries across artistic disciplines, making labels like physical theatre or imagistic dance redundant. Of course all theatre is physical and all dance engages a level of imagistic presentation in the overall expression of its particular world. Tanztheater captures the inter-, cross-, multi-disciplinary spirit of the age, infecting artists who break boundaries faster than critics and scholars can draw a line in the sand.

"But is it dance ... ?"

Richard Sikes

Originally published in *Dance Magazine*, June, 1984

To understand the success of Pina Bausch in Germany you must be aware of certain basic priorities of German theatregoers. Generally, the German public does not bring fantasy to its theatre, but rather goes there seeking to discover the fantasy of the theatremaker. A dance audience tends to look for meaning, content, or symbolism in a choreographic work; the American aesthetics of musicality and athleticism are minimal considerations. This is understandable when one considers Germany's long tradition of literature and the predominance of storytelling theatre and opera in German cultural life.

German society takes itself very seriously, questioning constantly the nature and meaning of existence. There is a mythological work ethic, a strong sense of financial awareness (read: materialism), a tendency towards cult adulation, and a history of terrible, destructive wars. Germany's geographical location between today's two world superpowers only heightens fears of a third World War, and with it comes a corresponding anxiety. No wonder that the Germans take their theatre very seriously.

Pina Bausch grew up in the wake of World War II, which ended in 1945. Few young Americans today can realize the totality of the destruction of the German nation after the defeat of Adolf Hitler and the Third Reich. In the city of Wuppertal, today the home of Bausch's *tanztheater* (dance theatre) movement, sixty-four percent of all private homes and forty-seven percent of the schools were destroyed – and this was light damage when compared with other German cities such as Frankfurt, for example, which was eighty-seven percent flattened. In the wake of the war, there was little food, practically no shelter, winters characterized by killing cold, and a chaotic economy. Mothers cut up the remains of curtains in their bombed-out living rooms to make diapers for their babies.

Thanks largely to American financial aid, Germany was able to rebuild, stone for stone. A strong Germany was important to European and American interests. The economy began to be rebuilt. A middle class began to emerge again and strive for the acquisition of material goods. People in Germany – as in many countries after the war – began to pin their hopes for happiness on the acquisition of cars, television sets, and furniture. About the time of Bausch's adolescence, comparing status symbols began to be a more potent form of personal communication than simple human contact. Today Germany is still suffering from the consumer mentality. And the country's economic weakness of the 1970s only exacerbated these social ills.

It is against this background that Bausch in 1973 took over the artistic direction of the then Wuppertal Opera Ballet. Instead of continuing the tradition of escapist entertainment, she began to seek her own way of expressing the world she perceived, of viewing with honesty the communicative failures in the society around her. Reaction to her work was immediate and extreme, both in positive and negative directions. That is only natural: A societal group such as a theatre public can get trapped by convention to such a degree that it no longer realizes that it is trapped. When an individual comes along who views the world from a vantage so radically different from the norm that a new reality becomes evident, then the most human reaction is *outrage.* Outrage at the artistic event itself and outrage at oneself for not knowing how, when, how long, which time, or even if one has been duped.

The crux of the problem lies with the acceptability of the rejection of various types of theatrical conventions. Throughout the history of dance there has been a thrust toward the expression of "reality," but the devices of expressing that reality to one era have become conventions to the next. Few, if any, dance works became "classics" immediately; most ballets fade quickly into the soon-dated, "old fashioned" period from which they arose. Only when certain ballets of rare qualities become old enough to be considered museum pieces can later generations of audiences accept the period convention as reality, and overlook some improbable continuum of events that constitutes a story or a style, and look for other beauties.

Today's dancemakers are forced to look for symbols and actions to which contemporary audiences can relate, or they must use theatrical devices that provide freedom from the constraints of the concomitant reality. This is becoming increasingly difficult in today's world. Human fantasy is going off in other directions; the formulae are changing. In short, the narrative ballet is in serious trouble.

Many of today's most influential choreographers prefer to skirt the issue. Jiri Kylián's ballets, for example, fall under the category of atmosphere or situational pieces. John Neumeier's *Lady of the Camellias* uses dream imagery to explore the psyche of Marguerite, drawing parallels from a ballet-within-a-ballet performance of *Manon Lescaut*. This was a formula that was successful in Germany partly because of the familiarity with operatic literature that one can assume with Germans. It did not work, however, in the United States. Neumeier tells the legend of King Arthur in a series of closely related atmosphere sketches, character relationship being defined at the beginning of the evening in a formal, danced genealogy.

Bausch avoids the traps of narrative dance by simply not telling stories. One could perhaps speak of progressions of atmospheres in pieces such as *Bluebeard – while listening to a tape recording of Béla Bartok's opera "Duke Bluebeard's Castle"* or *Komm, tanz mit mir*, which come near to narrative sequences, but that is not the point of the pieces. More important is the expression of the human condition. In works such as *1980 – a piece by Pina Bausch*, the sections are tacked together in a seemingly arbitrary order. Some of Bausch's works stay in a state of flux until very late in the creative process. For example, the two halves of the work *Bandoneon* were switched around in the dress rehearsal, with the second half coming first and the first half second.

What seems arbitrary on superficial viewing, however, is in actuality not so. Doris Humphrey defined the four raw ingredients of dance movement as design, dynamics, rhythm, and motivation. All of these elements are to be found in Bausch's work, albeit not applied to dance exclusively, but rather to the broader spectrum of movement. Strict dance movement relates to the whole of Bausch's work in the way that "passé" or "arabesque" relates to a classical variation: It is part of the whole vocabulary. What is fascinating and revolutionary about Bausch is the application of dance construction principles to that of a more all-inclusive theatrical presentation.

Design is to be found in the use of groupings of people, the usage of props, costumes, and sets. Dynamics and rhythm can be found in the increase and decrease of dramatic tension in scenes, and especially in the flow of ideas. Motivation is an ever-fluctuating element, sometimes tossed around with abandon, sometimes focused with the accuracy of a target-shooter. All these elements arc employed in the consequent usage of two theatrical devices: repetition of activity and absence of activity.

Many of the most striking moments in Bausch's work come when some very simple movement or gestural motif is repeated over and over again. This can have a kind of structural beauty, such as in the final circle in *Kontakthof,* a humorous effect such as when the troupe parades through the audience in *1980 – a piece by Pina Bausch,* or a dramatic effect as in *Bluebeard ...* when the female lead is continually pushed down to the floor by the man, each time to have a lonely hand climb back up his body, seeking a possibility for her to rise back up again.

Very important to Bausch's work is the use of "emptiness." When asked directly if she consciously provokes boredom in the audience, Bausch replied, "I don't think of it as boredom at all; I think of it as emptiness. And I don't find it boring at any time, but rather suspenseful." In this philosophy, Bausch approaches a John Cage-like view of silence, i.e. of "emptiness" being a valid constructive material to be shaped and used fully as much as activity. Bausch's sense of rhythm induces "emptiness," giving the following scenic crescendos their impact.

In the working process of most choreographers, there is an element that could best be described as the "choreographer's internal narrative." This is a series of images, ideas, references, often non-sequitur, that are linked together as a sort of mental foundation from which choreographic ideas are drawn. These images are often inspired by the music, but can just as easily come from other sources and can be tacked together with no particular regard for each other. The main goal of such a narrative is for the choreographer to know for himself who is doing what to whom, when they are doing it, and why. The choreographer shares only a part of this narrative with the dancers, using what he needs to get the desired results.

The dancers then, through their understanding of the narrative and of the choreographer, share a further portion with the audience. Naturally, the more complete the narrative in the first place, and the better it is communicated along the way, the more will filter through to the audience. Bausch cuts this whole process short by going straight to the images themselves and enlightening them in their original form as opposed to abstracting them through various levels of movement design. The result is a series of impressionistic pictures, though in no sense are they static. The audience has the feeling of going through a movable picture gallery of human experience. It is the sense of style, the sense of period, the sense of humanity, the sense of relationship, combined with the extraordinary emotional virtuosity of Bausch's dancers that make her works so gripping.

Bausch's contribution to dance is a process, not a product; tanztheater is in a constant state of change. It is unfortunate that too many people, including some influential critics, celebrate her work as if it were the next goal in the evolution of dance as an art form. Others argue, with good reason, that tanztheater is not dance but a separate, valid theatre form that grew out of dance and utilizes dance as one of its fundamental building blocks. It is performed by dancers and, according to Bausch, would be unthinkable otherwise. But when one talks about the future of European dance as an art form, one must speak of Kylian, Neumeier, Christopher Bruce, and Hans van Manen. These are all choreographers who have stretched the boundaries of dance from within. Bausch has packed her bags and stepped outside, taking along only what she needs for the trip. It is a fascinating, questioning, and controversial pioneering venture that has already exerted considerable influence, both on those who follow in her footsteps and on those who, like William Forsythe, walk parallel paths into the wilderness.

Please do it again, do it again, again, again …

Deborah Jowitt

Originally published in *The Village Voice*, 3 July, 1984

About Pina Bausch and the Wuppertaler Tanztheater: no conclusions about greatness or lack thereof. Nor do the works insist that you conclude anything about the import of what you've just seen, that you know "what happened." With the exception of *The Rite of Spring* (1979), the four works that the company has been showing to packed-in audiences at BAM are circular, non-narrative dramas. Events appear, repeat, disappear, recur in different configurations. Action is rendered static by repetition. In these vast, seemingly aimless jigsaw puzzles, a piece of sky may fit into a field of grass, a woman's body may snap onto a man's chest, while her head goes elsewhere.

I'm speaking figuratively, of course, but the most powerful impression that Bausch's montage technique supports is that of the isolation of human beings from one another and from their own impulses. In *Bluebeard*, a woman (identifiable as the last young wife) kneels between the legs of a man in an overcoat who is sitting on a chair (Bluebeard). He places one hand on top of her head and pushes her down, lifting his arm high in order to simulate great force. She immediately kneels up again. He pushes her down. These two actions escalate in speed and intensity until they dissipate in a blur. But, although the gestures become more brutal with every repetition, they also move farther away from their original status as expressions of devotion and rejection, and the performers don't seem to own them anymore.

It's not hard to imagine the shock among the bourgeoisie of Wuppertal, where Bausch went to work in 1973, when she began to branch out from opera choreography to something like *Bluebeard* (1977), in which the images are bleak, violent, and decadent and Bartok's opera is played murderously on a tape recorder by the leading male performer – stopped, rewound, punched on again. It's also not hard to understand the excitement in the German dance world, which has not produced anyone to equal Bausch in imagination and audacity for more than 50 years. Dancers can embrace her – those who do – as the contemporary offspring of the Expressionist dance-drama pioneers Mary Wigman and Kurt Jooss, while the theatre people can place her as a neo-Brechtian. Americans may also see her in relation to the Living Theatre, to they psychological ballets of Anthony Tudor, and to modern dance of the 1950s. (When Bausch's performers dance, which isn't often, the curving, suspended movements and intricate arm gestures immediately bring to mind José Limón, whose technique Bausch studied at Juilliard in the late '50s.)

It took me a while to realize that Bausch's work may be primal in a sense, but that these theatrical spectacles depend upon a notion of civilized behavior and the expectations of society that may then be exposed through irony or subverted by absurdity. No matter how much her performers hurl themselves numbly at walls or grovel on the floor, we never see them as members of preliterate societies, as we do Eiko and Koma or Kei Takei's company. Even in *The Rite of Spring*, the relations between the assertive, foot-pounding men and the frantic, nubile women have up-to-date overtones: the demeaning choosing that may go on at a dance audition or a secretary-wanted interview or a party, the eagerness with which the victim role is tried on by those unsuited for it.

The people in Bausch's pieces aren't terribly contemporary either. The collage of musical scraps that accompany *1980* contains no rock music. Benny Goodman and Judy Garland singing "Somewhere Over the Rainbow" are the most recent selections – used, as in every work but *The Rite of Spring*, to create atmosphere rather than to support dancing. The clothes people wear often suggest pre-World War II middle class. Like figures in a Cocteau film, these people wander through the brilliant surreal sets (all but the one for *1980* designed by the late Rolf Borzik); the lighting is no harshly bright, now dim, with only the audience lit. The effect is of a pungent, yet nonspecific 20th century in which people are alienated, preoccupied, and, generally grim.

Borzik's sets, and Peter Pabst's for *1980*, alter the stage space and the floor. For *The Rite of Spring*, the stage is covered with a red-brown dirt. The dancers' stamping raises little dust storms, and after a while, their sweat-soaked bodies are patched in brown. In *1980*, the floor is real turf, smelly and damp. *Bluebeard* takes place in a huge deserted room; dead leaves cover the floor and the sills of tall recessed windows. The set for *Café Müller* brings to mind the vaguely "modern" public rooms in universities – white walls, plate glass doors, a clutter of black chairs and tables.

In the relatively compact chamber piece *Café Müller* (six performers including Bausch), the BAM audience first comes to grips with the performers' formidable intensity and with some of Bausch's techniques. A woman (Beatrice Libonati) gropes about, blind or sleep-walking. An intent man (Jean Sasportes) hurls tables and chairs out of her way, dashing to anticipate her path. Is he protecting her? The furniture? He's so hasty, so clumsy, that at times it seems he'll do her more harm than stumbling over a chair would, and the sound of tumbling chairs seems to frighten her, make her more desperate and increase her anger. The repetition has no conclusions; it stops when Libonati bumps into a new-comer (Dominique Mercy). Later – this is another Bausch device – we will see Sasportes repeat the chair-throwing while Mercy hurls himself about in a repeating expanding "dance."

These kinds of repetition occur in all of Bausch's pieces. In *Bluebeard*, the men sit on the floor, backs to the wall: the women pull them away from the wall; the men scrabble back. Over and over. Later the doomed heroine (Libonati) sits against the wall, and "Bluebeard" (Jan Minarik) repeats the action with her. In the sprawling, less grim collage *1980*, one brief scene may be slipped behind another, but later a Xerox of it, clear or blurred, may appear in the foreground or off to the side. A woman who has been doing a loose, circling dance behind a line of people, later does it wriggling under the impact of a real sprinkler. In both *Bluebeard* and *1980*, Bausch ends the work by replaying high spots from it. In the former, these are frozen tableaux executed by a ghostly corps of women in taffeta dresses and men in dark suits. In the latter, they are blurred and increasingly messy reprises of events: a formerly tidy game of "Drop the Handkerchief" is repeated with far more chairs than people, and set amid a slew of other activities.

In *Café Müller*, too, we get a good look at Bausch's escalating repetition of form. Libonati and Dominique Mercy embrace. Minarik enters and efficiently, if elaborately, molds Mercy's docile arms into a carrying position, then hoists Libonati onto them. Mercy, expressionless, lets her slide to the floor. Minarik returns and repeats the action; again she falls. As they continue, the intervals between the molding, the falling, and the return of Minarik become shorter and shorter, the action more desperate. This device appears in *Bluebeard* (the head pushing bit, for example) and in *Rite*. In the more playful *1980*, it surfaces as Meryl Tankard dithers acquisitively about, regaling us with tales of her possessions, accumulating more boxes than she can possibly carry.

In *The Rite of Spring*, we're introduced to more of Bausch's compositional strategies. Her *Rite* is one of the best I've seen, and the grimmest. No promise of rebirth; the maiden chosen to be sacrificed falls dead on the last note of the music, and the lights bang out. At one point in the dance, each woman takes a turn moving out of a cluster, holding a red cloth. We realize that each is attempting to give the cloth to Minarik (the leader of the men); the one who dares this will be sacrificed. Within rigid parameters, each gets a chance to show minute individual variation. In *1980*, we see the same device used over and over. Each contestant in a funny (initially) beauty contest has to list three things his/her country is known for, two things he/she is afraid of. Each member of a sober group gets a turn to say a banal goodbye to one woman who is leaving.

We learn quite soon that Bausch is preoccupied with gender. The men may manipulate the women, the women the men, but never are they neutral about their male or female roles. It's hard to tell what Bausch believes; all you see is that she is savage on the subject. In *Bluebeard*, the men strip to their briefs and indulge in cartoonish musclemen preening. We're allowed to believe, in *1980*, that the amazing, theatrical, bass-voiced Mechthild Grossmann is a man, until she mockingly lets down her hair, opens her coat, and flashes her breasts at us. In *The Rite of Spring*, as one or another of the women tries on the role of the one to be sacrificed, doing steps we later see in the final frenzied solo, the men give each the once-over, as if they were judges in a beauty contest.

Some of Bausch's images are thrilling. In *Bluebeard*, the women charge at the walls, run up them, and hang there, stuck. (They're standing on brackets left over from long-gone bookshelves.) The tape recorder that Manarik manipulates is embedded in a wheeled table, its apparently limitless cord stretching up to a ceiling pulley and out through a side wall. It becomes his bulwark and his battering ram, as he races around the imprisoning room. In the first half of *1980*, which has to do with childhood memories and birthdays, a woman undresses a man (her son?), puts one stocking on him, makes up his face, sticks matches between the toes of his other foot, lights them, and says "Happy Birthday." Another woman lipsticks her mouth and kisses a man, over and over, until his face is scarred with lip prints.

I was feeling rather gloomy about Bausch's work – impressed by the performers, the startling images, wearied by the remorseless repetition, the grimness, the bitter underlining of gender, the goallessness. But, *1980* is lighter, funny, touching rather than gripping. And it gives us a closer look at the performers as they offer images from their childhoods, participate in sketches to do with being a performer, like the beauty contest, or a cheap, winning glad-eyed chorus strut through the audience. Its nearly four hours contain much clutter and many dead spaces, but also many wonderful things. The piece presents in a soft voice Bausch's harsh overriding message: running anguished in grooves of self-perpetuating emotion, we intersect only by accident or temporary contagion.

Dance Theatre

Rebellion of the body, theatre of images and an inquiry into the sense of the senses

Inge Baxmann

Originally published in *Ballett International*, January, 1990

> Who can tell the dancer from the dance?
>
> W. B. Yeats

> Pour éschapper à la figuration, il faut retrouver la sensation.
>
> Giles Deleuze

In the '80s dance has become the source of a new fascination with the expressive possibilities of the body. The boundaries separating dance and theatre are now less clear-cut due to this trend toward non-verbal communication. "Dance theatre," "movement theatre," "physical theatre," or "choreographic theatre" reflect the groping terminology of a practice that does not seek to represent, but rather serves to use movement, gesture, rhythm and space in order to come to terms with present-day forms of living – while simultaneously questioning the conventional hierarchy of the senses.

The return to the expressive powers of the body should not, however, be interpreted rashly as a "rejection of meaning," even if the image-laden productions somewhere between dance, pantomime and performance cannot be reduced to a single "message." A multitude of experimental forms have developed, influenced for the most part by Pina Bausch, Reinhild Hoffman and Susanne Linke. Yet this multitude has long since developed into a wide-ranging movement which has less in common with the classic conception of dance than with, say, the theatre of images of a Robert Wilson. An "aesthetic of the senses" would be one possible definition of this practice, as long as aesthetic were understood as a specific type of behavior and perception, rather than an ideal or a concept. Dance theatre can be understood as an "archeology of ways of life," which not only delves into the significance of cultural structure in the body but, at the same time, seeks oppositional forces. Its subject matter is drawn from daily experience and historical figures to myths. Myths of creation postulate an inquiry into possible new relationships to nature, and the rituals of *"sociabilité"* and the absurd torsions they demand of the subject also thematize the question as to the function of power structures and their anchoring in the body. Pictorial performance, pure dance passages, quick-changing thematic sequences – images, language and movement seem to be pitted against one another. Rather than the logical conveyance of meaning, language is quoted as gesture or serves to express by means of intoxication. Dance theatre – never completely dance – is an aesthetic of the constant crossing of boundaries, which both necessitates and demands a new culture of seeing beyond the established codes of perception.

In this connection, the current enthusiasm for dances oscillates between two poles that are indeed complementary and, at certain points, overlapping. On the one hand is the search for enduring rules in the return to myth, and a utopia that sees the basis for a "natural way of life" in the body and its rhythms. On the other is a deconstruction of physical expression, which questions the rule of the subject over her/his body, presenting it as a cultural construct. Who speaks through the body, what discourses are inscribed in it through styles of feeling, perceiving or moving? In what way are the "own" and the "other" woven together?

Tracking down lifestyles in the body

On the one hand, dance is more and more becoming the focal point of theatrical innovation, yet, on the other hand, there is less and less dancing in dance theatre. One could almost say that this is already one of the "conventions" of dance theatre. Others include scattered meta-commentaries and a dramaturgy that builds on patchwork-like combinations of sequences and movement images rather than linear narrative, the elements of which are borrowed from everything: from opera to pantomime, from spoken theatre to revue and, above all, from daily movement – but also draws movement material from the repertory of the *danse d'école* or ballroom dances for the odd ironic echo.

Through dance theatre, an investigation of subjectivity is set in motion by way of the body, where everything from the genesis of expression through to the smallest ramification of so-called "private-intimate" desires is seen as being completely influenced by society.

Often, striking images are found that trigger associations with the audience. Therein lies the special pleasure of dance theatre. Every spectator can rearrange the performed "image puzzle" according to his or her own personal experience or blindness, yet the images are not arbitrary. They liberate one's gaze to make unassumed connections and trip up a standardized perception that is continuously in search of ready-made, recognizable structures of meaning.

At the same time, dance theatre occasionally allows a "feast of the senses," an aesthetic delight – as, for example, the sight of a stage covered with earth, leaves and carnations awakens the desire to move among those elements.

The medium of narrative forms and ways of speaking which shatter the normal is the body: movement, gestures, gesticulation. If detailed directions for fox-hunting are given over a microphone and the dancers then set them in motion, then this transferal becomes a metaphor for the daily hunt or chase. It can, at the same time, be seen as a satire on "how to" literature, including the collective illusion that this continually elusive reality can be brought under control by doing the "right" thing.

A couple crawl to one another over the floor using all their strength, only to fall into lively party small talk – as if this were the appropriate stance for such activity (Pina Bausch: *Waltzes*).

The absurdity of ways of life can be seen in the torsions they wring from the subject. Dance theatre sniffs out the breaks in an image-riddled daily life by sabotaging rituals that repeat the image of an image through sudden, unexpected outbreaks of alien needs.

Our lifestyles are dictated by images that set conventional symbols to conventional poses in stereotypical situations as a counterpart to growing social differentiation. In dance theatre, contrary to this, the oppositional side of ambivalence is stressed. The non-categorizable, for which there is no expression in a world of emotional mannequins and style salesmen, is given a "voice." However, one is not involved here in the search for an "authentic gesture" beyond the realm of cultural codes, an "original human nature" in the expressive possibilities of the body, as was the case with the expressionist dancers of the 1920s. Indeed, it is the inseparable interweaving of "own" and "other" that is called into question when ways of life become (voluntarily adapted) body norms and stereotypical formulas for living.

The broken tableau

Dance theatre is less a case of stories being told than experiences being staged. The study of the relationships between lifestyle and body eliminates one basic requirement of classical dance aesthetics: the domination of the subject over his/her body. "Body control" becomes a problem when the question is raised as to who, or what, is speaking through the body – when the subject falls apart.

Then there are no longer any uniform perspectives to guarantee the unity of the composition – only ruptured and interrupted sequences of movement. One does not lead to the other. The interpretation of space corresponds to a daily experience that defies narrative structuring. It is characterized by interrupted movements, repetitions and constant movement without change. Movement is a ritual pattern that no longer has a goal. The disintegration of history into stories that are no longer held together by any doctrine or history-supporting subject, but rather are lined up in a more or less associative manner according to the principles of collage, reflects the fragmentation of everyday perception. Experience hardly allows itself to be shored up by structures of meaning, the vouchers for which are generally binding values and norms. The simultaneousness and the heterogeneity of the experiencing of reality dominate experiences that oppose "narration." The fact that "reality" eludes the subject as an unspecified, constantly isolated present becomes a structural principle in dance theatre. Again and again, situations are presented in which chaos emerges, structures of meaning fall apart and new episodes are patched together. The hectic, interruption and repetition of already begun movement sequences reflects the lack of control of our own living conditions – the uncertainty of our own perception and the reaction of others. Tenderness can unexpectedly turn into violence; the longing for closeness and warmth is immediately forced into the mold of the conventional couple. The many more diffuse and differentiated feelings and needs are raped. The transformation often occurs unnoticed. Moments of harmony, happiness and trust can mostly be found as utopian gestures in the return to one's childhood – in children's games, where worlds of one's own are built. Where everything is possible.

Subjective space and subjective times

Subjectivity of spatial experience can be seen in the play with everyday objects. In *Im Baden Wannen* (*Bathtubbing*), a choreography by Susanne Linke, it is a bathtub that structures the intercourse with space. It creates a subjective space and a subjective time, a little counter-world within the daily routine. At first, the dancer trips lightly around the object, dips halfway in balancing acts which seem to defy gravity, until the tub itself is finally set in motion, opening up new choreographic possibilities. One feels reminded of Reinhild Hoffman's

Solo with Sofa, a choreography in which the use of the space is predetermined by the inseparability of the dancer from the object. The slip-cover of the sofa was also the dancer's dress and dictated her sphere of movement. Perhaps in order to indicate subjective counter-worlds and their ambivalence?

In dance theatre, space is no longer understood as a connection between vectors, speed and temporal variability, as movement and room direction. It is a tapestry of movable elements, the result of activities that give it initial direction, i.e. it itself is expression. The spatial experience of dance expresses a specific relationship to the world that can be described by Merleau-Ponty's distinction between "geometric" and "anthropological" space. Spatial experience is a product of movement, that is to say, a cultural practice. However, space and time have another "direction" in dance; in this respect it is – comparable to dreams – another form of being within the cultural order. In dance, the body offers a kind of resistance – it can withdraw occasionally from the value system of a space-time experience, determined by effectivity and time-reduction, which shapes our ways of life.

Dance defines space as the location of the body, as a condition; as such it articulates how human perception experiences space. In dance theatre, spaces can become sensations, emotional conditions. The subjectivity of the spatial experience is emphasized. A bathtub or sofa as part of the "inner space" opens up new inner spaces and becomes a component of a bodily location. Yet this spatial experience is ambivalent; it can mean either the retreat or the assertion of a subjective space. On the other hand, it is the desire to experiment, a sounding of movement possibilities within physical boundaries of one's own construction.

The spatial stagings of dance theatre are part of an aesthetic that stresses the subjectivity of perception and processes the (postmodern?) experience of a-topia: that loss of a central perspective that presets an "order of things." At the same time they convey the experience of a widening discrepancy between body and environment, up to and including individual difficulties in coming to terms with synthetic living spaces.

Performance spaces are covered with water, earth, leaves or flowers and the resulting movement possibilities (and impossibilities) rendered presentable to the senses and incorporated as choreographic elements. In such a-topian spaces that make possible the shifting and crossing of boundaries, levels of (day)dream and reality become blurred in the true sense of the word. Trance-like, slow-motion movement sequences demonstrate that space-time relationships are cultural conventions that always base upon the exclusion of a specific human possibility; living in several times and worlds all at once – a capability that should perhaps be regained for the discovery of new ways of life.

Between expressionist and postmodern dance

Dance theatre moves between a renaturalizing of the dancing body that understands motion as the expression of emotions – as was the case with expressionist dance – and a denaturalizing that already understands the movement of the body in space as "expression" and content of the dance.

This is, above all, the heritage of dancers like Merce Cunningham and the subsequent generation of American postmodern dance. For Cunningham, the elimination of linear time characterized a dance that was free from all manner of literalizing and symbolizing. Every dance step, every movement should retain its own "meaning" as a comment on life or a communication with and through the senses. Even random movement conveys an experience of bodily presence rather than representation. "I have always felt that movement is expressive in and of itself, regardless of whether expression is intended or not," says Cunningham.

The liberation of dance from codes is also the goal of choreographers such as Alwin Nikolais, Paul Taylor, Carolyn Carlson, etc., who have opened up entirely new perspectives for dance. Experimentation with the movement possibilities of the body is considered a game that is intended to open the sense to movement and allow a "field situation" (Cunningham) to occur within the audience – a certain openness. The movement may not be random, but it can be connected by every observer with memories and associations in a different way.

The relationship between space and body in Cunningham's choreographies is determined by a space-time perception that breaks apart the unity of body (movement), scenic space and music.

Every element can be taken on its own and has its own intensity that does not result from the context. As such, Cunningham is a forerunner of the decentralization that has been labeled "postmodern."

Dance theatre makes use of these ideas, yet separates itself from the postmodern concept by once again employing movement as an expressive medium for emotions in coming to terms with current ways of life.

A developed and increasingly complex technique of movement phrasing, which always discovers new sequences and rhythms in the structuring of space into decentralized space. Dreams and daily pressures are inextricably woven together: a space of confusion and experimental possibilities.

Dance theatre leads both traditions (expressionist and postmodern dance) to a new synthesis. It makes use of a movement language that is not the expression of a metaphysical soul, but rather breaks through the pathos where ambivalences and dissonances are thematized. It creates utopian spaces that stage the loss of a standardizing "world model" – be it no more than a utopian vision – and the loss of orientation resulting therefrom.

From Utopia to the utopian gesture

An aesthetic of the senses that affects the sensibilities of the observer and wishes to convey associations and experiences rather than proclaiming messages – this does not seem capable of co-existing with political motives, at least as long as the political searches among generalized utopian remedies. The criticism of the dressage and mistreatment of the body voiced by dance theatre, however, questions an understanding of politics that is oriented by an "autonomous" subject, yet to be illuminated, as a strategy for change. However, when the resistance of ambivalence is stressed and body experience and subjectivity are experienced as being shaped by society in dance theatre, then no "alternative remedies" are possible. Yet, an eminently important political element is contained in the development of narrative forms and ways of speaking that break through cultural clichés. The search for a new culture of seeing that breaks open standardized models of perception to clear the way for new insights – an emphasis on playfulness and imagination in the discovery of new ways of life – is perhaps an adequate political strategy in our current cultural climate.

The fact that a predominantly female dance theatre scene dealt, for the most part, with power structures in inter-human relationships and thematized the dressage of women to femininity is an expression of the lack of socio-political alternatives and ideas in just this area.

However, the fact that dance theatre – precisely in view of the failure of utopian models and the perplexity in the face of the loss of a subject – also gains a new edge as political theatre can be seen in Hans Kresnik's production of *Macbeth* in Heidelberg. Kresnik poses the question of corruption as a questioning of the mechanisms of the reproduction of power-political structures and their way of "functioning." His choreography interprets Macbeth as a number in a continuum that runs through history right up to the Barschel affair.

The dressage of the body illustrates the way in which the desire for power is born. The anonymous character of power, which cannot be attached to individual persons, makes accusations of guilt impossible and allows Macbeth to appear as both victim and culprit. The action is arranged in a narrative sequence of images as they occur in the original text or the genesis of a contemporary biography. The brutal sequences are separated from one another by "curtains."

Gottfried Heinweing's set provides more than atmospheric characterization in this context. It becomes a component of the scenic action that demonstrates the "technical" functioning of political structures. Dead bodies lie in bathtubs on a stage covered in shiny white foil; the space is one of cold rationality. Blood-red liquid trickles through plastic tubes on walls that are as white as the stage; pumps are activated whenever a new victim is brought in through the enormous iron door that opens and shuts with amplified slams. A figure in a scholarly black gown appears at regular intervals and empties buckets and tubs full of blood into the orchestra pit. Human "garbage" – or the price of the reproduction of the system?

How are performers trained to power? They as well are no "doers," but rather the victims of an incomprehensible machine in which they have their parts to play. The witches, dressed in uniforms decorated with swastikas and sexy black lingerie, include Macbeth in their dance, undress him and stick him into oversized boots in which he helplessly hops about, his crown as symbol of power on his head. Thus do bodies and power-political structures grow together, mutilating the body, which knows nothing but this dressage. The rest of the figures are no different, gathered around huge conference tables reminiscent of Jooss's *Green Table*: places of treachery or bitter power struggles. The heads of the performers are wrapped in black; shears protrude from the bandages. Their large suitcases contain instruments of death; their way of moving characterizes their way of living – abrupt, greedy lunges for symbols of power such as crowns and daggers – staccato, diffuse, hectic and hurried hunts. Yet there is no real movement; the same thing is continually repeated.

These movements of the dancers are acoustically amplified and mixed with a sort of "noise music" that further intensifies the nightmare element of this vision. And the dances as well – drawing mainly on the classical movement repertoire – suddenly change from harmonious *pas de deux* to warlike confrontations, as do the group sequences. The unexpected nature of these outbursts, as inextricable components of a functioning reality, is taken one step further in the murder of Macduff's children. The chidren, dressed in play togs and tee-shirts, play at an oversized table with a giant coffee pot together with Lady Macduff. The family idyll is interrupted by amiably smiling men in white aprons and boots with crampons. At first they dance a merry ring-around-the-rosy with the children, only then to nail them to the table leg, rape them with the leg of a chair or drown them in the coffee cup. The "opponent" is not clearly identifiable – is he a scientist, a doctor? The obscurity and anonymity of a power that is not tangible. The brutality of the images presents an all-too-apocalyptic vision that could be an anti-utopia, without the shimmer of an alternative model.

Dance as exploratory journey in a world of ways of life

When ways of living change round to human self-destruction and ecological catastrophes and the danger of nuclear warfare force us to our senses, one turns to the body for clues as to an "original way of life" in keeping with the laws of nature. The one-sided concentrations on reason raises the question of whether the body could not lead to a new way of thinking. Suddenly dance is of interest as the residue of a "body knowledge" that opens up the gaze to new possibilities vis-à-vis a rationality reduced to functionality and efficiency. It is precisely the non-functional use of the body in dance that counts as a resistance to customary space-time economy. Subjectivity of spatial and time experience and playful dealings with everyday space allow the possibility of new experience. They are part of the new search for an anthropology based upon a new way of dealing with the senses.

Dance theatre has developed into such an archeology of ways of life. Gesture, movement and space are elements of an aesthetic of crossing boundaries, which seeks to develop a new way of perceiving in opposition to ready-made worlds of images that tamper with our ways of seeing.

The rediscovery of dance as an ontology of perception and of the aesthetic as an ordering of the senses attains meaning where sociological theories and utopian models of the future fear to tread.

However, the criticism of the dressage and mistreatment of the body does not, in dance theatre, lead to a "discourse of liberation" that seeks an authentic human nature beyond cultural edifices. Instead of this, the body is presented as a battlefield of cultural discourses, in which conformity and resistance are inextricably woven. Search and lack of orientation are the theme. Atopian spaces and interrupted and repeated movement sequences present a way of life that is determined by an experience of linear time without collective goals and constant motion without change. Yet wariness of the consolations of utopia does not mean a renunciation of the utopian gesture. A playful testing out of human possibilities and possible realities is a utopian gesture to set frozen structures back into motion.

A gesture that leads out of the captivity of outmoded ways of life – and that is the prerequisite for all change.

Gunsmoke

Anita Finkel

Originally published in *The New Dance Review*, October–December, 1991

In her art of the protean and transparent, Pina Bausch invites us to sample the experience of X-ray vision.

In one of those ironic juxtapositions of which only a power greater than ourselves is capable, Pina Bausch and her Tanztheater Wuppertal returned to the United States – to the Brooklyn Academy of Music, as part of the Next Wave Festival (September 30 – October 13) – just as the nation's attention was focused, for the first time in history, on sexual harassment. Men's intimidation of women through the mechanism of sexual shame – forced sexual compliance, sexual bullying – has always been Bausch's theme. She has never neglected the cost to men as well as women through the habit of sexual harassment. In her *Rite of Spring,* the man who lies wasted, depleted, and defeated on the earth as the Chosen One crumples in agony is in no better shape than she is, and for that matter, neither are the terrified, apathetic men and women looking on, wondering what happened. He said, she said. That the country of record should have the chance to savor *Bandoneon* and *Palermo Palermo* just as Anita Hill was bringing the red dress to Clarence Thomas, and he was putting it over her head with his eyes averted and his face hidden, is itself as extraordinary as the Paper of Record putting the story all over the front page, above the fold.

We haven't seen Bausch here in three years – she last appeared in June 1988 with *Viktor* and *Carnations.* She first came in 1984, a year after Balanchine's death, among other things, and was critically lambasted by an outraged and grieving dance community. I thought of Balanchine a lot during Bausch's season this year, in part because I also looked at a tape of *Viktor* during that time and noted that part of it is set to a large section of Tchaikovsky's Sixth Symphony. So were the last moments of Balanchine's creative life, Balanchine's last work, and the way Bausch ends *Viktor* is by replaying a large part of the beginning of the piece, but looked at in a compressed way, from the perspective of knowing that we are at the end.

In any event, the story of Bausch's creative development, her artistry, is a largely untold one. In 1984, Bausch brought four pieces to the U.S.: *The Rite of Spring, Café Müller, 1980 – A Piece by Pina Bausch,* and *Bluebeard*. In 1985 we had *The Seven Deadly Sins/Don't Be Afraid, On the Mountain a Cry Is Heard, Arias,* and *Kontakthof.* In 1988 came *Viktor* and *Carnations*; this year, *Bandoneon* and *Palermo Palermo*. Thus no piece once seen has been offered again. Certain elements of her work are, of course, the same in every piece – the same themes, the same imagery, the same sense of design. But in the area of structure Bausch has changed profoundly. *Palermo Palermo* is constructed in a way that far extends the less complex structure of *Bandoneon*. The sense of men and women in relationships, of the human body, sex, and pain – the subject matter of all her work – is the same in every piece. But the way these ideas and the images created by them are embedded in a work has deepened to communicate more of their richness.

Bausch's way of showing this is Bauschian. On her last two visits, 1988 and this year, she presented her most recent creation and a work somewhat older. Both times she chose to give the more recent work first and its predecessor second, the better, I imagine, to frustrate, or at least confound, our need to read her development in a linear, progressive fashion. Bausch is never linear, even when you think she surely must be *now*. Like the ultimate victim, she operates on a circular, completely closed basis. *Viktor* ends exactly the way it began, and *Bandoneon,* we discover, had its first and second acts switched just before the premiere – the work originally ended with the striking of the set that now takes place in the middle. And this, too, is why the "second" act of *Bandoneon* is, in complete reversal of theatrical tradition, longer than the "first." Learning this only after my first viewing of *Bandoneon,* I tried to use my second to figure out how those people got there. But it's a circle, with no beginning and no end. I still wonder – what would I learn if I could see all Bausch's pieces in the right order, first to last?

In the same way, there is no time and no place in Bausch's work, no importance to her observance of the classical unities, no progression of moments building to a climax, no progressive revelation of character or personality. There is nothing Argentine about *Bandoneon* (the *title* refers to the type of accordion traditionally used to play the tango), nothing Italian about *Palermo Palermo*. A wall crumbles. The life that was lodged in the crannies and niches comes scuttling out.

Nevertheless, within the three levels of reading in circles that this season afforded – *Palermo Palermo* back to the beginning of *Bandoneon* to the end of *Bandoneon* – a definite progression resides. It is an artist's progression, from one point of view, toward art and experience – deeply intertwined with life, stricken by mortality, concerned with temporality – to another that presents art as superseding reality rather than intertwined with it overriding mortality, overriding loss, overriding temporality. We see the same sense of transcendence in the timeless harmonies of Mozart and Shakespeare, the timeless geometrical precision and exactitude of Balanchine. Bausch's mode is primarily that of the visual artist – she works with visual images rather than sounds or poetic diction or even movement. I've always hated photographs of Bausch's work. Her work as depicted in photographs is uncomely and false – as "weird," in fact, as Robert Greskovic found it in a review in *Ballet News* in 1984. Photographs distort Bausch's work. Her images, ultimately twentieth century things, are fluid – and cannot be captured in stills. Her work is a kind of choreography, and it draws heavily from cinematography. It is an art form composed of images that melt into and give way to each other. In *Bandoneon* (1980), the focus is still on the content of the images – there is not yet the masterly focus on form that we see in *Palermo Palermo* (1990). Bausch is still close to loss in *Bandoneon*. It came close to the death, at age thirty-five, of her great love, Rolf Borzik ("Rolf was gone and Rolf loved life and I felt sad and calm and strong"). *Bandoneon* is still rough, ragged, occasionally lurching; *Palermo Palermo* is completely smooth, silken, blemishless, perfectly knit. There is no living suffering in it. There is only the joy of mastery, of self-affirmation, self-confirmation, at every potential hitch.

Progression is always invoked in discussing Bausch, and usually despaired of. Born in 1940 in Solingen, (West) Germany, Bausch grew up in the restaurant owned by her parents and was taken to her first dance classes by patrons of the restaurant, who also happened to be theatre folk and who noted her extreme flexibility. Indeed this trait made her an instant standout at her first class, her teacher saluted her as a "real serpent girl." She danced in operettas and was a young perfectionist; appearing in one show as a street urchin who sold the fictional "San Remo Gazette," Bausch mocked up a "real" San Remo Gazette with letters cut from actual newspapers. At the age of fifteen, she left home for the Folkwang School in Essen, working under the tutelage of Kurt Jooss; at nineteen, she left Europe for New York, "all alone, without knowing a word of English, without the slightest idea of where I was going to live in New York." She studied with Antony

Tudor and danced under his direction with the Metropolitan Opera Ballet; as Marcia Siegel has pointed out, her work with Paul Sanasardo, a colleague of Anna Sokolow, was surely another great influence. In 1961, Jooss summoned her back to Germany, offering her a job. She eventually began to choreograph, and was successful enough to attract the attention of the management of the theatre in Wuppertal. She devised a "Venusberg" there in 1972, and was appointed the director of the Wuppertal "Ballet" a year later. Bausch choreographed her first work as resident director in 1974; it was called *Fritz* and Fritz was portrayed by a woman. Some of the dancers still working with her today were in *Fritz* – Malou Airaudo, Dominique Mercy, and Ed Kortlandt.

In 1975 Bausch choreographed *The Rite* of *Spring*, the earliest of her works to be seen in the U.S. It followed Stravinsky's/Roerich's scenario pretty straightforwardly – "the most important thing to me was to understand what Stravinsky wanted. In *The Rite of Spring*, there is nothing to add to what's already there. There is a Young Girl, the Chosen One, and that young girl dances, all by herself, until she dies." (All quotations are taken from an interview with Bausch conducted in German by Leonetta Bentivoglio and printed in French in Delahaye/De Gubematis's 1986 *Pina Bausch*. The English translation is my own.) The break came the next year, with *The Seven Deadly Sins*. On the face of it, this should have been another cut-and-dried (for Bausch) assignment – a hallowed German text, hallowed German music, tried and true, a fixed scenario. But Bausch got to thinking, and

something happened between the company and me. For the first time, I was afraid of my dancers. They hated the work. They would not understand or accept it. Once, at the end of a rehearsal, Vivienne Newport shouted out violently, "Enough! I can't take it anymore! All of this, I hate it!" After the premiere, I had a terrible crisis. I wanted to give up, never work again. I decided to never set foot in the theatre again. And eventually I started to work in a little studio of Jan Minarik's, with a few dancers who accepted my methods.

With about ten loyalists – "less than half the company" – Bausch put together *Bluebeard – While Listening to a Tape Recording of Béla Bartok's Opera "Duke Bluebeard's Castle."* With Borzik she produced seven more "dance theatre" works, the last being *The Legend of Chastity*, never seen in this country. Then came *1980*, her farewell to Borzik and, in the last few days of 1980, *Bandoneon*.

Bandoneon is the dance that opens and closes like a fan. On one side it starts with a dancer, Janusz Subicz, coming onstage alone and standing awkwardly, uncomfortably, trying to engage us and at the same time avoid our gaze. Though he acknowledges, "I have to do something," finally he can't think of anything and starts to leave, but even as he opens the door to exit, he is met by a line of other men entering. Finally it is Dominique Mercy who "does something," taking over, putting on a romantic tutu, turning out, doing ballet exercises, telling us how good it feels to pee and also what pleasure it is to unbutton his pants when he has eaten a really big meal. Subicz never does get around to "doing something."

The other side of the fan opens with another solo dancer, Beatrice Libonati, coming in with a tiny mouse in her hand. She has no trouble finding something to do, crooning to the mouse, stroking it, inviting members of the audience to stroke it. This opening is quiet and still, and the vituperative atmosphere that soon begins to gather – for example, when Mercy and Silvia Kesselheim laugh at jokes on cards the audience can't see – is a deep, troubling disturbance of the peace, although, in fact, that peace had ominous, almost sinister connotations.

At the heart of *Bandoneon* are illustrations that have nothing to do with either opening. They are the delineations of several erotic postures unique to this work. In a method that foreshadows the artistic calm of her later works, Bausch takes all her leisure here to work out, trace, define, and shade these images.

The point of departure is the basic image of man and woman as partners in a dance, in general terms, the love embrace, in specific ones, dancers doing the tango. Here Bausch's consideration is rooted in the question that underlies all her work – "May I have this dance?" and all that is implied within it. In *Bandoneon*, there are four major studies of the position. Working them out, Bausch also brings out all the emotional aspects she can connect to the central image, both those with a logical connection and those where it is oblique or buried. One of the oblique connections consists of the threat and test implied in asking questions, and the rebellious resistance of those being tested, the combination of compliance and resistance. Bausch is famous for her questions, her post-*Bluebeard* method of composing her work by asking her dancers questions like "What did you eat for Christmas dinner?" Here the question is *"Dominique, qu'est-ce que tupenses de Maria?"* In time every dancer is asked this question, and their answers reveal their mixed feelings: "Tia Maria. Mary had a little lamb," (Jakob Andersen); "Mary Christmas. Marijuana" (Finola Cronin). Another oblique tracing of the image can be seen in the two long solo "waits" Bausch implants: once when Nazareth Panadero must squirm through the whole length of a tango before she can recite the poem beginning "in May," and again when Andersen endures a similar motionless period throughout the length of a tango – in the agony of a backbend in the middle of the stage.

But the moments when the image of the embrace is explicitly drawn and shaded are the most powerful. The first embrace doesn't come in a dance at all, but in a still, private kiss for Julie Anne Stanzak and one of the men as they stand surrounded by running, screaming, jumping dancers. Immediately thereafter, Julie Shanahan becomes frantic, trying to suppress an urge but finally pulling her dress up over her head and commanding Andersen to scratch her back. His nails rip at her. Shanahan was the touchstone woman this season – thin, mature, platinum-haired, complicated, not immediately sympathetic. As Andersen pushes his nails into Shanahan's skin, Kesselheim tries a similar maneuver on Mercy – she demands he rub her neck and stroke her hair. She never gets what she wants from him; the more insistent and infuriated she becomes, the more passively he resists with a feint at compliance. Unlike violence, tenderness cannot be compelled, and these women don't know any way to ask for it.

Lights lower for the "intimacy suite." In the first act, the whole company pairs off for an extended experiment in disclosure, vulnerability, and physicality. Couples enter, one at a time, look around the stage in a matter-of-fact investigation of a suitably private move off to their chosen spot, and undress slowly, incompletely – baring one shoulder, one leg, one carefully considered part of the body, self-protective gestures that emphasize the nakedness of the small area of bared flesh. Subdued and hesitant, they tentatively touch the exposed, naked places. The scene is troubling, the intimacy hard to watch – starting with the very undisguised, businesslike, unflirtatious, "unromantic" searching out of a spot to be alone and undress, including as well the "unromantic," fearful quality of the partial nudity. These aren't states of being human beings customarily observe, or ones where we fancy being observed and on display – in the lifelike revelation of these needs and our feelings about them. The postures are twisted and graceless at the same time that, as they turn into lifts, they require a great deal of complicity and trust. As each man lifts his partner so that she straddles his shoulders, his face pressing into her crotch, the dancers reflect no ecstasy. Their gazes are solemn and inward, their consciousness averted, evasive. However physically intimate the contact, the women are emotionally inaccessible to the men, who finally dispel the tension with nervous clicks of their cigarette lighters. The pose of the woman straddling the man's shoulders is the first major image of the dance embrace in *Bandoneon,* and it takes over the stage in waves. It ends as all the women scream, and the couples drop to the floor, still interlocked, "tangoing" on their hips. A second image, as grotesque as the first.

This image is developed further in the second half of *Bandoneon.* The lift that characterizes this act begins as the tension of Panadero's long wait for her poetic recitation is deflated by the reading of the poem itself, both her self-deprecating manner of reading it and the idea that "love is singing." A man and woman (Jan Minarik and Mariko Aoyama at BAM) step on the stage from the stage left wing. He kneels before her, but the courtliness of his gesture is at once qualified as he inserts his arm between her legs and, through some hidden trickery, lifts her in the air, apparently lifeless, feelingless, inert, passive, submissive, frozen – with terror? With horror? With ennui? It takes several couples repeating the lift before the shock wears off and we are able to take note of how it's done. The man grips the waistband of the woman's underpants and hoists her up by pressing on her vagina. When Cronin enters in a completely transparent black lace dress, the whole operation is completely exposed. Is it ugly – the unemotional depiction of the man forcing his hand and energy between the woman's legs? Is it peculiar? Is it inherently beautiful? May I have this dance? It can't be sustained long, and the "exit" is via the woman's wrapping her legs around the man's torso more or less as she did in the first act. But in juxtaposition to the gradual disclosure of act one, the plunge into intimacy here is abrupt; it's almost rape.

Badoneon's final image of the couple embracing and dancing is benign, almost, purgative, almost. It comes as the entire company lines up facing the audience at the end of the piece – well, almost the entire company, for Mercy is back in his tutu, lurking shyly in the rear. The scenario has ended with Minarik recalling the sadistic antics of a ballet teacher he had who demanded a smile at all times: "When onstage you can't breathe through your nose anymore, you must breathe through your teeth and smile. Jan, a dancer who doesn't smile onstage – it's no dancer!" And as the music bursts into a light, merry tune, the first joyful music of the evening, Subicz requests of Airaudo the honor of a dance. The two break into an almost ribald, hip-rolling, jolly dance, whose synchronized movements below the waist are explicitly sexual. A few other couples join in, there is some changing of partners, but eventually all fade back into the line – smiling, smiling, smiling. On one side of the fan, the ballet ends with Mercy, clad in his tutu, curled in a fetal position alone on the stage. On the reverse side, it is ended by Libonati, alone again as the lights black out.

Are these dancers, anyway? ("A dancer who doesn't smile onstage – it's no dancer!") The study of ballet figures largely in much of Bausch's work, and largely in *Bandoneon*. There are several ludicrous/comical invocations of the ballet studio in this piece. There is, of course, that grotesquely displaced romantic tutu. At one point, Kesselheim torments Panadero in the guise of a ballet teacher who plunges a girl's head into a bucket of water until she smiles – "Nazareth, are you smiling?" The beauty of ballet is always perverse – as when the stage is filled with dancers in street clothes, including Minarik in a three-piece business suit, doing a barre. Obviously the whole concept of desexualized, ultra-romanticized "lifts" is devastated by *Bandoneon*. In the first act, Kesselheim ties Panadero's legs together in passé and orders her to pirouette, an impossibility (Panadero just falls). Minarik recalls an employer's remark, "If you don't feel pain, it's not my choreography," and later impersonates a teacher who held a lit cigar close to his students' legs to force their extensions ("See! It is possible!").

Viktor (1986) is set in a quarry, the stage hemmed with walls of dirt down which cascade, from time to time, streams of sand, as if gravediggers were burying bodies. The showers of sand provide aural and visual punctuation for the action, coming unpredictably as reminders of the unpredictable nature of all things. There are numerous other images of flow, of flux, in *Viktor*, illustrating both the beauty and threat of mutability. These images, magnified a thousand-fold in *Palermo Palermo,* are potent and explosive in *Viktor*. Their beauty is as important as their sometimes sinister ominousness.

Within the quarry walls, a Japanese woman feeds breadcrumbs to paper ducks and at the same time "dresses" a chair and stands behind it, herself becoming an optical illusion of a well-dressed woman sitting on a chair, but only a little more real and reachable than those ducks. Later, she becomes a fountain, spewing bottled water from her mouth as two men wash up; at another point, she becomes another kind of fountain, squatting and feigning urinating at the shadowy rear of the stage. Her long dark hair flows around her to her waist.

During the "fountain" scene, as the men bathe in the stream that is Kyomi Ichida, Bausch slows down the pace to present a tableau in quiet stillness. Not quite a tableau, a flowing one. With Ichida to stage left, and a woman crisscrossing the stage stopping here and there to change from one dress to another (it recalls *The Rite of Spring* and foreshadows a section for Julie Shanahan in *Palermo Palermo*), two other women move from place to place, one of them Anne Martin, in heels, with a fur tied to both her ankles. She stops; a second woman reclines on the fur, they pause for some time, then move on, dragging the rug, stopping again elsewhere to compose another grouping. Bausch is purely the painter here, doing nothing more than arranging and rearranging the objects of her study. Once noted, this "tableau" method – trying an arrangement one way, then revolving it to study it from another angle – is characteristic of Bausch. It's notable in that section of *Bandoneon* where she tries having the dancers sit in chairs arranged first against one wall, then another, then a third. Which way looks best? They're all interesting, though the differences are subtle and unimportant, maybe, to any eye but an artist's.

The vituperation hurled at Bausch has been extensive and imaginative. Clive Barnes finds her "silly, empty ... stupid, self-indulgent, self-congratulatory," and describes her aesthetic as "tatterdemalion." In the *New York Times*, where Anna Kisselgoff has been a responsive sympathizer, John Rockwell stepped in with a slur at Bausch's "ultimately repetitive and narcissistic potpourris." Arlene Croce has contributed such descriptors as "glum despondent dabblings," "feminist paranoia, ritualistic amateurism," "meaningless frenzy," "an entrepreneuse who fills theatres with projections of her self-pity ... a little girl acting po'faced," "calculated audience voyeurism to a nicety," "yucky," "little fat girls in the company," and finally, "corny and tiresome." Writing in *Dance Magazine,* Joan Acocella maintained, "the women are pathetically reduced, all pendent breasts and stringy hair." I want to focus in on "tatterdemalion," "little fat girls," "pendent breasts and stringy hair," and note that a similar complaint is often made about the limp looseness of the performers' dresses and lingerie.

The complaints about the dancers' comeliness – their lack of conventional romantic allure, sleek seductiveness, and the absence of the usual guaranteed, reliable sensuality we count on finding in the dance theatre – is a definite provocation on Bausch's part. An identical charge was leveled at Nijinsky (and company) for the atypically baggy, loose costumes of *Le Sacre du Printemps*, 1913 version. There and then, the withholding of the sight of trim, lithe, young bodies, temptingly arrayed in skintight clothing, totally outraged Paris. One thing is clear – loose clothing on a ballet company incites frenzied outrage.

The question of the beauty, or lack of it, in Bausch's women deserves serious, dry, extended consideration. Hers is a world of women, indeed, a female-centered universe in which men, struggle as they will, can never be as interesting to look at, talk to, or think about as women. *Palermo Palermo* is obsessively feminine, Bausch's most female-focused mature work: *Viktor* comes close. It doesn't go too far

Figure 11 Keuschheitslegende (1979): Tanztheater Wuppertal. © Ursula Kaufmann

to say that Bausch finds grounds to reject men in part because they don't look very good in those sumptuously beautiful, magical garments, dresses (or high heels). She has certainly given them every opportunity to try!

In Bausch's company are many women who compare favorably to women in New York City Ballet (if not the Kirov), who far outshine the standard of pulchritude typical of ABT or the Joffrey or virtually any modern dance company in the world. Statuesque Julie Anne Stanzak, sweet-faced Dulce Pessoa, the fine-boned Malou Airaudo, a ringer for Suzanne Farrell – these women could hold their own with any stage beauties, as could Bénédicte Billiet of years past, not to mention Anne Martin – Martin was a truly intoxicatingly pretty girl. As far as their loose hair is concerned, the sweeping, well-tended falls of such women as Stanzak, Pessoa, Airaudo, and Panadero compare favorably with the loose heads of hair swinging free in *Tchaikovsky Suite #3*. Several of Bausch's women have short, neat, well-tended hairdos (Finola Cronin, Quincella Swyningan) or well-maintained, trimmed, mid-length hair (Shanahan, Kesselheim).

Today all the women in the company are extremely thin, with "twiggy" Shanahan as the standard-bearer. In the past, though, Bausch has pondered on plumpness (voluptuousness), as with Melanie Karen Lien, who featured largely in *Viktor* as the much abused, blowsy blonde. Generally, breast size falls within the dance world's conventions. Three things do genuinely distinguish Bausch's women from such busty dancers as Tina LeBlanc, Constance Dinapoli, or Karen Fink Radford – all of whom are much fuller on top than anyone in the Tanztheater Wuppertal today. One is that some of Bausch's women don't shave their legs or underarms. Second, while some are in their early twenties, many are in their forties. And then there is that loose clothing.

The assumption of loose clothing is the flashpoint, because somehow in the dance theatre, it breaks a taboo and makes dancers fair game – maybe, in denying us the kick provided by milliskin and decorative intimations of nudity, it arouses a latent hostility and jealousy that underlie all our attraction to dancers. Women of forty do lose the firm line of the breasts – it happened as clearly to Patricia McBride, as made visible in her *Raymonda Variations* tutu in the 1980s. But no one would have dreamt of commenting on the way McBride's upper body looked in this revealing garment. McBride was keeping up her end, and it would have been cruel to point out the ineluctable pull of gravity. Bausch will not allow us to deny nature, and we respond with anger. There are those who stay compulsively away from Bausch's theatre because the spectacle of real flesh is too painful to bear, and they're right to absent themselves – once inside, Bausch's sense of the body as vulnerable is inescapable, even when, as in *Viktor*, she dresses her women in a series of beautiful ball gowns.

The climax of *Viktor* is a triumphant one. While it can be seen ironically, onstage it plays lyrically, and it's that section of the second half where the women enter, dressed in froufrou concoctions of lace, satin. taffeta, and silk organza and sit at little tables, butter muffins and heap jelly on them, then move out to the audience offering these sweets to the customers. They do this smiling, highlighted by Martin's positively incandescent, inviting smile. When the muffins (or scones or crumpets) have been distributed, huge rings – like gymnasts' still rings – are lowered, men lift the women to the rings, and each swings in arcs that trail her hair and ruffles and ribbons through the air.

Martin is the first to go. The music is typical of Bausch – kind of crazy, but perfectly right. It's "The Way You Look Tonight," in an old-fashioned arrangement. "Light music is often serious," Bausch has said. "On the one side is classical music, on the other, contemporary. Between these two extremes is a great deal of other music – commercial music, musical accompaniment. It's always important music to me." As pretty, pretty Anne Martin swings, a man sings:

> Some day, when I'm awfully low
> When the world is cold
> I will feel a glow
> Just thinking of you
> And the way you look tonight.

The rhythmic sway of her body, high above the ground, is a dance movement as powerful and irresistible as the sweep of couples across the stage at the end of *Vienna Waltzes*. It is dance without dance steps. A still photograph, taken by Guy Delahaye and reproduced in his lavish book, betrays Bausch here, I think. He prints an image of Kesselheim on the rings, a close-up, and she is grimacing with effort. Yes, there is always an ironic interpretation to Bausch's work, but it is far from the only one, not necessarily the right one, and the frequent fixation with it covers up for Bausch's central awareness of sadness and beauty and the ways they are linked. Her women do labor to be beautiful. Those women soaring on the rings are butterflies – ephemeral, dazzling, transitory, and fair game.

It is just a moment in *Viktor*, a transcendent moment. In *Palermo Palermo*, Bausch extends the moment, interfusing it with everything in the work.

The air is filled with dust in *Palermo Palermo*. The trailing organdy and ruffled lace, the showers of sand – these are disintegrated into vapor, a cloudy billowing, veiling diffusion of substance into essence. In *Palermo Palermo*, everything hisses. The air is filled with noises, full of clouds. Even water, Bausch's favorite element, is superseded by vapor and mist. That vapor is seen in the perfume Swyningan sprays into the air with an atomizer in visible clouds; in the cigarette smoke a man breathes in front of him, to hide his face; in the hiss of a bottle of carbonated water that a woman suggests also represents the body's gaseous exhalations; in the fall of ochre powder that descends in dusty curtains; in the hiss of a steam iron; in the empyrean clouds that billow against a painted backdrop of clouds as six pianos pound out Tchaikovsky. Twice in the play a character fires a gun, and the atmosphere of *Palermo Palermo* is suffused with gunsmoke. Even violence transmutes into beauty. At the end of the work, the dancers bend forward from the waist and move in a slow parade, their hair falling forward in "weeping" cascades, and the red sand falls around them like tears. No other work of Bausch's is so subtly and completely unified around the metaphor of mutability, of dissolution, so sad and so diverse.

Crucial in *Palermo Palermo* are the clothes – here, specifically, the preponderance of diaphanous, transparent garments. The designer who made it possible for Bausch to reach her artistic maturity was Borzik. Since his death, her costumes have been in the hands of Borzik's former assistant, Marion Cito, who is, judging from photographs, a chic woman of Bausch's generation. In *Palermo Palermo*, she offers a set of gorgeous outfits that are as two-faced and deceptive as they are beautiful. In a proper afternoon suit with a string of decorous pearls, Panadero in an angry fit flings shoes across the stage. Shanahan, dressed in a ravishing fitted smoke-grey chiffon gown, carries a load of kitchen utensils across the stage and drops them in a pile. Right on stage, Swyningan releases herself from an orange evening gown with crinoline underskirts to emerge in a sleek black velvet sheath. Each woman has numerous dresses and changes frequently throughout the evening – standard in Bausch's work – but the cavalcade of dresses is overwhelming in *Palermo Palermo,* and by the end of the evening, it demolishes the men in their unvarying grey and white. Bausch has always liked see-through clothes, and all of her works contain some transparent lace or voile. But there is an uncommon number of them here: the transparent white pinafore Cronin wears as she reads a fairy tale to Minarik; Shanahan's grey evening gown, floating around her like a cloud, and her see-through red jumpsuit; someone's – her head is covered – transparent black floor-length dress. These costumes are coalescences, not solid, in the process of dissolving before our eyes.

Throughout the action, candles and flames fill the air with their smoke. Dressed in her see-through apron, Cronin dances with a cigarette lighter in each hand, flicking them on and off as she brings them close to her. Subicz describes the custom of dreamy young Polish girls setting candles afloat, and as he indicates they make a wish with each candle, he leers over what that wish might be, Minarik wears a crown of candles – a commentary on the circles of floating candles, the Statue of Liberty, and, indeed, the Virgin Mary (*"Qu'est ce que tu penses de Maria?"*). Candles are a threat when a man sticks six or eight of them, burning, on his arm and proceeds to play the saxophone. All the while, Shanahan, in the guise of a figure of Death (her head is covered with a stocking mask), stands by with a gun – but does not, finally, "fire."

Related, too, in the great coalescence of *Palermo Palermo*, are the images of granulation, such as the descending curtains of sand. Early in the work, Shanahan throws a box of ashes over herself. Later Swyningan sprinkles the stage with sugar. Another kind of dissolving is suggested in the snowballs Swyningan brings out from a freezer. The air is filled with objects that are large "grains," sometimes light (a feather), sometimes heavy (an apple impaled on a knife).

Bausch has cut the dance element to its barest in *Palermo Palermo*. It is possible, as a result, to study her method of construction. Her basic means of proceeding is to juxtapose moments of stillness and near immobility with "parades," passages of unison mass movement that come seemingly from nowhere and end suddenly, in stillness. It's a traditional technique in directing and a powerful one – to muster forces out of thin air and subsequently have them "dissolve." It takes great skill in timing, pacing, and, obviously, using large numbers of people. In a work as early as *Bandoneon,* the parades *are* less organized and diverse than they become later, but one thinks of the parade of individual "bravos" that the performers inflict on each other, of Airaudo's run down the center of the stage as she is cheered; of the group doing barre exercises, then vanishing; of the dismantlement of the stage set; of the dancers running and jumping uncontrolledly while somewhere a man and woman kiss.

In *Viktor,* the alternation between parades and periods of subdued action in small groups is clear and frequent. The first parade is the first auction scene, which fills every part of the stage with life; soon there is a cosmic line dance with a snaking double file of dancers in waltz position moving across the stage and into the audience; after a series of quiet scenes, another parade has the men carrying the women forward to the apron of the stage and back again. A magnificent parade in the second act occurs as the whole company crosses from wing to wing as if the stage were perilous quicksand, stepping on planks, boards, chairs, tables, pieces of cloth, anything they can find. There's another auction parade and then, of course, the grand défilé of the women on the rings.

In *Palermo Palermo,* Bausch has moved far enough away from her reliance on parades to hold her work together that she cuts down to only two – one at the end of the first act, one at the end of the second. What holds *Palermo Palermo* together instead is imagery, the network of images of vapor, sand, steam, dissolving. So imaginatively, richly, and confidently is Bausch able to explore this imagery that she is able to let go of her earlier methods – to become, in the process, more of a "painter" and less of a "dancer."

Bausch's work is life-affirming in part because it is enlivened by genuine artistic strides – it has the energy of forward momentum. The concentrated grey, white, and red palette of *Palermo Palermo* is a summation of twenty years of experimentation and development. It is also a work that finally upholds beauty, tenuous as it is. At the end of *Palermo Palermo,* branches covered with lavender flowers (a reference to *Tannhäuser*?) are lowered on ropes, half untied, and piled to the side of the stage. Like the snowballs in the freezer, they are artificially preserved and saved, set outside of the process of mutability. They are no longer part of the stream of nature, and they are both a tantalizing promise and a frustration any adult can see through.

Not this work only, but the whole world created by Pina Bausch sits neatly on the border between yes and no, so balanced we can easily take for granted the delicate precision involved in poising there. Poise is a good word for her work and for her women. They continually revolve poise in their hands, finding composure, complaisance, apathy, and despair within their roles, but also finding hope. There is irony, but there is also straightforward beauty. And there is always the image, the surprise, the enchantment of a moment on the rings that lifts us out of the everyday into an amazing and ephemeral transformation. I believe Pina Bausch means it when she says,

> Some day, when I'm awfully low
> When the world is cold
> I will feel a glow
> Just thinking of you
> And the way you look tonight.

"Come dance with me"

Interview with Pina Bausch

Nadine Meisner
Originally published in *Dance and Dancers*, September–October, 1992

It doesn't matter that Pina Bausch shies from publicity because she doesn't need it. Her work is revered and obsessively pursued by ruthless and determined hordes. It strikes such deep chords that it can turn the calmest people into hopeless addicts; because it bridges dance and theatre it attracts spectators who would not the seen dead at a conventional dance performance. Even her own remoteness has a mystique, adding to the allure of a figure that towers above all other European choreographers.

Where does her view of the world come from? From simply watching it, she says. People have suggested that her melancholy must come from an unhappy childhood, but she does not remember her childhood as being so – although she knows she was extremely timid and sometimes sad, without recalling why. She remembers being terrified of having large feet like her father, and she used to pray at night that they would stop growing. And she remembers hiding under the tables of her parents' restaurant, because she didn't want to go to bed. "For a child," she said in an interview with Leonetta Bentivoglio, "a restaurant can be an enchanting place: there were so many people and so many strange things happening." These are memories which surely fed *Café Müller,* the piece she recently brought to the Edinburgh Festival.

She was always hanging around, playing, jumping, dancing about in the restaurant, which was in Solingen, a town between Düsseldorf and Wuppertal, where she was born in 1940. Theatre people used regularly to eat lunch there, and with their encouragement she started dance classes. She used to appear at the local theatre in walk-on roles in operas, operettas and ballets. She remembers one role as a newspaper vendor where she had to shout "Gazzetta San Remo;" she was such a perfectionist that she made herself a pile of front pages, sticking together newsprint letters to form the correct title.

Aged 15, she started at the Folkwangschule (Folkwang School) in another neighboring town – Essen, where Kurt Jooss headed the dance department. There she studied an exhaustive range of dance – ballet, various modern techniques, folk dance, choreography. Aged 19, she gained a scholarship to study in New York and boarded the ship not knowing a word of English or where she would live, her tearful parents waving goodbye. She attended the Juilliard School of Music, where her teachers included Antony Tudor. She danced in Paul Sanasardo and Donya Feuer's company, she worked with Paul Taylor. She then danced with the New American Ballet and, under Tudor's directorship, the Metropolitan Opera Ballet.

Her two years in New York made a profound impression, not only because of the quality of teaching and experience she found there, but also because during that time she grew up, gaining an emotional strength and confidence. She was torn between staying and accepting Jooss's invitation to work with the Folkwangtanzstudio, a dance group linked with the school, which he had revived. She chose the latter: but New York, she has said, is the only city for which she still feels nostalgia.

After New York she found the pace in Germany lax. But in Jean Cébron, then teaching at the Folkwang School, she found a fellow workaholic; she worked with him, with Jooss and with Hans Züllig. She helped Jooss with the performance group, drawing up programmes, sometimes taking rehearsals, as well as performing. She taught at the Folkwang School, and she accepted engagements to dance for Tudor and Lucas Hoving.

In 1968, she choreographed her first piece, *Im Wind der Zeit* (*In the Wind of Time*), for the Folkwangtanzstudio, remembered by Hans Züllig as "very abstract, very dancerly, very graphic. Pina had a wonderful sense of polyphony in her choreography." This won the first prize of the Cologne Choreographic Competition the following year. During that time she also choreographed Purcell's opera-ballet, *The Fairy Queen,* at Schwetzingen and took over the running of the Folkwang-tanzstudio. (She later, in 1984, became director of the dance department of the school, and still maintains a link with the graduate group.)

For the group she made *After 0*, where the five dancers seemed like agonized, torn bodies, and *Wigenlied* (*Lullaby*), on the theme of war, showing horror behind the simple lilting lullaby music used. In 1970, she accepted a Dutch invitation to choreograph and showed her work in the USA where at Saratoga she met for the first time two French dancers, Dominique Mercy and Malou Airaudo, later to become two of her earliest and closest collaborators.

In 1971, asked by the Wuppertaler Bühnen (Wuppertal Opera House and Playhouse) to create a piece with the Folkwang group as performers, she made *Actions for Dancers*, a skit on classical dance. In 1972, again at Wuppertal with the same group, she choreographed the Bacchanale from *Tannhaüser* (Susanne Linke danced the lead); it was a big success and the theatre's then director, Arnold Wüstenhöfer, took the bold decision to invite her to direct the resident dance company, which after some trepadation she accepted. The company had never had a choreographer as director before, having hitherto been managed by rather obscure ballet masters, (At Essen her successors were Susanne Linke and then Reinhild Hoffman.)

Before taking her Wuppertal appointment for the 1973–74 season, she traveled, teaching in Saratoga, performing in Rotterdam, Manchester and London. (The editor of this magazine remembers seeing her dance at the Roundhouse.) She began as director with *Fritz*, a piece where childhood fears were a theme. Its cast included the now-familiar names of Mercy, Airaudo, Jan Minarik and Monika Sagon. Also listed in the program was an assistant costume-designer, Rolf Borzik, who became Bausch's scenographer and companion and died of cancer in 1980. Dancing *Fritz*, Mercy once explained, was a new experience for him, "For the first time I had the feeling that I, Dominique, was on stage and that I was giving and saying something of myself."

The Wuppertal public, on the other hand, accustomed to evenings of conventional dance, were not impressed – although Gluck's *Iphigenie en Tauride*, which followed a few months later, went some way to placating them. Bausch's production (revived last year at the Paris Opera with the original cast) placed the singers in the pit or auditorium, while the dancers mirrored their roles on stage. Josephine Ann Endicott, another future Bausch lynchpin, made her debut with the company, as Clytemnestra. Then at the end of 1974 came *Ich bringe Dich um die Ecke* (*I'll bump you off*), a short piece in which the dancers sang popular songs and evoked another Bausch preoccupation: relationships between men and women and the power struggle between them. To the same bill she added another short premiere, *Adagio*, which used five songs by Gustav Mahler.

In 1975 she choreographed a second Gluck opera, *Orpheus and Eurydice* presenting this time both the singers and the dancers doubling them on stage. (The production is also about to be revived at the Paris Opera.) In this she depicted the leading characters unsparingly, everything stripped away except their pathos; the design featured bare trees, a favored motif of subsequent works. Then came *The Rite of Spring*, the only successful post-Nijinsky version (assuming Nijinsky's was successful); *Seven Deadly Sins*; *Bluebeard*; *Komm Tanz mit Mir* (*Come Dance with Me*), *Renate Wandert Aus* (*Renate Emigrates*); *Er nimmt sie an der Hand und führt sie in das Schloss, die anderen folgen* (*He Takes her by the Hand and Leads Her into the Castle, the Others Follow*), based on the story of *Macbeth*; and *Café Müller*.

There also came international acclaim, making the Tanztheater Wuppertal one of the most traveled companies, with regular seasons in France, Italy, Greece and the USA. As a result, a grey industrial German town, hitherto known as the birthplace of aspirin and Friedrich Engels, has been etched on the cultural map.

Nowadays the company attracts an average audience of 94% in its home theatre, but it has taken time to persuade Wuppertalers not to hand back their tickets in disgust. To that end the company took to publishing reviews of their successes abroad in the local newspapers. But it was not just the audiences who were once resistant, it was also the dancers.

During the making of *The Seven Deadly Sins* in 1976 they rebelled, enraged at what they saw as the absence of dance. After its premiere, Bausch fled, wanting never to return. She began working with a small core of the company who did accept her style; they included Minarik, the only one to have made the transition from the pre-Bausch Wuppertal company. Using Minarik's own studio, they experimented with new kinds of work, evolving material that was to be recycled into *Bluebeard* a few months later. And all the while, a trickle of renegade company members returned to them, until they numbered about half the company. So they went back to the theatre, announcing to the rest "We're here! We already have material prepared!"

Her pieces in the last twelve years or so have resembled sprawling epics, less focused than the *Rite of Spring*, her last all dance piece, or *Café Müller* (the last where the dancers do not speak). The later pieces might include images just as bleak as in, say, *Café Müller*, exposing loneliness, egocentricity and ultimate futility; but they also celebrate the human spirit, man's tenderness and courage and laughter. All means are valid – dance, theatre, mood, music, comedy, sketches, visual jokes, a floor covered in grass or mud or water – to create a complete world that we can all recognize within ourselves. She refuses labels; she uses whichever device best serves to express her intentions at a given point; and having such a broad palette means being able to enlarge her scope, as well as make it more precise. Her critics may bemoan the absence of dance in its usual sense, but she sees dance as more than conventional choreography, believes that a performer standing still can be executing dance. Although she has sometimes employed actors (the best-known being Mechthild Grossman), she chooses professional dancers with techniques she can exploit.

Some of her material is selected from improvisations by the dancers. She sets them themes and tasks to work on, sifting through the results, rejecting, assembling, modifying. Consequently, her 26 dancers seem to bring themselves, their thoughts and experiences to the stage – even if it is often an illusion. And consequently she likes them to be highly individual; they are as diverse as people on the street, with their different nationalities, physiques and personalities, the very antithesis of a *corps de ballet*. That also means that when somebody leaves, they are not easy to replace. Even so, the company has changed greatly over the years: of the oldest guard, only Mercy, Minarik, and Nazareth Panadero remain. But wherever possible in restaging old works, former members are enticed back as guests to perform the roles they created, as happened with *Iphigéenie en Tauride* in Paris and *Café Müller* in Edinburgh.

Those who read her work as feminist are as misguided as those who interpret the old-fashioned dresses worn by her women as a sinister hankering for wartime Germany. It seems to me she favors these dresses because she deals with memories, with evocations of her childhood and adolescence through which she summons up universal emotions. Nor does she hold a brief for any one sex, she is interested in people, even if she displays a creative sensibility – allusive, subtle, atmospheric – that is distinctly feminine. She sees human relationships as difficult, but then that is what they are. She does not condemn either men or women: she portrays our failings, struggles and childishness with poignant humanity. She shows us lonely people trying to assert their existence in the world (which is perhaps why the taking of photographs is sometimes a motif in her work).

Bausch has gaunt Teutonic looks and a chain-smoking habit. She is not an easy interviewee; she does not have an easy social manner or small talk. But she gives the impression of great warmth towards those she knows. And to strangers like myself there was no ill-will or fussy selectivity about what she would or would not answer. On the contrary, she was exhaustively patient and helpful.

What follows is a fuller version of an interview for a feature in *The Sunday Times*, the only one she granted before coming to Edinburgh, her first British visit for ten years. The material for my introduction came from various sources, in particular *Pina Bausch*, photographs by Delahaye, texts by Raphael de Gubernatis and Leonetta Bentevoglio, and *Pina Bausch, Histoires de théàtre dansé*, by Raimond Hoghe.

D&D: Your training has been very varied, very rich. You have studied with Kurt Jooss, with Antony Tudor. Could you describe what your style was like in your early pieces?

PINA BAUSCH: I never had the thought or the wish to be a choreographer, I was a dancer, I loved to dance. There was a time when there was not enough work for me to dance, and I felt so much a need to express myself, so I thought maybe I will do a little piece, something for myself. So I started, and there were other people who also wanted to dance more; they asked me if they could join in. So I did it with a few others. But I never thought I would become a choreographer.

I worked with many different teachers, many different styles. And for me there was always a problem; I never wanted to copy anyone, I did not want to do something I had learnt. It was very difficult: in my first piece I even thought a step is impossible – to try to go from here to there – because I did not want to use the steps I knew! I made myself very different. It was not like a style of ballet – it was really far away – but it was also very far away from all the styles I learnt. It was not a style from Jooss or from anybody else.

You yourself perform now only in Café Müller. *Why is that?*

Because for many years I plan to perform roles and I never find the time, because everybody "eats" me up you know. Everybody wants so much to dance or to do so much work, that it never happens for me. So I am standing on the waiting list for many years, on my own waiting list!

When did you first incorporate speech into your work? I know you did a piece where the dancers sang – it was an early piece for Wuppertal, but then when did you use actual speech?

In *Fritz,* my very first piece in Wuppertal, there were already little words or sounds. Little things. Then a year later I did *Ich bringe Dich um die Ecke,* in which all the women had their little song: old popular songs. Then I did *Weill/Brecht* which was with singing and actors. So I always had a double strand of acting and dancing, because of working with Mechthild Grossman, or other actors I found. But really the very big change in my work was with *He takes her by the hand and leads her into the castle, the others follow*: a production with not too many people, but I had singers who didn't sing, dancers who didn't dance, actors who didn't act – each one did different work. It had as starting point a scene from *Macbeth*, but the piece is not Shakespeare's *Macbeth*. It was a coproduction between Wuppertal and Bochum, a town nearby.

From what I understand you work a lot by using the dancers' personalities, and questions and answers in the studio.

It is part of finding material. But it's only one way of finding material. I might throw it away, or I might find things in there.

When a member of your company leaves and you have to bring somebody else into a role, what happens? Do you modify the role, so that it takes on more of the personality of the new person?

It depends what it is. Sometimes it feels easy to forget the other person, and I think the idea underneath – my feeling, my idea – can fit very easily. Sometimes you have to find a way round. With each person it is different.

In the instances where it is difficult, do you feel happy to modify things?

Sometimes I like it much better after! But sometimes I cannot find anybody who can really do it the way it was.

The Meryl Tankard remark in 1980 *about three famous products of Australia – "Boomerangs! Kangaroos! Me!" – Does that remain?*

Oh yes, because the new person in that part comes from Australia. But if she had not come from this country, the sentence would not be there.

What made you diversify into other forms, beyond dance?

What I try is to find the pictures, or the images, that can best express the feeling I want to convey. And you have to find your own way to show these things, I am not telling a story in a normal way. Each person in the audience is part of the piece in a way; you bring your own experience, your own fantasy, you own feeling in response to what you see. There is something happening inside. You only understand that if you let that happen, it's not something you can do with your intellect. So everybody, according to their experience, has a different feeling, a different impression. Also on different days what you feel is different.

I think it can only work if we avoid anything explicit – anything where we see something and we all know what it means. We think oh, this is a sign for that: you know it in your head. But if we avoid this and if the audience are open to experience or feel things, I think there is the possibility of another kind of language.

I do not use only choreography for this, but for me the stage is important, the space, the time, the music, the personalities, everything has to be brought together. It is not only a question of "Why do you not do dance? Why do you do this?" Actually the reason is, I am interested in a certain feeling that I want to express, something that there is no word for.

And the means to this include not only dancing and language and singing, but also how the dancers walk, whether they make a noise – like in *1980* you cannot hear the steps, because of the turf, but if they walk in water it will be completely different, or if they sweat or have earth on their bodies – it all makes a difference.

Or the smell of grass.

The smell of the grass; or there are little mosquitoes circling in the theatre, all the millions of details.

Which add together to make the complete picture.

Yes, but it should not add up to "What did she think when she did this?" It is going to a different level than an intellectual level, it is a feeling – but a feeling which is very precise; it is not just some vague feeling, it is something absolutely precise. If you do it like this instead of like that, everything changes.

But you make the spectator enter a world.

Enter their own world. Everybody has their own interpretation. If you go outside here, you might say "Oh, isn't it terrible?" Someone else might say "Oh, isn't it fantastic?" You see the same thing but the reaction is different.

Does all this mean you don't see a future when you might go back and do a pure dance piece again?

Maybe I shall, but it will not be the same; it will not going be back, it will be going forward. If I decide again not to use words, it will be completely different. And it is completely open, there is no plan or system, it might just happen.

Is there a specific reason why you chose to go back to the operas and mount Iphigénie en Tauride *at the Paris Opera and will also be doing* Orpheus?

We have played many, many different pieces, we try to do as many as possible, and because there are so many we always lose some. The reason for doing this production again was that the Goethe Institute in Paris had its 25 years anniversary, and their wish was to show something in Paris which they didn't already know about there. It was also to help a certain situation. If I do *Iphigenia*, it is a whole orchestra and singers – we certainly could not do it at the Theatre de la Ville, where we have our regular seasons. So their wish was to show *Iphigenia* in Paris. I was scared a bit, because it was so long ago, and I didn't know whether I would now like it, what I would think when I see it again.

So I said "nein," and then "jein" – and then "ja" and we did it – not only in Paris but also in Wuppertal, Turin and Rome.

Was it a recreation or a revival?

I had several videos and we did it the way it was

Did you learn anything from that, was it a productive experience for you?

What I learnt was that it was so near, it felt like it was done a few months ago. There were dancers who were in the original production; without them really I would have felt less confident. It was one of the things that gave me confidence to do it, because I know that they wanted to do this too.

Was Café Müller *the last piece in which the dance content was so pronounced? Is it a piece that stands out as a dividing line?*

No, not really. What stands out is my piece about *Macbeth*, with actors and singers as well as dancers. I had to find a way to work with people who are not dancers – I had some experience with non-dancers before, but this time I found another way. From there on something in my work changed, somehow. But *Café Müller* is different because it is a little bit short – something like 45 minutes – it is a small cast, only a few people.

But after Café Müller, *never again did you use so much dance?*

What is dance anyway? First of all, dance is not only a certain style, there are so many different styles, cultures, needs why to dance; we can't only call certain modern or ballet techniques dance, or say this is dance, this is not. For me, much more is dance than other people think of. If you go to Japan, where you see Noh, you cannot say it is not dance, but it is completely different. The same if you go to India, or whatever culture or period.

You do tend to use dancers, although you have sometimes used actors …

But using actors is more exceptional.

… do they do a ballet class?

They do ballet and a modern class.

What do you look for in a dancer or performer?

For me, the person is very important. They are persons who dance – they are wonderful dancers and they have a very good technique – but also very important for me is the personality, what is them. If you come here and you just show me some tricks or a wonderful raised leg, that is not enough for this work. I like very much to have the possibility to use these beautiful things, if I want to. But the dancers must have more, must want to do this kind of work, to experience this. It must be a need for them to go into this, to try, to see what happens.

How do you know that a person is right?

That is the difficult thing!

Do you have a system of apprentices?

Not yet a system of apprentices, there is not yet the money for this. There is only this wonderful connection to the Folkwang School,

Are you still director of this school?

No, there is no director, the system for art schools has changed and now the department is differently organized; the teachers together have to find a way without a director. I take care of their postgraduate group. This is a small group, and they are performing with different young choreographers. Then some of them go to other companies, some go to Tanztheater Wuppertal.

Is this the same group where you started choreographing?

Yes.

Are you aware of an evolution in your work?

Oh yes, it is like a river – changing, but still the same. It is like life: time changes, your body changes, your thoughts. It happens organically. But I think I am still the same person.

Would you acknowledge any influences on you as a choreographer? Was Jooss an influence?

It is difficult to say, because life is already so much an influence, each person you meet, the technique you learn, or music you hear, or what you see. It is very difficult to take apart, it is in you, you don't know where it is. Altogether it makes you what you are. Of the people I worked with, Tudor was such a great person. I think the most important is the humanity, which was so important also for people like Jooss, like Tudor. The human side. But you see Jooss had to find his own way, Tudor had to find his own way; I find my own way too.

Figure 12 Two Cigarettes in the Dark (1985): Julie Shanahan, Michael Strecker.
© Ursula Kaufmann

IV

Bausch's reception

The influence of Tanztheater has been strong, and continues to grow, but the real question remains: What has Tanztheater given us? How has Bausch's and others' work reconfigured dance and theatrical practice to provide new arenas for expression and understanding? The answer to that question is twofold. First, Bausch's continued insistence on the expressive possibilities of subjective engagement has led to a re-orchestration of presentational structure, both in rehearsal and performance. Bausch provides the model for an entrance into a different sort of dramaturgy based on metaphor and association, and therefore necessarily draws on the developed expression of her performers as they enter into the process of performance as subjects. This attitude has far-reaching effects, both in the construction and presentation of performed events. The role of the performer shifts from one who actualizes material, whether that be through the expressive potential of movement or the delineation of character within a story, to one who brings ideas and emotions to presence, who makes emotions and attitudes manifest through her own presence on stage.

This idea is not so very new, and its practice has troubled the edges of dance and theatre practice for some time. What is new is Bausch's insistence on this mode of presentation as a working method. In so doing, she returns performance to its more mystical roots in ritual. The performers do create a part to play, and, far from abandoning technique, they require a heightened awareness of technical presentation, but they use those elements to enact a transformation of purpose and expression. Through recreating structures of feeling on stage, we are able to feel again and in our own way, rather than be told about a specific feeling up there with which we may or may not empathize.

The other part of the answer to our initial question lies in the degree to which this method both uncovers and makes invisible again the ways in which meaning is created on stage. To return to the basic elements of expression in an attempt to recreate feeling structures, rather than relying on codified forms of expression, requires an exploration of how those elements operate. That exploration of essential structure and expression remains present in the final work, though often hidden in the construction of a narrative of association. In exploring Bausch's work, I find I am exploring the vast history of performance, for she asks the same questions that led us to perform in the first place, and she utilizes the long history of methods open to her in creating her worlds. Those who would follow Bausch are most successful when they begin at that same elemental beginning and discover their own path through the creation of meaning, utilizing their own resources. More than jumping to something new, Bausch returns again to the roots of dance and theatre practice, and the means by which those arts function. The path towards meaning she creates falls somewhere between forms, or, perhaps more appropriately, behind them at the source from which they arise. She asks of expression the same thing she asks of her performers – what moves them and why? In concentrating on those fundamental elements of expression, her work gives us access to the structures of meaning. She also relies on and makes evident the desire to search for that expression, and the persistence with which we strive for some sense of completion.

Whether tanztheater will continue to exert a strong influence on dance and theatre practice in the years to come, or be eclipsed by the next new thing, is yet to be determined. But whether it will be considered as one of the few great dance movements when future dancers and critics look back upon this era or not, we have to recognize the force of its impact on the dance and theatre worlds as we know them now, and we see that in the ways in which critics and audiences alike gradually warm to the potentials that Bausch's work creates. Our first reaction is often confusion and outrage as our assumptions are challenged and our expectations of what dance or theatre are "supposed" to do are upended. As audience members, our job is to remain open to the potential for a newly constructed meaning and expression and meet it with our own engaged perspective. As critics, our job is to explore that meaning and expression in depth, in detail, and with eloquence. And as artists our goal is to find new means of asking questions, even while we borrow from and acknowledge the past, and to continue to try to move each other. For every act of connection is a moment of truth where we move past the dull veneer of our lives and recognize something within us that is larger than our own individual selves.

Bausch's reception has not always been easy, especially early on, when she enjoyed at least as many detractors as champions, especially in her home city of Wuppertal, where they were not keen to replace the comforting beauty of mediocre ballet with challenging and often violent explorations of human want and longing. But even those who didn't like her work, and wrote about it (some of which are included here), recognized that something was happening. She elicited a response.

This section proceeds chronologically, beginning with some of Bausch's earliest appraisals, and ends with appreciations of her body of work upon her death, and a few attempts to imagine what's next. I have tried to provide a representative sampling across sources and throughout the breadth of Bausch's career, though my focus is narrowed to primarily English-language pieces. As the sheer volume of work in the bibliography shows (and even this is a delimited sample of the reviews and considerations that might be included, particularly if the scope were widened to consider writing in other languages), the variety and impact of Bausch's work has been enormous. Love it or hate it, there has been more written about Pina Bausch and Tanztheater Wuppertal in the last 35 years than any other performing artist.

Tanztheater Wuppertal

Hörst Koegler

Originally published in *Dance Magazine*, February, 1979

It has been claimed that if Wuppertal were to be remembered for two people, they would be Friedrich Engels and Pina Bausch. At thirty-eight, Pina Bausch is definitely the most discussed German name on the national and increasingly on the international dance scene. She has been artistic director and resident choreographer of the Wuppertal Dance Theatre since the 1973–74 season. Strangely enough, there really is something Bausch and Engels have in common, apart from their being Wuppertalers: a strong and engaged sympathy for the misery of the underprivileged classes of bourgeois society.

Bausch, a large and bony woman with an unusually clean and clear face and penetrating eyes, comes from typical German middle-class stock. Born on July 27, 1940, into a family of innkeepers in Solingen, a small town between Cologne and Wuppertal, she studied at the Essen Folkwang School where Kurt Jooss undoubtedly influenced her whole outlook both in dance morality (dance with a message) and in dance technique (a medley of classical and contemporary).

As a dancer in the reformed German Folkwang Ballet she immediately drew the audience's attention whenever she was on stage. Her stark, earthbound personality, the stare of her eyes, which always seemed to look under the surface of things to reveal their innermost sorrow and pity, and the massive weight of each of her movements made it impossible to overlook her. And there were her inimitable screwing turns, with which she almost drilled her body into the ground. Not that she tried to star or to stand out – it was through no special will or effort, but just by her very nature that she stood apart from the rest of the dancers. She recalled the women Käthe Kollwitz has drawn; women carrying the burden of generations, who have been exploited through no fault of their own other than having had the misfortune of being born female in a male-dominated society.

From Essen she moved on a scholarship to New York where she danced with a company calling itself New American Ballet and for a season at the Met – which must have been hell for somebody like her. But really it was to study with different teachers that drew Bausch initially to New York. And study she did, with Antony Tudor, José Limón, Paul Taylor, Paul Sanasardo, and La Meri – though astonishingly enough not with Graham herself, but only with some of her protégés. Add to these her Essen experiences with Jooss, Hans Zullig, Lucas Hoving, and Jean Cébron, and one can form an idea about her school background. However, says Bausch, and not without a healthy dose of self-assurance: "I am not at all the disciple of anybody. I am just me."

Such fits of assertiveness are, however, extremely rare in her biography. Generally she is a very shy and aloof woman. She lives with Rolf Borzik, the designer of her pieces, but whether she has a private life, I very much doubt; anyway, nothing is known about it. In any event she leads such a discreet life that she refused to proffer any information at all when I started my German ballet dictionary, and it was only by subtly blackmailing her that I finally managed to draw from her some details about her family.

I first became aware of her as a choreographer during the late sixties when she did a couple of works for the performing group of the Folkwang School – rather withdrawn pieces with some enigmatic message and somewhat forlornly carrying on in beautiful formal patterns. There was a continuous flow to her movements, which were very beautiful to watch, and they had an undoubtedly contemporary quality that was difficult to categorize. There was something behind these movements, and if one couldn't say exactly what it was, it seemed to have to do with mute despair and mourning for a beautiful world in which man was going to seed.

Then Bausch did some experimental works for the Wuppertal house. One of them was called *Actions for Dancers*, in which she dealt with a rather freakish bunch of people and their reactions and non-reactions to each other – people who were obviously retarded or sick or derelict. I couldn't refrain from calling the work a sort of *La Syphilide*. However, in 1972 she did the *Tannhäuser* bacchanal in a Wuppertal production of the opera that was propelled by such a climactic, erotic urgency and so marvelously matched to Wagner's rising flood of music that it earned her a contract for the next season as Wuppertal's ballet director. The contract also had the provision that she could bring in most of the dancers with whom she had been collaborating in her Folkwang ballets.

Bausch started her Wuppertal directorship with programs that she shared with Jooss (*The Green Table, Big City*) and Agnes de Mille (for what must have been the first European staging of *Rodeo* in its original version). She herself contributed *Fritz*, a piece about family oppression and the way it cripples its children; a revue of pop songs from the twenties, which devastatingly revealed the idiocy of the texts (with the songs belted out by the dancers themselves); and a Mahler ballet simply called *Adagio/Five Lieder by Mahler,* referring to the Fifth Symphony and the *Kindertotenlieder*, respectively, which deals with the isolation and loneliness of modern man and his desperate unsuccessful attempts to communicate.

Reactions were sharply divided, and though there was never any doubt about Bausch's strong and stark individual gifts and her emotionally charged personal vocabulary, some found her unrelieved sense of drabness and doom just a bit too much – especially in the context of the Wuppertal repertory, which since the second program has not admitted a single choreographer other than Bausch. After *Fritz* and Mahler and their "us poor people" ostentatiousness, I accused her of her kitchen-sink outlook.

I was much happier, though, with her subsequent stagings of Gluck's operas *Iphigénie in Tauride* (1974) and *Orfeo ed Euridice* (1975), which were completely choreographed productions, dance-operas (as Bausch likes to classify them). In *Iphigénia* all the singers and the chorus were placed in boxes in the auditorium, in *Orfeo* the soloist singers moved among the dancers while they were simultaneously mirrored by dancers. These were productions far from the Balanchine or Ashton approach and in a strictly contemporary idiom, with the dancers not so much illustrating or emphasizing the drama as commenting on its emotional implications and at the same time focusing on the central issues of the opera's individual scenes. Thus, for instance, the four scenes of *Orfeo* were called "Mourning," "Death," "Peace," and "Dying." Of course Bausch dropped the happy end. These were certainly landmarks in the chronicles of Gluck production in our century.

Next came a fascinating Stravinsky program in 1975, a triple bill which consisted of the *Cantata* (under the title *Wind from West*), some smaller concert pieces (including the famous *Tango*) called *The Second Spring*, and *Sacre du Printemps*. The first is one of those enigmatic essays on people constantly on the move who search for new contacts, which nonetheless are dropped the minute they are established; the second, a farce about the amorous remembrances of an elderly middle-class couple on the eve of an anniversary; and *Sacre* rather closely adhering, if not to the original libretto then to the original sequence of scenes. Bausch's *Sacre* lacks any connotations of ancient Russia, set instead in an unspecified modern society. With only twenty-six dancers it emerged as a vision of the blackest terror and despair rather than as a purifying rite of hope and rebirth. For the first time, or so it would seem, Bausch had taken the title literally with the idea of spring (in the person of a hopeful and innocent young girl) being brutally sacrificed in this transmogrification.

Next followed her Brecht–Weill double bill, consisting of *The Seven Deadly Sins* and *Don't Be Afraid* (1976), the latter a concoction of the most popular songs from *Threepenny Opera*, *Mahagonny*, *Happy End* (the title song, which refers to a Salvation Army hymn), and *Berlin Requiem*. Some of these songs were sung by the dancers themselves, while others were attributed to legitimate actresses. Both are very grim and acid comments on the plight of women in a male-governed world; both plead for pity for those poor creatures who are the disposable products of a phallocratic society of male consumers.

Early in 1977 Bausch presented *Bluebeard – while Listening to a Tape Recording of Bela Bartók's Opera Duke Bluebeard's Castle*, which was exactly what the title said: a blow-up of Bartók's fifty minute opera to almost two hours of nonstop music coming from a tape recorder wheeled about the stage, with certain passages of the piece being constantly rewound and played all over again. To this music a couple who cannot separate and yet are unable to live together act out the various stages of their estrangement, with projections of themselves on the crowd of fellow-dancers. It's one of those embittered love–hate relationships that spares its participants no humiliation whatsoever. In the ensuing attacks and fights, the display of brute, physical force reached unprecedented heights, even for Bausch. There were some strong objections against such rape of Bartók's music, but I must say, even though I am a great lover of the opera proper, I was spellbound throughout the piece's excessive duration.

I parted company with Bausch, however, in her following *Come Dance With Me*, another one of her intermissionless two-hour productions, this one based upon nursery rhymes and children's songs, which, of course, were once again sung by the dancers themselves. In spite of its title there was very little actual dance in it. In fact this was the piece's very aim: to show how difficult even the most simple of human contacts have become, how utterly everybody is left to his or her own despair, despite everybody's frantic search for some personal happiness shared with a matching soul. It was a production that imprinted itself upon one's memory more through its scenic effects than through its dancing content – with an overwhelming sliding wall dominating the background, which people either toppled down or frantically, though in vain, tried to ascend. As in all her productions, starting with the Gluck *Iphigenie*, Bausch collaborated with Borzik as her designer.

One of Bausch's latest works is called *Renate Emigrates*, and it is classified as an operetta, set to songs and evergreens from musicals, films, et cetera, stretching from "Some Enchanted Evening" to the intermezzo from Franz Schmidt's *Notre Dame*. This lasts almost four hours and is set in the white-white surroundings of washing detergents. There is no character who could be identified as Renate. Instead we have a group of girls who, inspired by the songs' promises of eternal bliss and happiness, are not so much growing up as stagnating in fantasies of their true lover and who are constantly being disappointed – even shattered – in their completely unrealistic expectations. It is really a piece about the consequences of refusing to grow up and being forever imprisoned in the cocoon of one's childish dreams. In this work the dancers have to speak a lot, hold imaginary telephone conversations, write fictitious love letters, and so on.

Again the wealth of pictures completely dwarfs the dance content, which is reduced to some chasing around the stage. Bausch's by now notorious screwing turns inevitably finish with the collapse of the dancer and a couple of ballroom dancing steps. One's general reaction was mixed: admiration for the outcome of Bausch's unremitting probe into the follies of today's society and the force and power of her (and Borzik's) visual iconography which temper one's frustration of being offered so little dance.

Being invited to all sorts of festivals and sent abroad more and more by official German cultural institutions, Bausch and her devoted troupe of dancer–actor–singers – of which one must single out the Australian Jo-Ann Endicott, with her non-dancer's body an artist whose commitment to everything she does can move even hardboiled theatregoers to tears – have become one of the most talked about companies of the European contemporary theatre scene. At the same time she moves further and further from the confines of dance. It is very interesting to accompany her on her lonely path through today's theatre-scape, and her iconoclasm explains the success she and her troupe enjoy wherever they appear for a couple of guest performances. But it is as an alternative that a dance audience responds to her offerings, a sort of antidote against too many Balanchine and Ashton and Cranko and MacMillan and van Manen and Neumeier performances. However, as Wuppertal, the company's home city, has no chance to see any other form of dance and ballet, one can easily sympathize with the local subscribers getting thoroughly tired of being offered exclusively Bausch's black visions of our modern world where all one's hopes and wishes and dreams are constantly slaughtered.

Personally I can only, agree with what Edmund Gleede has written about Pina Bausch in an article dealing with her pictures and her ideology in the German ballet annual *Ballett* 1977:

> One can only wish that Pina Bausch will extend the range of subjects during the years to come. That man and woman are not destined for each other and also that all males are criminals may conform to her own individual and subjective truth. However, after four years of incessant indictment without concrete proof, the time has arrived to start hearing the witnesses. That men do own a penis doesn't turn them automatically into rapists. ... Where hope for tenderness between humans is so constantly ignored or simply refused, the result is finally untrustworthiness and massive resentment. ...
>
> To return to the aspect of tenderness. In contrast to differing opinions in our age of pornography, I am convinced that tenderness is a spiritual quality – even where it has physical consequences, I therefore do ask for more spirit, more tenderness and more charity from Pina Bausch for her choreography and for her audience because I am tired of having to consider suicide after every Bausch performance. And as long as she refuses me (and others) this thimbleful of hope for the reason of an objective truth, I will reject her.
>
> What we do need is a new Bausch. A Bausch who could stage *Samson et Dalila* – and this by adhering to the old story and not by having Samson cutting the hair off Delilah and piercing her eyeballs.
>
> To sum it up: What a pity for so much talent!

New York City

Amanda Smith

Originally published in *Dance Magazine*, September, 1984

The eagerly anticipated New York debut of Germany's Pina Bausch Wuppertal Dance Theatre at the Brooklyn Academy of Music June 12–24 was marked by the healthiest kind of controversy: Whether you loved it or detested it, it provoked you to think.

Based in an opera house in an industrial city on the Ruhr river and rightly regarded as one of Europe's most important choreographers, Bausch makes work that is controversial on several counts. Her theatrical mix is a combination of old and new. *The Rite of Spring,* the work for which she is best known, is radical in its unadorned primitivism – it is danced on a stage covered with earth – yet the source of much of its movement is surprisingly old-fashioned: Limón technique, garnered from Bausch's Juilliard days. Also time-worn is Bausch's world view. In an era when angst isn't stylish, she pursues her bleak vision; the vision makes us squirm at the same time we admire its rendering.

Controversial, too, is Bausch's form. Student and spiritual descendant of Kurt Jooss and Antony Tudor, Bausch now makes neither abstract nor strictly narrative works. Instead, her pieces, like those of Meredith Monk and Robert Wilson, are layerings of disparate elements, dreamlike stream-of-consciousness collages of dance, drama and music. *Tanztheater* (the company is called *Wuppertaler Tanztheater* in Germany) means dance and theatre, not one or the other, but both, enmeshed. *The Rite of Spring*, made in 1975, is the only pure dance work Bausch brought to America. Her later pieces – *Bluebeard, Café Müller, 1980* – are imagistic, theatrical voyages into the interior of fantasies, dreams, nightmares, where childhood and adulthood and the knowledge of death collide, where the loves and fears and vulnerabilities of men and woman are exposed and examined in all their sadly comic and brutal aspects.

In a press conference given upon her arrival here, virtually the first thing Bausch said was that her work was "about the relationships between man and woman. The pieces are about how much we want to be loved. We are all afraid of death." In *The Rite of Spring*, the gown the sacrificial victim wears is blood red – blood, the sap of life, and menstrual blood, the coming of age into womanhood. As she dances herself to death in the unstopped and unstoppable action of the dance, a strap of her thin gown slips down to reveal her naked breast. Sex and death are inextricably intertwined in the world of Pina Bausch.

Because *The Rite of Spring* enacts a primitive ritual, its outcome is resolved, definite. The later pieces are more enigmatic. Relationships are permanently tormented; there is no exorcism. In the dingy white walls and the leaf-strewn floor that comprise the late Rolf Borzik's set for *Bluebeard*, the central figures, a man and a woman, grapple compulsively with one another as others pass through like ghosts of their ancestors, their past lovers. Once the woman kneels before the man, between his legs as he sits on a chair, and as she reaches up his chest towards his face, he violently and repeatedly pushes her back to the floor.

In *1980,* at three and three-quarters hours the most ambitious and complex of the works Bausch brought to America, the images of masculine and feminine roles are multifaceted and ever shifting. A woman undresses a man as if to make love to him but instead puts a nylon stocking on him and applies makeup, lipsticking his nipples before she sadistically places matches between his toes and lights them. Elsewhere, couples stroll arm in arm and dance together on the grassy sod that fills the stage. Men and women sit on chairs, smoking and drinking and talking, as the lights fade like dusk descending before you go home to make love. Even in the midst of love, there is menace. Once, an authoritarian figure appears in the opera house balcony and commands those below on-stage to name their fears. The dancers offer various answers: rats, deep water, darkness, "when someone says 'I love you,'" fire, slaughterhouses, becoming blind, to be a soldier and go to war. "Madness and death," one woman says. "Is that all?" the Hitler figure asks contemptuously. "That's enough!" the woman replies angrily.

Bausch is at heart a choreographer, and even where there is not much pure dancing, physical imagery is at the very core of her work, expressing the little and the large dramas that are played out on her stage. What is perhaps her most stunning single physical image occurs in *Bluebeard* when phantasmal women in tawdry Victorian dresses, their long hair hanging and snarled with leaves from the floor, suddenly step up onto unseen rungs and cling to the walls of the room like moths.

Linked to the physical expressionism is the extraordinary and diverse musicality of Bausch's work. Her musicianship in *The Rite of Spring* contributes to its reputation as one of the best versions ever done. She plumbs the heft and weight of Stravinsky's great score, her dancers dropping forward like injured beasts to the thud of the bass drum. At the ritual's conclusion there is a moment of enormous impact when the sacrificial maiden plunges face forward to the floor on the music's final chord like a tree toppled in a forest. The full title of *Bluebeard* is actually *Bluebeard – While Listening to a Tape Recording of Bela Bartók's Opera, "Duke Bluebeard's Castle."* There, the man frenetically punches a tape recorder on and off, conjuring the sounds of Bartók's opera and thereby the plot of a man who locks up and murders his wives serves as a gloss on the brutal male-female relationship unraveling in Bausch's drama. In *Café Müller* the intermittent interjection of soulful, grief laden Purcell songs establishes and maintains the brooding, dreamlike atmosphere of the work as a sleepwalking woman stumbles through a ghostly café.

Bausch also manipulates the mood with music in *1980*. Weaving in and out of the proceedings is countertenor Alfred Deller's melancholy interpretation of "Willow Song," Desdemona's air as she readies herself for bed. Elsewhere, Judy Garland's recording of "Over the Rainbow" plays as the dancers disport themselves on the grass in various eccentric sunbathers' poses, an earthly paradise of sorts. Bausch's brilliant juxtaposition of music and physical image becomes a comment on the poignancy of the human condition.

The rendering of Bausch's work is in the hands of an extraordinary international company of twenty-six dancers, and if I yearn for more of the pure-dance pieces, it is because they are an assemblage of beautiful and diverse movers. Among them are Josephine Anne Endicott, a wonderfully lush dancer, even as her terror grows in *The Rite of Spring's* sacrificial solo; Meryl Tankard, showing her gorgeous feet in an exquisite dance as the red-haired floozy who patters through *Café Müller*, yet dippy and seductive in *1980*; Lutz Forster, bounding gleefully back and forth across the stage making a salad in *1980*, and, there too, Mechthild Grossman with her throaty voice, a motorcycle moll proclaiming everything "fantastic"; Beatrice Libonati as the battered lover in *Café Müller* and *Bluebeard*; Jan Minarik as the obsessive Bluebeard figure; and Bausch herself, the haunting presence in the background of *Café Müller*, thin and long-limbed and gaunt, like a figure in an Edvard Munch painting.

If Bausch's *Rite of Spring* has the quality of a prolonged scream, her later pieces seem like sentences half-uttered in sleep. Her work, imperfect – because the human condition is – but indisputably rich, recalls a legendary scene. On her deathbed, Gertrude Stein is reported to have asked, "What is the answer?" and then, sinking back into the pillows, "What is the question?"

Bausch's theatre of dejection

Arlene Croce

Originally published in *The New Yorker*, 16 July, 1984. © Arlene Croce

In the Louise Brooks movie "Diary of a Lost Girl," a sadistic matron in an orphanage makes the girls spoon up their soup to a metronomic rhythm. The rhythm of a Pina Bausch piece is obsessively regular. Bursts of violence are followed by long stillnesses. Bits of business are systematically repeated, sometimes with increasing urgency but more often with no variation at all. At every repetition, less is revealed, and action that looked gratuitous to begin with dissolves into meaningless frenzy. "Café Müller," which opened the Bausch season and set the pattern for it, is thirty-five minutes long and feels ninety; its subject is duration and repetition is its only device. The café – apparently it is meant to resemble a real place – seems to be the canteen of a mental hospital. A small cast of inmates gives us intermittent doses of violent/apathetic behavior while a woman who may be a visitor scurries noisily about in high-heeled shoes. Music from Purcell's operas drifts over the loudspeakers, doing its best to solemnize the goings on. "Café Müller," with its thin but flashy shtick, is a how-to-make-theatre handbook. It enshrines the amateur's faith in psychopathy as drama. Bausch herself is in it, entering the set at curtain rise and remaining onstage throughout. A thin, spectral figure in a nightgown, she is also sightless, and she creeps along a wall and huddles in the dark until the end, when she staggers dimly downstage and starts bumping into the furniture. It takes a considerable ego to cast yourself as a pathetic, sightless, wandering creature. When I saw Bausch playing the blind princess with the sad smiles in the movie "And the Ship Sails On," I thought she was a typical piece of hammy Fellini invention. But Bausch evidently sees herself as this wan, wasted Duse; the blind-seeress act is perfectly in keeping with the inverted romanticism of her theatre. There have been numerous clinical analyses of Bausch's Theatre of Dejection; they're beside the point. Bausch may have her hang-ups, but basically she's an entrepreneuse who fills theatres with projections of herself and her self-pity. Since there's nothing between us and her – no mediating dramatic rationale, no technique to transfigure and validate raw emotion – we think that she's somehow authentic, that her suffering, at least, must be real. She can't be just a little girl acting po' faced.

Bausch's power lies in having calculated audience voyeurism to a nicety, and those sad smiles have a way of curling up contemptuously when it comes to her favorite theme of men and women. In Bausch's theatre, men brutalize women and women humiliate men; the savage round goes on endlessly. The content of these bruising encounters is always minimal. Bausch doesn't build psychodramas in which people come to understand something about themselves and their pain. She keeps referring us to the act of brutalization or humiliation – to the pornography of pain. Presumably, the superficiality of it all is what allows the Wuppertaler Tanztheater to call itself that; *dance* is something it hardly ever shows us. (One of the great jokes of the season was the choice of this supremely unathletic company to open the Olympic Arts Festival.)

When the Wuppertalers do dance, they're strangely inhibited. They usually begin by standing in place and stretching and swerving the upper body this way and that, their hands locked over or behind their heads. They don't move their feet much except when they run, and then it's usually pell-mell. But it seems they only run in order to halt. Either they halt stymied (by banging into something or somebody) or they halt dead, feet slanted apart, eyes cast down, as if they'd suddenly realized they were violating the ground by running over it. The run motifs and the halt motifs are used in Bausch's version of "Le Sacre du Printemps." Running in herds (the Tribe) is opposed to running alone (the Sacrifice). The catalogue expands as the piece goes on: sweating, heavy breathing, clammy bodies slapping against each other, peeling wet clothes from clammy bodies. We'd already seen these motifs in "Café Müller," but there the stage was completely filled with little black tables and chairs, and in the "Sacre" it's covered with packed-down dirt, like a camping ground or like a Peter Brook set.

Bausch's covered floors have become famous, and I imagine the clinicians really do have something to say about this need to fill the floor end to end and wing to wing with objects or foreign substances: dead leaves are used in "Bluebeard," live grass in "1980." Another aberration – or perhaps it is an extension of the littering compulsion – is Bausch's use of sets with walls and ceilings that completely enclose the stage picture. For someone in search of dance theatre – or, indeed theatre of any kind – all this is just so much window dressing, and it's of the same order of unpleasantness as everything else. By getting sweaty dancers dirty, the earth floor adds an element of yuck to "Sacre" which the other pieces don't have, but the dead leaves and the grass are bad enough: they made the Brooklyn Academy, which isn't air-conditioned, smell like a stable. Naturally, you don't dance on such stages.

In spite of its yuckiness, the "Sacre" remains in memory as the only tolerable Bausch piece. But if the Stravinsky score sets limits on her tendency to maunder and repeat, it also amplifies and energizes her theme of female persecution. This must be the tenth or twelfth "Sacre" I've seen in the past five years. Every one but Paul Taylor's has used the score to whip up an excitement the choreography could not have sustained on its own. Bausch's version, which is about ritual murder with no reference to fertility, has no more feel for the rhythms of the score than Martha Graham's version did, earlier this season. In the Sacrificial Victim's dance, it reaches its wit's end long before the music runs out. If Bausch has a choreographic technique that she disdains to use in her "theatre" pieces, here was the place for it. But she produced a run-of-the-mill "Sacre." The only moment of tension – I found it agonizing – came when the choice of the Victim seemed about to settle on one of the little fat girls in the company.

The Bausch troupe contains quite a few members who don't look like dancers and are none too pre-possessing physically. They look their best in "1980;" the women dress up and comb their hair and put on makeup, and even the men seem civilized. When the whole cast of eighteen comes on like a chorus line; snaking through the audience and grinning in all directions, we can see that they mean to be likably batty, but then they go on to do vaudeville turns and little skits reminiscing about or reverting to their childhoods, and they're corny and tiresome. The casting is so determinedly egalitarian (everyone gets a chance to bore you) and the material is so clownish or so literally childish (actual children's games and songs, actually played and sung) that the fact that some, if not all, of these reminiscences are biographical has no weight. And why is it that everyone seems to have had a sad childhood? Because everyone belongs to the Theatre of Dejection, that's why. "1980," named for the year it was first put on, suggests what life in the Bausch company must be like: "Animal House" with *weltschmerz*.

The Theatre of Dejection builds down from the Theatre of Absurdity and the Theatre of Cruelty and other manifestations of the sixties; the cycle has come back to the raw pulp of abuse it started with. It is hard to believe in mental-asylum metaphors twenty years after "Marat/ Sade;" in audience-involvement techniques fifteen years after the Living Theatre; in bleak despair, in the prankishly surrealistic, in

monomaniacal simplicity, and in all the affectless contrivances of
avant-garde fashion which Bausch puts on the stage after two full
generations of American modern dancers have done them to death.
She is a force in European theatre, and perhaps that explains everything. (It explains quite a bit of Carolyn Carlson, an American choreographer now working in Europe, in the European mode. In exchange
for the dirt floors Bausch has from Peter Brook – who probably got *his*
from Gurdjieff's headquarters – Bausch gives Carlson madwomen in
lingerie.) To judge from the Eurotrash that has poured in on us in
recent seasons – a partial list would begin with all those terrible ballet
companies that preceded Bausch into the Brooklyn Academy, and
include Brook's "Carmen," Maurice Béjart, Jirí Kylián, and Patrice
Chéreau's "Ring" – there is not much resistance to such a force.

I can't say I was surprised by anything I saw done by the Wuppertal
Theatre, but there was one element I was surprised not to see. Bausch's
publicity has exaggerated the scandal and salaciousness in her work.
Some mild ribaldry, some rather unappetizing nudity are all she has.
As a theatre terrorist, she gets her main effects by repetition. People
throw each other against the walls not once but many times. Women
are caught in a sling and swung round and round and round not once
but many times. Men are undressed, paraded naked, and smeared with
lipstick not once but so frequently and maliciously that the point
reverses itself: the worm turns once too often, and Bausch's vengeance
becomes seemingly that of a woman who not only has hated to expose
herself for male delectation but has feared to. Body shame is a sub-
theme of the female exploitation theme. In "Café Müller," "Le Sacre
du Printemps," and "Bluebeard," the women most of the time wear
filmy slips without bras, which makes them look like a bunch of sad
sacks, and they use a characteristic Bauschian gesture: they hang their
heads and let their hands creep up the front of their bodies, lifting the
garment exhibitionistically as they go. Skirts are sometimes lifted
without implications of shame but never with implications of pleasure,
and it's typical of Bausch's males that they show no interest whatever.
It's typical, too, that when they strip they have nothing to show us.
I was unable to hold myself in the theatre for more than an hour of
"Bluebeard," the most concentrated of Bausch's feminist tirades, and
an hour and a half of "1980" (which was four hours long), but I should
be surprised to learn that Bausch was able to turn but one credible,
attractive image of masculinity. Having made women look worse on
the stage than any misogynist ever has, she is under no obligation
to men.

Wuppertal in London

Judith Cruikshank

Originally published in *Dance and Dancers*, October, 1987

Strangely, it is as a dancer that I remember Pina Bausch when she made her first visit to London several years ago as director of the Essen Folkwang company. Certainly she choreographed some items, but it is the memory of the performer that remained with me: tall, spare and commanding.

Nowadays it is as a choreographer that she is known, directing the Wuppertal Dance Theatre, and known as much by theatre as by dance specialists. Much of the advance publicity for her season at Sadler's Wells came from theatre critics, and there were a number of them in the audience at the performances I attended.

But, although her work involves speech, magic, eating and drinking, and little in the way of conventional dance, I think it must still be classed as ballet. Not just because the participants are dancers, all I believe with a mainly classical training, but because the works themselves are so carefully structured, the various elements added in such precisely measured doses, and the mood and pace so skillfully manipulated, and all this in a completely planned and set fashion.

The company brought two works to London for its two-week season: *1980, a piece by Pina Bausch*, and *Kontakthof*, both made within the last four years. *Kontakthof* is the older, premiered in 1978. In each piece Bausch uses similar devices, but producing a totally different effect.

1980 is given on a bare stage, but not quite bare since the entire floor is covered with real, growing green grass. According to the programme note (which I read only after seeing the ballet) it is a "Proustian exploration of childhood dreams and their destruction in adulthood." It starts with a single man wearing a dark suit sitting on a platform in the middle of the stage and feeding himself with what looks like Benger's food out of a large tureen, muttering with each mouthful "Une cuillére pour Papa, une cuillére pour Maman ... ." A beautiful girl in an elaborate evening dress sits on a chair and sings "Happy birthday to me," blowing out the flame from her cigarette lighter in place of birthday-cake candles.

Meryl Tankard, clad in a satin outfit of wondrous complexity and accessories that would provide a small exhibition in the theme of Kitsch, delivers a piercing monologue in true Edna Everage style. There is a great deal of processing up and down the stage by both men and women. Every now and again the entire cast, women in elaborate, slightly outdated evening dress, men in formal suits, descends in procession into the audience and, to the accompaniment of a maddeningly jolly little tune, they go through a routine of arm and head movements which reminded me of the kind of dances that used to be done in discotheques some twenty years ago when the dance floor became so crowded that actual body movement was impossible.

This routine was accompanied by the one attribute which, despite their varying physiques, styles, nationalities, every single dancer in the company could lay claim to: a knowing look. I suspect it must be the prime requirement of each new recruit, though I have to say that every member of the cast is a really first-class performer, and if I do not mention them all by name it is for lack of space, nothing else.

Bausch uses a similarly meaningless routine, but this time with the dancers walking round in a circle, in *Kontakthof*. Having performed it once, one of the women cries "That was so good – let's do it again in black!", and promptly the dancers rush off stage, to reappear with the women all in black dresses and go through the pointless arm-waving, bottom-scratching series of movements once more.

In *1980*, Bausch has certainly created a very atmospheric piece, full of gentle nostalgia. Events occur in a random fashion, rather like a process of recollection, where one memory leads to another, not necessarily in sequence, and childhood memories awake comparisons with adult life.

There are a magician, a gymnast, a violinist, a tea party. Tea is even served to members of the audience. The first half finishes as two of the dancers play an endless series of complex children's games involving territories and penalties in an atmosphere evoking twilight falling on a long summer evening. Meanwhile a wonderfully funny scene has almost the entire cast sunbathing in attitudes that show their determination to ensure that every last inch of flesh is a nice even brown, except Tankard resolutely hiding from the sun.

The second half begins with a beautiful dance, only glimpsed earlier on because of the surrounding watchers, in which Anne Martin dances like an ondine with a lawn sprinkler. But the innocence is retreating, and competitiveness is the order of the day with leg shows, talk shows, and everyone jostling for first place.

There is a certain amount of role reversal too. Some of the men have their clothes removed, or their faces painted. There is a flasher, but it is the lovely Mechthild Grossman rather than any of the men, and both sexes struggle to prove that they have the best pair of legs. The majority of the spoken part was given for London audiences in English – one exception being Janusz Subicz, the gruel eater, who confines himself to Polish or French.

The dancers tell you about their fears, their scars, their nationalities, at the end of the ballet you feel – rightly or wrongly – that you know them quite well. I was left with a feeling of gentle melancholy, although I had laughed a great deal, and regret for some of the lost days of my own childhood. Certainly Bausch is able to involve you in the ballet to such an extent that almost four hours pass without difficulty.

Kontakthof, too, strikes chords in the watcher, but far harsher and more bitter ones. According to the programme note it is set in a seedy German music hall. To me it looked like the kind of church or school hall where "young people's dances" were held in my youth. A very solid set with doors and windows, a curtained stage, all painted a dull grey, with institutional wooden chairs arranged around the walls.

The title of the ballet means, I believe, a meeting hall, or contact place, perhaps even the area of a prison where the inmates can meet. The theme seems to be the impossibility of ever really meeting honestly, without barriers or defenses. Anne Marie Benati and Dominique Mercy sit on opposite sides of the stage and shyly but eagerly remove their clothes as if in preparation to make love. But their consummation is interrupted by the rest of the cast and, still sitting on their chairs, they struggle back into their clothes. Later, by now fully clothed, each one drops to the floor in the middle of a group dance, taking up the attitudes of love, but quite separately, as if secretly embracing a lost memory.

Kyomi Ichida constantly begs members of the audience for a coin so that she can ride the mechanical horse which stands at one side of the stage – what about all those theories about young women and horses? But here it is no splendid white stallion, only a tacky child's toy.

Josephine Anne Endicott and Meryl Tankard have a series of duets, one of which consists of a promenade round the stage on three-quarter point, but in bare feet, so as to demonstrate the unnatural stance forced on the wearer by high-heeled formal shoes. Meanwhile, they are tugging at the strapless bras, the tight roll-ons and the chafing suspenders that they might be expected to wear under their formal gowns.

I found *Kontakthof* a very moving piece in many ways. Being of the generation that wore those dreadful dresses and went to those terrible dances may be part of the reason. Oh lucky young women of today, who have learned that the number of men who ask you to dance is not the most important thing in life! But it seemed that there was another underlying theme, the crippling constraints that society puts on truth and honesty, especially between men and women.

In one episode Tankard is surrounded by all the men in the cast, all of whom touch or caress her, but in a fashion which implies that they are taking from her rather than giving her comfort, affection, or whatever, and not one takes notice of the agony on her face. In a lighter vein Tankard and Endicott have a series of dances as slightly batty bacchantes clad in pink chiffon and lace; there is a long episode in which, like children, the dancers think of nasty little tortures they can inflict on one another, all done with a great deal of cheerfulness and resource. *Kontakthof* is a serious, and in some ways a bitter work, but it is far from being dull or unfunny.

Seeing these two pieces, it would seem that Bausch has discovered a vocabulary and a way of structuring her works that allows her to express her themes very clearly and entertainingly. Just how far she can take it I shall be very interested to see. The development from early works like *The Rite of Spring* is tremendous, and it will be fascinating to see just what kind of work she is producing three or four years from now. One final thought; a moment of pity for those good dance-loving citizens of Wuppertal who feel, deep down inside, that dance is really about pink satin slippers and swan feathers. I think it will be a long time before they see either from their local dance company.

Exits and entrances

Leonetta Bentivoglio

Originally published in *Artforum*, April, 1990. Translated from the Italian by Marguerite Shore

Pina Bausch's Tanztheater Wuppertal rejects the notion of an ideal body. Operating outside aesthetic imperatives, against ideologies of the "proper use" of the body, the mother of European dance-theatre violently reveals the transgressive power of movement. Every element of gesture finds expressive space in her world: elastic, infinite borders are restored to the body, which, freed from the role of mediator of significances, may outrageously fabricate emotions onstage. If archetypal tales are told in traditional ballet, if music is visualized through the inscription of pure signs in space in abstract neoclassical dance, if subtextual associations between expression and its form are constructed in historical modern dance, Bausch leaps over these conventions with unprecedented impudence. In her performances, everything that moves about onstage has an implicit dramatic autonomy, which is inscribed in the quality of gesture, in that dynamic relationship between bodies that makes up the fabric of the fresco, in the obsessiveness of the leitmotivs and the dead zones, in the polymorphous perversion expressed by bodies that can never be homologous, but instead are strongly individuated. The body, in Bausch's work, is personified; it does not assume a role as it might don a costume. Freeing itself from symbolic functionalism, discovering a lost unity in its own irrational components, the body becomes an agent of its own history.

The associative criterion that guides the montage of images, by which each of these bodily histories is communicated, is determinably elliptical. In Bausch's theatrical collages, a freedom of connections is in force, recalling a flow of memories or of consciousness. Seeking out the matter that forms dreams, she pursues the mysterious law that leads to their development. Thus, for Bausch, "dreaming" about Palermo does not involve looking at its exterior elements – the facades, the artworks, the folklore. As revealed in *Palermo, Palermo*, her newest creation (the piece had its Italian premiere in late January at Palermo's Teatro Biondo), the city is by no means the land "where lemon trees flower," in Goethe's romantic phrase. Rather, *Palermo, Palermo* is a land of gray cement blocks (the upsettingly dynamic set design is by Peter Pabst), which end up carpeting the stage after the terrifying collapse of the wall that claustrophobically covers the proscenium when the curtain goes up. And if the image cannot help but recall the Berlin Wall, other influences, from Peter Stein to Peter Brook, reverberate in the blanket of ruins. There is omnipresent in Bausch's work a willingness – a need – to plunge into the most unpleasant effluvia of a civilization and a culture: more than the dream of lemon trees we have the nightmare of incomplete constructions scattered like diseased excrescences along the Sicilian coast joining Palermo to Bagheria (in Bausch's work, every vision is by its nature polysemous.)

But *Palermo, Palermo* is also an infernal wave of tolling bells, or of cicadas driven mad with thirst, or of sorrowful marches. Or fireworks of some religious festival, which seems to move in rhythm more to the warpath than to the ways of the Lord. Or a group of men holding up an emaciated widow – shadows of an ancient male tyranny, one of the most potent and insistent themes in the piece. Or the advance of a multitude of people (self-absorbed as the Sicilians can be) who rhythmically throw to the wind bundles of garbage – threads of an everyday intimacy in an urban ritual of sowing, a fecund appeal to a suffering city. Or, yet again, it is a large, half-naked man-tuna, who swims on land, to the rhythmic accompaniment of a noisy soundtrack, perhaps attempting to save himself from the *muttanza*, the bloody tuna harvest of Sicilian custom.

Many other sacrificial acts are consummated in the concentrated metropolitan "Casbah" of *Palermo, Palermo*, between views of interiors grazed by the spectral gleams of televisions and pieces of flesh that fill the pockets: revolvers aimed in the dark and exploding bombs, large white puffs of smoke seen against a dome of stormy sky, and red earth that rains down like an erupting volcano.

Palermo, dreamed by Bausch, is a city that is both prostituted and holy, baroque and extremely violent, in harmony with history and infested with decay, seductive in its contradictions, which burn with the same intensity as the row of lighted candles, as in a church, which are supported by the arm of a man who plays a saxophone. And his heartrending lament tells of all the pleasure of death to be found in the heroine's "holes." At the finale, a procession of women, bent over, legs crossed, faces hidden in their laps, interlace in a long collective sob.

This interior diary of Palermo, as interpreted with the unspoiled eye of a foreigner, was the result of a sojourn of several weeks that Bausch made to the city. But this fact should by no means lead one to infer that Bausch's work has taken a narrative turn. More precisely, here perhaps with greater force than ever before, Bausch's hallmark assemblage of images is revealed to the spectator with a dry, obsessive transparency and a disarming shamelessness that dispenses with her usual irony, or black humor. This time, the parade of visions displays with absolute, despairing crudeness, the grand themes of auteur theatre: the submergence in memory, the pursuit of innocence, the conflicting relationship between the sexes, the violence of the world, the anxious need for answers to existential questions, the inexhaustible need for love.

Dance view
The Bausch imagination still bedazzles

Anna Kisselgoff
Originally published in *New York Times*, 20 October, 1991

Nowadays, The Pina Bausch Tanztheater Wuppertal is greeted with the kind of anticipation reserved for a cult classic at a film festival. The atmosphere around the recent and fourth visit by the German company to the Brooklyn Academy of Music had none of the controversy that accompanied the troupe's New York debut in 1984.

Progressively, the imprint of Miss Bausch's brilliant imagination has made itself felt: We expect her pieces to contain an unflinching look at painful male–female relationships, the bitter humor of human existence, repetitive structures with confessional vignettes, the use of trained dancers who virtually do not dance but who move with nuances of gesture and timing that only a choreographer could conceive.

This time, Miss Bausch presented two pieces created a decade apart, "Bandoneon" (1980) and "Palermo, Palermo" (1990). It is now evident, as it was not in 1984, that each Bausch work is a chapter in a continuing serial. We are under the impression that we know the players; we wait to see what they will do next.

Yet the idea that we really do know the dancers as people is an illusion. The moments in which they recall actual experiences are theatricalized and put in unfamiliar contexts – raw material brought to a boil. Look at the performers off stage and they appear much younger than the mature types they play on stage.

Nonetheless, the childhood recollections recited in each piece have a recognizable resonance. For her detractors, Miss Bausch is merely playing high-level charades, but she has taught audiences how to look afresh at a performance, to avoid impatience, to wait for her dissociated images to add up.

"Palermo, Palermo" has even less of a thread of continuity than usual, although those who have visited the Sicilian capital say the rubble-filled stage evokes that city. The piece's structure is rooted in a series of vignettes, vivid and polished enough to communicate on their own. But several leitmotifs serve as metaphors for the world at large.

Jan Minarik, a Bausch veteran, portrays a transvestite who cooks food on a steam iron; Julie Shanahan orders men to love her and also to pelt her with tomatoes; a real dog comes in and then exits; women in bathing suits do handstands; Beatrice Libonati, in her Anna Magnani phase, is mistreated by macho men. A sense of overall disjunction is emphasized.

Nonetheless, a piece that begins with the collapse of a cinder-block wall (designed by Peter Pabst) ends with the promise of rebirth as trees are lowered to the stage from the grid above. Like it or not, a Bausch piece is not boring.

"Bandoneon," which has the unity of early Bausch works, derives its title from the accordion used to play Argentine tangos. The piece appears to be about training and virtuosity. Training in ballet is equated with training for other pursuits, including life and love. The only time the dancers actually look as if they are doing a tango is when they are on their knees or sitting down.

The set by Gralf-Edzard Habben is the interior of an old European café, with large photographs of prizefighters, circa World War I. Yet Marion Cito has dressed the men in modern-day three-piece suits and the women in 1950's dresses. This sense of the past in the present, augmented by scratchy phonograph records of tangos, suggests a timelessness about the emotions on view. Whatever the era, individuals seek out partners for companionship.

"Bandoneon" also becomes an examination of the nature of performance. Dominique Mercy, one of Miss Bausch's most nuanced male dancers, begins and ends the piece doing pliés in a romantic tutu. Miss Libonati sings "I Pagliacci" to a mouse in a glass tank. Mr. Minarik, Silvia Kesselheim and Nazareth Panadero demonstrate how ballet teachers tied their feet together to perfect turns or encouraged a leg to go higher by lighting a cigarette under it.

The search for love as a theme makes its entry with several depressed couples. The images grow increasingly powerful as the intimate is made public. Strangers go through loveless rituals.

A blackout suggests an intermission but signals only that time has passed. Stagehands strip the stage bare in full view of the audience, and a second blackout links acts I and II. Miss Panadero opens up a piece of paper as if to read from it, but does so only after the intermission. Her rendering in English of a poem by Heine expresses yearnings for love that are contrasted with crude images of women as inanimate objects – live mannequins lifted straight up by partners reaching under their dresses.

The pain underlying the beauty of love and performance is suggested by having Miss Panadero lie on the floor and roar from time to time. Spontaneity made formal is expressed when the dancers repeat a sequence immediately: every detail is reproduced with exactness. Does an artist seek applause or simply the satisfaction of performing? The thirst for applause is implied by a diva who keeps taking bows.

Training in ballet is equated with training in sports: Mr. Minarik teaches men how to play soccer but trips them up. Yet the goal of sports is hardly the goal of art.

Virtuosity takes many forms. Jakob Andersen holds a backbend for nearly 10 minutes, but the applause from a simulated audience onstage is feeble. Mr. Minarik maneuvers himself in and out of a sweater with his wrists tied. "A dancer who doesn't smile on stage is no dancer," says Mr. Minarik, quoting his folk-dance teacher in Czechoslovakia. The cast advances toward the audience with pasted smiles, and Mr. Mercy is in a tutu again.

That art is artifice is no secret, but Miss Bausch has something to add, as usual, to the restating of a truth.

Theatre of despair and survival

Chris de Marigny

Originally published in *Dance Theatre Journal*, November, 1991

The two hottest tickets in Paris this June were for Pina Bausch's Wuppertal Dance Theatre and William Forsythe's Frankfurt Ballet. These two companies were playing opposite each other at the Théâtre de la Ville and the Châtelet Theatre, selling over 3000 tickets a night between them. Forsythe has been lionized over the last few years, whereas Pina Bausch has now been a major figure in the dance and theatre world for at least twelve years. The fact that it is now necessary to go to Paris to see either company is a sad reflection on the current problems faced by British producers who would like to present overseas work. Stephen Remington of Sadler's Wells Theatre said at a recent press conference that to present Pina Bausch in London, which he would very much like to do, would mean having to find over £250,000 in sponsorship, that being the difference between the box office on a sold out season, and the cost of presenting the company. This autumn, Sadler's Wells will present the American Paul Taylor Dance Company, and the sponsorship for that is for a very similar amount.

Bausch's latest production *Palermo, Palermo* is co-produced by the Theatre Biondo in Palermo, and Andres Neumann International. The work was started in Wuppertal, and then developed in Palermo during the long residency. Nearly eighteen months old, this production has seasoned and is now being presented for the first time in a major dance capital. It is ten years since I last saw Pina Bausch live, mostly due to the vagaries of international travel commitments and above all, to the problems of English presenters mentioned above. This prolonged gap is useful in one sense only, in that it does provide one with an opportunity of assessing how she and her company have moved on in the decade.

On walking into the large open auditorium of the Théâtre de la Ville, the first thing that confronts you, even before you sit down, is a large traditional curtain. This is a surprise, as the great stage of the

Théâtre de la Ville is usually used without any cross arch or any other performer/audience divide. Eventually the curtain opens in total silence to reveal a solid grey breeze-block wall rising from the floor to ceiling and across the full width of the auditorium. A deafening silence extends the tension interminably until, without any warning, the entire structure literally collapses backwards onto the stage with a tremendous roar – rising clouds of dust enveloping the stage. This collapsed structure dominates the action for the next three hours. During and after the show I pondered much on the significance of the wall. Clearly no German artist can invent such a structure without knowing that it will be taken by many as a reference to the Berlin Wall. This device was conceived before the Wall came down, but was first presented in Palermo after that event. According to the dancers with whom I talked, they did consider for some time if they should keep the wall or not, and eventually decided that they had to. Whilst this association is unavoidable, it would be a mistake to conclude that this is its sole meaning or reference (of this more later.)

As the dust subsides, dancers and various other characters, who turn out to be stage hands, start to remove some of the more unstable sections of the collapsed wall. But very quickly it becomes clear that the debris of bricks covering the stage is in large measure going to stay in place. For the rest of the evening it is an obstacle course, particularly for the women in their very high stiletto heels (a Bausch trademark), or occasionally in bare feet as they strut, stride, run, and skip across the space. As the piece develops, the stage will become even more cluttered with the rubbish of urban life – plastic bottles, paper wraps, decaying food, a mountain of apples, until the entire environment becomes a visual metaphor for the green movement. In fact, as the piece progresses, it becomes apparent that the rubble of the wall is also a metaphor for the degeneration of urban life in the western world. No doubt Palermo has its breeze-block slums and decaying housing estates as does virtually every other major city. Against this background we have the now familiar series of short episodes, acted out by the company, largely in solos, often in duets, and occasionally by the entire group.

So what in the Bauschian theatre has changed, and what remains the same? The men still wear suits and sensible shoes, the women still wear their little shift dresses, changing occasionally into more glamorous outfits. The men and women still alternate between flirting with the audience and drowning in a sea of their own personal and seemingly private angst. The stage floor, as in so many of Bausch's works, is covered with a substance unfriendly to dance (previous floors have included grass lawns and fields of carnations). But this floor is by far the most threatening. This obsession with the floor could only have been dreamed up by a choreographer, and a contemporary one at that. One is never allowed to forget the ground – no chance here, as in ballet, of gravity-defying leaps, or floating up into the spiritual ether.

What has gone is the element of repetition. Scenes and events now follow each other in short bursts. Each scene offering a new idea or visual image, each one alternately arresting or entertaining the audience. Ten years ago, in works such as *1980* and *Kontakthof*, events were often drawn out for excruciatingly long periods of time, or endlessly repeated. Bausch has junked all this in favor of a format that reminds you of the revue music hall. Performers strut confidently to the front of the stage to deliver a poem, a story, or some other trick and walk away smirking, or occasionally ignoring the audience completely, nose in the air. On the other hand, some scenes still bear a huge emotional load and are affecting and upsetting at the deepest level. What has happened is that Bausch has now become a master of theatre. She knows exactly how long a scene should last, when it should be changed, when to crack a joke, and when to make the audience ponder and reflect upon the events it is witnessing. It is this mastery of theatre that distinguishes her from the literally hundreds of choreographers who have been influenced by her during the decade. In fact it is hard to conceive of the new European dance theatre without taking into account her seminal influence. Admittedly there are other important influences: the American Robert Wilson, Japanese Butoh and Bausch's own historical antecedents in Expressionist German dance theatre of the Twenties and Thirties. But none dominate in the way that Bausch has, and seemingly still does. In France one can hardly think of a choreographer apart from the work of Bagouet, Cremona, Duboc, Hallet-Egehan and Hervé Robbe, who has not come, in part, under her influence. Notable artists who have taken some of the best aspects of her work included Anna Teresa de Keersmaeker, Ian Spink, Lloyd Newson and Wim Vandekeybus.

It is in the attitude of the dancers, the protagonists themselves, that the real sea change has occurred. In one of the early scenes after the wall has collapsed, a tall, thin, blonde haired woman (Julie Shanahan) looking rather vulnerable, walks to the middle of the stage and sits facing the audience. Two men arrive and empty a bag of dirt over her head. Unmoved, she demands that they now throw tomatoes at her. The demands become increasingly aggressive "at my stomach! – now! – more!" She continues "Kiss me! … *Kiss me!* … KISS ME! … *KISS*

ME! … STOP!" The men do as they are told, dutifully, humbly. They are told to go away, commanded to return, to continue. A few scenes later, Nazareth Pandero strides onto the stage in a deceivingly "pretty girl" pink lace dress, clutching a large bunch of extremely long spaghetti. She addresses the audience confidently in a deep throaty voice: "These are *my* spaghetti. *All* of them. This one is *mine* (showing a spaghetti strand). And this one … *and* this one … *AND* this one. I never lend *any* of them! Because they are MINE." This speech continues in a like vein for several minutes in a highly aggressive manner and then, flashing a charming smile, she quickly leaves the stage, negotiating her way across the rubble.

Bausch's women are now demanding, self-confident and aggressive. Julie Shanahan may be a masochist, but she is a demanding one, fully in control of the action. This remains largely true for the whole of *Palermo, Palermo*. The men on the other hand, remain unassertive, obedient, and for most of the time, led by the women. In the present ensemble, there are a whole host of remarkable female performers with strong personalities. Amongst the men, only the veterans Dominique Mercy and Jan Minarik hold their own. Whilst the rest of the men are adequate performers, they lack any real individuality. Gone are the days when the women clung to the men imploringly, in what Roger Copeland has referred to as "the Bauschian unrequited embrace." This personality change amongst the sexes completely alters the feel and character of Bausch's work.

The first half of the show lasts nearly two hours, and scenes such as the ones above follow each other with extraordinary rapidity. As the debris of the wall is being cleared at the beginning of the evening, Beatrice Libonati, a small, dark, stocky woman with unusually strong legs in a plain black dress dances a short running-skipping solo. She criss-crosses the stage in bare feet, making me want to shout "watch your ankles!" Her next appearance is straight after the masochist's scene with the tomatoes, when she arrives on stage looking like Anna Magnani in a Sicilian peasant drama, clutching a large plastic bottle of water. She appears menacingly before a rather aggressive-looking group of men in dark suits. Slowly she places the bottle at an angle between her legs, pointing towards the floor. She undoes the cap and stares intensely at the men while the water "pisses" away. This image mesmerized the audience, and indeed it seemed to be a powerful metaphor for what was now clearly becoming the dominant attitude between the men and women. Water reappears as symbol and metaphor in various scenes throughout the evening. In the South water is precious, in the North, it is a symbol of purity and cleansing; in other cultures, it is a symbol of the untamable quality of nature. Following this they dance a septet where she is picked up and manipulated by the men, who turn her upside down and carry her about in a variety of positions. At one moment she lies across an assembled line of their feet, from which they raise her from the ground, and rock her as if in a lullaby. She bounds up, runs round them, over their hands, straight onto and up the side cross arch of the stage, seemingly running in a full circle through the air, and back down to the ground again, aided almost invisibly by one of the men.

Of the men, Dominique Mercy is highlighted as a character through the close relationship with Nazareth Panadero. A quiet, but insistent presence on the stage, he is unbearably meek and neurotic, clutching his individual spaghetti, compulsively breaking it now and then. Jan Minarik is the only man who stands in opposition to this version of masculinity. Tall and heavily built, he starts the evening in a number of blustering and fairly comic routines, after which he moves to the extreme left of the stage, where, throughout the rest of the first half, he watches television, fries eggs on the back of an iron, and gradually changes his outfit. As we come near to the end of the first half, Minarik now becomes a late Sixties, San Francisco type drag. He flirts more and more openly with the audience, in an outfit nothing less than a parody of the Statue of Liberty. Smiling tauntingly, he carries a large sign across the stage in Marcel Marceau style, on which is scrawled the word "Pause." Bausch knows the transformatory aspect of theatre, and can make political statements without ever being literal, whilst allying them to the personal and the particular. I counted over sixty such scenes in the three hours. While a few were resumed with variations in the second act, this is still an extraordinary catalogue of invention. Very few were dull or unmoving, many were mesmerizing or at the least highly entertaining. The Sicilian theme recurs, particularly in a march towards the end of the first half, to music played on a Jews Harp, and those strange, off-key trumpet-like instruments that are so often used in the South. Space prevents me from recounting much else. Towards the end of the evening there is a final procession and an Italian-style dirge where the entire cast jump bent forward on one leg like some broken bird of prey. Meanwhile upended cherry blossom trees descend from the flies. Out of the ensemble strides Janusz Subicz, an older dancer with a disarmingly naive young man's smile. He proceeds to tell a story about the geese who saved their lives by persuading the fox to let them finish their story – the geese went wah-wah-wah – but you know geese, they never stop, the story continues …

Bausch's view of humanity is still characteristically bleak, but whereas before the struggle between the sexes was uneven, it is now posed in equal opposition. Whereas before the view of the world was one of despair, there is now a sense that it is worthwhile continuing, perhaps even with some wry humor, even if there is no real hope. This is a theatre of despair and survival.

Bausch's inferno

Joan Ross Acocella

Originally published in *Art in America*, January, 1992

In two works, created a decade apart but seen together recently at BAM, Germany's Pina Bausch showed signs of tempering her trademark ferocity with poetic images of an expanded emotional range.

An evening with the German "dance theatre" artist Pina Bausch and her Wuppertal Tanztheater is like nothing else. The typical Bausch piece is three hours long, with a cast of about 20 people, men and women such as you might encounter on your public transportation system. One is chubby, one is thin. One has glasses, one is balding. The men are dressed in business suits. The women wear dresses, often luxurious dresses, and high, high heels, though at the same time they look a little the worse for wear, as if they had just run the two-minute mile or been saved from drowning.

There's rarely a story, though there may be a dominant motif, such as love or death (indeed, usually love or death). Basically, a Bausch piece is a collection of skits, and the subject of the skits is cruelty or absurdity. None of the action is realistic. It is surrealistic. It works by displacement, disjuncture. A woman kicks a man in the rear, and he reaches inside his jacket, produces a package of meat and throws it to the floor. She kicks him again and again, and each time he reaches inside his clothes – now up his sleeve, now up his pants leg – and pulls out another package of meat, which he surrenders. A woman begs two men to throw tomatoes at her. They do so, and she yells, "Throw more! Throw them in my face!" In between peltings, she yells, "Hug me! Take my hand!" They do, and then she starts yelling for more tomatoes.

All this takes place, typically, on a stage covered with something you don't normally find on a stage, such as water or dirt or flowers. (Bausch's newest piece, *Palermo Palermo*, opens with a five-ton concrete wall falling backward; the rubble covers the stage throughout the work.) This not only heightens the sense of strangeness, but impedes the performers, forces them to pick their way through something, watch their step. We feel their difficulty and danger. The lighting is typically dim, cold and dirty, as if the action were transpiring in some back alley, lit by a distant street lamp. In the background, music plays: snatches of jazz or, more often, of opera, songs of love and beauty from a bygone world of meaning.

But what is most distinctive in Bausch's theatre, wholly her own, is the atmosphere of embarrassment, of exposure and discomfort, that pervades the action. Rarely do five minutes pass without our looking up a woman's dress, and that's not all we look up. The performers show us the insides of their mouths, the insides of their noses, A man reaches down a woman's dress front and pulls out her breasts. Another man tells us how much he likes to take a good piss, and unbuttons his pants as if to do so. A woman pretends to fart. A man comes in with something hanging out of his nose. There's often a puddle on the floor, with everyone walking around it and trying to act as though it's not there.

The embarrassment is forcibly shared with the audience. Bausch makes us feel it – makes us remember the time we made a puddle on the floor, the time we peeked at something we weren't supposed to look at. A woman turns her back to us and pulls up her dress, and a man puts his hand on her – we can't see where. Then slowly, slowly, they turn around, and we see that his hand is only on her abdomen. We're forced into voyeurism, then accused of voyeurism. The front rows of the audience are forced into more direct action. The performers are always coming to the edge of the stage and asking the people in row A to give them money or take their picture or pet their mouse. Elsewhere the audience's collusion is simply taken for granted. The performers look out at us with that knowing smile so typical of German art, as if they owned a brothel that we had just entered with a very special request.

But I am summarizing 15 years of work: the 13 pieces, extending from 1975 to 1990, that Bausch has brought to New York in the course of her four visits to the Brooklyn Academy of Music (1984, 1985, 1988, 1991). One can safely make such a summary, for Bausch is very consistent. Her themes are always the same. Somebody's always kicking somebody else. Somebody's always sticking porridge in his ear. Nevertheless, the work has changed, as was made very clear by Bausch's fall season at BAM, which consisted of two works made 10 years apart, *Bandoneon* from 1980 and *Palermo Palermo* from 1990.

Above all, there has been a let up on cruelty. When Bausch first brought her company to the United States in 1984, this was the thing in her work that amazed everybody: the sheer, stark brutality, usually inflicted by men on women. Perhaps the most indelible image of that first season was the episode in *Café Müller* where a man and a woman took turns picking each other up and hurling one another directly into a wall. Again and again they did it, as if they were souls in hell, condemned to do this for eternity.

The following year, Bausch returned to BAM with a piece called *Gebirge* in which she did herself one better. Here a woman came out in a black slip, pulled her slip up over her head and lay face down in a pile of dirt, whereupon a man came and slashed her back with an unseen weapon, leaving a huge red gash. (This was done with a crayon or something, just as the wall in *Café Müller* was padded, but it was very convincing.) Then the woman got up and pulled her slip back and forth between her legs as if she were masturbating. Then she lay down again, pulled her slip up again, and he slashed her again. This too went on and on, and it only ended because the man left. The woman lay down again, waiting for him to slice her, but apparently he got tired of it. In these pieces the women got some revenge, usually in the form of humiliation, pulling the men's pants down or painting their faces with lipstick. Or the men were shamed by having to wear women's clothes: dresses, girdles, tutus. But the power was definitely not equal, and regardless of the power balance, the image of male–female relations was unrelievedly brutal.

Bandoneon comes from that period in Bausch's work, and though it has no gashings, it has the same feel for cruelty. It is also heavy on another form of aggressiveness that Bausch used to favor, and that is the tale of childhood woe. With seemingly autobiographical directness, the performers tell us how their ballet teachers used to hold lighted cigarettes to the undersides of their legs to make them raise their legs higher, how their nursemaids used to punish them by holding their heads down in buckets of cold water. This is the same sort of gun-to-the-head appeal to the audiences feelings that the performance artist Karen Finley habitually uses, and its effect in Bausch's work, as in Finley's, is one of self-pity, which rubs off on the more potent images of cruelty and makes the whole thing start to look like a temper tantrum – a big long personal complaint by Pina Bausch about how hard life is and how everybody was mean.

The note of complaint is underlined in these early works by what was then Bausch's fondness for repetition, and particularly for canonic form: she will have one couple start a series of actions, then another couple start the same series of actions a few seconds later, then another couple and another, so that we can see how mechanical human behavior is, how we do everything by rote. In both content and form, then, these early works have a kind of relentlessness, a truncheon-like quality, that is probably supposed to be an image of life but which finally looks like a failure of imagination. *Bandoneon* is no exception. I saw a lot of people sneaking up the aisle during the second half, and I know why.

But *Palermo Palermo*, which Bausch made last year, is different. Commissioned by the city of Palermo (hence the title), it does not seem to be about Palermo or Sicily or Italy or anything other than what Bausch's work has always been about. But the emotions have become less insistent at the same time that the imagery has become more varied, more complex. The images are not pinned so tightly to their emotional origin. They don't yell at us "This is how bad men are!" or "This is what my mother did to me!" They range more freely; they obey internal laws; they flower.

Here is a moment from the piece. A lovely man named Geraldo paints his nails bright red, then goes to the back of the stage, where he disrobes and proceeds to take a bath. In the meantime a man named Francis takes off his shirt, washes it, puts it back on soaking wet, affixes a number of wax candles to his right arm and lights them. A woman named Quincella appears, smears her lips with white powder and orders Francis to play music for her. He goes and gets a sax-ophone, comes back, sits down and plays the whole of "Stormy Weather" – plays it very beautifully, considering that hot candle wax is coursing down his arm the whole time. Now and then during the song, Geraldo waves at us from the back and holds his hand up to show how nice his nails look. Quincella stands implacable. The scene also includes a woman with a stocking over her head and a gun in her hand. She sits and listens to the song. When it's finished, they all go away.

That scene includes most of Bausch's regular themes – cruelty (Quincella issuing orders), humiliation (the feminizing of Geraldo), emergency (the woman with the gun), visceral discomfort (the wet shirt against the skin, the candle wax dripping down the arm) – but the emotions involved are softened, and mixed into an ambiguous and poetic whole. The scene is *composed*: it has many parts, and they all fit together and are true to the scene rather than to some pressing single message. The same is true of other scenes. Cruelty is still there, but it seems to have dived down into itself and found a more complicated inner life. At one point the veteran Bausch actor Jan Minarik takes a knife and seems to cut off a piece of his hand, whereupon he takes this slice of meat, cooks it on the surface of a hot iron and eats it with a smile. As with the woman ordering the men to pelt her with tomatoes – the scene that opens *Palermo Palermo* – you can no longer tell just who is the victim and who the aggressor.

I wish Bausch would get over her *hypocrite lecteur* obsession. In much of *Palermo Palermo*, Minarik is on the sidelines giving us that I-know-what-you're-thinking smile, I know what I'm thinking, too, and it's not about eating a piece of my hand. This constant need to implicate the audience seems to me a mark of insecurity that Bausch can now afford to give up, the same way she has given up ranting. As for her linear structure – her habit of building her pieces just by tacking one scene onto the next – I have stopped wishing she would give it up. Apparently it is the result of her compositional method. (She assembles the company, asks them questions about their lives and their feelings and then builds scenes out of their answers.) It is a part of her, and to complain of it is like complaining of morbidity in Poe or banality in Roy Lichtenstein. Furthermore, now that she is no longer so attached to repetition, it is less wearying. (Now, instead of AAAABBBBB, we get ABCD.) Finally, it is her metaphor for duration – for the way things in life just go on and on.

What has changed is her sense of how they go on and on. At the end of *Palermo Palermo*, one of the actors (Janusz Subicz) tells a story. A bunch of geese are caught by a fox, and the fox says he is going to eat them. "Okay," say the geese, "but first you have to let us say our prayers." So the fox waits, and they begin to pray. And they are still praying, says Subicz. End of story. So that's how Bausch sees it now. Before, we were getting eaten every minute. Now we're praying, prior to getting eaten. It's not a big shift – you can't get much done in either circumstance. You just go from moment to moment. So the structure has stayed the same, but the tone has changed, and the work has thereby become freer and deeper.

Pina, queen of the deep

Valerie Lawson

Originally published in *Sydney Morning Herald*, 17 July, 2000

Pina Bausch is a beautiful woman. She is also obsessive, exhausting, elusive, occasionally infuriating and magnetic. This German queen of dance theatre fixes her subjects with deep-socketed blue eyes and, well, they melt. Dancers fall in love. So do audiences, who greet her work with ritualistic slow clapping. On their feet. Twenty-minute curtain calls. Pina grips her dancers' hands. She gazes into the auditorium, her pale face a mixture of gratitude and exhaustion.

Her setting is Wuppertal, a rainy city in the Ruhr Valley, where she has run her company for a quarter of a century. It's not far from Cologne, but unlike that city, has no awe-inspiring cathedral. In fact there's no reason at all to visit except for business (chemicals, pesticides), to boggle over the mechanics of the unique overhead railway, or to see Bausch.

I went there in May, primed for the best and worst. A former dancer with Tanztheater Wuppertal Pina Bausch, Australian-born Jo Ann Endicott, had promised on the phone: "You meet Pina, you fall in love." A few days later, I asked ballet superstar Sylvie Guillem if she had ever worked with Bausch. She shook her head. "Pina? You work for her … I think it's like joining a cult."

There was no knowing how a meeting would go. Some had warned that Bausch never answered direct questions. Perhaps a few crumbs might be forthcoming over supper with lots of coffee and cigarettes. The one certainty, clear from watching rehearsal videos of her company, was that Bausch would be chain-smoking Camels or Lucky Strikes.

After the build-up came the reality. We talked in a meeting room at the theatre, two days after the premiere of her latest work, *Wiesenland* (*Meadowland*). The opening night had not gone well; Bausch was still making structural changes to the piece which was then without a title. She wore black and sat, impassively, waiting for the questions.

Her face has been accurately described as "an early Picasso" long, white, chiseled. Her slender fingers were never without a cigarette. Questions on her work were met with a disconcerting silence. A very long silence.

At last came the right question and the sun came out. The change was as unexpected as it was a relief. The transformation from an anguished 59-year-old into a blithe young woman arrived when I asked how she felt when she went to dance class for the first time, as a child.

"I loved to dance because I was scared to speak. When I was moving, I could feel."

Other questions brought out a third Bausch, not anxious, not nostalgic, but tough. "I am," she says, "somebody who never gives up."

That is probably her greatest strength and greatest weakness. Australian dancer Michael Whaites, who worked with her for four years, knows she is "obsessive like any genius".

Genius is taking it a bit far, but Bausch does matter. She's much more than a choreographer creating in a rarefied field. Her work has influenced many other directors and companies as far apart philosophically and geographically as Lloyd Newson's DV8 from England and Lin Hwai-Min's Cloud Gate from Taiwan. Coincidentally, all three companies are appearing in the Olympic Arts Festival, with the Bausch company staging *Masurca Fogo*.

Bausch's productions blend speech, song, circus tricks, gymnastics, brilliant visual images, and monumental sets. Often, dance plays only a supporting role. Her works refer to Bertolt Brecht's theatre of alienation, the political cabarets of the Weimar Republic, American musicals, and the expressionist dance history of Germany, in particular, the choreography and philosophy of Kurt Jooss and Mary Wigman.

Audiences react with a shock of recognition because her dance dramas seem to reach into the subconscious. Each is a patchwork quilt of episodes all to do with love, bodies, and alienation, the search for fulfilment, desire and thwarted desire. The German critic Manuel Brug sums up her philosophy as "the interpretation of the soul and the battle of the sexes".

Surely all the praise she has won along the way is enough to reassure her? But no, says Bausch, "it has been beautiful, and I am very, very happy. But when I do a new piece it doesn't help me. Nothing helps me. Not what I have already done. It is done. Each time, you are a beginner." Bausch tapped out a cigarette and lit the next. "I want to give up, actually, but I don't … It's complicated. It all takes so much strength. I'm so fragile. It's emotional. I get little sleep, you try to sleep but you can't." She laughed but looked wretched. "I am thinking too much. It's like my head is in the way. It seems simple, but I make it so complicated.

"It gets worse when I am coming out of a work. There comes a point when I think 'This is the last time. I am never going to do this again'. And afterwards, you think 'I should not stop now. I should right away do a new piece'. I go to all the extremes, deep down ... " Her voice fades away. "It's so terrible, horrible, you go down, down, down, but you can't give up, because the dancers are always there and expect you to do something."

Who does she talk to at this point?

"At that moment, nobody."

It's no wonder she's exhausted. Whaites says that the company works from 10am to 10pm every day in the three-month lead-up to each premiere. Outside, in the rehearsal room above Wuppertal's McDonald's, there are few distractions. Bausch says it's the perfect place to create. The climate encourages a certain work ethic, and Wuppertal (population 400,000) is relatively rich. Nearby are the headquarters of the chemical firm Bayer, which was founded in Wuppertal and maintains a pesticide factory in the town. Wuppertal is also the hometown of the German Federal President and Head of State, Johannes Rau. Bausch's troupe attracts generous subsidies from the city itself, and from the State of North Rhine-Westphalia, totalling 3.7 million deutschemarks ($3 million) a year.

Yet behind this small and serious city, there is an element of the surreal, summed up by a fascinating piece of engineering, the century-old Schwebebahn, a monorail suspension system once described as a "flying millipede". Years ago, a circus elephant called Tuffi, on a promotional tour of the town, thrilled the locals when he survived a jump from one of the carriages into the slow-moving Wupper below.

Pina (short for Philippina) was born nearby in Solingen in 1940, three years before the Battle of the Ruhr. Her parents ran a modest restaurant with a small hotel attached, and sent their little girl to ballet class.

At 14, she studied at the Essen Folkwang School, directed by Germany's most influential choreographer, Jooss, known, Bausch says, as "Papa Jooss".

"He was like a papa, in a way, very, very kind, very, very warm, with a lot of humour, very much joy for things, people. A very beautiful man," she says. "He knew so much about history, music. His school was special, with an opera department, acting, pantomime, graphic arts, photography, sculpture, all together."

Figure 13 Vollmond (2006): Tanztheater Wuppertal. © Ursula Kaufmann

Bausch became interested in "forms, materials", which later influenced her distinctive sets, such as the sea of flowers in her work *Nelken* (*Carnations*), the heaped leaves of *Bluebeard*, the water-flooded stage of *Arien*, or the mounds of peat in her *Le Sacre du Printemps* (*The Rite of Spring*). "I also saw José Limón's company [from the United States] in Dusseldorf and I was really very impressed."

When she graduated, Bausch won a grant to study at the Juilliard School in New York, where her teachers were the choreographers Limón, Paul Taylor and Antony Tudor.

Tudor, a tortured man, cold with most dancers, was "not tough with me, but very kind. He was very beautiful, a great man. There was a reason if he was rude. He believed if people were too comfortable they couldn't dance".

Without prompting, she added: "I don't do this kind of thing."

In 1962, Bausch returned to Germany, joining Jooss as a soloist at the Folkwang Ballet where she succeeded him as director. Eleven years later, she was asked to become director of municipal Wuppertal Dance Theatre. In the beginning, things were tough. Audiences didn't understand her choreographic language and dancers rebelled at the lack of dancing. Bausch was not deterred. She found an ally in Rolf Borzik, a designer, whom she married. He died in 1980. Their son, also called Rolf, is studying music.

Bausch now lives with Ronald Kay, a poet. He looks after her, says Whaites, does the cooking. But the two are thought to lead rather separate lives.

I wanted to know more, but suspected that a Mona Lisa-like smile would be the result of more direct questioning. As Whaites says, "she plays her cards close to her chest." For him, that proved to be a sticking point.

"One day," he recalled, "I told Pina 'I feel you know all about me' but I was sad because I knew nothing of her. I was scared of her reaction. She says she felt the same way." But Bausch told him she had "no time to give".

It's easy, though, for her to see into the souls of her dancers. Since 1978, she has been working on her question-and-answer technique. Bausch asks her dancers to enact a mood or desire, and, from their responses, she builds a collage.

The questions are "very difficult to answer", says Whaites. Among them:

- Copy someone else's tic.
- Do something you are ashamed of.

- Write your name with movement.
- What would you do with a corpse?
- Move your favourite body part.
- How do you behave when you've lost something?

Sometimes, of course, the technique does not succeed, and the resulting piece is derivative of her own earlier works. Critics were tough on Bausch's latest for this reason. In the newspaper *Die Welt*, Brug wrote: "Seldom has a piece from Pina Bausch been so nice, cheerful and so meaningless, because it fails to disturb." *Wiesenland* had "leafed through the formidable pattern book of the Bausch collection, choosing, trying out, and returning to previous pieces".

Like many of her works, *Wiesenland* featured water everywhere. It's danced in front of a giant green mossy bank, dripping with rivulets of trickling water. Water is also poured from buckets, into miniature baths, from hoses, from bottles into mouths. Men holding vessels washed women who blew smoke from cigarettes through the stream of water. A lot of mopping up was required. The sexual allusions are obvious, but not overdone. Bausch treats sex lightly, but takes romance very seriously.

The dancers approached the front rows and expressed their hopes or fears. They asked audience members if they were in love, how many children they had, if they loved the person next to them, or, if not, if they would like to go backstage with the dancer. This kind of work is confrontational for both audience and dancers, but then if they work for Bausch, they are already stripped of their defenses and prepared to take risks.

Reflecting the spirituality of Bausch, many are Christian or Buddhist, says Whaites, who is one of four Australian dancers to have done well in her company. The others are choreographer Meryl Tankard, Sydney-born Endicott, a member of the Australian Ballet before leaving for Europe in the early 1970s, and current company member Julie Shanahan, from Adelaide, who seems to be a kind of alter ego for Bausch, often dressing in glamorous evening clothes yet speaking quite directly of her feelings to the audience in a strong Australian accent.

Woven throughout Bausch's 34 works is the use of dress to send sexual messages. She often portrays women in vampy, girly clothes, with pointy-toed and stiletto-heeled shoes, and in long, sweeping, silky dresses. Other signatures are her love of romantic pop songs, the ritual of cigarette smoking, and social dance, especially the use of snaking dance lines. Much of this seems to recall her girlhood of the 1940s and 1950s.

But Bausch's inspiration does not come only from within. Since 1986, she's been staging co-productions collaborative efforts made with the input and influence of other cities, mainly European. Her company bases itself for about a month in a city, with the dancers absorbing the atmosphere for ideas to feed Bausch. *Wiesenland* was a co-production with Budapest, while *Masurca Fogo* arose from the company's 1998 visit to Lisbon. Says Whaites, "it reflects Lisbon's seafaring past, its adventurers and explorers". The title *Masurca Fogo* refers to a simple dance from Cape Verde, the islands off West Africa, a former Portuguese colony.

Before Bausch choreographed this work, she asked the dancers to express themselves through various phrases, among them: "something forbidden", "water and stone", "something about love", "a long deep tone", "first impressions", and "write the word sunshine with your body".

Bausch still has her own yearnings, among them, to work with dancers in classical companies, to "learn a lot in other countries. I would love to learn. But my wishes are much bigger than my strength. I just hope I am strong enough to do a bit more of what I wish".

But it is hard to see her leaving the security of Wuppertal permanently, ever. "I never changed anything in my house. Every year I would think 'I am leaving tomorrow'. It was like I was just passing by. But I never had time to think of anything else. We just went rolling on."

Dancing in the dark

John O'Mahony

Originally published in *Guardian*, 26 January, 2002. © Guardian
News & Media Ltd 2002

Backstage at the Wuppertal Opera, Pina Bausch is making preparations
for the final performance of *Iphigenie auf Tauris*, a revival of her 1974
dance-opera based on the Gluck opera. A little earlier she has given
the company a point-by-point critique of the previous night's performance. "Mostly I tell them what was not right," she says gently. "I sit
in the auditorium every night. I make many notes."

Now, as they file past Bausch's willowy, almost sepulchral figure in
the corridor, the dancers seem somewhat bashful and apologetic,
though one or two give playful military salutes. With an astounding
range of physiques, types, sizes, personalities, ages, it's immediately
obvious that this is not a typical troupe of flawless ballet drones. The
angular, imposing figure of the Brazilian Ruth Amarante, who plays
Iphigenie, is in striking contrast to the tiny birdlike Asian dancer,
Na Young Kim. And, despite the incandescence of their performances,
Beatrice Libonati, Nazareth Panadero and Bausch veteran Dominique
Mercy – all well into their 40s – have reached an age when they would
have long since been put out to pasture by more conventional companies.

As they take up positions for *Iphigenie*, which dates from Bausch's
more traditionally balletic early period, the choreographer breaks into
a radiant smile: "Each of them is such an individual personality," she
says proudly. "It is difficult for them to dance in a piece like *Iphigenie*.
I love everybody in the company so much and everyone is so special,
that I wanted to find something different for each one to do. It is
necessary to see what they can do in the other works, where everyone is
just themselves."

One of the seminal performance figures of the 20th century, Bausch
is a choreographer who has expanded the possibilities of modern
dance, opening up the genre to snatches of dialogue, stage visions and
chaotic intrusions from everyday life. Her influence is evident not only
in those such as William Forsythe and Maguy Marin, who have

consciously followed her lead, but in practically every corner of the dance world where overtly theatrical elements have simply been absorbed into the idiom: "She has basically re-invented dance," says William Forsythe. "She is one of the greatest innovators of the past 50 years. Pina needs to examine the world this way. She is a category of dance unto herself. Dance-theatre didn't really exist before she invented it."

Meticulously unstructured and freeform, the works themselves lack any of the usual, reassuring reference points such as plot, character, even coherent meaning. Invariably dressed in evening wear of the 1930s, the dancers appear on stage, tell simple, often mundane stories, engage in childish games and exaggerated courting rituals, fling themselves on the ground, scream, whoop, giggle, growl and cry. The males seem to spend a disproportionate amount of time in drag, while the females tend to occupy grotesque, overblown caricatures of female sexuality. Accompanying music can range from German folk songs to Stravinsky to PJ Harvey.

Yet, from this improvised chaos, beauty bubbles to the surface – the serene, semi-naked accordion player who roams through *Carnations* (1982); or the poignant scene in *Legend Of Chastity*, first performed in 1979, when a lone figure tells the story of a goldfish trained to live on land that almost drowns when returned to the water. Bausch's themes are positively Strindbergian: loss, loneliness, grief, death, leave-taking and the tortuous relations between the sexes. But there is also wicked humour too, in the fluttery bourrées of 1986's *Viktor* performed with a bloody hunk of meat protruding from the dancer's pointe shoes, or in the mermaids' swimming lesson of *Masurca Fogo*, which opens this week at Sadler's Wells.

Much of this material is carefully distilled from the dancers' own experiences, using Bausch's famous question-and-answer approach: "Pina asks questions," says Jo Ann Endicott, who has been with the company for almost 30 years. "Sometimes it's just a word or a sentence. Each of the dancers has time to think, then gets up and shows Pina his or her answer, either danced, spoken, alone, with partner, with props, with everyone, whatever. Pina looks at it all, takes notes, thinks about it." Famously, Bausch refuses to discuss the work explicitly and in rehearsals never reveals its underlying themes or possible future direction: "Even the dancers have no idea," Endicott claims. "It's like a real big secret existing inside her – waiting, simmering, exploding."

Given the difficult and disorienting nature of the work, critical reaction has not always been enthusiastic: "Silly, empty, stupid, self-indulgent, self-congratulatory," railed Clive Barnes, theatre critic of the *New York Times*. *New Yorker* dance critic Arlene Croce dismissed the work as the "pornography of pain" and Bausch herself as "an entrepreneuse who fills theatres with projections of her self-pity".

The most ferociously negative reaction came from citizens of the German city of Wuppertal, where Bausch and her company have been based since 1973, who, right up to the early 80s, viewed Bausch as an avant-garde anti-Christ: "They would bang the doors and leave," remembers dancer Meryl Tankard. "Sometimes they would throw oranges at us when we were trying to dance. Once a man got up on stage and took a bucket of water I had as a prop and tried to throw it over one of the other dancers who was repeating a poem over and over. But she ducked and the water went all over the audience."

This was more than compensated for by the luminaries who began making pilgrimages to Wuppertal, among them those who became avid Bausch supporters – Susan Sontag, Robert Wilson, Peter Brook, Robert Lepage. "Pina's accomplishment is enormous," says her friend, the American choreographer Paul Sanasardo, "and it is amazing that she has managed to do it all in Wuppertal. I mean, who ever heard of Wuppertal before Pina, except as some little industrial city in Germany? It's hard to believe she pulled that together away from the traditional metropolitan centres of London or New York."

Even more intriguing is the fact that all of this has been achieved by a woman who is, at least on the surface, shy and reticent. Dressed invariably in dark tones, always sucking on a Camel cigarette or draining a cup of coffee, Bausch speaks in a low, halting, gentle voice. Tankard recalls: "When I first came to Wuppertal, I spoke absolutely no German, but I did notice that there was one word she kept saying again and again: 'vielleicht.' And I thought this must be a word that meant a lot to her whole approach. So I asked one of the others what it meant, and it turned out that 'vielleicht' was the German for 'maybe'." However, this fragile-looking woman controls almost every aspect of the Wuppertal Tanztheater: "No decision is made without her involvement, from the temperature of the heating system to the colours we use on the poster," says Matthias Schmiegelt, the company manager.

During the process of creating a new piece, she is engulfed in a miasma of uncertainty and self-doubt: "The anguish that she goes through is enormous," says her partner Ronald Kay, who lives with her in a modest Wuppertal apartment not far from the theatre. "She comes home like a heap of ashes. I have learned to look at it from a distance. To be absolutely outside of it is the only way I can help."

But these insecurities are always tempered by Bausch's ferocious determination, which pushes her to demand miracles from herself and her dancers: "She works in the rehearsal room from 10 in the morning, and rehearsals don't end till late in the evening," continues Kay. "She comes home at about 10 at night, we eat, and then she sits there till two or three o'clock getting an idea of what it was all about, what can be kept, what are the little jewels of the piece. And then she gets up at seven, sometimes even earlier, to prepare. She always manages to keep the same intensity."

Philippina Bausch was born on July 27 1940, in the small German town of Solingen, not far from Wuppertal, the third child of August Bausch, proprietor of a small hotel and restaurant, and his wife Anita. Pina's brother, Roland, and sister, also Anita, were both almost a decade older, and her parents were often absorbed by the family business, which meant that the young girl was often left alone to amuse herself: "My parents didn't have so much time for me," Pina remembers, "so I was always around the restaurant very late. You have no family life. I was always up till midnight or one o' clock, or sitting under a table somewhere."

From a very young age, Bausch was constantly dancing, and her aptitude soon came to the attention of performers from the local Solingen theatre: "People from the chorus came sometimes to eat in the restaurant," Bausch recalls, "and they saw me always hopping about and doing handstands. So they took me to the children's ballet. All the children had to lie on their stomachs and put their legs behind their heads. And it was so easy for me to do that the teacher said: 'Du bist ein schlangenmensch,' which means something like 'You are a snake-person or a contortionist'. I thought that it was fantastic to be like that and afterwards always wanted to go back."

At 14, she a won a place at the Folkwang Ballet in Essen, which was run by the renowned German choreographer Kurt Jooss, one of the founding fathers of German Expressionist dance or *Ausdruckstanz*, which combined movement, music, and dramatic elements. Consequently, Essen exposed Bausch to a variety of artistic disciplines: "At this time at the Folkwang, all the arts were together," she says. "It was not just the performing arts like music or acting or mime or dance, but there were also painters, sculptors, designers, photographers. If you just went to a little ballet school, the experience would have been entirely different."

Following her graduation from the Folkwang in 1958, Bausch won a scholarship from the German academic exchange service to continue her dance studies at the Juilliard School in New York. For a teenager who had barely ventured outside Westphalia, it was a daunting adventure. "I was just 18 when I stepped on that ship," she recalls now, shaking her head in disbelief, "I couldn't speak any English." Choreographer Donya Feuer, who took Bausch under her wing and became a life-long friend, remembers a young woman somewhat intimidated by New York: "She was very shy and cried a lot," says Feuer. "Everything was so foreign to her. We would have to walk her to the subway every evening until she felt secure. But once we saw what a gifted person she was, we did everything we could so she could be at ease."

Once in the rehearsal room, Bausch's timidity melted away, and her grace and radiance as a dancer immediately impressed her Juilliard teachers, who included Graham disciples Louis Horst and Mary Hinkson, as well as José Limón and Antony Tudor, who made her a member of the Metropolitan Opera Ballet company. She also worked with Paul Taylor at the New American Ballet.

However, it was in the 19th-Street studio of Feuer and another budding progressive choreographer named Paul Sanasardo that Bausch did her most interesting work. In 1961, they collaborated on a piece called *Phases Of Madness*, a series of consecutive solos danced to a score by Edgar Varèse, and later on a second evening-length ballet entitled *In View Of God*. Sanasardo, who had also seen Bausch dance at the Met and at Juilliard, remembers her magnetic quality in these pieces: "Pina had a great gift," he says, "She was an extremely beautiful dancer. Tudor had staged this piece at Juilliard in which Pina danced a section called *500 Arabesques*, and she did it on point and it was wonderful. She had great flexibility. She was very lyrical and she also had a tremendous intensity."

As the collaboration blossomed into friendship, in the autumn of 1961 Bausch practically moved into the enormous loft that Feuer and Sanasardo rented above the studio. Almost immediately, however, it became apparent that she was not well: "Pina became extraordinarily thin,"says Sanasardo. "We were very concerned because we had great difficulty getting her to eat. It was confusing because we were all young and Pina didn't speak very much English. We were not sure if something was bothering her. And when we tried to talk to her, she would just say 'No, I'm fine, I'm fine'." In the end, Sanasardo and Feuer called on the help of Lucas Hoving, a dancer with the José Limón company and former teacher of Bausch's at Essen, who organized Bausch's safe passage back to Germany.

Bausch herself has never spoken about this probable eating disorder or to what degree it may have influenced themes of gender identity in her work, so exact details of its causes, course or consequences remain obscure. On her return to Germany she joined Kurt Jooss's new Folkwang Ballet in Essen and appears to have been well enough to dance the role of Caroline in Antony Tudor's *Jardin aux Lilas* when he visited Essen in 1962. But she was still uncomfortably thin, and her condition soon drew the attention of Jooss himself: "She was so thin that she had no strength," remembers Jean Cebron, who was a teacher at Folkwang at the time. "She lost a little control and she didn't look good really. So Kurt Jooss said that either she put on some weight or get out of the company. After that, she seems to have got better quite quickly."

Once recovered, Bausch established herself as one of the principal soloists while assisting Jooss on many of the pieces. On Jooss's departure at the end of the decade, Bausch took over as artistic director of what had become known as the Folkwang Tanzstudio, and began choreographing pieces of her own: *Fragment* in 1968 to the music of Béla Bartók, and *Im Wind der Zeit* in 1969, and in 1971, *Actionen für Tänzer*. "I never thought of being a choreographer," she says. "The only reason I made those pieces was because I wanted to express myself differently and I wanted to dance." Even in these early works, Bausch was already breaking away from Jooss and *Ausdruckstanz*, and forging her own heretic style: "I didn't want to imitate anybody," she says. "Any movement I knew, I didn't want to use."

In 1973, Bausch was offered the post of director of the Ballett der Wupperthaler Buhnen. At first Bausch was reluctant – Wuppertal was grey and provincial and its inhabitants renowned for their conservative tastes: "Here, there was only a classical tradition," she says. But she was ultimately seduced by the immense potential of building up her own company as well as assurances of total artistic freedom, and began conscripting core members.

Her first production in Wuppertal was a strange little piece called *Fritz*, that was so eccentric and outlandish that even now she balks at reviving it: "There was hardly any music. It was like a suffocating atmosphere," says Jo Ann Endicott, who danced the role of the daughter in the piece. "It choked the audience it was so overpowering and strong, and nobody at the time was used to her style. There were weird characters and Pina herself played this huge grandmother who sat for most of the time in a chair, and then suddenly arose, big and pale and imposing."

After a reaction that spanned disbelief and open hostility, when the sparsely attended performances were interrupted by the jeers of outraged spectators, Bausch wisely retreated for her next pieces, the "dance-operas" *Iphigenie auf Tauris* and *Orpheus und Eurydike* (1975), both straightforward and overwhelming pieces of pure, diaphanous choreography. The culmination of Bausch's experiment in conventionality came with *Frühlingsopfer*, or *Spring Opera*, a movement triptych based on Stravinsky that climaxed with the classic Bausch version of *The Rite Of Spring*. In the piece, Bausch transformed the original narrative into a dark, ritualistic battle of the sexes in which sacrifice is symbolized by a red dress. Performed on a layer of topsoil, the dancers seem to write the incantatory movements into the dirt, panting audibly throughout.

After a version of the *Seven Deadly Sins*, the Brecht/Weill opera, which boasted a very precisely choreographed gang-rape scene, Bausch began work in 1977 on *Blaubart* – *Bluebeard* – a milestone in the development of her work. Voraciously inclusive of elements from opera to mime to regular straight theatre, *Bluebeard* was the first to fully realize Bausch's cross-genre ideal of dance-theatre, and largely replaces a "balletic" vocabulary with simple, repetitive everyday movements.

The dancers groan and scream or simply babble phrases from the arias that Bluebeard plays on a tape-recorder tethered to him like a leg iron. At the very onset Bluebeard brutally, almost casually rapes his wife and then repeatedly shoves her head into his crotch in a deeply disturbing scene of ritual humiliation: "It is not that I wanted to confront people," Bausch protests. "The misunderstanding is not that I love violence, it was quite the opposite. I was terrified of violence, but I wanted to understand the person doing the violence. That was the exploration."

By now, Bausch was beginning to formulate the question-and-answer format that would become the basis of her subsequent work. However, there were those among the company who found that the grueling new approach left them battered and emotionally brutalized. In the period after *Bluebeard*, which produced *Come Dance With Me*, an exploration of sexual conflict loosely structured around traditional German folk songs, and the "dance operetta" *Renate Wandert Aus*, a deconstruction of gender stereotypes, the company was on the verge of meltdown: "At one stage I went on strike with one of the other dancers," says Jo Ann Endicott. "She was just asking us to do these amazing, weird, strange, brutal, sick kinds of things. On stage it all felt so naked and exposed, and I think it was just having an effect on us." Meryl Tankard, who joined the company in 1978, was also taken aback by the extent of Bausch's demands: "In one rehearsal, all the men in the company had to do six ways of groping you and kissing you and it was just like being raped. I was very disciplined and I would do as I was told. But I finally broke down crying."

To escape this increasingly tense atmosphere, Bausch briefly relocated, along with a select group of dancers, to the Schauspielhaus in nearby Bochum, for her next work, an adaptation of *Macbeth* entitled *He Takes Her By the Hand and Leads Her into the Castle, the Others Follow*. In a piece that seems fixated on childhood squabbles over the toys littering the stage, only a few motifs survive from Shakespeare's play. Bausch again chose a small group of dancers for the classic *Café Müller*, a starkly beautiful and unflinching 45-minute piece, in which the dancers hurtle through a stage littered with chairs. As they approach, the chairs are scrambled out of the way by an anonymous figure, while Bausch herself, dancing for the first time since 1973–74, slams herself against a wall.

After the claustrophobic intimacy of *Café Müller*, Bausch moved directly afterwards into a wide-open fin-de-siècle expanse for *Kontakthof* (*Contact Yard*), a riotous full-company work that satirized the courting rituals of the ballroom. The decade ended with two pieces that were particularly striking for the spectacular visual effects employed: *Arias*, in which the sodden dancers splash and gurgle their way through an onstage pool inhabited by a wallowing hippopotamus; and *Legend Of Chastity*, in which the performers scoot around in armchairs on castors while life-size alligators crawl across the stage.

None of these quirky, vivid tableaux would have been possible without the Dutch-born set and costume designer Rolf Borzik, who had forged the visual style of the Tanztheater right from its inception. Her romantic as well as professional partner, Borzik had been crucial in supporting Bausch through the frequent crises of creativity and had insulated her against the hostility of the Wuppertal audiences. So, it was cruel that just as the company was beginning to gain international recognition, Borzik was diagnosed with leukemia: "Very few people knew at first," says dancer Lutz Forster. "People in the company only got to know on a south-east Asian tour when he got too sick to continue and Pina had to stay with him."

Borzik's death in January 1980 was a huge blow to Bausch, and threw the whole future of the company into doubt: "I was so scared I wouldn't be able to continue," she says. "It was so important for me to do a piece right away, so that I wouldn't even have the chance to worry." The result, simply entitled *1980 – A Piece By Pina Bausch*, is a wistful elegy that deals primarily with nostalgia and childhood games. Company members attribute the strangely upbeat tone to the desire to "distract ourselves from what had happened".

Bausch's personal life seems to have rebounded with equal rapidity. While touring Chile in summer 1980, she met a Chilean poet and professor of aesthetics and literature at the University of Chile named Ronald Kay: "Rolf Borzik died in January, and I met her at the end of July," says Kay, "so you can imagine that it was a very hard time for her. Borzik and Pina lived together, he was the stage designer of the company and his collaboration was essential to what became the Tanztheater. She lost a companion and a co-worker. In that sense she was a widow twice over."

Kay and Bausch met at a reception in the German embassy, there was an immediate affinity, and a relationship soon followed. "I met Pina without having seen any of her work," says Kay, "I didn't even know who she was. But we began talking and we continued talking and we are still talking." The two got together in 1981 and shortly afterwards Bausch gave birth to her only child, Rolf-Salomen, named after Borzik.

Since 1980, Bausch's work has grown steadily more joyous and cele-bratory, in particular the plaintive, comic *Danzón*, created in 1995 around a Cuban dance and featuring Bausch onstage for the first time in over a decade; and *Viktor*, an ode to the city of Rome, which was seen at Sadler's Wells in 1999. Some put this development in her work down to the birth of her son, though Bausch herself attributes it more to the infusion of youth that has come from the younger members of her company.

And while critics regularly objected to the darkness and violence in the works, many now mourn the passing of that era: "There was a time when everybody lived and worked together and everything grew out of that," says ex-company member Marika Aoyama. "Now Pina needs her own taxi and her own hotel suite. And I think she more than deserves that, but it does change the complexion of things. And the new members of the company are much cooler. They don't get involved the way that we used to." On the other hand one of the original members, Dominique Mercy, feels that what has happened has been a necessary evolution: "You cannot expect a company that has been alive for so many years to stay the same. It has just continued to grow."

One thing that hasn't changed is Bausch's lacerating self-doubt. As the company prepares to occupy Sadler's Wells with *Masurca Fogo*, she is creating a new piece, under her usual working title of *A Work By Pina Bausch*. "It is very difficult," she whispers. "At this point, I don't know anything, I just can hope. I feel my way and try not to be afraid. It is not just that the dancers don't know where we are going, it is that I don't know where we are going also. It is not just that they have to trust me, I have to trust myself too."

Pornography of pain

Dancer Pina Bausch's turbulent career

Zoë Anderson

Originally published in *The Independent*, 23 January, 2008

In Stravinsky's *The Rite of Spring*, the change of seasons is violent. Ice cracks to reveal the earth; a chosen maiden dances herself to death. In Pina Bausch's celebrated production, which comes to Sadler's Wells next month, the earth is there already. The stage floor is covered with a thick layer of peat. As the dancers drive themselves through a frantic ritual, heading towards sacrifice, peat is churned into mud, marking their clothes and their bodies.

When Bausch created her *Rite* in 1975, she was already controversial. In 1973, when she took over the ballet company in the German industrial city of Wuppertal, her work provoked furious reactions. Audiences walked out, banging doors as they left. Sometimes they threw things. Bausch kept going. By the early 1980s, she had established herself as a major figure in 20th-century dance. She is famously aloof, reluctant to give interviews: the high priestess of tanztheater.

Bausch was born in the German city of Solingen in 1940. Her early training was with the choreographer Kurt Jooss, best known now for his expressionist anti-war ballet *The Green Table*. Winning a grant to study in New York, she worked with a range of choreographers before returning to Germany. Working with her own company, she quickly established an international reputation. From 1974, she collaborated closely with the set and costume designer Rolf Borzik, whom she married. Borzik died in 1980.

Though Bausch has ardent fans in Britain, her company hasn't performed here regularly. There were long gaps between its visits to Sadler's Wells or to the Edinburgh Festival. The current Sadler's Wells season has two London premieres, *The Rite of Spring* and *Café Müller*, both created in the 1970s. *Café Müller* is also one of the few works in which Bausch, now 67, still dances.

Bausch's influence stretches far beyond the dance world. Her admirers include the directors Peter Brook, Robert Wilson and Robert

Lepage, the singer Bryan Ferry, and the actors Fiona Shaw and Richard Wilson. The film-maker Pedro Almodovar is another fan: his 2002 film *Talk to Her* begins and ends with scenes from Bausch works. The autograph that appears in the movie is Bausch's own, given to Almodovar six years previously.

Yet Bausch has always had detractors. The American critic Arlene Croce described her work as "pornography of pain". One of the first times I saw a Bausch piece, I went with a friend who stood swearing in rage in the foyer afterwards. Why so much vehemence? Bausch's vision and approach are immediately distinctive, and often angst-ridden. *The Rite of Spring* was the last of her works to feature a coherent narrative. Since then, she's created collages of movement, fragmented sequences of speech and gesture.

Bausch has said, "I keep making, time and again, desperate efforts to dance." When her performers do dance, it's often ironic or humiliating. She has created several mocking ballet scenes, as when a dancer stuffs bloody meat into her pointe shoes. Bausch's dancers can show masochistic levels of commitment. In *The Rite of Spring*, they are ready to dance to the point of exhaustion.

More than that, they're part of a very personal rehearsal process. Bausch questions her dancers, who answer in speech or movement. The questions cover memories, relationships, responses to particular situations. She might ask them to imitate one another, to do something they are ashamed of, to act out a mood. Sometimes the prompt is just a word or a sentence. The answers give Bausch her raw material: gestures, dialogue, scenes, which she builds into stage works.

It's a relationship that her dancers cherish. Describing her own training, Bausch recalled working with the ballet choreographer Antony Tudor, who could be cruel or unsettling in rehearsal. He had been kind to her, Bausch told the journalist Valerie Lawson; if he was rude to others, it was because "he believed that if people were too comfortable they couldn't dance". But, she added, "I don't do this kind of thing." Bausch's own chosen dancers are devoted and loyal. Some performers have stayed with her company for decades.

Her main theme is relationships, often with an atmosphere of violence or shame. Bausch's men are often in drag, while her women are regularly dressed with exaggerated, fetishized glamour: impossibly high heels, corset knickers, 1930s evening dress. The performance style can be intensely personal, with a sense that these dancers are acting out their own troubles and fears. They play children's games, scream or babble. In more recent works, Bausch has shown signs of lightening up. The Sadler's Wells season, however, shows two of her earliest and most intense works.

Café Müller, created in 1978, draws on Bausch's own memories. As a child, she played in her parents' restaurant, watching but not understanding the relationships between the adult customers. In the piece, everyone is needy but nobody manages to connect with anybody else. One couple dance together, the man lifting his partner, swinging her across his body before putting her down. They repeat the move, not stopping even when they reach the wall – which means that the woman is repeatedly smashed against it. A playful step becomes a battering.

The sets for Bausch's work are often monumental. *The Rite of Spring* has the aforementioned peat-covered stage. *Palermo, Palermo* starts with a wall of breeze blocks, which collapses in clouds of dust. *Nelken* has hundreds of carnations on stage, an artificial field of flowers. Her dancers romp through the carnation field, watched by guards with Alsatian dogs.

This choreographer can invent astonishing stage pictures. At the same time, the neurosis can seem self-indulgent: so much introspection, so much angst. Must all smiles be mocking, all relationships brutal? In *Café Müller*, Bausch casts herself as an anguished sleepwalker, unable to negotiate the furniture around her. Trying to get through a glass door, she just bumps into it, again and again. I remember wondering how she would get in: it would break the mood if someone held it open for her. Just as I thought that, a crash of furniture made me look at the other side of the stage. When I looked back, there was Bausch, coming through the door, air of sacrificial mysteriousness intact. That's cheating.

Yet Bausch creates images that stick in your mind: the carnation field, the couples whose games get stuck in a rut. Her performers are committed, daring and raw. Audiences argue about Bausch: exasperated by her fractured collages, or swept along by her creation of pictures, of relationships, of unspoken atmospheres.

In memoriam

Pina Bausch (1940–2009)

Deborah Jowitt

Originally published in *The Village Voice*, July 1, 2009

The death of Pina Bausch on Tuesday, June 6, came as a shock. She had been diagnosed with cancer only five days before. I thought not just of the dance world's unexpected loss of a brilliant, influential, controversial figure, but of her works and perhaps of her company – a particular, intimate extension of her own body and creative mind.

My first memory of Bausch, oddly, is of her as a young dancer in the early 1960s, when she was studying at Juilliard (having already graduated from the Folkwang School in Essen). One of a small group of women in a piece by Antony Tudor, she was wearing a black tutu of sorts and black tights and looked like a glamorous spider; I had never seen anyone so thin. Tudor admired her and took her into the Metropolitan Opera Ballet, which he directed (she danced briefly, too, with Paul Sanasardo and with Paul Taylor). When Tudor staged his great *Lilac Garden* for the Folkwang company, after Bausch returned to Germany, she played the central figure of Caroline.

Nothing prepared me for the first New York appearance of her Wuppertal Tanztheater, brought by Harvey Lichtenstein to the Brooklyn Academy of Music in 1984 for the first of many visits. One can only imagine the ruckus she may have caused in the small industrial German city in 1973, when, as a prize-winning young choreographer, she took over as director of the local opera house's dance company and gradually transformed it. The group certainly shook things up in New York. Audiences were mostly thrilled, critics divided. In 1985, BAM and Goethe House sponsored a symposium in which the debate touched on whether what Bausch was making was dance, whether new German dance was "deeper" than current American dance, whether Americans were concerned only with movement and form. Issues such as naturalism, abstraction, symbolism, violence, misogyny, and meaning were batted about among the panelists, and between them and members of the audience. The moderator, *Times* critic Anna Kisselgoff, often engaged German dance critic Jochen Schmidt, one of the panel members, in a dialogue (Schmidt grew increasingly red in the face with anger throughout the session as they debated American dance values versus those of German Tanztheater).

Yet appreciation of Wuppertal Tanztheater grew here, as year after year the company showed us works that had premiered in Germany in the 1970s (it took us a while to catch up). Whether you loved Bausch's work or hated it, you wouldn't dream of not going to see it. And many young New York choreographers, schooled in Merce Cunningham's the-movement-is-the-meaning principles, were both impressed and excited. As Jane Comfort remarked in a 1988 interview, "When we saw Pina Bausch, it was a shock; it was almost like she was giving Americans permission to use expressive movement again."

Bausch redefined expressiveness in ways that meshed with post-'60s ideas about distancing and coolness. She didn't construct her pieces as extended narratives, but as short—often very short—and enigmatic "acts." Cruel, heartrending, disturbing, funny. Her collage structures derive less from the art world than from revues and vaudeville turns. The dance numbers, the monologues, the songs, the bizarre games, contests, and ordeals don't influence one another. When one scene ends, the performers walk away from it and the next one starts. Within a sequence, repetition is often used mercilessly. I think, for example, of a woman repeatedly turning her back to the audience and pulling down her dress so that a man can lay a lipstick stripe across her back; they repeat this action without any sign of hostility until her back is a network of red lines. Or a group of men attempting to caress and soothe a woman, until their accumulated patting and stroking becomes painfully oppressive.

The brief sequences, however, have underlying themes: the often antagonistic relationship between men and women, loneliness, longing, the perils of childhood. In *1980*, a woman removes a man's shoes and socks while he's seated on a chair; she puts a woman's stocking on one of his legs and sticks little candles between each toe of his other foot; then she lights them and, in a noncommittal voice, sings "Happy Birthday to You." That kind of distanced performing is a crucial ingredient of her style, and the occasional, realistic fits of anger or grief become transformed by repetition or excess.

Bausch's world is essentially a bourgeois society reminiscent of the 1950s. The women wear short dresses or long flowery evening gowns and, often, high heels; the men appear in suits and ties. Many of the music selections are another generation's favorites. But Bausch frequently alludes to rehearsing and to the act of performing. Dancers break through the fourth wall, addressing spectators flirtatiously or aggressively from the stage or moving among them.

Figure 14 Danzón (1995): Pina Bausch. © Ursula Kaufmann

The hours-long pieces that astounded us in the 1980s were, in a sense, postmodern spectacles (the early ones wonderfully abetted by Rolf Borzik's set designs). Remember the floor flooded with water in *Arien* (1979); the enormous proscenium-filling wall that crashed down to begin *Palermo, Palermo* (1989); the moist, smelly turf that covered the stage in *1980*; the flower-garden vision of the 1982 *Carnations* (through which, at one point, men in party dresses frolicked like rabbits).

In the 1990s, Bausch made pieces that can be seen as snapshots in an album or video clips—with images and sounds inspired by cities to which Wuppertal Tanztheater had toured, or by a country that intrigued her. The last one seen here, in December of 2008, was *Bamboo Blues* (2007), with its allusions to India (draping fabrics, the cooling power of water, Bollywood films) mixing with her familiar visions of ordeal and absurd tasks. In these works, Bausch returned to dancing. One after another, her company members would appear in fluid solos that reminded me that Bausch had studied with José Limón while at Juilliard. It was as if each dancer had been given a theme to develop in individual ways.

Oh those dancers! Bausch's oeuvre cannot be considered without their input. In the studio in Wuppertal, they responded to her leading questions, dredged up memories of childhood, of passions, of their most embarrassing experiences. She chose, edited, added to, and orchestrated the facts of their lives and their desires and fears. Meryl Tankard, Dominique Mercy, Beatrice Libonati, Jan Minarek, Lutz Forster, Nazareth Panadero, Josephine Ann Endicott, and many many more; they brought her work to unforgettable life. In a work never seen here, *Action for Dancers*, made before Bausch took over the company in Wuppertal, the action centered on a woman lying shrouded on a white hospital bed, which, wrote Schmidt, "sooner or later the entire ensemble will climb into." The image haunts me now, of course, in relation to her death, but also because I feel for the brilliant performers who, in another sense, climbed into bed with her and helped her work to become the phenomenon it is. Their loss is ours too, and in losing her, we lose them. Although never—not ever—our memories.

Kontakthof, Tanztheater Wuppertal Pina Bausch, Barbican Theatre

Ismene Brown

Originally published in *The Arts Desk*, April 4, 2010

A house of contact, a place to make contact – this bare, evocative title sits on one of Pina Bausch's most appealing works, and also its most elastic. Brought this week to the Barbican posthumously, staged by her company on two amateur casts, *Kontakthof* didn't look 32 years old, it looked both timeless and as fresh as fledglings cracking out of their egg shells.

In 1978 when this surreal and exact spinner of magical webs created the piece, the Berlin Wall was as impregnable as it had been for a generation and meetings carried less casual insignificance than today. *Kontakthof* then was danced by young professional dancers in her company born in the 1950s, to parents who were in the war. Now *Kontakthof* has been given two further existences, for amateurs – a version for over-65s, people who shared that life, that world, that same half-fearful childhood that Bausch knew, and one for teenagers born since the country's reunification.

When pensioners perform *Kontakthof*, the village hall on the stage (high windows, curtained stage, ropey upright piano, black bentwood chairs) becomes a day centre, a dance-hall of dreams and memories. They wear the same style of dresses as the kids do – glamorous, vaguely Fifties, satin cocktail dresses, and heels, of course (where would Bausch works be without high heels?) – but old people being old people, they are highly non-conformist. Some live more in the past than others, some are greater fantasists, others don't want to remember.

As they stand up before us, offering their teeth and hands for us to inspect, we're clinicians, casting agents, border officials, a quarter expecting to see faded concentration camp tattoos, or proof that the old folk are fit enough to work. When the youngsters do the same, we're parents, we're seeing kids worried they don't look grown-up enough, or enough like their idols, or secretly wondering if they'll have to have sex with their new boyfriend on the first date. It may be this effortless way that *Kontakthof* peels the skin off souls young and old, and responds with love and nostalgia to their differences, that makes it such a piercing joy to experience. Could anyone but Pina Bausch put a masterpiece on amateurs and make it look even more like a masterpiece?

The nearly three hours fly by, borne along on a series of old café songs, tangos, love songs, strains of romantic classical music, like a soundtrack of memories. The characters appear to be auditioning for (maybe) an amateur performance set somewhere in Alice's crazed Wonderland. They tell a snatch of story in German or cracked English, or climb carefully up on a chair and laugh in a way that is discomfitingly pitched between hilarity and hysteria. After their three seconds at the microphone, the others applaud politely. They carefully learn their social dancing, switching between partners in games that seem like a speeded-up version of a life of missed opportunities, a sort of musical chairs where you must find a spare partner, or be lost. Or they fall over, to be totally ignored.

Lovers in pairs demonstrate different shades of relationships by performing the same series of caresses, in increasing gradients of violence, so that what is tender in the first pair by the fourth has turned into a mutually sadistic war, with the male slapping the female's bottom hard, while she grinds her stiletto into his foot. As Bausch said in an interview "for some people life would be boring without violence in their relationship".

Then there are the shades of the brothel, the meat market, that come unbidden to mind watching the teenagers (aged 14 to 19) strutting with their hooker-red lipstick, their mothers' evening dresses, or for the boys their too-soon learning of physical domination of girls, itemizing their date's attractiveness (pulling up her arm, pulling her head around) like a Magimix demonstrator expecting a sale. With the older folk, this is pregnant with embarrassment, like when your mother dressed too daringly when she was middle-aged, or a senile old granddad suddenly unleashes an adolescent sex drive.

As usual, this is a dance-play rather than a contemporary dance, and as usual it is a paean to woman-watching, their plumage, their mating rites, their power-sex games. The movement sequences are meticulously fashioned from observed body language, the little tics of discomfort and adjustment that women automatically adopt, hitching a bra strap, surreptitiously hiking down their pants when they stand up, or trying to smooth a wandering girdle. Bausch's eye misses nothing – she makes an entire tango of silly walks from a foot-grinding motion that I swear is derived from having stepped in stilettos in muck and trying to wipe it off them on a doormat. The bottom sticks out, the knee bends, the heel grinds, wipes awkwardly either side while the hips push unstably from this side to that, the hands bunch as if doing the twist. All together now – and there is a dance of pure Jabberwockian glory, vividly and hilariously eloquent about human beings' little unconscious ways.

The differences in physical strength that are marked and interesting in the older performers with their wide age range – the powerful old lady, the withered old man – become in the younger cast differences in that crucial quality, aplomb. The eye-catching thing with the teenage cast is what very strong stage personalities are already evident among them – several of them could effortlessly translate up into the "adult" version of *Kontakthof*, it seems, particularly the adorable, irresistible two girls, one skinny and blonde, the other voluptuous and chestnut-haired, who lead these daffy, perceptive and wholly entertaining revels. How Bausch will be missed. But *Kontakthof* holds out a promise that life and her captivatingly absurd and truthful work continues without her.

Tanztheater Wuppertal Pina Bausch

Luke Jennings

Originally published in *The Observer*, 28 March, 2010.

No one had a greater influence on postwar European dance than the German choreographer Pina Bausch, who died of cancer last June. Since 1973, she had been based in the Westphalian city of Wuppertal, surrounded by a tight-knit troupe of performers who, for more than three decades in some cases, followed wherever her vision led, into ghostly territories of memory and loss (*Café Müller*), flower-strewn battlefields of human misunderstanding (*Nelken*), surreal nightmares of murder and rape (*Seven Deadly Sins, The Rite of Spring*).

Many of these pieces didn't look like dance works, in that there was little "dancing", in the understood sense. Instead, the performers, often dressed as if for some formal event, processed enigmatically across the stage to sentimental tunes, or enacted dream-like scenarios which often involved sexual violence. Central to Bausch's oeuvre was the traumatized interplay of its performers, who often seemed caught in conflicting narratives. There were excruciating spoken confessions, acute physical and emotional self-barings, incontinent litanies of personal detail. Profoundly troubling and occasionally beautiful, this was dance as absolutist experience: the traumatized psyche of middle Europe made flesh.

In the early days, forcing her dancers to more and more extreme degrees of self-revelation, Bausch brought the company close to implosion. In the mid-1970s, she created *Come Dance With Me*, an exploration of gender stereotypes and sexual violence set to German folk songs. Preparation for the piece left many of the dancers feeling distraught. "In one rehearsal, all the men in the company had to do six ways of groping you and kissing you and it was just like being raped ... I finally broke down crying," said the Australian dancer Meryl Tankard.

Before Bausch, modern dance had taken its lead from America, from George Balanchine and Martha Graham, for whom the expressiveness of the moving body was paramount. Tending to plotlessness and abstraction, their work offered a severe form of joy, and when

Bausch's company toured the US in 1984, the tenders of the sacred flame were unimpressed. The *Village Voice* dismissed her work as "a crock", Alan Kriegsman of the *Washington Post* wrote of her "specifically Teutonic attraction to the powers of darkness, to an alliance of art, disease and malevolence", while Arlene Croce of the *New Yorker* described Bausch as "an entrepreneuse who fills theatres with projections of herself and her self-pity".

After an uncertain start – in her first Wuppertal production, the audience threw fruit at the stage and banged the doors – Europeans came to regard her work with awe and respect. With their more dark-accustomed eyes, they were sympathetic to her baroque theatricality and to the brooding sense of the past with which her productions were infused. Bausch's 1975 *Rite of Spring*, which saw a terrified female victim sacrificed by her tribe on a stage spread with black soil, made a particularly forceful impression. By the end of the piece, the dancers are streaked with sweat and dirt and audibly panting. Never had the war of the sexes been so graphically depicted. "I am terrified of violence, but I wanted to understand the person doing violence," Bausch explained.

Her creative style quickly bled into the landscape and today it's hard to find an avant-garde choreographer whose output doesn't reflect her influence. According to William Forsythe, probably the most important living choreographer: "She has basically reinvented dance." The British choreographer Wayne McGregor acknowledges his debt to her, and there are echoes of her work in the productions of dance-makers as diverse as Alain Platel, Angelin Preljocaj and Anne Teresa de Keersmaeker.

Recently, I travelled to Wuppertal to see *Kontakthof*, which Tanztheater Wuppertal are bringing to London. At first sight, the industrial city with its graffiti-streaked streets is an unlikely site for experimental dance-theatre. But it suited Bausch, who admired its toughness and authentic nature. Crucially, it boasts an opera house with a vast stage, capable of accommodating her grand-scale flights of the imagination.

When it first appeared in 1978, *Kontakthof* showed a dozen men and a dozen women as they prepared for a formal dance, with the action spinning off into surreal flights of fantasy, frustration and regret. When the piece was revived in 2000, however, Bausch decided to up the ante by presenting two different casts. In one, the performers were teenagers, in the other they were over 65 years old. Both casts are coming to the Barbican; I saw the teenagers.

The piece is set in a school hall where the boys, spiky-haired and coltish in suits and ties, face a contingent of girls in pastel satin evening gowns. Hopeful of connection, but unable to effect it, they stalk one another to a soundtrack of schmaltzy 1930s songs. Tentatively they essay the roles and attitudes that seem to be expected of them: the mating rituals and the desperate objectifications of self.

The performers may be teenagers, but they swiftly draw us into the traumatic world that Bausch made her own. Their movements are measured, spectral, purposeful. A young woman has hysterics as the rest of the cast stare resentfully at the audience. A second mimes orgasm, or perhaps agony, as the others applaud. A third borrows money from the audience to operate a mechanical rocking horse, on which she finds a lonely, fleeting pleasure. Love, Bausch seems to be saying, is a sentimental construct: we are hard-wired for conflict and alienation.

As always, the mood is orchestrated with a sure touch. In one sequence, a young cast member named Joy Wonnenberg simply repeats the word "Liebling!" for minutes on end. Whining, pleading, increasingly shrill, she turns from naive teenager to harridan before our eyes. It echoes a chilling earlier moment when the whole cast march on wearing masks of their older selves.

Kontakthof offers a bleak prognosis, but the journey is exhilarating and the cast deliver it with precision. They've been rehearsed by Josephine Ann Endicott, who has performed with Tanztheater Wuppertal since 1973, and enjoyed "a close love–hate relationship" with Bausch. To her dancers, Endicott says, the choreographer was at once devouring mother, spirit guide and addiction. They'd leave the company at intervals, hollowed out by her demands, but they almost always came back. "It was hard, that balance. There was Pina and there was real life … I could never quite get rid of her."

And then, suddenly, she was gone. "We all thought she was one of those people who'd never die," says 59-year-old Dominique Mercy, a founder member of the company. After the initial shock, the dancers turned to Mercy, who agreed to lead the company into the future. For the immediate future, he says, Bausch's works will continue to be performed as scheduled. In the course of time, however, it's probable that the company will acquire new work. "After all, we have to move forward."

For Jan Lade, a 17-year-old who performs in *Kontakthof*, Bausch's work has been a revelation. "It's so emotional I sometimes start to cry." Like his fellow cast members, he is looking forward to performing in London. "It'll be a change," he says. "In Wuppertal it's always raining."

Figure 15 Vollmond (2006): Dominique Mercy. © Ursula Kaufmann

V

Critical perspectives

Critics and dancers often meet arguments against dance for its anti-intellectualism with a defense of the human body in its ascendant form, where, for once, ideas are antithetical to the sensuous immediacy of the event. Dance becomes removed from life and ideas, and only approaches that life through the intermediary of the dancer's body in motion, which stands as a sign to be interpreted. Dancers worked long and hard to achieve this autonomy of movement, but this concentration on movement values negates our bodily placement in the world and creates of the dancer's body an instrument for movement. As much as we might try to remove ourselves from our bodies to become detached, rational subjects, or, conversely, to lose ourselves in sensuous experience, it is through and with our bodies that we are placed in the world and through which we derive our experience of self. It is of and through sensuous experience that we maintain a thought process. Trying to remove sensuous experience from this thought leaves us with a hollow, mechanical mind that is unable to conceive of self and unable to incorporate that self into the creation of ideas. If we retreat into a purely sensuous consideration of dance, however, then our bodies are not aspects of our selves, not the means through which we experience the world, but are efficators of movement, similarly mechanical and removed things which, though lauded within the context of dance, remain separate from our selves as other.

This separation of body and self comes out of the dominant influence of Cartesianism in the Western world. Descartes sought to take truth out of the abstract and develop it within each individual. In so doing, he elaborated on the concept of the soul as a distinct entity encased in our bodies, and so led to a development of an individual self capable of managing and interpreting the world. But Cartesianism hacks off its own structure of the self as an individual phenomenon by taking that newly developed self outside of its body and situating it in an ethereal soul. This emphasis on the soul as independent from the body is never complete, however. As the flesh is derealized, the body becomes extraneous. But without the ability to be completely eradicated, the body continues to exert its influence from the periphery, troubling the space from which it has been banished. Bausch's work enacts that battle to reclaim the body's position in the understanding of self, where each individual's engagement with the world is not simply the reading of information through the lens of the body, but is an act of interpretation that implies a subject not merely located in a body, but as body.

Bausch's work has been considered from various critical perspectives and feeds into contemporary issues surrounding bodiliness and presence, but owing to a lack of critical discourse surrounding dance in general, much of the work is cursory or thin, or worse – unnecessarily laden with dense jargon of theory as an attempt to prove dance's worthiness to play in the critical sandbox. Dance studies, as a more solidified academic discipline, is only just beginning to take hold, and Bausch's work is often in the middle of new attempts to place dance within a critical spectrum, with particular interest in feminist, psychological and particularly phenomenological theory. Many essays are available in anthologies on various aspects of dance and culture, or Bausch's work is considered as part of a larger argument centred on a particular perspective, and so I have not included them here. I have focused on a few seminal essays that place Bausch's work in critical perspective, beginning with the discussion surrounding Bausch's work and Tanztheater in general, surrounding her cataclysmic first visits to America. The dance world in America at the time was still on the heels of the formalist stance coming out of the Postmodern dance movement, while German dance had more fully embraced the emotive tradition of Ausdruckstanz, and taken it to a new level of expression.

The issues at stake were not simply ones of historical precedent, but struck deep at the critical divide between an abstracted or embodied presence as the core of new performance expression. The increase in the consideration of dance as critical inquiry followed an explosion of critical theory throughout the 1980s, and the use of cultural artefacts, both high and low, as a means for understanding our place in the world. The body took on a newly important role in discussions of cultural theory, and dance was ready to claim a complex consideration of the body as its birthright, even if the record did not always jibe with the claims of the theorists. Bausch's work was not only useful in furthering this discussion, it became fashionable. Bausch stayed away from attempts to wrest her work into the camp of feminism or any other ideological preference, but her very silence created an aura of critical mystique that carried the work on to academic legitimacy.

Each essay in this section provides a way of thinking about Bausch's work from a critical mindset. Again, I have left out those essays readily available in other published sources, or already anthologized in previous works. The result is an idiosyncratic mix of works, ending with Norbert Servos's poetic rendition of the collision of Eros and Thanatos in contemporary performance. Servos was writing about the Zeitgeist of the mid-1980s, but his words could not be more resonant today. "The battle still rages between the heights of the spirit and the 'depths' of the flesh, between humble dwellings and palaces. And we still aren't sure to what end. Nevertheless, dance theatre seems to have a notion of what will transpire: a misty morning sunrise and fresh morning air. It poses the question generously, persistently; always anew." What more can we ask of critical theory, of art, or of ourselves?

Tanztheater
The thrill of the lynch mob or the rage of a woman

Edited and with a postscript by Ann Daly
Originally published in *TDR*, Spring, 1986

Editor's note: Goethe House New York and the Brooklyn Academy of Music co-sponsored a symposium, "German and American Dance: Yesterday and Today," on 8 November 1985. This transcript, edited and abridged by *TDR* Managing Editor Ann Daly, is the second half of the symposium, concerned with current dance trends. Anna Kisselgoff, dance critic of *The New York Times*, was moderator. Participants were West German dance critic Jochen Schmidt; Reinhild Hoffmann, artistic director of Tanztheater Bremen; American choreographer Nina Wiener; and dance critic Nancy Goldner of *The Philadelphia Inquirer*.

Tanztheater in historical perspective

SCHMIDT: We lost a big part of our past, of our history, in the '30s, '40s, and '50s. I'm not quite sure if we lost more of it during the Nazi Third Reich and World War II or during the period of reconstruction in the Adenauer era. As a matter of fact, we lost more buildings and houses in the '50s than during World War II. To me, it looks as if we lost our dance tradition of the '20s not during the world war, not during the Nazi time, but during the '50s.

It was really dead in the '60s. All the German dancers, all the public, wanted to dance ballet and see ballet. There was a big, big boom of classical ballet in Germany with John Cranko [artistic director of the Stuttgart Ballet] and others. In 1967, Dore Hoyer, one of the great personalities of the '20s and the Ausdruckstanz, committed suicide. Nobody knows exactly why she did, but we all supposed it was because her dance was dead.

At that time we had a lot of influences from American modern dance. It came over with the Dutch companies, mainly from the Netherlands Dance Theatre, which was at that lime led by Glen Tetley and Hans van Manen. So we saw a lot of our own past transformed by Americans coming back. At that rime, we didn't want to do it ourselves.

I think that there was a new life for German dance for the tradition of the '20s. It has to do with the student revolution at the end of the '60s. It's no accident that most choreographers of the first generation (Reinhild is somewhat from the second generation already) – Hans Kresnik, Pina Bausch, Gerhard Bohner – were in a way connected with that social debate.

The break really came in 1973. In that year, Mary Wigman and John Cranko died. We all thought Cranko's death was just an accident that wouldn't disturb the flourishing of the ballet, but for German ballet it was something like an end. At the same time, Pina was appointed director of the Wuppertal Ballet, not tanztheater at that time. That was really the break. It was she who made tanztheater. Without her success, which was not an easy success, there would not have been tanztheater.

Now we have about ten companies in our stadtheatre system which are seen as tanztheater companies – not ballet companies – and about 30 ballet companies. All the big companies, of course, are ballet companies. I think the Stuttgart is doing good work, but it is just doing traditional things.

In a way, Pina and the tanztheater have influenced even the classical ballet. William Forsythe, who is an American working now in Frankfurt, is a ballet choreographer. But I think he is much, much closer to Pina and Reinhild and Susanne Linke than he is to John Neumeier or George Balanchine or other classical choreographers. So at this moment, of 100 performances in Germany, 70 percent are ballet, and 30 percent are tanztheater. The fame of Pina Bausch created a climate for tanztheater, so we are speaking about it, but the public likes *Giselle* and *Swan Lake*.

Is content taboo in American Experimental Dance?

KISSELGOFF: I'm going to read something that Jochen Schmidt wrote in *Ballett International* (June/July 1982:13): "And the Germans? How are they distinguished, if at all, from the American New Dance choreographers?" He says there's a certain similarity to Meredith Monk and Kei Takei. "But there is a decisive difference to the most recent generation of New Dancers, which can best be described in a statement by Pina Bausch. The New Dance choreographers, as we have seen, are interested above all in movement.

Pina Bausch, however, has expressly determined that she is less interested in how people move as in what moves them – and that applies, by and large, to her German colleagues Reinhild Hoff-mann and Susanne Linke. Whereas the young Americans – inas-much as they are descendants of the Cunningham-Nikolais generation which defined dance as 'motion, not emotion' – are fascinated by dance in itself, their German dance colleagues want to learn something and transmit something about their surround-ings, about people's daily lives, their cares, fears, problems and joys. Dance serves them as a means for release and humanizing. They therefore have a more realistic, earthy and heavy – but also more concrete, social and political effect than their American counterparts.

"Is the 'German nature' in dance again to be described as primarily 'deep'? Without a doubt, but for once that is no drawback. And if I interpret the reactions to this German dance rightly – especially in Italy and France – this 'depth' and gravity are not considered even abroad to be a drawback, but rather as a necessary corrective to the American art of lightness, which all too quickly becomes an art of insignificance."

Elsewhere you write that content is basically taboo in the American experimental dance. Do you not feel that content can be expressed as form, that form and content can be one, that you can have abstraction which also deals with life around us?

SCHMIDT: I am sure one can, but I can't do anything with that "experimental dance." I think every art has to find out new things, things that haven't been said before. If not, it's not art. I think the new German tanztheater is trying to find out new things with movement. Sometimes with words, too, and with singing and film and other things. They are trying to find out new things about people, I think.

KISSELGOFF: We rarely see pure dance coming out of West Germany. There must be some reason why there are directions that are being taken in America and Germany which are so opposite. Do you feel that formal concerns are of no interest to German choreographers?

SCHMIDT: I think there is a lot of form in all the works of Pina Bausch.

KISSELGOFF: But not in themselves. Used for another reason.

HOFFMANN: I think it's just a question of emphasis. I think in everything is form and in everything is motion. Sometimes you put more accent on this or more accent on that. It's a choice, that's all. Maybe we in Europe are much more connected to the theatre tradition. In each town there is an opera house, which has all the traditional theatre pieces. Maybe that is a reason why we're still dealing with telling stories, showing characters, saying something about human beings beyond just presenting form or movement.

Each person must find her/his own movement. If that is new or not, I cannot say. It's just that we try to find our own language. I think we are full of things we have learned from our teachers, from the tradition, and also we react personally to what we have learned and what we experience daily. Through that comes a new construction. We maybe have tried to separate ourselves from movements we feel are too decorative. We try to speak as directly as possible or to find a translation that the stage allows. The stage is a world, a platform for translations, a place to say something about daily life.

KISSELGOFF: Reinhild, dance theatre often discards a dance vocabulary in favor of other kinds of movement.

HOFFMANN: Sometimes I just think it's not necessary. If there is a person over there and I am here, I just go to this person. Why should I [undulates arms forward]? [Applause]

LUTZ FORSTER (MEMBER OF WUPPERTAL TANZTHEATER AND ASSOCIATE ARTISTIC DIRECTOR OF THE JOSÉ LIMÓN DANCE COMPANY): When we started doing *Arien*, it looked like a dance piece. There were about ten movement phrases Pina gave us that we did for a long time over and over again. In the finished piece, they all concentrated into these two big dancing scenes, which I think are some of the most beautiful things we've choreographed in terms of movement. In these scenes, the dancers form couples.

One person is screaming at and chasing the other one, who is dancing different versions of those original phrases. The second such scene eventually dissolves into solo dancing. But the other things we worked on – the children's games, the women in a row being made up by the men – were much stronger than all these other movement things, so we just cut them out. Pina always starts with a lot of movement, and during the process she finds out things that are much stronger. She always tries. It's not a conscious effort not to move.

GOLDNER: Very generally speaking, I think that the chief characteristic of American dance is that choreographers are interested in movement values. Every gesture and every step has an inherent validity, beauty, and expressiveness. It's all there, all you have to do is use it.

These American ideas come from two men in the warring camps of ballet and modern dance: George Balanchine and Merce

Cunningham. I think it's extremely fortunate for younger choreographers that they have these two very, very large influences from different areas of dance.

I think younger choreographers – and some of them aren't so young anymore – have always used the idea, first, that movement is interesting in itself. That we dance not so that we can express something but first of all we dance so we can move. The idea is to move – how are you going to move, how many interesting ways can you do it.

The second idea is that movements have in themselves an expressive quality, and I want to use that term expressive in a very loose and ambiguous way. All you can say maybe is movement has a quality about it. Even Merce Cunningham, who has been very adamant about his dances not having content, has written that we jump and we also jump for joy, and there's no way to get around the second idea that we do jump for joy.

WIENER: I came out of the Cunningham postmodern tradition, which was trying to break away from some old concepts of moving. The exploration of new vocabularies came out of trying to break away from those old concepts, and people got very preoccupied with that.

What's happening now, and I can only speak for myself, is that I'm starting to move into exploring emotional expression in a more public arena. In my early work my private concerns were my emotions, which I wasn't willing or interested in sharing; my public concerns were my form and my structure, which came out of the postmodern tradition and were interlinked through different kinds of material manipulations – which goes back to "We can move a box, and that's O.K."

Now I feel so secure in my structural and formal concerns that they are becoming very private for me. Today I don't care if the audience sees these concerns or that they are recognized. I am currently more into sharing my emotional concerns.

KISSELGOFF: Emotion is the new word among American choreographers. I can tell you that American choreographers of the '30s and '40s are laughing their heads off. I would just like to ask Miss Hoffmann if she in fact began with plotless, pure movement work.

HOFFMANN: Well, I did one early piece of choreography – more like an exercise – which was pure movement. It was like splitting two or three people like a mirror picture or like a wave movement. But I am not able to separate a personal feeling or a personal movement from a form. It always comes together. That's the impulse.

KISSELGOFF: American dance has tended to go in the direction of formalism, and the German dance as we see it is a form of neo-expressionism. These are labels, and they're too pat, but they are general categories. Do you accept them, Jochen?

SCHMIDT: Not that of neo-expressionism, because it's much more than that.

I think there have been two lines in American modern dance. One is more realistic – Martha Graham, Doris Humphrey, José Limón and Anna Sokolow. But it was lost after Graham, I see a lot of younger American choreographers now doing things which classical ballet can do better. They are always trying to become brilliant and fast. I ask: why don't they do ballet?

For me, some of those dancers and choreographers are like hamsters. These little beasts in a wheel go around and around and around but always remain in the same spot.

KISSELGOFF: You feel Graham and Humphrey were realistic. I feel they are totally not realistic. Realism is a word that you and your fellow critics use very often in writing about dance theatre. That's very interesting to me, because I don't find tanztheater realistic. Bausch's work is expressionistic in that there is a very strong distillation of a prime emotion in every episode and every character. It's personal experience as expressed in a form of distortion, which is very common to expressionistic art, especially expressionism in Germany.

GOLDNER: It seems to me the action in Bausch alternates between large mass things and small things, where the action breaks down and there is a lot of small individual gesture. There is a lot of individuality. I think in that sense, it's quite realistic.

SCHMIDT: I know that realism can't be naturalism. We all know that. I am sure Bausch is not naturalistic, but German dance theatre is closer to daily life than the dances of Nina Wiener or Douglas Dunn or Laura Dean.

KISSELGOFF: Why is Dean separate from daily life? To me she is very in tune with her generation. That's what I see, Laura Deans all around me in the street.

SCHMIDT: Just spinning?

KISSELGOFF: The symbol is spinning, but the sensibility is what her generation expresses.

SCHMIDT: Spinning is all I see.

WIENER: I think what Bausch does is extremely simple. The emotions presented are not the whole range of the emotion you could look at.

In all her dances I see the conflict or confrontation between men and women. Each time it's the same thing. That kind of angst emotion is not something that I want to participate in. That has nothing to do with whether I think she's brilliant, which I do. That angst emotion goes on for too long for me to want to participate in it.

I also have a difficult time with the sense of editing. I think the sense of time in European work and American work is very different. It may have to do with this sense of speed – in New York we go fast.

I think one of the reasons why American dance got so focused on the abstraction of pure movement has to do with the fact that we underwent the same kind of revolution that the original modern dancers underwent when they found that the ballet was very limiting for them and they had other, more earthy concerns. Modern dance became completely connected to this emotional thing, and in order to make that break, the postmoderns switched to the other side.

Postmodern dance was about establishing individual vocabularies. There was a tremendous pressure for new patterns of expression, which has just started to let up. American dance has been extremely diffuse, pushing out in all directions.

People are now trying to work more in the framework of sharing how they feel and sharing things that are more common on a personal level. It doesn't happen to be taking the form of dance theatre, but it is taking another form.

GOLDNER: I think there are certain emotions which Americans think are the proper emotions to show on the stage, and they are very different from what the Germans think. There's a common American sensibility now that says: the heavier you get, the more trivial you are, and the lighter you stay, the more intelligent it will be. I think this also comes from the Balanchine/Cunningham tradition. Americans have trouble with the heaviness of German emotion or expression, because we find the heaviness rather "lightweight." You might feel the same way about the lightness of American dance. You find us trivial because of that lightness.

HOFFMANN: Really, I think Merce Cunningham's work is very interesting and very intelligent. I enjoy it immensely. But I also think that it isn't good to say you will not deal with the problems you have. I often hear that what you see in our pieces is only about man–woman relationships. It's not meant to be so narrow. It stands for problems that human beings have, nations have, the world has. It stands for more than just man–woman.

For what I hear and see when I walk through the streets in New York, there are a lot of problems here. When young choreographers living here choose *mainly* just to move and not to relate strongly to what they see daily, then I ask: why?

SCHMIDT: Balanchine's type of choreography was in a certain sense finished because he never could make any ballet last more than one act. If you want to tell things and to make longer ballets, you need a new form. The German dance theatre found a new form. It wasn't really new in the arts, because it was in painting and film. It was the form of collage and montage. The works of Pina Bausch are much closer to an Eisenstein movie than to classical or narrative ballet. The Bausch pieces are narrative. They tell things, but they don't tell stories. They tell: then it was this, then that, and that. There are always things going on, and you have to put it together in your head. She knows very well what she is doing and all the things she does are very, very formed.

Maybe some of you remember a scene in *Café Müller* with three people – man, woman, and one who helps them. They do it again and again. They become faster and faster and faster. It's a very sad scene in the beginning, and in the end when it's very fast it's very humorous. For me, she's not doing things ten times in the same way. There's always really a difference. If not, she knows why not.

KISSELGOFF: Could I ask George Jackson, do you feel the Living Theatre played a role in German dance theatre?

JACKSON (CONTRIBUTING CRITIC, *WASHINGTON DANCEVIEW*):   Perhaps by way of Pina Bausch. I know she was over here. I do not think she saw any of the early Judson experiments. At least she said she hadn't. But I do believe she went to the Living Theatre.

Certainly the sprawling structures of most of Pina Bausch's works and what I saw in Hoffmann's *Callas* last night remind me very much of the Living Theatre. I fail to see form. That's the weakness. The material is interesting, the methods are interesting, but ultimately most of these pieces repeat themselves because they lack a competent form – compact and significant. The works go on and on, and everything that has been created is destroyed at the end.

Form means significant change. An organic structure that makes emotional sense. Emotion not as the expression of a literal, realistic feeling but a formal implementation or diminution. I would say Balanchine did succeed in creating a ballet that is more than one act and that has formal unity and formal emotion. That is his *Don Quixote,* probably his greatest ballet, I'd say. I don't see this mastery of form in the Living Theatre and the current German dance theatre. I don't see that as it goes on it becomes more meaningful. I just don't see it.

Violence

KISSELGOFF: What really disturbs American audiences and dancers – especially about Bausch's work – is the violence depicted. Some say Bausch may be condemning violence but that she revels in depicting it; they say she works up the audience so they are thrilled, and it's the thrill of the lynch mob in watching people bang their heads against the wall or hit each other. Is that a characteristic of German dance?

SCHMIDT: I'll answer with a question. Would you think that way about cinema, television, drama, and literature – or only dance? I think Bansch is doing what all other artists are doing. She is not attracted by violence. I'm sure she's not. She hates it, but she shows it and she shows it in a very comic form. You really have to see the pieces more than one time, and you will find them more comical every time.

GOLDNER: It's not only the violence. It's also certain sexual aspects of the work. In *Callas,* there was much humor in the men's costumes and in the way they held themselves in the dresses and in the bathing suits. There is also something very disturbing about that. I think that's also a part of the violence you're talking about. It's not just men and women fighting each other but a certain depiction of men as women.

HOFFMANN: I want to come back to my question. I felt I didn't get an answer. Why do so many people here in America try not to be confronted in their art with human problems? For example, violence, you have it daily. I hear the sound of sirens every day. I always hear it – it never goes away. It's like a fear of dealing with it, questioning it. Isn't it important to confront it?

FORSTER: I'm surprised when people talk so much about violence in Pina's pieces. I'm always surprised, because I see in so many American companies a lack of tenderness. In all Pina's pieces people are tender to each other.

American critics are really obsessed with violence. I am appalled to see the news in America. They really dig into everybody who's lying there on the ground. That would never happen on German television.

GOLDNER: In tribute to Bausch, what we see on the stage – and also in *Callas –* is much more powerful than what we see on television. To Americans, when we're seeing people shoot-'em-up, it's an age-old convention, it's stylized. We're eating our cereal and ironing our clothes. This is background music. We're not taking it seriously. But when we see this on the stage, it has a truth, it has an immediacy, and a power.

KISSELGOFF: In *Gebirge,* many people told me they left because they could not take the image of Josephine Ann Endicott lying down repeatedly and having her back slashed with red. I saw it as a statement of a Pavlovian response in which the victim can be taught to submit. People accused me of being overly cerebral about something that was extremely disturbing to them. I would like to deal with that image. What is comic or tender about it?

SPECTATOR: I think what we see a lot in Pina Bausch, which is the antithesis of American television, is the rage of a woman.

[MURMURS OF DISSENT AND DISINTEREST.]

KISSELGOFF: Wait a minute. Don't go "ah." I didn't hear any female voices going, "ah."

SPECTATOR: We would not see Maria Tallchief dancing with hairy armpits. The level of reality of violence and of sex all wed together in Bausch makes it very exciting and revolutionary for an American audience. And, I think, very hard for people to take. I thought the scene from *Gebirge* which you talked about was very powerful. We hear repeatedly about women who are beaten, tormented by their husbands and then sent to jail for killing them. That doesn't seem so real to us or upsetting, but when Pina Bausch distills it through art on stage, people get up and leave.

I don't think these dances are realistic in the way Emile Zola's novels are, but the dancers running across the stage in wet, dripping satin evening gowns destroy a certain kind of dramatic illusion that we're used to staying behind on the American stage.

SPECTATOR: The fetishism of women's clothes is nowhere better revealed than in Bausch and also in *Callas,* when you see men stripped of their gender, all coming out wearing red evening gowns. In *The Seven Deadly Sins* the men come out in women's underwear. On the women we think it looks just sexy and dynamite, baby, but on the men they look jerky. I noticed in *Callas* that the dancers were used as dancers irrespective of gender. To me, that's very, very thrilling. To my friend who was there with me, it was terrifying.

I think the people who don't like the violence are really responding to some deep-seated horror. Is it possible that there is no difference between men and women – it's just clothes? Is it possible that the clothes we wear are nothing but convention that we can throw out? I think that's frightening, and not simply because of the violence.

JACKSON: One objection that people here have voiced about tanztheater is that it looks too practiced. When William Dunas threw himself against the wall in the '60s, he was doing an experiment. In the Bausch work, it looked too rehearsed, and hence the moral ambiguity.

JOAN ROSS ACOCELLA (SENIOR EDITOR, *DANCE* MAGAZINE): Sometimes the violence looks simply like theatrical kilowatts rather than a human problem we are seriously exploring. Also, I do think it should be considered that it's not just banging people into walls that feels violent. For instance, the opening image in *Gebirge* when Jan Minarik takes the balloons out of his swimsuit and blows them up. There's surely some relation to genitals and his nose is cramped down, and then they pop. There is a large amount of sexual humiliation that takes place in a soft, comic way – someone brought up comedy supposedly offsetting the violence in these things.

I think the problem is not so much with the subject matter – though I certainly also feel my nerves screech with that gashing in *Gebirge* – as with the way it's dealt with artistically. It's the episodic character, the fact that we can count on it. That every four minutes you're going to be hit over the head with a hammer, whether it be somebody being banged into the wall or some terrible business of a man's pants being pulled down, which eventually looks more violent to me. It's not repetition that bothers me. It's repetition without development, variation, exploration. Development is something that we in America associate with intelligence. It starts to look after a while like something that is cheap – just a theatrical firecracker.

SCHMIDT: Can you imagine that you and the American critics are using the wrong criteria for those pieces?

ACOCELLA: It's possible that you come from one culture and we from another.

SCHMIDT: It has nothing to do with culture. We had the same problems in the beginning, because this is a new form. What you are saying about development does not concern these pieces. It's not the point.

Please remember what the public thought about Cunningham when he worked first in New York City and then when he came to Europe. Remember that people thought Nijinsky was a very bad choreographer. Now, 70 years later, we are beginning to think maybe he was 50 years ahead of his time. I think it's something that happens to all great artists at the beginning. They set a new border.

Postscript

The initial refusal of the Goethe House audience to deal with the "rage of a woman" in Pina Bausch's work is not atypical for the New York dance community. I have seen similar concerns with the way women are represented in dance dismissed at another dance critics' symposium. The dominant male/submissive female stereotype is mutely upheld in practically all American dance criticism.

But the real subject is not the rage of a woman; it is the *unheard* rage of a woman. In Bausch's pieces, violence comes in bursts of dense repetition. These acts of violence are neither conventional nor naturalistic; rather, they exist on the plane of metaphor. They deal with the violation of women's bodies but, more so, of women's autonomy.

In *Kontaktkof*, a group of men surround a woman; their initial caresses turn into tweaks and pulls and tugs. She offers no protest. They literally pick at her for what seems a very long time. In *Gebirge*, a madman makes his way through a line of women, making each one say "Uncle" with whatever amount of force is necessary to overcome her resistance (or lack thereof).

The way Bausch uses repetition both intensifies and anesthetizes the response to the violence. At the same time that her repetitions accumulate emotional force, they also undercut emotional impact with the overtly theatrical (repeatable, therefore acted and "make-believe") behavior. That's why some spectators sweat through these sequences while others laugh.

The effect varies from spectator to spectator. I was horrified by that passage in *Gebirge* in which a woman repeatedly gets down on all fours, pulls up her dress to bare her back, and gets slashed by a man with a red lipstick or crayon. The animalistic position of the woman, the slashing movement, the thickening red marks on her back – all signal to me quite plainly a violent encounter made doubly despicable by the complicity of the victim. Kisselgoff, viewing this scene as a model of Pavlovian response, ignores its full and strident political–social–sexual content.

There is in the dance community a resistance to Bausch's use of repetition. It's chauvinistic to dismiss such a fundamental formalist technique as formless and boring just because it serves expressionist ends. The same holds true of Bausch's collage structure, which is neither as formless as the Americans say nor as unique in dance as the Germans would have us believe: the works of Yoshiko Chuma and The School of Hard Knocks and Stephanie Skura's *Travelog*, for instance, are collages.

While some American critics seem unable to read the formal and structural properties of Bausch's work, German critics seem unable to read the expressive qualities (and not necessarily emotional expression) of postmodern American dance. The symposium concretized the very different ways two cultures have of reading movement.

And yet the anti-formalists at the symposium were arguing against a straw man. American formalism today is not the rigorous formalism of the Judson days. Even the Judson Church choreographers – Lucinda Childs, Trisha Brown, most notably – are now making overtly theatrical dances. And rarely do you find a young, experimental choreographer dealing with "pure form" (if there can be such a thing). Bebe Miller, for example, gives full rein to the expressiveness of her dances. *Trapped in Queens* is a high-energy, limb-flinging dance, but it also suggests a community of generous relationships: if these people are trapped in Queens, they are doing their darndest to help each other get out.

Bausch's work brilliantly embeds powerful dramatic imagery in formal repetition. In sequences when I realized that something would happen again and again and again, I experienced a very unsettling but at the same time pleasurable suspension of time. Instead of going forward, time expanded in another dimension. The spatial metaphor is apt, because the experience has to do with a sense of a totally enveloping, absorbing space. What's out there on stage becomes very internalized: inside/outside, before/next become one.

But what is out there on Bausch's stage is women's acquiescent powerlessness. (A psychologically unsatisfying strategy for survival: "Don't resist your rapist, and you may live through the attack.") Nearly without exception, the violence is done by men to women. Nearly without exception, the women remain passive. And it's crucial to remember that the content of the repetitions are verbatim. There is no register of change, of the woman's movement toward freedom. She remains utterly powerless, without any recourse or prospects of enfranchisement. Frustration, desperation – they're the emotions of Bausch's nihilist imagery, which bespeaks not just the physical but emotional, social, political and economic oppression of women.

This repeated imagery can tease the spectator's heightened sense of anticipation and expectation into dread. In *Gebirge*, every time a balloon blew up in the face of that man in swimming trunks – and he must have burst at least four in his face – I jumped a foot, even though I consciously prepared myself for it. Every time the madman in *Gebirge* made another woman cry "Uncle," I winced – not just because of what was in front of my eyes but because I dreaded the thought of going through it again. Only in *The Seven Deadly Sins*, perhaps because it was the last production of the run or because it is unselectively shrill, was I disengaged. Such a flood of emotion on stage – *Sins* didn't have the power that the stark repetitions lent the other pieces. Or maybe familiarity makes Bausch's violence just as numbing as it has the 6 o'clock news.

Bausch apologists charge that American critics shouldn't be so supersensitive to the violence in her pieces when there is so much violence on American television. They overlook, however, the essential difference between the violence in these two genres.

On American television, violence is undeniably a main attraction. But the violence is always presented within a mediating ideology which espouses that "violence is immoral and illegal. Violators must be caught and punished," Most cop and adventure shows (*A-Team*, for example) are virtual morality plays. Good guys win; bad guys lose.

In Bausch, what's the mediating ideology? There is none. Though I admire Bausch's formal techniques, what they express is repugnant. Early in her season, I felt it unfair to require that an artist go beyond depicting provocative images to providing the spectator with ways of processing them. But the more I saw, the more the violence began to undercut its own impact and the more the "unheard rage of a woman" became debilitating and even insulting. To state the obvious – that women collaborate with their victimizers – over and over again without exploring the reasons for their passivity or the ways in which they do/can/will fight back makes violence, oppression, and passivity look inevitable and "natural." Bausch may be displaying violence, she may even be confronting it, but she certainly isn't questioning it. It's as if she's built violence and oppression into a massive wall without allowing us any cracks to break it open and see what's supporting it.

She scrupulously avoids inscribing her pieces with anything that would guide her spectators toward a resolution of their emotional response by structuring each piece as a string of discrete scenes or bits. What holds each of her works together is not any point of view but rather the mise-en-scène and the heightened theatricality of it all. (Ironically, Bausch's works could be construed as even more theatrically hermetic and self-referring than the American formalist works, whose lack of overt reference to the "real world" the tanztheater proponents disdain).

Without a framework that helps us resolve the stew of emotions she provokes, we're left to deal with them through our own prior assumptions. If Bausch is aiming to foreground the horror of men's violence against women, she doesn't succeed in changing the mind of anyone who doesn't already agree with her.

Artifice and authenticity

Gender scenarios in Pina Bausch's Dance Theatre

Marianne Goldberg

Originally published in *Women and Performance*, 1984

In Pina Bausch's Dance Theatre, confessions are simulations, unique identities assemblages of gender stereotypes, heartfelt gestures fiction. Bausch's company from Wuppertal, Germany offers the lure of authentic emotional expression. Her repertory could be considered a revival of the "Ausdruckstanz" tradition of Mary Wigman, Rudolf Laban or Kurt Jooss, in which "inner necessity," a kind of emotional kinesthetic-honesty, was considered the choreographer's most important resource.[1] Yet Bausch's dances communicate an overriding tension between artifice and authenticity – particularly in her deconstruction of gender identities. The humanist model of self-expression that fueled the Ausdruckstanz choreographers is under critique in her work, as much as she reiterates it as a form of nostalgia. Bausch defamiliarizes "spontaneous" emotional and kinesthetic responses and rejects the idea that they stem from an essential inner self. She scrutinizes the social constructs that separate men and women into opposites.

To dissect solidified gender meanings, Bausch employs various strategies: juxtapositions of simultaneous, incongruous activities, a defiance of the time and space conventions of realism, and narrative fragmentation that disrupts the contexts of human behavior. She distorts ordinary patterns of movement and speech and isolates events into bits that will not gel into conventional meanings. Bausch's work shares concerns with the dance formalism that evolved from New York City's Judson Dance Theatre in the 1960s, in her focus on codes and conventions of communication, task and game structures, pedestrian actions, and minimalist repetition.[2] But unlike dance formalism in the work of Trisha Brown, Lucinda Childs or Laura Dean, Bausch emphasizes the overlay of psychological and social motivation on kinesthesia, never attempting to isolate the elements of dance (time, weight, or space) from a highly charged, emotional context. Until recently, the American dance formalists have erased gender differences by giving performers androgynous roles. Bausch's pieces have been laden with gender clichés and the symbiosis and violence they provoke between men and women.

Although Bausch's dances show the influence of both the Ausdruckstanz expressionist tradition and the formalism of the 1960s, she effectively disempowers both systems. In a Bausch work, formal gestures become subjective as they accumulate new meanings with each repetition, while expression becomes a highly coded language that simulates authentic experience. Movements lose authenticity to become histrionics rather than Ultimate Truth, mocking the authority of introspection. Bausch makes it clear that the self, including the body, never exists prior to its gendered acculturation.[3]

Bausch's works involve the audience in the kinds of intense sensory experience that Antonin Artaud might have had in mind for his Theatre of Cruelty. In *Arien* (1979), the spectator is greeted with the dank odor of a stage covered with three inches of water; in *Gebirge* (1984), with the dust rising from a stage filled with dirt and the musty air of a fog machine. Yet equally important, Bausch uses Brechtian alienation devices to disrupt these experiences at their points of greatest intensity.[4]

There are jarring shifts from the immediacy of sensation to reflective thought.

Bausch foregrounds the theatrical experience and skews its contract of seduction between male viewer and female object. In *Kontakthof* (1978), Bausch makes the usual contract blatant: a woman approaches a man in the front row and asks him for spare change to put into a mechanical rocking horse so she can take a ride. But early in *Arien*, she reverses convention: a male performer seduces a woman in the box seats, calling to her, "I'd rather get you alone. Café au lait? Croissant? Would you like to ride in my car?" In *Viktor,* which had its U.S. premiere at the Brooklyn Academy of Music, dancers are carted to the front of the stage like statues and auctioned off to the audience. They occasionally escape from the stage into the house to sell postcards or to serve buns with jam. In much of Bausch's work the performers seem to be like the mannequins dressed up in windows to seduce passersby. But if Bausch makes it clear that the audience is buying and the performers are selling, she doesn't exactly give the spectators what they paid for. She presents the ungraceful body, making usually repressed physiological obscenities blatant – her performers spit, smoke, scream or squirt water from their mouths.

All of Bausch's performers – both male and female – seem to be on exhibit for the audience's consumption. Both *Arien* and *Kontakthof* feature a photographer who takes pictures of the stage action and then offers them to the audience as souvenirs. The interaction is more gruesome in *Gebirge* when a man's arm serves as bread for a fresh cold cut sandwich and he offers spectators a bite. In all these situations, Bausch reveals the performer's exhibitionism and the audience's voyeurism by breaking the proscenium's pictorializing function. There is no fourth wall in her theatre – performers confront spectators by speaking to them directly.

At one point in *Kontakthof*, Bausch gives a parable for the theatrical experience. The performers pull up chairs to face backstage, where an inner set of curtains opens to reveal a movie screen. They watch a film of young ducks on a lake, going through the paces of socialization in the bird world. As the performers watch the ducks onscreen within their theatre and we watch them within ours, an analogy becomes evident between the predetermined patterns of both groups. Each seems equally contrived, equally natural.

Bausch's performers disrupt the moat of safety that separates the world of stage fantasy from the comfortable seats of the ticket holders. They inhabit the theatre as if it were their living space. They use the proscenium frame as a prop, slamming themselves into it, or performing stunts for the audience at its edge. The house lights are turned up as part of the ongoing events. To indicate the end of the first half of the program, a performer simply calls out "intermission!" Bausch carries out Brecht's call for a "smoker's" audience, aware of itself in the theatre as it would be at a sporting event.

Much of Bausch's work subverts the romantic infatuations that are the soul of ballet. She shows their dark sides. In *Viktor*, the stage is a pit, surrounded by high earthen walls, from which dirt is shoveled constantly onto the stage throughout the performance. Within this open grave, a woman lines the inside of her toe shoes with strips of steak. As she rises on pointe, the red oozing from her feet evokes the infamous blood of ballerinas who have deformed their own bodies to become cultural icons of grace. At another point, women in fluffy dresses and high heels grasp gymnastic rings, swinging though the air to the tune of "Dancing Cheek to Cheek." Bausch sensationalizes the filmically clichéd moment when a person rushes forward to meet a lover. In Bausch's version, the women strain despite their relentless smiles; they flinch only a little after repeating the passionate onrush. These women are trapped in an oppressive Hollywood version of romance that prevents any true flights of passion. For an American audience, nihilism is the greatest foreignness in Bausch's work.

Through her use of irony, Bausch not only prevents glorification of her performers, she also breaks the barrier between the performer's body and the bodies of the spectators. In *Carnations*, which is a sort of patrolled Arden where dancers can transgress the constricting rules of ballet, the stage is filled with a garden of pink silk carnations guarded by German shepherd dogs ready to attack trespassers. A man in a sundress performs balletic tricks that are designed to draw applause. Suddenly, he drops what he's doing and tells the audience, "If that's what you want I'm not going to do it – do it yourself." Later, the dancers give a ballet lesson to the audience, asking everyone to stand up and open their arms to the count of four. The audience complies, and when the performers spill off the stage, their stylized arm gestures turn into embraces as they hug the spectators in the front row. In this unexpected closeness, Bausch has trespassed into the void that traditionally separates dancer from viewer, European troupe and American audience. When performers break from the puppet-like tasks Bausch usually imposes on them, they audience glimpses their humanness. But still, there remains the gulf of artifice. Even an embrace, one of the few acts of potential grace on Bausch's stage, is ambiguous: touch can intensify either intimacy or isolation.

Kontakthof reiterates the cynicism of earlier Bausch works – the incessant male–female battles of *Bluebeard* (1980), *Rite of Spring* (1975), and *Café Müller* (1978). *Kontakthof* presents a society degenerating in self-exhibition. Intimate conversations and emotional outbursts are melodramatically amplified by microphones. Masochistic stunts gain approval. A man determinedly slams his hand in a door and everyone applauds; people humiliate one another by poking armpits, nipples or any other private zone of the body available. A chorus of men and women appear ludicrous as they advance toward each other by scooting on chairs while gesticulating in motions of sexual seduction. The one tender encounter is between a shy man and woman who risk undressing only at long distance, from opposite ends of the stage.

Arien presents a more humorous, tongue-in-cheek play on some of the same themes. This time, sexuality and vulnerability are explored as adolescent fantasies. Hollywood romance, children's rhymes and games, and the exotic temptation of tropical paradise evoke an "in utero" nostalgia on the shimmering surface of a water-filled stage floor. The sides of the stage are lined with mirrors and huge dressing room tables. *Arien* opens with the performers preparing for the evening's show in colorful robes and dressing gowns, their own eccentric versions of glamour.

Reflective surfaces are everywhere. Mirrors triple the image of women who put on make-up, fall repeatedly to the ground with great splashes of water, or engage in conversation with their own multiplied reflection. When the lights darken, the watery shadows on the back fire wall look like a river and for a moment the stage seems to dissolve. The projection spills onto the walls outside the proscenium frame, as far up as the balcony. Water, shadows, mirrors, and multiple identities combine into a reflexive make-believe. The possibilities for sexuality that society holds up to its adolescents are constructed and reconstructed as the performers parade in front of the mirrors.[5]

Bausch pairs these adolescents off as romantic misfits, critiquing the "naturalness" of conventional male–female romance. A man walks across the stage locked in a prolonged kiss with a woman little more than half his size. Her feet dangle around his knees as he holds her up to his mouth. The moment is refreshingly lighthearted and tender for a Bausch piece, and it sets the tone for much of *Arien*. There are further romantic incongruities when a young woman falls in love with a hippopotamus who is oblivious to her advances. The life-size replica of a hippo wanders around, perfectly at home in the water-drenched environment. The woman sunbathes and takes a swim in an onstage pool Just wide and deep enough for a few athletic strokes of the back crawl. Leaning her arms and face languidly over the pool edge, she eyes the animal, looking as though she has just materialized from a 1940s Hollywood pin-up poster. To the strains of "Night and day, you are the one," she seductively splashes water over the hippo's back.

Our nostalgic pleasure continues as she slips into an elegant, romantic dress and escorts the hippo to a banquet table that is assembled on the spot. This banquet in a field of water is as odd and delightful as Alice in Wonderland's Mad Hatter banquet or Fellini's banquets for entire dislocated societies. Guests arrive and take their seats with exaggerated gestures of social greeting. Throughout the banquet, an empty chair remains for the hippo, but he stays tentatively off to the side. The enamored woman spends a lot of time surreptitiously waving to him behind her back. In the end, she is left dejected. The hippo saunters away without reciprocating her infatuation.

The now-drunk banqueters don clowns' masks and the men dress as women in colorful, wacky attire. Amidst the antics, the rejected woman nurses her broken heart. She lies submerged in the water and sobs, as others monitor her pulse. A man in a woman's fluffy green robe and floppy white hat self-times a camera and dashes to pose next to her with a huge rubber swan.

As is often the case when Bausch includes cross-dressing in her work, men in women's clothing are funny. To masquerade as a woman demands that a man surrender his masculine privilege and step down in social prestige. In other works, Bausch dresses the women in men's clothing. In *The Seven Deadly Sins*, the women wear suits along with the men in a procession. But their movements are violent rather than funny, as they join the men in playing rapists. Bausch's use of cross-dressing makes the gender politics of power obvious. "Feminized" or "masculinized" gestures communicate differently when performed by men or women. Movements telegraph power relations according to their conventional gender uses.[6] In crossing genders, Bausch foregrounds these differences in power. She chips away at the authentic "natural *truth*" of patriarchal culture.

The final moments of *Arien* equate romantic fantasy with death in eerie images of tenderness and drowning. The men lie down in the water and the women join them, letting their weight sink into the surface of the floor. The couples explore each other's faces with gentle gestures, embracing to the slow rhythm of piano music. They shift positions comfortably, lovers drifting into a deep, warm sleep, entwined in each other's arms, until they almost look dead. Closeness becomes submersion, symbiosis, death.

To end the piece, the cast repeats the dressing table scene of the opening, reminding us that this was all masquerade. In framing the piece with pre-performance behavior, Bausch points to the paradox that the "behind-the-scenes" glimpse is not spontaneous since it can be repeated as a coda. She suggests that everyday behavior is a performance – the impulses that precede theatrics have their own artifice.[7]

In a 1985 interview, Bausch told me, "Because I also am the audience, I want to live with it." But *Gebirge* was the only piece that tipped my involvement as a spectator from detachment to emotional experience. In this piece, Bausch mixes the everyday and the fantasy in a way traditionally associated with dreams or visionary cinema: jumps in time, unexplained dissolves from one image to another, abrupt interruptions of scenes, and the use of slow or fast motion induce disorientation.

In cinema, more than in theatre, the spectator is constructed as the origin of staged representations. The movement of the camera becomes analogous to the spectator's own eye and so can replicate the perceptual mechanisms of fantasy.[8] Images are hermetically sealed on the screen and their illusions difficult to disrupt. But Bausch uses sensory experience to engulf the audience to an extent not possible in the movies. In two fog scenes in *Gebirge,* she blurs the boundaries between the visual realm of the stage and the sensory experience of the spectator. If images are sealed on the screen, in Bausch's theatre they extend beyond the frame of the stage to envelop the audience. Onscreen, fog can obscure vision but in live theatre it can congest our lungs.

The full title of *Gebirge, Auf Dem Gebirge Hat Man Ein Geschrei Gehort*, translates, "On the Mountain a Cry Was Heard." Yet if the stage is covered with the dirt of a mountainside, many of the gestures are derived from swimming, rowing, or canoeing. Forming a line seated on the ground, groups of men or women mime a crew boat skimming across water. A woman flaps her whole body like a fish out of water; another woman is carried through the air in a wave-like path, paddling as if on a canoe. This incongruity creates a friction between stage action and scenography that indicates fantasy: land can be defined as water simply by activities that stake out territory. The displacement of this amphibian society onto dry land continually estranges even the most mundane action.

In a prelude, the performers run as if terrorized through the area behind the audience, again including us in the frame of their action. A hefty man in a swim cap, fins, and goggles pulls one balloon after another from his red bathing briefs and blows them up until they pop. Suddenly, a gang of men in white shirts and black trousers brutally force a resisting man and woman together into a kiss. This scene of enforced heterosexuality is repeated over and over to a fanfare of strident, heroic classical music.

The grotesque portrayal of phallic/patriarchal sexuality develops into sadism that permeates the piece. Billie Holliday sings about a pastoral scene in the American South that is disrupted by the "sudden smell of burning flesh" – and we are all implicated as voyeurs in a sadomasochistic spectacle. The burning flesh serves as a metaphor for the performers' display of violence and pleasure in a theatrical marketplace. Sometimes the cruelty is obvious – the man in the red briefs slowly and repetitively tosses lit matches into a group of people who stand immobile. Sometimes vulnerability is tinged with black humor. Two women in flouncy green dresses perform "innocent" cartwheels that reveal their underwear and sexy little dance phrases that make them available commodities. A man in a black leotard with glitter trim and bare legs, his hands forming the shape of a tiara over his head, steadily bourées across the stage. "Why are you looking at me?" he anxiously asks the audience.

At times the black humor turns to cruelty and the audience is dependent on gut response to grapple with the oncoming images. A lethargic group of women sits in a row leaning against one another as a crazed man twists them one by one to the floor shouting, "Say uncle!" When he has dominated them all, he screams at the top of his lungs. "I want to kill! I want to murder them!" Abruptly, the scene shifts to rock and roll music and men gyrate across the stage to the beat of "Baby, don't you know my love is true …" At the height of immersion in this scene, Bausch cuts to throbbing violin music. A woman in a black negligee travels alongside the grotesque man in the red briefs, her hair covering her face. She prostrates herself, raising her gown to bare her back so that he can slash it with red paint. They perform this ritual over and over again. She continues even after he has left, like a prisoner who remains in an unlocked cell when the guard is no longer watching.

These images follow one another so quickly that there is no time for thought. The three scenes are so abruptly edited that one erases the next. Only in retrospect does it become clear that the rock and roll scene is sutured in between two sado-masochistic sequences in which men dominate women. Bausch walks a fine line between spectacular exploitation of the victimized woman and consciousness-raising.

Parody depends on the awareness of both performers and audience. If either considers Bausch's deconstruction of gender roles as pastiche rather than parody, her cultural interrogation could degenerate into a bizarre entertainment that re-inscribes oppressive values to the detriment of the woman who is sadistically displayed.[9] Contemporary audiences familiar with MTV – or the TV news for that matter – could easily experience Bausch's work in this way. In this case, sex and violence become mired in the very sensationalism Bausch seeks to critique. For those spectators who do reflect on the sequence, she makes it clear that "gut response" is actually a form of perceptual ideology. We make sense of the chaotic oncoming events according to systems of meaning-making that are controlled by perceptions of sex and power.

While the woman still wants to be slashed with the red paint, the man in the red briefs slits a table down its center and opens it. The stage erupts in fog and a density of action. Another woman runs on screaming, clasping a red dress to cover her exposed body. A man grabs it and flashes it at her like a bullfighter. The bursts of red in fog repeatedly signal her desperation. A chorus of men and women scoot along the floor to popular instrumental music when, suddenly, the music stops; in mid-scene the curtain closes, again breaking the illusion of the fourth wall. The disruption points to the arbitrariness of stage conventions for viewing theatre. It also points up the artifice of conventional gender roles and their resultant violence: their inevitability can be halted, even if only momentarily, by closing a curtain.

When the fog has cleared, a woman in a black negligee runs in a circle that encompasses the empty stage. As she runs, she comforts herself, fluidly crossing one arm to touch her shoulder then folding her body forward. Her limbs seem to flow from the middle of her body outward, and metaphorically from the center of her soul out into the world. She runs for a long time, heroically, her head high, until she falls to the ground in exhaustion, pauses a moment, then tries again. This is one of the most moving passages in *Gebirge* – endurance, bravery under duress, the indominitable determination of the human spirit despite a world that crumbles around her. We are privy for a moment to seemingly authentic acts. Yet the passage also calls to mind the elevation of woman as muse of freedom – the Winged Victory of Samothrace, the Statue of Liberty – symbols that serve to rationalize our violence as often as they fuel inspiration. Our mistresses of liberty can be foils that conceal refractions against freedom. In eulogizing woman they also defile her by forcing her to become a symbol of political systems that may withhold her actual power in everyday political life.

Bausch isolates these heroic dance phrases as one of the few elements of formal dance that she retains. She quotes bits of them, just as she clips fragments of everyday social gestures. The physical language system that produces these heroics is based on a subjectivist model: the impulse radiates from the inside outward, embodying the modern dance manifesto of moving from the inside out.[10] Although the movement language illustrates Wigman's concept of "inner necessity," in which the subjective impulse of the dancer determines the positioning of her body, in Bausch's world it becomes a vestige of dignity that nostalgically recalls a time when the body was conceived as an integrated whole or a reservoir of ultimate truths.

As the first half of *Gebirge* comes to an end, a woman stands motionless, her eyes closed. A man approaches her and kisses her, but she does not reciprocate. He continues, as Bausch's men often do, kissing her as though he owns her. He is replaced by another man who brushes her hair with chalk, turning it white, aging her before our eyes. She begins to sing peacefully, responding to the tenderness rather than to the implied cruelty. Her song could be about the time it takes to grow old, or it could just help her to be oblivious to everything, finding shelter in her internal world. The chalk gives off a slight mist over her head, recalling the mystery and violence of the fog scene. She remains motionless like that, center stage, eyes still closed, throughout intermission. By having her persist in her intensity of inner involvement while the audience enters the non-theatrical reality of intermission, Bausch amplifies her stillness, her victimization, her enforced passivity. The woman is both tenacious and extremely alone. Most spectators forget about her as they become distracted by more pedestrian priorities. Just as she refuses the visible realm by closing her eyes, she becomes invisible to the audience by becoming peripheral. Yet by breaking the convention of intermission, Bausch foregrounds her marginality and places it center-stage, making us aware that woman's experiences are often ignored and left to exist between the acts.

In the second half of *Gebirge*, Bausch offers an alternative view of masculinity in a male duet that counters the grotesque phallic imagery of the first half. A tall, slim man executes a Romantic flourish that sets his body in locomotion, his arms pulling him into space in search of something solid to lean on. He is a lost Siegfried, displaced from *Swan Lake*, or a Don Quixote in search of a Dulcinea who will never materialize – the Romantic hero seeking the unattainable to pacify him. A shorter man attempts to find him something to attach himself to – a piano bench, the proscenium edge, a blanket, finally his own shoulder. Together they perform a little Chaplinesque two-step, arm in arm, another Bauschian pair of romantic misfits, one tall, one short. They turn toward us, then away, like a couple walking into the distance at the end of a movie.

The end of *Gebirge* is surreal. Bausch recycles motifs from earlier sections as if they have been sifted through strata of the unconscious of patriarchy. A transition into dream state is made by a droopy woman who aimlessly rests her head on her bent arm and points into nowhere – the kind of tedium that precedes fantasy. A man in a turban with veils appears. An eccentric version of a female belly dance costume, with deflated balloons hanging like breasts, completes his attire. Incongruously, he wears eyeglasses, and washes dishes in a bucket. A woman in a blue business suit gives him a long passionate kiss, but he gazes at the audience, distracted. The grotesque man who pulled balloons from his red briefs at the opening of *Gebirge* reappears. Now he wears a suit, and nose plugs. As he lights a cigarette, the turbaned man joins him, and the two smoke side by side in profile. The surreal and the ordinary exist together, neither more "real" than the other.

The turbaned man begins an awkward little stepping dance while chanting "Potatoes are left, tomatoes are right", as if planting a dirt field with his feet. He is interrupted by a chorus of men who drift across the space like the "lost Siegfried" character of the male twosome. A woman in a black ruffled dress continues the planting theme, bent over digging a narrow furrow in the earth with her fingers, her arms covered with black formal gloves. Her burrowing brings on a crew of men who haul pine trees onto the stage and topple them over like angry construction workers, until the whole terrain is filled with a horizontal forest. The scent of fresh pine makes its way into the audience. One of the young women who did the sexy cartwheel dance in the first half of the piece cavorts amidst the trees, coquettishly appearing and disappearing.

The seduction of the gaze of the spectator – particularly the male spectator – is underscored as the scene continues.[11] The woman who remained onstage throughout intermission saunters on, swathed in white bedsheets, her naked shoulders protruding. She spreads out the sheets and reclines amidst the foliage. Bausch here replicates one of the most recognized scenarios in the visual arts – the reclining female nude in pastoral paradise: woman as nature, undressed, in a scene of men's construction. While the 1538 *Venus of Urbino* reposed contentedly within the frame of her painting, merging with the foliage and the draperies on her richly decorated couch, Bausch's Venus repetitively addresses the audience: "Hello! Come on. Nah." As she persists in breaking from the frame of the theatrical apparatus that attempts to turn her into a visual display, the men remove the pine trees, literally "deconstructing" the forest as abruptly as they had constructed it. The whole scene lasts perhaps ten minutes; and such large-scale changes in such a brief time create a great sense of spectacle.

The recycling of themes continues, beginning to point to societally condoned erasures of woman's power. The reclining woman returns, dressed in the blue dress she wore during intermission. She lies down, brushing her hair and putting on lipstick. She looks like a corpse spruced up for viewing. This image is interrupted by a mysterious woman in a formal white evening gown who leans against the proscenium frame and paints her arms and upper chest with lipstick. The marking of the woman's body again serves as a segue into fog, as it did in the first act when the man in the red briefs slashed his partner's back with red paint. This time, the cast walks in a procession, echoing the scooting processional of the first fog scene. Within the fog, the woman in the white gown seats herself in a chair and a man wraps her whole head with white gauze, an elimination of her features that recalls the victim in the slashing scene.

The last sequence of the piece places Bausch's gendered world in the context of a larger world – that of earth, death, the human life cycle. Returning to the digging/burying theme, in silence a woman in black, bent over with age, shovels dirt over a chair. Simultaneously, a man marks the length of his body on the ground. The images are cryptic; perhaps he is measuring his own coffin and she is digging his grave. Bagpipes break the silence. Just as the sound of a man blowing balloons opened *Gebirge,* the sound of inflating and deflating bagpipes closes the dance – two sounds of human breath filling the stage, one grotesque, one strangely hopeful.

As a sort of coda, the lights come up on the grotesque man who lies on the ground, supporting a woman who stands on his hands. She attempts to walk. There is a desperation in her struggle to maintain balance and her fall is inevitable. Her failed effort leads to a repetition of the scene in which a gang of men forces a man and woman together in a kiss. The cyclic return makes it evident that nothing has progressed in the course of the evening's performance.

There is no closure or resolution to Bausch's montage of events. There is no anticipation of resolution. The rationale of dreams and obsessions dominates. In the time flow of watching, visual, kinesthetic, or aural motifs go in and out of focus and evoke moments of contiguous revelation. One image supplies the context for another; the receding image imprints itself on its successor. Gestures often recur with altered meaning, the new ones overlaying the previous ones in harmony or troubling contradiction. Connotations intermingle and steadily accumulate. Sometimes time stops in intense sensation or emotion; sometimes the cascade of perception obliterates time. There is no narrative desire to "see what happens next" beyond the short term of an episode. Time becomes routine: the daily time that Bausch leaves unedited to expose the banalities of social experience. Or time is surreal; anything can follow anything without cause. Repetition stalls time, or keeps it in a perpetual present. History is forfeited in a society steeped in the nostalgia of some indefinite yet close past, as songs from the '30s mingle with the faded furnishing and dress of the '40s.

Bausch's pieces take place in the circularity of perception, memory and recurrence, rather than the linerarity of historical change. In all the pieces I have seen, she has never introduced an alternative to the gendered behavior she so acutely critiques. When I asked her whether she wanted to accomplish social change through her theatre work, she responded, "I'm not trying to change anything. I don't know anything better – I am just trying to see what happens to us and how each person wants to be loved." She gave me the impression that she conceives herself and her performers not as consciously in control of the connotations of their performance texts, but as unconsciously a part of social patterns that are beyond their abilities to understand or to change. She seemed to negate her authority as the "auteur" of her own work, pointing up the problematic position of being a director in an age when the authentic "self" of the author is in question.[12]

When Bausch opens and closes the curtains of her stage arbitrarily, rather than to begin or end an act, she accentuates the constructed nature of theatrical fantasy and shows that performance events can stop or proceed at will, rather than at the mercy of an illusory spectacle. Yet with no way out, her performers reiterate the details of their inexorable social and psychological patterns. They are trapped in the polarities and power relations of the artifice of "masculine" and "feminine". It is as if Bausch does not allow them the possibility of change through expressive, imaginative, or moral will. Yet she points – by default – to the need for a society that exceeds the limits of the one we inhabit.

Notes

1　For further information on Ausdruckstanz, see Mary Wigman's books, *The Language of Dance* (1966) and *The Mary Wigman Book* (1973), both translated by Walter Sorrell and published by Wesleyan University in Middletown, Connecticut.

2　Judson Dance Theatre was a group of choreographers who performed at Judson Church in New York City's Greenwich Village in the early 1960s. The group evolved from a class taught by Robert Dunn and sponsored by the studio of dance experimentalist Merce Cunningham. Dunn's compositional strategies were influenced by Cunningham's collaborator, composer John Cage. Several of the Judson choreographers were also influenced by San Francisco dancer Anna Halprin.

3　For a discussion of expressionism as a language that simulates immediacy, see Hal Forster's essay "The Expressive Fallacy" in his book *Recodings: Art, Spectacle, Cultural Politics*, Bay Press, Port Townsend, Washington, 1985.

4　For an introduction to Brecht's theories on alienation techniques and theatre as social critique, see *Brecht on Theatre*, Trans. John Willett. Hill and Wang, New York, 1964, particularly his essay, "A Short Organum for the Theatre."

5　Here I refer to Jacques Lacan's reworkings of Freudian theory, in which he suggests that the child's identity is established in a "mirror stage." See Jacques Lacan, *Ecrits: A Selection*, Trans. Alan Sheridan, Norton, New York, 1977.

6　For an analysis of gesture and its relation to gendered power relations, see Nancy Henley and Marianne La France's "Gender as Culture: Difference and Dominance in Nonverbal Behavior," in *Nonverbal Behavior: Perspectives, Applications, Intercultural Insights*, Aaron Wolfgang, Editor, Hogrefe, New York, 1984.

7　Erving Goffman developed the idea that everyday life is like a performance in his *The Presentation of Self in Everyday Life*, Doubleday Anchor Books, Garden City, New York, 1959.

8　For a further exploration of differences in cinematic and theatrical ways of seeing, refer to Noel Carroll's "The Power of Movies," *Daedalus*, Fall 1985, pp. 89–90.

9　For an analysis of the distinction between pastiche and parody in post-modern art, see Frederic Jameson's essay, "Postmodernism and Consumer Society" in *The Anti-Aesthetic: Essays on Postmodern Culture*, edited by Hal Foster, Bay Press, Port Townsend, Washington, 1983.

10　For background information on expressionism in American modern dance, see essays by Martha Graham and Doris Humphrey in *The Vision of Modern Dance*, Jean Morrison Brown, Editor, Princeton Book Company, Princeton, New Jersey, 1979, pp. 49–64.

11　I base this analysis on previous feminist writings in film theory about the dominance of the gaze of the male spectator, male actor, and male camera operator. See Laura Mulvey, "Visual Pleasure and Narrative Cinema," *Screen* 16 (Autumn 1975): 17; and E. Ann Kaplan, *Women and Film: Both Sides of the Camera*, Methuen. New York, 1983, especially her essay, "Is the Gaze Male?"

12　Bausch seems to deflect the task of understanding her performance to the spectator of her work – and she includes herself as a spectator. Each night I saw her out in the audience observing the dancing with attentiveness.

Roland Barthes has suggested that "a text's unity lies not in its origin but in its destination" – in the person who receives the text. That person is "simply that someone who holds together in a single field all the traces by which the written text is constituted." See Roland Barthes, "The Death of the Author" in his *Image Music Text*, Trans. Stephen Heath, Hill and Wang, New York, 1977.

The weight of time

Marianne van Kerkhoven

Originally published in *Ballett International*, February, 1991

> The weight of this sad time we must obey;
> Speak what we feel, not what we ought to say,
> (William Shakespeare, *King Lear*, V, 3)

Seven reflections concerning the theatre of our time, stemming from a line of Shakespeare.

1. Political upheaval

For several months our image of Europe and the relationship between East and West has been turned head over heels. The balance between communism and capitalism has been altered, or rather, knocked out of balance. Moreover, this relationship cannot be considered as being typically European; it is part of a global political vision spreading throughout the entire world – in other words, it is part of that most visible, most recognizable part of our world view.

The euphoria with which the West has greeted this revolution leaves us ill at ease. Capitalism considers this defeat of communism – whether provisional or not – to be the incontestable proof of being "in the right." While Helmut Kohl – to take the Federal Republic of Germany as only one of many possible examples – belches out grand words like solidarity and democracy, he plays with relish the most vulgar of power games. East Germany is bought and paid for on a grand scale by West Germany; already the foundations have been laid for the future difficulties of a united state that shall be peopled by first and second class citizens. The colonization of the East by the West is in full swing. And it is nothing to be proud of.

The political parties of the West – those of Christian as well as those of social-democratic origin – are flooding the east at this very moment with masses of typewriters and all manner of propagandistic material; why didn't they do this ten years ago, for example, in order to support that courageous minority which, already then, was opposing the oppression of its regime? At least the West could be a bit more selective about its help.

Wolf Biermann: "Vengeance is cried out for by those who never raised a hand in opposition. Those who never opened their mouths are now foaming at those very mouths ..."

The experience of the past should have taught us of the fallacy of the good (or the bad) masses – which do not exist – and that it is essential to maintain a critical point of view, a vigilance over every new development in all affairs political.

All of a sudden – both here and in the East – socialism seems to be devoid of content; all of a sudden – both here and in the East – Marxism, which is still one of the most interesting aspects of our philosophical patrimony, has been wiped off the map.

However, when I consider the daily practice of the dramaturg, I affirm that many Marxist notions have a very permanent worth:

– the primacy of practice, which I experience day in, day out;
– that production conditions determine the product, confirmed daily;
– that search for a whole which is greater than the sum of its parts seems to be one of the essential characteristics of the work of many artists;
– that art is created by the manipulation of material elements rather than by the visualization of ideas becomes clearer day by day;
– that there is still a notion of alienation, an alienation against which one must fight every day both at work and in the world around us;
– and that other battle against social injustice, as necessary today as it was in Marx's day;
– and finally, there is that utopian force of Marxist ideas that wish for another world which would bring us all further.

We can only hope that the radical changes in Eastern Europe will lead to a rediscovery of historical conscience in the West, a conscience that has been a bit lost since 1968. Yet many artists have retained that historical and political conscience, in many, productions it was even present in a very direct manner – we need only think of Peter Sellars's *Ajax*, of Ariane Mnouchkine's *Sihanouk*, of *L.S.D.* by the Wooster Group or *Need to Know* by the Needcompany. I believe it is one of the responsibilities of the artist today to construct a counter-current, be it direct or indirect, to the banal euphoria that surrounds us.

2. Upheaval in other places

There are other aspects of our worldview that have been exposed to profound changes, changes which go well beyond the borders of

Europe. These have been spoken of on other occasions – but are important enough to be repeated here.

Throughout this century a number of discoveries in the scientific domain have completely reversed our ways of thinking, yet they are still only known and recognized by a minority of the world's population. Their influence on social life remains minimal as a result, which creates tensions – sometimes invisible but no less real – between "those who know" and "those who don't know." More on this later. We are referring here to discoveries in the realm of chaos theory, the expanding universe, the principle of uncertainty, which rules the sciences, and, more recently, the reversibility of time.

The theory of the expansion of the universe destroyed the principles of the Newtonian model; our sun is no longer the center of the universe. In an infinite universe each point can be considered the center. What influence can this theory have on aesthetics based on equilibrium and harmony?

Alongside the disorder in the sky, chaos theory questions organization and order on earth. Today in the world of science we are convinced of the fact that closed systems ruled by a perfect state of equilibrium are a minority and that the majority of structures one comes across in nature have an open and unstable character, at the interior of which bizarre mutations of an unforeseeable nature can occur. Nature is considered to be an auto-creative force; science researches creativity as method, a research that could possibly throw light on may facets of the arts.

Heisenberg's principle of uncertainty says that the natural sciences cannot avoid the random and the unforeseen; this theory completely reverses all our ideas concerning the existence of an objective truth or a conformity to universal laws.

Today many roads lead from A to B; that which our senses convey to us can no longer be interpreted unequivocally. Multiple values and synchronism have long since made their debut in the arts.

The world as it is described to us nowadays by the natural sciences is infinitely more complicated than the Newtonian model made it seem. Modern man must learn to manipulate that complexity. One cannot disregard all these questions, all those moments where theories were justified by reality or the intellectual stimulation provoked by these inventions. All these ideas need to be spread and popularized.

3. Complexity

In what way are theatre, dance, and even the opera going to respond to the pressure exerted by modern times in the direction of a greater complexity? How can art show not just a mirror image, but rather a reorganized and well-reflected-upon double of what is occurring in the real world?

Many years ago Rilke wrote: "No, no there is nothing in the world which can conceive of itself ... Realities are slow and indescribably encumbered." To this György Konrad adds today: "it is impossible to know what is happening ... Each instant has a far greater value than the traces it leaves behind."

How can the theatre, which exists only for the moment, the here and now, grasp the complexity and polysignificance of the moment? How can the artist respond to a life experienced as a bombardment of sensations occurring at great speed and in innumerable, ever-changing combinations?

The simultaneity of actions, of movements, of events and so on is present in many contemporary productions. In Jan Gabvre's opera, *Das Glas im Kopf wird vom Glas*, the choir's dancers and singers all function at different rhythms that intercept and overlap one another. In *Stella*, the latest production by Anne Teresa De Keersmaeker, each of the five women have an own sequence, the lines of which cross in an unforeseen pattern which is – above all – devoid of symmetry. In the second section of *Ça va*, directed by Jan Lauwers with the Needcompany, the characters gathered together in a small house all talk at the same time, telling superimposed stories whilst participating in the same situation.

Contemporary theatre's awareness of the ephemeral and continuously variable essence of each moment gives rise to – or so it would seem to me (with prudence) – a dramaturgy based more on partial structures than on the global structure of a work. As if one more and more wished to arrive at the tiny entity of "the full instant." The "great edifice," the structure in its entirety, long remains unknown, incomplete, open to modification. In assembling the mini-entities, that is to say the more or less stable basic materials, one experiences, one slowly circumnavigates the greater structure. The movement of improvisation is situated above all in numerous attempts in ever-varying combinations, in the continuously changing reorganization of cornerstones, until the form attains purity and is more or less stabilized in an organization that is the final and global structure of the work.

This is an entirely different method of working than proceeding from a pre-established concept which, during the period of rehearsal, is elaborated upon in all its interpretive consequences; this method also differs from rigorous analysis (of a text, for example) or totally free improvisation, which sometimes barley leads to a structure.

Perhaps words such as density, condensation or concentration are more adequate for describing the approach – or one of the possible approaches – of may artists today.

4. Abstraction as a working method

Efforts at controlling mounting complexity seem to lead art much less towards the use of concepts such as content, analysis of meaning, psychology or narrative; their reality is often too concrete, too limited or too anecdotal. They tend too strongly towards linearity – it is too difficult to keep reassigning them a place within the totality. The working methods that develop from a process of repetition are increasingly based on the manipulation of abstract elements that one could almost qualify as musical.

According to the dictionary, abstract means: "that which has no relation to visible reality." A geometric pattern in space, an absolutely monotone rhythm for the recitation of a text, a contrapuntal or parallel structure for organizing text or movement sequences – these are all routes, or detours, for finally arriving at a form and (thus?) a meaning.

Abstraction as a method leaves its traces, its fingerprints on the material; the quality of the method employed determines the final result. Thanks to the use of abstraction, the nature of things changes – they are attributed a new value. By means of this added distance we are able to see them differently and become aware – with time – of their complexity.

5. Insufficient psychology

Abstraction has long since been adopted by the art of painting and sculpture. Classical ballet as well and certainly its "counterpart" modern dance have realized that, as a medium, they had rather an affinity to abstraction and that their efforts at imitating literature and trying to tell stories "as one is used to telling them" was taking them down a one-way street.

The sought-after interiority was achieved in passing rather by the detour of abstraction than by way of the narrative ballet.

As regards the theatre, one has always been convinced that abstraction was impossible, since it was about exchanging concrete contents between living beings. Abstract psychology or abstract narrative – this was unimaginable.

Today this seems less certain. How would the theatre, with its infinite repetitions of stories of relationships, with its interminably regurgitated psychological structures, ever be capable of embracing complexity and plenitude? How would it be capable of seeing its basic materials with other eyes in order that its audience, for their part, perceive it in a different way?

To arrive at this, will a revision of Freudianism have to follow on the heels of a revision of Marxism?

I feel that Freud's models are, on the one hand, still valid, yet, on the other hand, insufficient for describing modern reality, that is to say, for describing how an individual and his/her interior life function today.

Marxists and structuralists, such as Claude Lévi-Strauss, have made essential contributions to our view of humankind in the course of this century.

In an essay on the family, Lévi-Strauss demonstrates that marriage, considered by us – by intuitive idealization – to be the most intimate state between a man and woman, has never been a private affair, but rather an affair of a social nature.

Without society, the couple, the family, does not exist. In order to achieve a marriage, one family is needed to offer a man and another willing to offer a woman. These three families together already form a small society.

"Society," he says, "only permits the existence of families for a certain length of time, short or long, according to the case in question, but under the explicit condition that its elements – the individuals of which it is composed – are constantly displaced, lent and borrowed, given or given up in such a way that new families can arise from the remains of previous families before these, for their part disappear. ... The biblical commandment that all must leave their fathers and mothers expresses the irrevocable rule prescribed to each society so that it can exist and thrive." Lévi-Strauss's vision makes an essential contribution to the theories of Freud; it relativizes in a fundamental manner the Oedipus theory and other complexes.

But recent psychiatry has also offered nuances of its own. In one of his remarkable books, *The Man Who Mistook His Wife for a Hat*, the English professor of neurology Oliver Sacks describes individual interiority in a manner interesting to the theatre: "Each one of us is a story constructed by us in a permanent fashion within ourselves – by way of our experiences, our feelings, our thoughts, our actions and, certainly not least, by what we say, by our spoken narratives. From a biological point of view, or a psychological one, we hardly differ from one another; from a historical point of view, as stories, as narratives, each of us is unique."

This definition seems wider and more open than one that reduces people to their traumas of youth or their inherited personality traits.

Also remarkable is the fact that Sacks uses terms in his vocabulary borrowed from the vocabulary of the arts. He talks of our music or of our internal beat; he refers to the entirety of our personal modes of life as "the script" or the "score" of our personality.

In other words, the notion of identity covers a reality much larger than the notion of psychology. Psychology is only one minimal part of our being. Moving away from psychology in the direction of the essential, in the direction of that interior narrative spoken of by Oliver Sacks, can lead to a new manner of telling stories on stage.

In order to narrate the world one must be convinced that the world is describable. At present, we are involved in telling and describing without considering the question as to whether this conviction is present or not. There is a need to understand, if only to maintain the illusion that it is at all possible to understand.

Today a new form of narration is being born that, enriched by the fruitful route or detour of postmodernism, is finding a new way of telling stories; by way of complex, non-linear structures, or within a situation of synchronism.

6. The monumentality of opera

For a long time the opera was considered the most complex of our art forms. Wagner's ideas concerning the "Gesamtkunstwerk" – where all artistic disciplines would be combined – or his aspirations of arriving at an identification between concrete dramatic events, on the one hand, and the absolute form of music on the other, are still important today – even though the multi-disciplined in the theatre today is of an altogether different nature than Wagner's Gesamtkunst. The current multi-disciplined is more pragmatic, more practical and, above all, more materialistic.

The opera, however, has not succeeded in renewing itself with the same speed and intensity as theatre or dance. In the last few years the opera has tried to bridge this gap; it has sought the aid of the theatre to reanimate its petrified forms. The Théâtre Royal de la Monnaie in Brussels has given, in the last years, a good example of this maneuver.

Directors and playwrights made their appearance in the opera. Working with singers also became actors' work and dramaturgy was seen as being more important.

However, these renewals have not touched the very root of the problem; the lack of mobility in the opera is due to reasons of a more structural nature.

Making an opera requires lots of money: the organization is too consuming, too expensive – so they say – for it to be open to experimental artists. More often than not, one does not want to take risks in the opera. Artists are chosen who have a proven and successful track record. Opera puts all its eggs in one basket of stable values; it is based on gains. Reproducing already approved or successful formulas eventually kills creativity.

The omnipresent idea that opera must be grand and monumental has impeded the development of a small or marginal opera. Because of this, the opera has been denied the fruitful contradiction and dialectic of an official versus a marginal art – a contradiction from which theatre and dance have been able to benefit.

I feel that the possibilities of opera on a small scale must be researched if the opera is to develop as a genre.

Yet its very grandeur and monumentality render the opera extremely qualified to respond to the current tendency towards greater complexity. Large forms are difficult to fill, but they are particularly well qualified to give an audience a total perception of a very complex event, the structure of which could not be discerned in a smaller framework.

I feel it is one of the tasks of the times to give the opera a thorough artistic check-up; but I am sure that a fundamental evolution of the opera can only be achieved if its current organizational structure – i.e. the production conditions under which artistic work is obliged to develop – is reviewed and changed in a fundamental manner.

7. A new realism

The theatre, as described above, attempts to embrace our complex reality – or better: that which we know or are able to know of present-day reality.

To attempt to show the complexity of modern reality on stage – this seems more real to us today than the approach of mirroring reality known to us from the realism/naturalism at the end of the 19th and beginning of the 20th century. This naturalist approach still has its influence, which can be seen on the stages of many modern theatres.

The positivism or determinism on which this realism was based was mainly interested in all that information which our senses were capable of conveying to us. One attempted to imitate or reproduce that information with the greatest possible precision. One believed what one saw. Today we are convinced, in the presence of an immense series of phenomena in the world and universe, that our senses are not – or not yet – capable of perceiving. Reality no longer has just one meaning or reading. Entire worlds exist beneath or behind our perceptions.

I do not know if contemporary art's manner of talking about the world can be called realist, if one can speak in terms of a new realism. This term seems paradoxical, even misplaced, if one confronts it with the large quantity of abstraction present in said art.

However, the introduction of this term, the inauguration of a new vocabulary can be much more than a simple tool. It can become a means of provoking a discussion within the art.

In an interview with Jean-Claude Gallotta, Claude-Henri Cuffard asked him why he had called himself a choreographer from the beginning, although his work deviated considerably from that which was normally considered a part of that profession. Gallotta replied, "it was only much later that I realized how important this stance – the fact that I referred to myself with conviction as a choreographer – actually was. Take Kandinsky and his abstract forms. If he had called himself a graphic artist, no one would have minded. By calling himself a painter, he provoked and prevented the world of painting from sleeping tranquilly. The choice kept me from doubting. I simply told myself that dance could have new rules."

Perhaps one should take the same approach today; deliberately use a provocative vocabulary, cause a discussion and, in this way, make clear that the theatre today can respond to other options than those that we have been dragging behind us for almost a century.

The role of criticism and thought is of overwhelming importance in this matter, but we must confirm – certainly as far as Flanders is concerned – that it has fallen far behind the events in question.

The world of science is seriously facing the problem of the popularization of its new ideas. If the basic concepts of recent discoveries do not reach more levels of society, we will have a science detached from social reality, which continues towards the future without the contact, and correcting influence, of humane society. This seems to me a dangerous situation.

Art is faced with a similar problem between the avant-garde and the rest of the milieu; each day "marginal" theatre fights for an audience. Fortunately, there exist small groups of organizers who are aware of what is at stake. Fortunately, a new public is growing little by little. But it is a slow, long-winded process, whereas the artists strain impatiently to go new ways. Thus it remains important to develop a criticism that assumes its responsibility in the work at hand.

The weight of the times

"The weight of this sad time we must obey." I feel that this time is putting us under a lot of pressure; much work lies ahead. I won't call the times sad, but jumbled, full of questions, fascinating.

The feeling that we are capable today of seeing the world differently, in the political realm as well as those of philosophy, science and culture, gives artists today an enormous reservoir of things to say. The post-modern concept of fragmentation, the feeling that "everything has been said" is starting to dissipate and fade. Perhaps it will soon be replaced by a new sentiment more in keeping with the quantity of things to tell. A quantity we will never be able to master or penetrate.

"What we ought to say" according to the codes of the past is unimportant. What is necessary is to lend an ear to our own times, with as much sensitivity and vigilance as possible. These times must be told, along with what we feel about them without forgetting the truth and relevance of that other phrase of Shakespeare's, formulated in another place, i.e. that "there are more things in heaven and earth … than are dreamt of in your philosophy."

The totality of the body

An essay on Pina Bausch's aesthetic

Kay Kirchman

Originally published in *Ballett International/Tanz Aktuell*, October, 1994

To talk about Pina Bausch in terms of "the body" is like taking coals to Newcastle. There are countless essays, discussions and critiques that set the body centre stage in Pina Bausch's art; it may seem that there's not much space to say anything else. Even so, here we're concerned with a concept of physicality that's not congruent with any conceptual delineation by which the debate over physicality in Pina Bausch's work has long been dominated. It's much more relevant to show that the concept of body that the Wuppertal choreographer works with is, in the best sense of the word, more than the up-to-now restriction of the human frame to the role of simple carrier of meaning. The misunderstanding here of what Pina Bausch means by the body origi- nates in the seventies when German dance theatre, with Pina Bausch as its leading protagonist, began to attract public notice. At that time every innovation, whose effect can be seen until today and which reduced the multifariousness of the Wuppertal Tanztheater concept of the body to the formula current at that time, impulsively introduced the body as shorthand.

That meant that dance theatre was seen as a medium for politicizing art. Pina Bausch's productions were above all else interpreted against the background of what dominated the realm of verbal discourse in the seventies: sexual liberation, the women's movement, critique of the forms of male dominance in general. Pasolini's pregnant formulation, "Throw your own body into the struggle," was taken as an authentic program for dance theatre, particularly for those whose roots in the West German dance scene of the late sixties (Stein, Grüber, Zadek) were appealed to by such manifestos. "The discourse of bodies" was one of the current slogans with which Pina Bausch's aesthetic was sup- posed to be reduced to an artistically articulate striking of an attitude in the struggle against hierarchical structures. The discourse of bodies in the symbology of the times referred above all to the oppressed female body in a male-dominated world, with the proclamation of a sensuality (rashly limited to women) to stand against the oppressive mores of a hierarchical, technocratic society. *Blaubart* in particular, one of Pina Bausch's first pieces to achieve widespread recognition, was interpreted as a manifesto for a feminine, and therefore feminist, aesthetic.

To the extent that details of the Wuppertal Tanztheater's production methods became known, they were celebrated as the expression of a deeply democratic decision-sharing process, the later manifestation of a program that had been tried out in drama in the late sixties but that had come more or less to grief. Just as numerous were attempts to characterize the work of the Wuppertal Tanztheater as "self-discovery" or collective therapy; also easily digestible in the seventies.

To sum up: Pina Bausch's specific aesthetic was callously hitched to an ethos that in retrospect can only be described as dogmatism. Concomitant with this, the labels with which the Wuppertal Tanztheater was plastered were prefixed with anti: anti-bourgeois, anti-illusionist, anti-patriarchal, anti-puritanical, anti-anti-sensual etc. That Pina Bausch desperately tried to set herself against such pigeonholing, that she continually claimed that her work was based on totally different premises – all this was hardly recognized, or was dismissed by the sneering arrogance of the know-alls.

It's curious then that hard on the heels of this political instrumentalizing came an instrumentalizing of interior discourse. This was celebrated in Pina Bausch's work as the triumphal march of the no longer communicable, the absolutely inarticulable. Every attempt to approach an understanding of the Wuppertal Tanztheater's aesthetic praxis was mocked by the champion of this monopoly of significance as a sinful presumption, trying, with the cold instruments of rationality, to conquer or even rape subtleties that only could be comprehended through feeling, purely intuitively.

The esotericism of this discourse brought about a situation whereby the construction of meaning for the Wuppertal Tanztheater could only be gleaned from carefully disseminated intimations from the choreographer's closest circle. If these explanations were hazy, if the "inexplicable genius of the mistress" were to be once more solemnly sworn to, the assembled company would be even more prepared to take this as proof of her doctrine that it could only be understood when one was allowed "to feel this just through the body" and only "from within." (One certainly can't spare the choreographer herself from the criticism that her own reticence and a conspicuous fear of an examination of her work provided fertile ground for this kind of insubstantial mystification.) So the choreographies were quickly caught up in the spell of a remoteness that it was difficult for the public to bear, of a therapeutic process for the

Figure 16 Für die Kinder ... (2002): Rainer Behr, Julie Anne Stanzak. © Ursula Kaufmann

observer (certainly also for the professionals). And suitably "moved," one had to eavesdrop on ecstatic performances where this or that scene "had, of course, reminded one of how one had once been sprayed with the garden hose by one's brother."

The political and the private preoccupations of Pina Bausch's aesthetic were as inseparable in the seventies debate as the demo and the coffee shop. And the body was as suitable and pertinent (i.e. mute) a metaphor of the political struggle as the legitimatization of the withdrawal from the world and avoidance of communication. That's what it was like, back in the seventies ...

This attempt should, however, set the concept of the body, so badly comprehended in the past, in the light that it deserves and present it as the all-defining spirit of the Wuppertal Tanztheater. But it isn't to be understood as an end in itself; but as a totality, a wholeness, the collective term for an organic world view within which the human form presents only one, even if significant, manifestation.

Pina Bausch's dance theatre is thereby essentially a physical theatre because it elevates the figure as an indivisible totality to an aesthetic program in every respect. To observe the body as presented as merely a symbol immediately destroys all the multilingualism of the living form that Pina Bausch's work with and on the human body is dedicated to and reduces it to a one-dimensional perspective, which Pina Bausch has, within and away from her choreographies, rightly and vehemently resisted.

An organic aesthetic can always be understood as being opposed to a mechanistic fragmentation of the world (and the arts), as tending towards a mystical antithesis of the rational examination and division of being into categories and linear sequences. Since Descartes's foundation of the new occidental philosophy, the western worldview has been dominated by erroneous and thus irreconcilable dichotomies: perception – understanding, culture – nature; sensuality – abstraction; feeling – expression; body – soul etc. This mechanistic apportionment of humanity in separate, that's to say no longer belonging together areas has dogged the entire occidental cultural oeuvre, as seen in the division of stage arts (dance – theatre). The antique ritual theatre was in this way alien until, through the reductive "Socratic" method, it arrived at the theatrical, which Nietzsche characterized in the "Birth of Tragedy" as the beginning of the decline of antique tragedy. The young Nietzsche had great hopes of a reconciliation of cognition and sensuality in Wagner's concept of opera, and that it would provide a synthesis of all the arts that the unmythical cultural praxis of the occident had sundered (Nietzsche felt himself, finally, to have been grievously deceived in this). His findings, however, were concerned with areas of being, in which dance and theatre were to be included well into the modern era. Dance as the domain of the physical and sensual (however it may be obfuscated within classical ballet) – theatre as the domain of the literary, spoken, argumentative and rational.

The simple formula is: there's a place for the mind and a place for the body. The revolutionizing of dance at the beginning of the century managed, nevertheless, to dismantle the trappings of ballet and insist on the true sensuality of the dancing body, but the separation of spirit/ language from body in an unchanged form soon became apparent in the cosmological content of German expressive dance. The expressivity of the body seemed henceforth a guarantee of communication that was supposed to operate as communing with a long-lost godhead: "Life from the original spring resonates in the gestures of the dancers. And so they are all seekers of God and pathfinders to God for their imprisoned brethren." (Böhme, F., *Tanzkunst*, Dessau, 1926, p. 40ff). What remained was the strict division of the body from the word, which was emphasized as being in diametric opposition to the truth of the body: "But the word sounds no more from the kingdom of the Mother; it is no more nourished from the spring of fecundity but is set and imprisoned, is rigid. The word has become stone." (Böhme, p. 39ff).

It's not difficult to rediscover such antagonism toward the spiritual and verbal in the above intimations of Bausch's aesthetic. In this, Pina Bausch can be credited with having discovered the body as a multi-expressive form that includes thought and speech just as much as movement in its narrower sense. That compounds the modernity of her dance theatre precisely in that it again brings to the fore the previous juxtaposition of a stage art tied to speech and to movement. This works to the benefit of an integral physical theatre that opens up all the possibilities for articulation at the disposal of the human form. Pina Bausch has recognized that "what speaks there" isn't a separate, abstract great "spirit," but our body itself, an organic whole to whom the categorical division into soul – body – spirit is inimical. The human form is understood in reality as an organic synthesis whose multilingualism – also in its complexity or even self-contraction – is the motor of the choreography.

Movement doesn't serve Pina Bausch as an end in itself: the dancers' gestures never degenerate to a simplistic celebration of physical beauty. Her oft-quoted remark, that it didn't interest her how people moved, but rather what moved them, must be understood as programmatic. Movement is a manifestation of what is stirring, whether it figures as "thought," "feeling" or "physical stimulus." Bausch's work insists that these divisions are obsolete in terms of our physical reality, that they can only be experienced as a totality. The "spoken passages" of Bausch's choreographies are always original movement and physical theatre, even when the performers freeze on stage and "only" speak or sing. The choreographer culls from speech, song and dialogue the same things as from mimic, gesture and dance-like elements in their most exact sense: all these are equally weighted articulations of the greater whole that stands at the center of her work, of a work that can best be described as physiognomous, as a quest in the houses of the body; a quest that accepts and contains the body because within its totality it also expresses displacement, exclusion and fragmentation. If the body can't lie then it's because in all its articulations (even the spoken ones) something undeveloped, unexplicated is made flesh, an inter-relationship that shines out of our divided perspective as "mysterious." Pina Bausch gives voice to all that appertains to humankind. To make the invisible visible is the beginning and end of her movement aesthetic. Whether these "components" of the totality of movement through speech, song, gesture or dance are brought across depends on whether and to what extent these diverse impulses – feeling, thought, will – can come to a representational form of the "I."

That there isn't and can't be a learnable Bausch technique is, in the light of all this, logically consistent inasmuch as a technique assumes the existence of an unambiguous, consistent form of expression for a defined content that can be called up at will and reproduced. Against this the Wuppertal choreographer insists on the idiosyncrasy of the body in seeking out other unforeseeable forms and channels of expression.

A simplistic schema of stimulus and reaction is just as alien to her art as a static content–form balance. Criticism of the training rituals of classical ballet, often a noticeable part of Bausch's choreography, can be traced to its roots in the critique of dividing the body into discrete sections. In the mechanisms of ballet training the alienation of the body from its own impulses has become just as manifest as the isolation of the limbs from one another. In Pina Bausch's aesthetic, however, there aren't any "parts of the body" or movements that originate in only one part. On the contrary, in her choreographies the fragmentation of the body is always depicted and indicted as pain, grievous injury. Where people – and that always means where dancers – are only observed through the functions of the separate parts of the body, the essence of the body as an organic multiplicity and thereby the human being itself is fundamentally betrayed. Ann Endicott's furious solo in *Walzer* demonstrated this particularly impressively: her desperate appeal to the audience – in the standard receptive mode of dance – to be so kind as to look at the unremarked "parts" of her body and to recognize them as part of the wholeness of her body demonstrates the injury which is done to the dancer's body by the way it's generally set apart in the isolating gaze of the spectator. To deal with the body as a multiplicity implies denunciation of male domination through separation and splitting off and to formulate accusations. Against the mechanistic arrangement of the form as a reproductory apparatus of complacent aesthetic pleasure in this, as in other pieces by Pina Bausch, the production sets up what's diametrically opposed to the functional constraints on the divided self: weakness, "ugliness," discontent, revulsion, pain and betrayal.

However, Pina Bausch is worlds away from the essentially romantic cosmology of expressive dance and the naïve belief in building a counter-world in the aesthetic of the dancing figure. What singles her out as a modern artist is that she doesn't depict the schism that runs through modern life as being easy to heal; reconciliation in a holistic constellation can only be dealt with in her pieces as a (mainly unattainable) quest.

The Bauschian figure's deepest yearning is to once more become whole and to be accepted as an entity, to gain admittance to the context of oneness. The desperate searching and striving for love as it's depicted in, for instance, the Schubert sequence in *Nelken* is the way towards experiencing at least an idea of the organic self in a world that presents itself as merely divisive and divided. This is the background of the individual and collective reminiscent work of the Wuppertal Tanztheater: the remembrances of childhood and children's games that are such a significant part of the choreographies are, in the last analysis, desperate and hopeless attempts, in conjuring up memories of childhood, to recreate the certainties of belonging. This is precisely not, as it's often been misinterpreted, a plea for a regressive perspective, but much more the painful exposition of the impossibility of regression – a work of mourning that can at best be only superficially summed up in political or introspective terms. What's presented is a body whose multifariousness the world that surrounds it is deaf and blind to. What remains is a concept of physicality that's as far removed from logical-rational physical terms as from the ahistorical cult of naturalness as it appeared possible on Monte Verità. Pina Bausch's aesthetic is neither Dionysic in Nietzsche's sense nor ritualistic in Artaud's. Nature indisputably appears in her pieces as a force to be respected and honored as well as something spoiled. The preponderance of natural phenomena (animals, plants, the elements) in Bausch's staging is counterbalanced with images of destruction: the death metaphors in *Viktor*, the poison-spraying toy helicopter in *Ahnen*, the destruction of the world by hammers, shovels, steam drills, the confinement of the world within aquarium walls in *Two Cigarettes* and so on. With all her obvious respect for the natural body, Pina Bausch never forgets that it bears the livid scars of dislocation, dissection, and injury. Physicality is never to be understood as natural mysticism but as a mythical construction of wholeness that's only imaginable as a chimera, a (provisional?) object of hopeless yearning.

This concept of physicality manifests itself as a collective body, as the release and tracing back of the divided self to the aesthetic figure of an original unity. On the other hand it's modernistic to recognize that a reconciliation of internal and external nature is only thinkable as an aesthetic ideal and certainly not as a realizable retracing to the cosmic source, as was once claimed in the manifesto of expressive dance. The collective body as an aesthetic mythos is Bauschian choreography's frame of reference in many respects. Within the last few years the intro-duction of mythological motifs and ethnic and archaic elements into the Wuppertal Tanztheater has been unmistakable. This is anything but fashionable cross-culturalism. It's a broadening of horizons, not an aban-donment of previous concerns for something completely new. In turning to the ancient, archaic archetypes the perspective widens to include the physiognomic quest for the collective human body, the configuration of our togetherness in the totality of human history. The title of the piece, *Ahnen* (suspecting, guessing, having a foreboding but also, concerning descent and genealogy) refers to this genealogy of the collective body as well as to the intuitive drawing of connections that, in contrast to the prevailing world view, are seen not as historical and lost but as everlasting. It's a kind of archeology of the wholeness of the human body that Pina Bausch is undertaking here. In the gestures, rites, words and sounds of other cultures she tracks down every movement that expresses the collectivity of thought, feeling and will. Also here it would be a flagrant misinterpretation to see this as an indication of regression from or avoidance of the present. It's more productive to see this alteration of perspective as the mature realization that the present can only be understood in terms of what has come to pass, on an individual as well as a collective scale.

The history of the body is on both levels always the history of what has been written in this form: as injuries, as hopes, as disappointments, as any experience at all. The mythical body of the human totality doesn't act here as a contradiction of the new but as an articulate, and therefore legible and askable, data-bank of human experience. And it's precisely the confrontation between archaic and absolutely current material within one piece that opens this data-bank, makes it transparent – not for the dissecting eyes of the anatomist but for the comprehension of the seekers, the archeologists and the physiognomists.

The collective body – that also includes the total stage presentation in which the performer's body, lighting, setting, music and also the auditorium are bound up in a unity, a body that bears the name, "A piece by Pina Bausch." Whoever has tried to separate the wealth of simultaneous movement and scenes of a performance from each other won't have got very far. It's the totality that is being offered to us as audience and it's only to be understood as such. Every fragmentation of its perception, every concentration on detail is bound to interfere with the essential – a receptive experience, even when painful, that anyone who's come across Pina Bausch will have gone through.

When, however, one observes oneself as a spectator, it also becomes clear that after a while one's self-perception alters and widens; that one doesn't persist in trying to recognize details and grasp them analytically but instead gives oneself over to a perception of the aesthetic gestalt, the totality, the whole that is presented. As dance theatre, Pina Bausch's is also a synaesthesia, one that allows us to see, hear and smell in equal degrees. (One remembers the scent of the earth in *Auf dem Gebirge hat Man ein Geschrei Gehört* or in *Palermo, Palermo*, and the sound of water in *Arien* or of rustling leaves in *Blaubart*.)

This production principle can't be described within the usual categories of collage and montage, inasmuch as montage denotes that the total arises from a summation of isolated pieces. With Pina Bausch, however, the relationship of the whole to its parts isn't additive but organic. This implies that one cannot – in contrast to a mechanistic relationship – remove any of the parts without substantively altering the totality. Bausch is right to insist that no element of her dance compositions can be taken in isolation or even symbolically interpreted with regard to the denouement as presented.

When addition in the sense of "single" scenes is an inadequate way of understanding the Bauschian aesthetic, this must also be true for an entire evening's performance. Also here – and any spectator would substantiate this – the whole doesn't arise from the chronological progression of the "single" scenes. When these choreographies have often been misunderstood as "a disjointed assortment of separate events" this has often been founded on the presumption that dance is always presented as narration. With Pina Bausch, however, there isn't (at least there hasn't been since *Blaubart* at the latest) an expositionary or any other kind of straight line; her aesthetic form has more in common with a spiral or circle. (*Walzer* in particular repays study on this basis: a continual variation on the cyclic form as a communication principle). This also makes the repetitions, variations and reprises with which each piece, as well as the total Bauschian oeuvre is permeated, possible. The currency and revival of more or less complete works (repertoire = what's repeated) expresses less the demands of the institution and much more how Pina Bausch sees herself. In the revivals, the character of the oeuvre is once more emphasized as a whole.

In this connection it seems that the exposure of the stage machinery, the making transparent of the aesthetic process within the piece with the common reference to Brecht's alienation technique (or the self-reflexivity of contemporary theatre in general) has been by no means exhaustively dealt with.

When, in *Walzer*, Jan Minarik quoted passages from rehearsal; when the scene change in *Bandoneon* was emphasized as being part of the production; when the stagehands striking the set of *Palermo, Palermo* were included in the dance of the performers – all this should be read as body against the background of these choreographies. They are, so to say, glimpses of the innards of the body of the "dance evening" that are granted to us; a revelation of the traces of the piece as something that has become, has been made.

The movements that are performed show what has been thought, felt, and willed into physical manifestation in the form of a "piece by Pina Bausch," which is now offered to our perception. From an encompassing perspective arises the need to bring these elements of the totality of the body on stage. The transparency of the stage action reclarifies the corporeality of the choreography, its cellular multiplicity and its organic maturity.

Consequently the production of an evening of dance by Pina Bausch is performed as a dynamic, organic, growing process that even at the premiere hasn't reached its final form. The choreographer has often intimated that her pieces don't develop linearly, from beginning to end, but rather grow outwards from the centre. An examination of the dancers who are chosen for this method of production gives rise to an understanding of the aesthetic product as a collective entity. Inasmuch as the choreographer presents the company with questions and notes to which the members of the Wuppertal Tanztheater respond with move-ments and games, both spoken and sung, she consults the collective body of the company. Even the rehearsal work is devoted to this phy-siognomic search for traces of the totality of the body. And it is part of the immense achievement of Pina Bausch that this way of working seems – and this is only an apparent paradox – to emphasize the indi-viduality of her dancers. One of the irritations of production that the Wuppertal Tanztheater has resolved is that the classic definition of role has just as little leverage as the trivial equation of person with portrayed. The specific function of each performer within a piece can only be understood by referring to the form of the whole company.

The individual portrayal is neither alien (role) nor self (person = performer), but rather common, a cell in the organic whole of the body of the performance, and the company, in whom this inseparability is once more inscribed. Egos and collective don't operate antipathetically; neither is the latter the sum of the former. As a collective body, the Wuppertal Tanztheater realizes what Gert Mattenklott has aptly described as the functioning of a mythical body, namely "the interplay of an empathetically responsive ensemble, a constellation of the most disparate physical, psychic and spiritual energy," whereby the differences, the individuality of each member of the ensemble aren't seen as divisive but as belonging to the collective body, and are thus made to bear fruit.

The choreographer's questions and the dancers' subsequent responses give birth to a body, so to speak, that grows in the course of rehearsal, that's to say that the almost formless assumes a form within this process. The material that lies to hand isn't simply assembled or added, rather it is, in the best sense of the word, tried out – what "fits" with, beside and after what. Pina Bausch stresses the experience so gained, that the particular context demonstrates the relevance of the material: only from the totality can the suitability of each element be estimated. In the web that grows during rehearsal, some parts of the original material lose their aesthetic dynamic and others gain prominence.

The material that's thrown out in this way (according to the choreographer, the majority of what was originally available) doesn't necessarily disappear forever – it isn't "waste" – but can later be recalled for another piece. The essential criterion remains the attitude during the growth process The same is true for the other elements – music, dressing, lighting and scenery – that are incorporated in the further gestation of the piece. These are neither posited at the beginning of the process nor simply added on. Because they are also elements of the body "dance evening," the same conditions apply to them.

They're "questioned," above all as to whether the traces that they contain are compatible with those which are gradually evolving in the body of the piece. Neither music nor props nor scenery is simply "used," wrenched to an alien purpose, but only finds a means of entry to the piece when it reflects the growth process organically and advances it, and it's always fascinating to see how well all this coalesces in the stage event to a homogenous whole that, from the lines of music through the props to the movements and positioning of the performers, produces a unity in multiplicity. It's almost unimaginable for me how such an organic harmony could be produced through another, more additively organized production method. In accord with the basic understanding of an organic world view the whole is contained in each of its "parts"; the totality of the stage impression doesn't arise from addition but from the equation of its elements or body cells. The piece, and the bodily presence within the "dance evening," really does grow from the centre outwards. Linear sequence, typical of a mechanistic aesthetic, is here secondary; one of the last things to be defined is the order in which the developed scenes will be presented on stage, and this, even after the premiere, is still subject to alteration. It is and remains a changing, changeable, living being.

The heavy touring schedule and the frequent guest performances of the Wuppertal Tanztheater are well known. In the last year this has become apparent in production praxis, in the form of co-productions with theatres in Rome, Palermo, Madrid and Vienna. What has evolved are pieces "about" these cities, in each of which the company spent a certain part of the rehearsal phase. Pina Bausch's fascination with this way of working is just as clear as the inspiration that she gathered from these journeys, encounters and work in the places. The source of inspiration is anything but random; rather it reflects a broadening of horizons that were already being extended. Thus the view of somewhere else in the pieces is neither exotic and remote nor superficial. To find oneself in the alien and the alien in oneself would perhaps be the best way to describe this aesthetic attitude. The ways and means whereby the city of Rome found itself in *Viktor* and Palermo in *Palermo, Palermo* is as far from annexation as from looting. Being somewhere else is more to be understood as the expansion of a collective physicality that combines self and other, home and abroad equally and impartially.

Bausch and phenomenology

Susan Kozel

Originally published in *Dance Now*, Winter, 1993/94

When Friedrich Nietzsche wrote that the spirit of a philosopher could wish nothing more than to be a good dancer, he adopted a perspective from which he saw the philosophy in dance and the dance in philosophy.[1] In this article I reaffirm the value of such a perspective. It is common in articles on the philosophy of art to outline the theoretical concerns first and then illustrate them with concrete examples. Here I try a different approach. I begin by describing the dance, and I let the philosophical issues emerge from the heart of the description. I am not interested in taking a philosophical paradigm or model and imposing it upon either dance or dance writing. It is my belief that dance is inherently philosophical and this only needs to be drawn out from within. In the first part of this article I discuss the work of Pina Bansch. In the second part (to be published in the next issue) I will look at the writing of Rudolf von Laban, and finally provide an account of the philosophy that emerges from the first two sections. I look at the work of Bausch and Laban with the interest of drawing out specific philosophical themes, not with the intention of providing a general overview of their work. The themes that I identify are those of the philosophical practice of phenomenology. Not only does their work illustrate three themes central to phenomenology, but it provides a ground from which these themes can be evaluated. The three themes that structure my investigation are:

(i) the concern with essences
(ii) the return to lived experience
(iii) the hyper-reflective moment in phenomenology

Pina Bausch

Norbert Servos writes that people are bewildered by Bausch for two reasons: her choice of subject and the merciless way she asks her

existential, social or aesthetic questions.[2] What is striking about the qualities of her work that Servos identifies as distinguishing Bausch from other
choreographers is that they correspond to qualities of a phenomenological
investigation as distinguished from other philosophical approaches.

The question of essences

Firstly, Servos identifies the powerful subject matter of Bausch's work:

> Her pieces deal with love and fear, longing and loneliness, frustration
> and terror, man's exploitation of man (and, in particular, man's
> exploitation of women in a world made to conform to the former's
> ideas) about remembering and forgetting. They are aware of the dif-
> ficulties of human coexistence and seek ways to reduce the distance
> between two (or more) individuals.[3]

Bausch is less concerned with conveying a story or a series of events
than with presenting precisely what we are all about. A famous quote
from Bausch is that she is not concerned with how dancers move, but
with what moves them.[4] This amounts to saying that she is interested
in what lies under the surface, or, in phenomenological terms, with
essences. Pina Bausch explores the essence of the human condition,
particularly as it unfolds through the relations between men and
women in social contexts.

An essence is traditionally hard to come by, whether it is an essential
oil, pressed from a flower or herb, or the essence of a politician's
speech. Essences are notoriously shrouded in layers, which must be
peeled back in order to reach them. They are elusive. In some respects,
psychoanalysis is a procedure for discovering the essence of an individual, and it is fraught with difficulty. Human beings seem to prefer to
remain protected, insulated, even if this means they are insulated from
their essences, in a happy sort of oblivion. Essences are not always
pleasant – like essential oils, they are more easily assimilated when
diluted. Pina Bausch, however, in her concern with essences, is not
inclined to dilute them. Through movement she explores the absurdity
of human social behavior, our longings and fears our inability to
communicate, our private despair and all-consuming desire for self
affirmation. These are difficult topics, painful topics even, but if it is
pain which lies below the surface of composure, then it is this that
forms the matter for her choreography.

Her commitment to exploring the human condition pervades and
shapes all aspects of her work, from the technique (or, some would say,
lack of technique) to the music, costumes and set design. Her dances have

a raw physicality that differs from the physical strength, or sheer vitality, we have come to associate with physical theatre (such as DV8, or Volcano Theatre). The rawness of her physicality lies not in strength but in weakness. Bausch's dancers are like exposed human nerves. They are often thin, or haggard looking. They do not preserve the myth that dance is graceful or effortless, nor, by extension, do they preserve an idea that life is easy or effortless. They are exposed to the audience in their vulnerability, and on stage they dance through, and often exploit, each other's vulnerability. The costumes Bausch selects are taken from highly charged social contexts such as the bedroom or the ballroom. When the dancers wear evening attire it is made to appear like the thin layer of civilization covering the heart of darkness: the taffeta ball gowns are frayed, ripped, dirty, falling off, or at the very least, horrendously uncomfortable, like the high-heeled shoes into which the dancers often have their feet forced. The thin white slips, which have become a common sight in much contemporary physical theatre and dance performances (for example, DV8 or The Cholmondeleys) were used by Bausch in the 1970s as a simple but powerful way to challenge theatrical and social conventions, while at the same time conveying human pain and vulnerability. Her dancers are further challenged by the confines of the stage. The set design for her pieces is often monumental and minimal at the same time. She rarely works with wings or flats, so the performance space is not softened in any way and takes up the whole shell of the stage space. In *Bluebeard* (1977), for example, the set is a huge and palatial room with high ceilings, imposing windows and doors, but it is devoid of any comfort. It is empty and the floor is covered with dry leaves.

By having the dance surface covered with leaves, soil, grass or water, Bausch's stage designs challenge the distinction between inside and outside, and complement a form of dance in which the inside and the outside of the dancer are entwined together and presented to the audience. She claims that her pieces grow from the inside outwards. In an interview from 1982, Bausch describes how she always begins with questions, which is not the easiest way to work. In her opinion it is easier to begin with a movement and to avoid the questions, but doing so does not allow the essences to emerge. In dance, as in philosophy, contact with essences is inextricably linked with an unflinching ability to question. For Bausch, dance begins with questions, it is a form of interrogation.

The return to lived experience

The second reason Servos believes Bausch's work to be bewildering for audiences is the merciless way she asks her existential, social or aesthetic questions. He writes, "Bausch makes no excuses, nor does she allow the spectator to do so. To everyone, her critics included, she is a constant reminder of our own inadequacy, a constant annoyance."[5] Her work is merciless because it is so real. Being in the audience of a Bausch performance is participating in it. Her work is not removed from life, it is a part of life. It does not pretend, it is. This distinction corresponds to the second phenomenological tenet to play a role in this discussion: phenomenology is a return to lived experience.

In Bausch's hands, dance theatre developed into a "theatre of experience," a theatre that by means of direct confrontation makes aesthetic reality as tangible as a physical reality. Her performances are long. The dancers tire, the audience also grows weary. No concessions are made to giving the audience what it expects, even intervals are frequently omitted – for when do we get an interval from our own lives? The viewer is assailed by the authenticity of the emotions and by their strength. Her work is not primarily concerned with abstraction, with presenting an interpretation or reality, creating a dramatic illusion or telling a story. It introduces real time and space into theatrical time and space, and takes the audience member through the motions with the dancers. In *Arias* (1979), for instance, the water that covers the stage is a real force in opposition to the dancers. Their movements are made difficult by the resistance of the water, and by the weight of their soaked costumes. Servos aptly describes this piece as one in which the dancers are involved in a "sensuous and tangible feat," they are not conjuring up a dramatic illusion, they are too occupied working against resistances. Exhaustion of the dancers combines with the highly emotional content of the pieces and lends them an authenticity seldom encountered in a theatrical context.

Bausch's work is not an invitation to escape from life, but to plunge even deeper into it. It would be wrong to view her choreography as simply variations on the themes of pain and despair, for there is much humor in it. But it is not the escapist humor of the slapstick comedy, it is the humor that illuminates the struggles of daily life; the laughter that keeps one from crying; the laughter that recognizes the absurdity of our struggles, and affirms the precious moments of beauty and light that animate them.

To be in the audience of a Bausch performance is to participate in it. Passive reception of her work is impossible for one important reason – her work is by nature incomplete. It is not a seamless and sculpted whole presented to a passive audience. Starting with the daily, social experiences of the body, she translates and alienates them into sequences of images and movements that only make sense once the audience member relates this to his or her personal physical experiences. It is in this sense that her work is incomplete; it needs to be completed by each audience member's own thoughts and emotions. A lot of the complex metaphors she uses would, if viewed in purely a rational light, not make much sense. For example, in *Bluebeard*, when the Bluebeard character himself dresses his newest wife in layers and layers of women's clothes, he is not simply insulating her from the cold, he is binding her, suffocating her by imposing upon her the roles and expectations imposed upon each of us according to our sex, class and race. An image which could seem simply surreal or meaningless becomes powerful once each person develops it with his or her own experiences of being forced into stereotypical roles against our wishes, be this the role of wife, secretary, heir, heterosexual, or breadwinner. Similarly, a famous Bausch sequence on film is that of a woman dressed as a playboy bunny wearing stiletto heels and struggling through a freshly ploughed field. This would be merely silly or comical if it were not for the understanding that we are each able to bring to it.[6] For anyone who refuses to contribute thoughts and emotions derived from their own experience, Bausch's work will remain incomplete. She presents an offer to the audience which is not without risk, for it is never guaranteed that when you are invited to look at your own life from a different perspective you won't find something disturbing. Again, the inside meets the outside through her choreography: the inner experiences of the viewers are invited to rise to the surface and engage with the spectacle on stage. The very designations of what is "outer" and what is "inner" are called into question along with corresponding notions of the domains of the public and the private.

One of the strongest implications of the real, or lived, quality of her work is that it challenges theatrical conventions. Once again referring to the watery stage for *Arias*, Servos asks, "And what could be more incredible and at the same time appear more real than an operatic stage under water – in which people move with the utmost matter-of-factness?"[7] The incredible aspect is that a stage should find itself under water, the reality is the way the dancers move through the water – just the way anyone would if they found themselves in such a situation. Bausch collapses the distinction between life and theatre, but does not produce works that are pedestrian. They are instead highly expressive and dramatic. She neither turns life into drama, nor renders theatre mundane. She calls attention to the dramatic, and incredible qualities of life, and to the concrete, non-illusory side of dance theatre.

In the light of how Bausch challenges theatrical conventions, I should add another reason to Servos's two reasons for being bewildered or disturbed by Bausch's work. This third is particularly significant to the phenomenological position I will set out in the next issue of *Dance Now:* it is her self-reflexivity.

Self-reflexivity

Bausch's work exhibits a strong self-reflexivity. She does not just question and expose the tensions in social and personal dimensions, but she turns the gaze upon her own activity and questions the conventions of dance and theatre in and through her choreography. She does not preserve the comfortable distance between spectator and performer. She dismantles the conventions of theatre and causes questions concerning the nature of art to mingle with those concerning the nature of society. In dance theatre the contradictions of the theatre themselves become themes. The first thing to be challenged is audience passivity in the face of activity on stage. Bausch challenges this in several ways, for example, by having the dancers run to the front of the stage and then stand there silently gazing at the audience, or by extending the action of the performance into the auditorium. In other instances the dancers discuss with the audience what will happen in the next scene, or confide their fears and insecurities about performing. Further emphasizing that theatre does not stand apart from reality, she parodies the theatrical compulsion to exhibitionism, and demonstrates how similar it is to the compulsions of everyday life. She rejects the frontier between rehearsal and performance by making it clear that the performance is not a polished or finished product; instead, like life it is a process. As Servos effectively summarizes, "by baring the creative process and its tools to view, dance theatre destroys the slick theatrical illusion."[8]

Bausch's style of self-reflexivity in both film and stage has been called "a game of gazes" in an illuminating essay by Ana Sanchez-Colberg.[9] In this game of gazes the activity of seeing and the passivity of being seen are explored and set off against one another. The dancers address the fact that they are watched by the audience and confront the viewers with their own intrinsic voyeurism. The audience is forced to admit that they engage in a reversible relation, that they are seen as well as seeing, by "objects" that see as well as are seen. Bausch exposes the chasm between audience and performer directly through having her dancers strike obvious poses, take each other's photographs, and arrange themselves in mirrors. The blanket of darkness that insulates dancer from viewer no longer sustains the one-directional gaze, it harbors a cross-current of entwining gazes with a corresponding plethora of power structures constantly being formed, dissolved and re-formed, as the dominance of "seeing subject" over "object seen" is reversed and reshaped.

Bausch's concern with the role of dance is intimately tied up with her concern with understanding human beings. I have already claimed that the essence of beings was at stake in her work. Here I add that she is not just concerned with the distortions that seem to dominate the relations between people, but is equally worried about whether dance has cut itself off from its own source of meaning through becoming empty or mechanical:

> Why do we dance in the first place? There is a great danger in the way things are developing at the moment and have been developing in the last few years. Everything has become routine and no one knows any longer why they're using these movements. All that's left is just a strange sort of vanity that is becoming more and more removed from actual people. And I believe that we ought to be getting closer to one another again.[10]

Thus, for Bausch dance is about human relationships, and her interrogation of human relationships happens simultaneously with her interrogation of the convention of theatre.

Notes

1 Friedrich Nietzsche. *The Gay Science*, trans. W Kaufmann (New York: Vintage Books, 1974), p. 346.
2 Norbert Servos. *Pina Bausch Wuppertal Dance Theatre, or the Art of Training a Goldfish* (Cologne: Ballett-Bühnen Verlag Rolf Garske, 1984), p. 13.
3 *Ibid.*
4 *Ibid.*, p. 227.
5 *Ibid.*, p. 13.
6 See also Ana Sanchez-Colberg for a discussion of these scenes in the context of film. "You can see it like this or like that. Pina Bausch's *Die Klage Der Kaiserin.*" *Parallel Lines: Media Representations of Dance*, ed. S. Jordan & D. Allen (London: John Libbey, 1993) pp. 217–33.
7 Servos, *op. cit.*, p. 132.
8 *Ibid.*, p. 25.
9 Sanchez-Colberg, *op. cit.*
10 Servos, *op. cit.*, p. 227.

On the seduction of angels

Conjectures about the Zeitgeiz[1]

Norbert Servos

Originally published in *Ballett International*, December, 1985

The Zeitgeist. The topic is loosely woven, large and impalpable. As a transient attraction, it haunts the arts and leisure sections and creates much fuss. The Zeitgeist is in vogue now; it imitates a rise, and twists and turns, here and there. Everything is fine and dandy. There are festivals everywhere: German dance theatre – and not only that, but dance in general – is craved at home and abroad. The choreographers in the middle of the summer lull: on tour, on tour … Everything is fine and dandy?

A flashback to the beginnings, more than fifteen years ago, at the end of the sixties; the first steps of dance theatre, which were taken not only to change the form – to blow open the field. To many it was particularly shocking and bothersome that a deficiency was laid bare. Choreographers stated that something essential was missing; that there was something fundamentally wrong with human interaction and that this problem could be better explained through the body than through words. Something continually went amiss in relationships, something that had to do with the body and its innate feelings – something unreal, peculiar and removed. And in spite of quite a few good and a considerable number of bad comments about this issue, choreographers clung to their claims about the failure of love and tenderness, and to their conjectures about the cause. On the contrary, they continued to bring their painful experiences of reality on stage, put them into the spotlight and revealed them nakedly without nice packaging – which made them indecent and shameless. Sometimes, in the most perfidious cases, they even moved the events so far to the front of the stage that they seemed to be bigger than life. Consequently, they lost their veracity and became enormous exaggerations, to be discarded. There were, therefore, more than a few people who had an image of the choreographers of dance theatre as bizarre exhibitionists, abstruse soul sorcerers, exaggerators of sorrow and braggarts.

Meanwhile – and this is how the times change – everyone has become successful: the choreographers and their audience. The Zeitgeist reveals itself as generous and is even inclined to bestow high cultural consecrations on this type of creativity. In the meantime, every premiere, whether it is in Bremen or Heidelberg, Wuppertal or Frankfurt, is a major event; and Hoffmann, Bausch, Kresnik, Forsythe and Gilmore are selling tickets for the cultural Olympus. But still – many contemporaries observe sullenly – the choreographers tell of the same painful conflicts with reality and the same sad losses. But it's more than that. The atmosphere in Pina Bausch's still untitled piece seems even colder, the ritual in William Forsythe's *LDC* seems even more estranged from people, the entanglements in Rosamund Gilmore's *Blaubart* seem even more convoluted and hopeless, the destruction of the myth of happiness in Reinhild Hoffmann's *Föhn* seems even more definitive and the way to suicide in Johann Kresnik's *Sylvia Plath* seems even more compulsory. If one is to believe the choreographers of dance theatre, who are apparently unteachable, then the bad state of affairs that compelled them years ago to introduce unusual means of portrayal has hardly changed. There is avarice and deficiency everywhere. Happiness is rare, and forgiveness of the old wounds is rare. And hope, which has always played a role in dance theatre, flickers – so it seems – only well below the surface. This hope is fired on by an equally tenacious persistence, not letting itself be discouraged by the increasing number of failures in the pursuit of happiness. Then the willingness to expose oneself to sadness in dance theatre is equal to the persistence of desire. Fear and rage go hand in hand. The seriousness of the situation can't suffocate people's pleasure in mocking the comical travesty with raucous laughter.

How it all began: Christian mythology documents the fall. Lucifer, at first still one of the angels, at home in the heavenly other world, didn't want to join in the praises of the Lord's power. Punishment followed immediately; he was banished and thrust into Hell. From then on the "incarnate one," the one who is identical with his body, lives in the underworld. From there he threatens as Satan, the Devil, luring people into sin with every conceivable type of physical temptation. The Devil doesn't seduce through the spirit, but through the flesh. And the flesh is obedient but weak – obedient in submitting to the dominance of the spirit, but too weak to stand up against the allurements of bodily desire. And as long as there is life in this despised body, it must time and again fall into "sin" – and each time crawl to the Cross, to that highest court of appeals which gives it absolution. There is no escape from this vicious circle; the body has the brand of Cain – guilt.

From then on the other world was divided in two; into a spiritual upper level and a bodily, lusting lower level; into Heaven and Hell, the world of angels and the world of demons. The body was also divided; into a spiritual "pure" upper half and a "soiled," threatening lower half. From then on there was war. What came from the lower half was the work of the Devil, and frightening; what came from the upper half was a gift from God, and reassuring. Thus, without any toil, the division of classes could be legitimized; "lower" on the one hand, and "upper" on other – both of them created by God's grace. And the same irreconcilability reigned from then on – it was compulsory on both sides; between the humble dwellings and the palaces, between the heights of the spirit and the "depths" of the flesh.

Lucifer's descent into Hell sealed a fate that still has consequences for us today. High above, the patriarchal Heaven of the spirit is enthroned above the matriarchal "Hell of lust." The Eros became subservient to the Logos; sense prevailed over sensuality. Since then the paradise on earth, that has yet to evolve, has been off-limits to the body. Access has been denied since Lucifer no longer graces the sides of the Celestial. Paradise has moved to the heavens and can no longer be attained by the body. It is only death that allows one to enter the domain of heavenly grace. It is only when the body, the seed of the Devil and of vice, is left behind that one is thrust into eternity. Paradise is incorporeal, like ideal knowledge.

Culture, which is rooted in this ideal, affirms death, not life. Being opposed to the body, it remains estranged from human nature, and can hardly have a positive effect on the exterior world. Exploitation rules, inside as well as outside. And everywhere there is only one law – that of the economy of things. The body has been considered a "thing" for a long time now, a commercial object without any rights or franchise. It can find no quarter between the heavens of incorporeal angels and the hells of the incarnate ones. For it's entire existence, it is banned from Heaven, and Hell is forbidden to it because of the threat of eternal damnation. There is no interplay between the two poles: Heaven and Hell, reason and emotion are eternally divided. Subservient to the spirit and other masters, the body has up to now served only alien masters.

Hardly anywhere else is this clearer than in dance. Because if the dance takes this seriously, there is nothing left to do but to take account of the betrayal of the body in the economy of things and to fight the same old battle once again. The rebellion of the emotions; the rise of Lucifer from the depths of Hell: the seduction of angels. In dance theatre, the debased move up to the top, and the celestial must plunge into the "depths" of confused passion. The world is turned upside down – and for the first time has a chance to find its balance. The games of dance theatre are diabolical. Instead of symbolically mending a torn world, it breaks the wrong agreements and throws itself into the stream of evil that is inherent in the world. It brings the wheels of the deficient economy to a halt – if only for a few moments – and creates a time and place for unfulfilled wishes. In doing so, it is always exposed to the greatest pain: to be a body and not to possess one – to carry daily one's own flesh to different markets. This is why all attempts at reaching personal happiness are doomed to failure in dance theatre. Because of the pain, the imagined ways never converge, but diverge. The head and the body, the heart and the hand, aren't allowed to ally with one another, says the unwritten law. But dance theatre does carry the contradiction of the divided world to extremes – towards a resolution. The sphere of ideas starts moving in circles, and the realm of emotions is able to break through, but in no way indiscriminately or aimlessly, and definitely not without a goal. Dance theatre acts neither symbolically, creating signs, nor does it thrust one into an unconscious delirium. Certainly, it achieves the same "depth" of feeling, but only to lift passion out of the gloomy hell of naked lust and lead it into the light. Certainly, it dives down into the wide spectrum of everyday experience, but its discoveries are displayed in the bright light of understanding. It isn't Nietzsche's Dionysian frenzy that dance theatre recommends as the last stop. It is only in the Apollonian clearness of consciousness that the riding murmurs of the depths of the body find their direction and goal. But understanding transcends the body. As long as the intellect is only at home with the incorporeal angels, the world will remain stagnant, let alone be changed. On the other hand, Lucifer's fire of passion is nothing without celestial clairvoyance, which turns mere lust into rebellion, and only in the fire of passion does mere knowledge grow into understanding and solidify to intervene in the affairs of inherent evil. Heaven defines where we are to go; Hell, from where we came. The angels show us the way, and Lucifer gives us the driving force. Instinct begets impulse; vision begets the view of a possibility beyond serfdom. Appearance becomes reality and heralds the end of contradictions. The seduction of angels and Lucifer's emergence from the underworld both have one goal: to bring both Angel and Devil to the here and now, where they can be effective. For in infernal banishment, emotions are only a faint whisper. In the ivory tower of heavenly abstraction, thinking only produces dead spirituality.

Dance theatre probably has a vague idea of this objective, but doesn't comprehend it and consciously pursue it. But when it takes its work seriously, such a task must inevitably become visible. Since dance theatre no longer tells stories with the body, which are alien to the dance, but through the body its own story, it necessarily runs into the ubiquitous world of contradictions. These contradictions appear unexpectedly during investigations of normal experience, and dance theatre tries to act them out literally, step for step, and it becomes necessary to transform the pain that is everywhere. For with every step the body makes on the dance stage, it apparently only gets caught in yet another trap. With every step with which the body envisions its own possession, it finds itself once again outside in the wilderness of the dance theatre industry. Supply and demand call the tune from which classical ballet always believed it could escape on light fairies' feet.

Dance theatre doesn't succumb to illusions. It insists that the body is unmistakably led astray. It is neither conscious of itself nor is it in its own possession. With unbroken élan, dance theatre continually deals with this deficiency anew from piece to piece and asserts the right of the body to self-determination and to self-confident action and movement. It keeps the wound open (and doesn't try to hide it), which has to heal before there can be happiness. It keeps alive the memory of the betrayal of the body, whose expiation still stands out. It makes the gravity of the situation utterly perceptible. But amidst the Devil's laughter, it extends far past the given and holds the prospect of the magnificent realm of possibility.

Seriousness and laughter, sorrow and joy, failure and pleasure – these are the extremes of longing in the dance theatre of feelings. It is at these extremes that the defeats and victories occur. In its quest for freedom from its dilemma, dance theatre does not beat around the bush. Its longing is not rooted in sentimentality as that of the Romantics; its hope is not based on "virtuosity" as was the Classicists' cult of Genius; its "sensitivity" is not one of sentiment, but passion. Its sorrow allows it to sink deeply into the painful experience of the have-nots, whereupon joy suddenly flashes like lightning in the firmament. Fear is sustained and rage experienced: there is indignation at the angels who vanished into the abstract other world. The Devil returns and the angels are seduced. Thus the dark whisper of lust ascends to a state of consciousness; the body is enlightened. Rage becomes fury – the fury of resistance. Fear turns into fright, with the diabolical antagonist in plain sight. There is no longer any question as to who has the upper hand: the Spirit or the body, the angels or the Devil.

From behind everything lurks a heretical suspicion. For it is not necessary, as we are in the habit of assuming, for the spirit to take up residence in the body and to treat it with condescension. In fact, the body can have its own conception of the spirit. After all, aren't both made out of the same substance, the spirit and the body, subject and object? Didn't both originate from the same matter?

To alter the traditional roles would make the spirit a function of the body, and the body would be conscious of itself. The body would no longer be a mere vessel for the spirit, but rather its coeval. The spiritual would unveil itself in the corporeal – in the body itself, and with it the emotions would become the subject. But the future is obscured unless alienation can be abrogated. There can be no change unless serfdom is abolished. Being oneself necessarily implies possessing oneself. So it is with dance, which by now is subservient to other aims: dance would be the place where the corporality of being finds itself and becomes conscious of itself. The impotence of the mere physical existence of the body would emerge powerfully as a possession of the body. Furthermore, if people were conscious in this way, they would bear the torch of change proudly to the outside world, and they would be capable of doing something that they otherwise couldn't to fulfill their unquenched wishes; to create a reality. Lucifer's fire of passion is fused to the Promethean light of understanding.

All of this is a perspective for the future. Both Prometheus and Lucifer were punished for their deeds. Meanwhile, the battle still rages between the heights of the spirit and the "depths" of the flesh, between humble dwellings and palaces. And we still aren't sure to what end. Nevertheless, dance theatre seems to have a notion of what will transpire: a misty morning sunrise and fresh morning air. It poses the question generously, persistently; always anew.

Note

1 "Zeitgeiz" as opposed to "Zeitgeist" (spirit of the times) is a play on words referring to the meagerness of the times.

Further research

Important works (primarily in English) directly connected to Baush's output and legacy, broken down by section to facilitate further investigation, and including full bibliographic information for material included in the text.

List of works, biography and awards

A complete and updated list of works, biography and awards is available at the Tanztheater Wuppertal website: http://www.pina-bausch.de/en/index.php

I. Dance and theatre roots and connections

Aloff, Mindy. "Two continents: two approaches to dance", *BAM Next Wave Festival Souvenir Program*, 1987, 64–73.

Anderson, Jack. "By word of mouth, dancers find new eloquence", *New York Times* (7 October, 1990), H10.

——. "Choreographic violence may be getting out of hand", *New York Times* (10 November, 1985), 9–10.

——. "Just what is this thing called dance", *New York Times* (12 August, 1990), H6.

Banes, Sally. *Democracy's Body: Judson Dance Theatre, 1962–1964*, Durham, NC: Duke UP, 1993.

——. *Greenwich Village 1963: Avant-Garde Performance and the Effervescent Body*, Durham, NC: Duke UP, 1993.

Bentivoglio, Leonetta. "Dance of the present, art of the future", *Ballett International* 8(12), (December, 1985), 24–28.

Borzik, Rolf. *Rolf Borzik und das Tanztheater,* Wuppertal: Tanztheater Wuppertal Pina Bausch GmbH, 1980.

Confino, Barbara. "The theatre of images: Pina Bausch and the expressionist temperament", *Cityweek* (18 July, 1988), 41–42.

Daly, Ann (ed.) "What has become of postmodern dance", *TDR* (Spring, 1992), 48–69.

Fischer, Eva Elizabeth. "Reflections of the times: the inter- and multimedia of Tanztheater", *Tanztheater Today: Thirty Years of German Dance*, Exhibition Catalogue, Seelze/Hannover: Kallmeyeresche, in association with Ballett International/Tanz Aktuell, 1998.

Galloway, David. "The stage as crossroads: Germany's Pina Bausch", *In Performance* 13(6), (March/April, 1984), 39–42.

——. "Visionary dance or total theatre?" *New York Times*, (10 June, 1984), C1 and 26.

Honegger, Gitta. "Form as torture: found meanings between Bausch and Kantor", *Theatre* 17(2), (Spring, 1986), 56–60.

Kisselgoff, Anna. "Dance that startles and challenges is coming from abroad", *New York Times* (13 October, 1985).

——. "Dance; the vision is European", *New York Times* (28 November, 1982).

——. "Dance view; American modern isn't at home in Germany", *New York Times* (22 October, 1989).

——. "Dance view; does dance reflect current concerns?" *New York Times* (12 January, 1986).

——. "Dance view; how much does dance owe to Jooss?" *New York Times* (11 July, 1982).

Langer, Roland. "Compulsion and restraint, love and angst: the post-war German expressionism of Pina Bausch and her Wuppertal Dance Theatre", *Dance Magazine*, trans. Richard Sikes (June, 1984), 46–48.

Leach, Robert. *Makers of Modern Theatre: An Introduction*, London: Routledge, 2004.

Lelli, Sylvia. *Körper und Raum: Pina Bausch, Reinhild Hoffman, Susanne Linke, William Forsythe, 1979–1999*, Wuppertal, Germany: Verlag Müller und Busmann, 1999.

Mackrell, Judith. "Hurt's so good", *Guardian* (23 January, 2002).

Manning, Susan Allene. "An American perspective on Tanztheater", *TDR* (Spring, 1986), 57–79.

——. *Ecstasy and the Demon: Feminism and Nationalism in the Dances of Mary Wigman*, Berkeley: University of California Press, 1993.

——. "Pina Bausch Wuppertal Dance Theatre and Jooss: a documentation", *Dance Research Journal* 17(2) and 18(1), (Fall 1985/Spring 1986), 93–94.

Manning, Susan and Melissa Benson. "Interrupted continuities: modern dance in Germany", *TDR* (Spring, 1986), 30–45.

Milz, Bettina. "Side leaps, quantum leaps: how an actor moves on stage. Choreographers and musicians bring a new sense of form to the theatre", *Ballett International/Tanz Aktuell* (April, 1998), 21–23.

Müller, Hedwig. "Expressionism? 'Ausdruckstanz' and the New Dance Theatre in Germany", *Festival International de Nouvelle Danse, Montreal, Souvenir Program*, trans. Michael Vensky-Stalling (1986), 10–15.

——. "The twisting spiral", *Ballett International* 8(3) (March, 1985), 16–20.

Nugent, Ann. "The Green Table and Café Müller" *Dance Now* 1(3) (Autumn, 1992), 34–41.

Odenthal, Johannes. "From Isadora to Pina", *Ballett International/Tanz Aktuell* (May, 1994), 34–36.

Partsch-Bergsohn, Isa. "Dance Theatre from Rudolph Laban to Pina Bausch", *Dance Theatre Journal* (October, 1987), 37–39.

——and Harold Bergsohn. *The Makers of Modern Dance in Germany: Rudolf Laban, Mary Wigman, Kurt Jooss*, Hightstown, NJ: Princeton Book Company, 2003.

"Pina Bausch in America", *Ballett International* 7(11), (November, 1984) 14–18.

Regitz, Hartmut. "Beyond the mainstream: everything else you find in Tanztheater", *Tanztheater Today: Thirty Years of German Dance*, Exhibition Catalogue, Seelze/Hannover: Kallmeyeresche, in association with Ballett International/Tanz Aktuell, 1998.

Robertson, Allen. "Close encounters: Pina Bausch's radical Tanztheater is a world where art and life are inextricably interwoven", *Ballet News* 5(12), (June, 1984), 10–14.

Schaik, Eva van. "The bemused muse", *Ballett International/Tanz Aktuell* (November, 1995), 36–45.

——. "The mistrust of life: relations in dance: connections between Butoh, Ausdruckstanz and Dance Theatre in contemporary experimental dance", *Ballett International* 13(5), (May, 1990), 11–14.

Scheier, Helmut. "What has Dance Theatre to do with Ausdruckstanz?" *Ballett International* 10(1), (January, 1987), 12–16.

Schlicher, Susanne. "The West German Dance Theatre: paths from the twenties to the present", *Choreography and Dance*, 3(2) (1993), 25–43.

Schmidt, Jochen. "From Isadora to Pina: the renewal of the human image in dance", *Ballett International/Tanz Aktuell* (May, 1994), 34–36.

The Search for Dance: Pina Bauch's Theatre with a Difference, Documentary Video, Script Direction: Patricia Corboud, Bonn: Inter Nationes, 1994: 28 min.

Servos, Norbert. "The emancipation of dance: Pina Bausch and the Wuppertal Dance Theatre", trans. Peter Harris and Pia Kleber, *Modern Drama* 22(4), (1981), 435–47.

——. "Whether to resist or conform: Ausdruckstanz then. And now?" *Ballett International* 10(1), (January, 1987), 18–20.

Siegel, Marcia B. "Carabosse in a cocktail dress", *Hudson Review* (Spring, 1986), 107–12.

Stein, Bonnie Sue. "Butoh: 'Twenty years ago we were crazy, dirty, and mad'", *TDR* (Spring, 1986), 107–25.

Thomas, Emma Lewis. "Choreographing Brecht", *Ballett International/Tanz Aktuell* (February, 1998), 56–61.

Warren, Larry. *Anna Sokolow: The Rebellious Spirit*, Princeton NJ: Dance Horizons, 1991.

Weiss, Uli. *Rolf Borzik und das Tanztheater*, Siegen, Germany: Druckerei Bonn und Fries, undated.
Wright, Elizabeth. *Postmodern Brecht: A Representation*, London: Routledge, 1989.

II. Creating Bausch's world

Adolphe, Jean-Marc. "Corpus Pina Bausch", *Pina Bausch*, Heidelberg: Editions Braus, 2007, 9–24.
Bartlett, Neil. "What moves: Pina Bausch", *Dance Theatre Journal* (January, 1999), 4–7.
"Bausch, Pina." *Current Biography* (September, 1986), 3–6.
Bausch, Pina. "Choreografin Pina Bausch über ihre Arbeit", Interview with Edmund Gleede, *Ballett-Jahrbuch des Friedrich Verlags*, 1975.
——. "Everyday a discovery … ", Interview with Christopher Bowen, *Stagebill: Cal Performances* (October, 1999), 10C–11A.
——. "The evolution of Pina Bausch", With Sylvie du Nussac, Reprinted from *Le Monde, World Press Review* (October, 1989), 91.
——. "Gespräch mit Pina Bausch im Goethe-Institut Paris", Interview with Dr. Ros, trans. by Susanne Marten, Goethe Institut Paris, 1994.
——. "Ich glaube nur, was ich gesehen habe", Interview with Ulrich Deuter, Andreas Wilink, *K. West* (October, 2004), 5–10.
——. "I'm still inquisitive", With Jochen Schmidt, *Pina Bausch Wuppertal Dance Theatre or the Art of Training a Goldfish*, Cologne, Germany: Ballett-Bühnen-Verlag, 1984, 238–39.
——. "'Man weiß gar nict, wo die Phantasie einen hintreibt': Ein Gespräch mit Pina Bausch gefürt von Jean-Mark Adolfe", *Pina Bausch*, Heidelberg: Editions Braus, 2007, 25–39.
——. "My pieces grow from the inside out", With Jochen Schmidt, *Pina Bausch Wuppertal Dance Theatre or the Art of Training a Goldfish*, Cologne, Germany: Ballett-Bühnen-Verlag, 1984, 234–37.
——. "Not how people move but what moves them", With Jochen Schmidt, *Pina Bausch Wuppertal Dance Theatre or the Art of Training a Goldfish*, Cologne, Germany: Ballett-Bühnen-Verlag, 1984, 227–30.
——. "Pina Bausch: an interview by Jochen Schmidt", *Ballett International* 6(2), (February, 1983), 12–15.
——. "Pina Bausch über Lust", Interview with Eva-Elisabeth Fischer, *Süddeutsche Zeitung* 223 (25/26 September, 2004), 8–12.
——. "The things we discover for ourselves are the most important", With Jochen Schmidt, *Pina Bausch Wuppertal Dance Theatre or the Art of Training a Goldfish*, Cologne, Germany: Ballett-Bühnen-Verlag, 1984, 231–33.
——. "'You have to keep totally alert, sensitive, receptive.': Pina Bausch talks with Norbert Servos", *Ballett International/Tanz Aktuell* (December 1995), 36–39.
——. "Zu extrem, um nachahmen zu können", Unlisted Interviewer, *GI-Intern* (March, 1998), 19–21.
Bentivoglio, Leonetta. *Il Teatro di Pina Bausch*, new edition, Milan: Ubulibri, 1991.

—— and Francesco Carbone. *Pina Bausch oder Die Kunst über Nelken zu tanzen*, Frankfurt am Main: Suhrkamp, 2007.

Boccadoro, Patricia. "Interview: working with Pina Bausch", *Culture Kiosque* (16 October, 2007), http://www.culturekiosque.com/dance/inter/pina_bausch. html

Brown, Ismene. "A place where life happens", *The Telegraph* (19 January, 2002).

Buchwald, Karlheinz. "If I tried concentrating on getting my arm right, then my feet went wrong", *Kontakthof with Ladies and Gentlemen over "65"*, Paris: L'Arche, 2007, 30–35.

Cattaneo, Anne. "Pina Bausch: 'You can always look at it the other way around'", *Village Voice* (19 June, 1984), 93–95.

Chamier, Ille. *Setz Dich Hin und Lächle: Tanztheater von Pina Bausch*, Cologne, Germany: Prometh, 1979.

Climenhaga, Royd. *Pina Bausch,* London: Routledge, 2009.

——. "Pina Bausch, Tanztheater Wuppertal in a newly commissioned piece: *Nur Du (Only You)*", *TPQ* (July, 1997), 288–98.

Daly, Ann. "Pina Bausch goes west to prospect for imagery", *New York Times* (22 September, 1996), 10–20

Delahaye, Guy. *Pina Bausch*, Kassel, Germany: Bärenreiter, 1989.

Farabough, Laura. "Nur Du (Only You): A piece by Pina Bausch", *TheatreForum* (Winter/Spring, 1997), 60–62.

Felciano, Rita. "Pina Bausch: the voice from Germany", *Dance Magazine* (October, 1996), 68–71.

Förster, Lutz. "An individual path to movement: interview with Lutz Förster by Birgit Kirchner", *Ballett International* 12(6), (June, 1989), 57–60.

Hamilton, Stanley. "Strength to endure", *Dance and Dancers* (April, 1986) 18–19.

Hoghe, Raimond. *Pina Bausch: Tanztheatergeschichten*, Frankfurt, Germany: Suhrkamp, 1986.

——. "The theatre of Pina Bausch", *The Drama Review*, trans. Stephen Tree (1985), 63–74.

Kapitanoff, Nancy. "Pina goes West", *In* (February, 1996), 48–51.

Kaplan, Jay L. "Pina Bausch: Dancing Around the Issue", *Ballet Review* (Spring, 1987), 74–77.

Kaufmann, Ursula. *Getanzte Augenblicke: Ursula Kaufmann Fotografiert Pina Bausch und das Tanztheater Wuppertal*. Wuppertal: Verlag Müller and Busman, 2005.

——. *Nur Du: Ursula Kaufmann Fotografiert Pina Bausch und das Tanztheater Wuppertal*. Wuppertal: Verlag Müller and Busman, 1998.

——. *Pina Bausch: Nur Du*. Wuppertal, Germany: Verlag Müller and Busmann: 1998.

——. *Ursula Kaufmann Fotografiert Pina Bausch und das Tanztheater Wuppertal*. Wuppertal: Verlag Müller and Busman, 2002.

Kew, Carole. "Swimming with Pina", *Dance Theatre Journal* 17(4), (Winter 2001/02), 4–7.

Klett, Renate. "In rehearsal with Pina Bausch", *Heresies* 5(1), (1984), 13–16.

Kontakthof with Ladies and Gentlemen over "65": A Piece by Pina Bausch Tanztheater Wuppetal. L'Arche, Paris, 2007. With DVD.

Linsel, Anne and Rainer Hoffman. "Dancing dreams", DVD, Tag/Traum Production, 2010: 89 minutes.

Loney, Glenn. "Creating an environment: Pina Bausch redefines dance with peat moss, autumn leaves, sod, tables, and chairs", *Theatre Crafts* (February, 1986), 30–37.

——. "'I pick my dancers as people'. Pina Bausch discusses her work with Wuppertal Dance Theatre", *On the Next Wave* (October, 1985), 14–19.

Manuel, Diane. "German choreographer Pina Bausch in rehearsal", News Release, Palo Alto, CA: Stanford University, 20 October, 1999.

Meisner, Nadine. "Come dance with me", *Dance and Dancers* (Sept./Oct., 1992), 12–16.

Nugent, Ann. "Altered states", *Dance Theatre Journal* 12(2), (Autumn, 1995), 16–20.

Nutter, Tamsin. "A Conversation with Pina Bausch", trans. Rieko Yamanaka, *The Arts Cure* (Winter 2004), 30–33.

Orpheus und Eurydike by Christoph W. Gluck, Dance-Opera by Pina Bausch, DVD, BelAir Calssiques and Opera National de Paris, 2009: 104 minutes.

Pabst, Peter. "Design and Collaboration: an Interview with Peter Pabst", Interview by Theodore Shank, *TheatreForum* (Winter/Spring, 1997, 79–83.

Panetta, Janet. "Interview: Janet Panetta: the ballet master parts the curtain on Tanztheater Wuppertal", Interview by Gia Kourlas, *Time Out New York* (July, 2009), 16–22, http://newyork.timeout.com/arts-culture/dance/42732/interview-janet-panetta.

Parry, Jann. "Wuppertal goes West", *Dance Now* (Summer, 1996), 66–71.

Perlmutter, Donna. "Pina Bausch comes to town", *Performing Arts* (October, 1996), 53–59.

"Pina Bausch." *Women and Performance,* 2(1) (1984), 97–100.

Pina Bausch: In Search of Dance, Documentary Film, Dir. Patricia Corboud, Inter Nationes, 1993. 29 minutes.

Pina Bausch: One Day Pina Asked … Documentary Film, Dir. Chantal Ackerman, Bravo International Films, 1984. 40 minutes.

Regitz, Hartmut. "I'm far too self-critical: an interview with Josephine Anne Endicott", *Ballett International/Tanz Aktuell* (August/September, 1998), 51–54.

Robertson, Allen. "Close encounters: Pina Bausch's radical Tanztheater is a world where art and life are inextricably interwoven", *Ballet News* 5(12), (June, 1984), 10–14.

Scheier, Helmut. "The woman from Wuppertal", *Dance and Dancers* (September 1982), 14–15.

Schmidt, Jochen. "Learning what moves people: thirty years of Tanztheater in Germany", *Tanztheater Today: Thirty Years of German Dance,* Exhibition

Catalogue, Seelze/Hannover: Kallmeyeresche, in association with Ballett International/Tanz Aktuell, 1998.

——. "Pina Bausch: a constant annoyance", *Pina Bausch Wuppertal Dance Theatre or the Art of Training a Goldfish,* Cologne, Germany: Ballett-Bühnen-Verlag, 1984, 13–16.

——. "Pina Bausch and the new German Tanztheater: movement from the inside out", *Festival des Nouvelle Danse, Montreal, Souvenir Program*, 1985, 59–65.

——. *Pina Bausch: Tanzen gegen die angst*, Munich, Germany: Econ Verlag, 1999.

——. "The Wuppertal choreographer Pina Bausch – the Mother Courage of modern dance – turns fifty", *Ballett International* 13(6–7), (June/July, 1990): 40–43.

Schmiegelt, Matthias. "A conversation: Matthias Schmiegelt, General Manager, Tanztheater Wuppertal", Interview by Lara Farabough, *TheatreForum* (Winter/Spring, 1997), 63–66.

Schulze-Reuber, Rika. *Das Tanztheater Pina Bausch: Speigel der Gesellschaft*, with Fotografien von Jochen Viehoff, Frankfurt/Main, Germany: R. G. Fischer, 2005.

The search for dance: Pina Bauch's theatre with a difference, Documentary Video, Script Direction, Patricia Corboud, Bonn: Inter Nationes, 1994: 28 min.

Servos, Norbert. "The emancipation of dance: Pina Bausch and the Wuppertal Dance Theatre", trans. Peter Harris and Pia Kleber, *Modern Drama*, 224) (1981), 435–47.

——. "In the emotions factory", *Ballett International*, 8(1), (January, 1985), 6–12.

——. *Pina Bausch: Dance Theatre*, Photographs by Gert Weigelt, Munich, Germany: K. Kieser, 2008.

——. *Pina Bausch: Tanztheater*, photographs by Gert Weigelt, Munich, Germany: K. Kieser, 2003.

——. *Pina Bausch Wuppertal Dance Theatre or the Art of Training a Goldfish,* Cologne, Germany: Ballett-Bühnen-Verlag, 1984.

——. *Pina Bausch – Wuppertaler Tanztheater oder die Kunst, einen Golfisch zu Dressieren*, Kallmeyer, Germany: Seelze – Velber, 1996.

Stendhal, Renate. "Pioneer dance", *San Francisco Focus* (October, 1996), 66–70.

Sullivan, Scott. "The laugh is on us: Pina Bausch is modern choreography's tragic joker", *Newsweek* (13 June, 1994), 45–47.

"Tanztheater Wuppertal", *Festival International des Nouvelle Danse, Montreal*, Souvenir Program, 1985, 40–43.

"Thoughts on the creation of *Nur Du* and Bausch's world", *The University of Texas College of Fine Arts Performing Arts Center Program*, Pina Bausch Tanztheater Wuppertal – Bass Concert Hall, 22 October, 1996.

"Twenty questions". Interview with Pina Bausch, *American Theatre* (May/June 2008), 96.

Viehof, Jochen. *Pina Bausch: Ein Fest*, Wuppertal, Germany: Verlag Müller and Busmann, 2000.

Vogel, Walter. *Pina*, Munich, Germany: Econ Ullstein List Verlag, 2000.

Was Tun Pina Bausch und Ihrer Tänzer in Wuppertal? Videocassette, Dir. Klaus Wildenhahn, Inter Nationes, 1983. 60 minutes.

Williams, Faynia. "Working with Pina Bausch: a conversation with Tanztheater Wuppertal", *TheatreForum* (Winter/Spring, 1997), 74–78.

III. Tanztheater – a new form

Abell, Jeff. "Toward a new dance-theatre", *Dialogue* (May/June, 1991), 14–15.

Bausch, Pina. "Come dance with me", Interview with Nadine Meisner, *Dance and Dancers* (Sept/Oct, 1992), 12–16.

Baxman, Inge. "Dance Theatre: rebellion of the body, theatre of images and an inquiry into the sense of the senses", *Ballett International* 13(10), (January, 1990), 55–60.

Bentivoglio, Leonetta. "Dance of the present, art of the future", *Ballett International* 8(12), (December, 1985), 24–28.

Brooklyn Academy of Music. *Next Wave Festival Catalogue* (October–December, 1985).

Carr, C. "The essence of dance." *Ruhr Works: The Arts of a German Region*, Promotional Brochure, Ministerium für Arbeit, Soziales und Stadtentwicklung, Kultur und Sport des Landes Nordrhein-Westfalen, 1985, 24–27.

Cohen, Selma Jeanne. "Visit to another world", *Dancemagazine* (May, 1988), 48–51.

Finkel, Anita. "Gunsmoke", *The New Dance Review* 4(2), (October–December, 1991), 3–10.

Garske, Rolf. "Modern times", *Ballett International* 11(6–7), (June/July, 1988), 34–39.

Gradinger, Malve. "Dances of disillusion", *Ballett International/Tanz Aktuell* (October, 1995), 24–28.

Jeschke, Claudia. "Reconstruction/deconstruction: currents in contemporary dance", Walter Sorrell (ed.), *The Dance Has Many Faces*, 3rd edn, Pennington, NJ: A Capella Books, 1992, 192–201.

Jowitt, Deborah. "Please Do It Again, Do It Again, Again. ... " *Village Voice* (3 July, 1984), 93–94.

Kerkhoven, Marianne van. "Dance, theatre, and their hazy boundaries", *Ballett International* 16(1), (1993), 11–15.

——. "Merging of all boundaries: on the autonomy of dance", *Ballett International* 12(1), (1989), 13–18.

Köllinger, Bernd. "What really counts", *Ballett International* 8(12), (1985), 49–52.

Linke, Susanne. "Dancing really does make sense: interview by Birgit Kirchner", *Ballett International* 6(12), (December, 1983), 22–26.

Lelli, Sylvia. *Körper und Raum: Pina Bausch, Reinhild Hoffman, Susanne Linke, William Forsythe, 1979–1999*, Wuppertal, Germany: Verlag Müller und Busmann, 1999.

Manning, Susan Allene. "Generation and gender in West German art today", *Next Wave Festival Catalogue*, 1985, 5–10.

——. "German *Rites*: A History of *Le Sacre du Printemps* on the German Stage", *Dance Chronicle* 14(2/3), (1991), 129–58.

Müller, Hedwig. "Accepting differences", *Ballett International* 9(2), (1986), 30–31.

Nugent, Ann. "Living up to its promise?" *Dance Theatre Journal* 13(2), (Autumn/Winter, 1996), 20–25.

Percival, John. "Dance along the Rhine", *Dance and Dancers* (July, 1977), 24–28.

Regitz, Hartmut. "As though the devil were a dancer: the choreodrama of Nada Kokotovic", *Ballett International/Tanz Aktuell* (April, 1998), 30–31.

——. "The Caucasian Chalk Circle in Bonn", *Ballett International/Tanz Aktuell* (February, 1998), 61.

——. "Darie Cardyn: I'm a stage person: Harmut Regitz talks to dancer and actress Darie Cardyn", *Ballett International/Tanz Aktuell* (April, 1998), 32–33.

Schlicher, Susanne. *Tanztheater*. Reinbek bei Hamburg, Germany: Rowohlts, 1987.

Schmidt, Jochen. "Ballet after the fall from grace", *Ballett International/ Tanz Aktuell* (8 September 1996), 20–25.

——. "Ballet and dance today: in the public eye but artistically in the doldrums?" *Ballett International* 11(1), (1988), 18–19.

——. "The choreographer's fear of the ensemble", *Ballett International/Tanz Aktuell* (March, 1996), 36–39.

——. "The granddaughters dance themselves free", *Ballett International* 6(1), (1983), 12–19.

——. "Learning what moves people: thirty years of Tanztheater in Germany", *Tanztheater Today: Thirty Years of German Dance*, Exhibition Catalogue, Seelze/Hannover: Kallmeyeresche, in association with Ballett International/ Tanz Aktuell, 1998.

——. "Movement is powerful, language concrete", *Ballett International* 9(12), (1986), 30–34.

——. *Tanztheater in Deutschland*, Frankfurt a. M.: Germany: Propyläen Verlag, 1992.

Servos, Norbert. "The heritage of freedom", *Ballett International* 9(7/8), (1986), 50–54.

——. "The rigid indifference of things", *Ballett International* 10(7/8), (1987), 14–15.

Sikes, Richard. "'But is it dance … ?'" *Dance Magazine* (June, 1984), 50–53.

Tanzland Nordrhein-Westfalen, Special promotional publication, Cologne, Germany: Ministry of Employment, Social Issues and City Development, Culture and Sports of the State of North Rhine Westphalia Office of Public Affairs in association with the NRW State Office for Dance, 1999.

"Tanztheater", unpublished transcript, 28 October, 1989, Sp. Lincoln Center Library for the Performing Arts, Participants: Reinhild Hoffmann, Susanne Linke, Susan Manning, Susanne Schlicher, Marcia Siegle, Moderated by Madeline Nichols, New York, 1989.

Tanztheater Today: Thirty Years of German Dance, Exhibition Catalogue, Seelze/Hannover: Kallmeyeresche, in association with Ballett International/ Tanz Aktuell, 1998.

Trembeck, Iro. "1995 Festival International de Nouvelle Danse", *Dance International* 23, (Fall 1995), 4–9.

Wesemann, Arnd. "Joachim Schlömer: it has to flow", *Ballett International/Tanz Aktuell* (April, 1998), 24–27.

Witzeling, Klaus. "Jan Pusch: the silence of the roles", *Ballett International/Tanz Aktuell* (April, 1998), 28–29.

IV. Bausch's reception

Acocella, Joan Ross. "Bausch's inferno", *Art in America* (January, 1992), 50–53.

——. "Dance: a kinder, gentler Pina Bausch", *The Wall Street Journal* (29 October, 1997), 17.

——. "Dancing: city lights: Pina Bausch returns to BAM", *The New Yorker* (25 December, 2006), 140–43.

——. "NYC Reviews", *Dance Magazine* (March, 1988), 42–45.

——. "Ordinary cruelties", *Seven Days* (20 July, 1988), 46–47.

——. "Play it again: Pina Bausch and William Forsythe at BAM", *The New Yorker* (14 January, 2002), 80–83.

——. "Reviews: New York City", *Dance Magazine* (March, 1986), 20–24 and 40–43.

Als, Hilton. "Pina und Kinder", *Ballet Review* (Winter, 1985), 78–80.

Anderson, Jack. "Fake flowers, real critters and, oh, yes, a mountain", *New York Times* (28 September, 1997), H6.

——. "New York Newsletter", *The Dancing Times* (December, 1991), 226–27.

——. "On love's scales, the pain outweighs the pleasure", *New York Times* (10 October, 1991), C18.

——. "Plotless dance-drama that deals in emotions", *New York Times* (26 June, 1984), H16.

——. "Pina Bausch? Funny? Yes, funny. Funny and very heartbreaking, too", *New York Times* (5 October, 1996), C15.

——. "Posies and rubble: designing 'reality' for Pina Bausch", *New York Times* (22 September, 1991), H23.

——. "West German dance: faddism and hippos", *New York Times* (21 November, 1985), C17.

Anderson, Zoë. "Pornography of pain: dancer Pina Bausch's turbulent career", *The Independent* (23 January, 2008).

Anonymous. "Dance legend returns", *Daily Mail* (29 January, 1999), 50.

——. "A feast in Wuppertal", *Ballett International/Tanz Aktuell* (October 1998), 27.

Ben-Itzak, Paul. "Breathless Pina meets the French Press", *The Dance Insider* (6 April, 2004).

Bentivoglio, Leonetta. "Exits and entrances", *Artforum* (April, 1990), 19–20.

Bidisha. "Pina Bausch, the genius of dance", *Guardian* (1 July, 2009). http://www.guardian.co.uk/ commentisfree/2009/jul/01/pina-bausch-dance.

Bir, Yvette. "Heartbreaking fragments, magnificent whole: Pina Bausch's new minimyths", *Performing Arts Journal* 20(2), (1998), 68–72.

Bleiberg, Laura. "Bausch, company lead journey of self-discovery", *The Orange County Register* (7 October, 1999).

———. "Wuppertal's Pina Bausch tackles a city epic", *The Orange County Register* (4 February, 1996), C1.

Bowen, Christopher. "Dancing in the dark", *The Scotsman* (March, 1995), 22–23.

———. "Flowering of an extraordinary talent", *The Scotsman* (31August, 1995).

———. "Influential choreographer brings her theatre of the mind to Berkeley", *San Francisco Chronicle. Datebook* (29 September–5 October, 1996), 40–41.

———. "Pina for your thoughts", *The Scotsman* (12 August, 1995), 6–7.

———. "Pina wears the pants", *The Times* (19 January, 1999), C1–2.

Brennan, Mary. "Dance: *Nelken*, Playhouse, Edinburgh", *The Herald* (1 September, 1995).

Breslauer, Jan. "Open-eyed in L.A", *Los Angeles Times* (17 March, 1996), 3–4.

Brouk, Tricia. "Insider audition: Ms. Bausch is casting", *The Dance Insider* (October, 1999), 14.

Brown, Ismene. "Bausch says it with flowers – thousands of them", *The Daily Telegraph* (9 September, 1995).

———. "Dance to the limit", *The Daily Telegraph* (28 August, 1995).

———. "Entranced by the mistress of misery", *The Daily Telegraph* (29 January, 1999).

———. "*Kontakthof*, Tanztheater Wuppertal Pina Bausch, Barbican Theatre", *The Arts Desk* (4 April, 2010).

———. "Living on a knife edge", *The Daily Telegraph* (26 January, 1999).

Bush, Catherine. "Pina Bausch makes a splash at BAM", *Theatre Crafts* (February, 1986), 14.

Chin, Brian. "Great performances", *The Daily Californian* (23 August, 1999).

"Choreographer Bausch dies aged 68", BBC News (30 June, 2009). http://news. bbc.co.uk/ 2/hi/entertainment/arts_and_culture/8128380.stm.

Citron, Paula. "Danzón brings Bausch's dance back to life after her death", *The Globe and Mail* (27 November, 2011), http://www.theglobeandmail.com/ news/arts/theatre/danzn-brings-bauschs-dance-back-to-life-after-her-death/ article2251180/

Climenhaga, Royd. "Realigned presence", *HotReview* (12 November, 2009), http://www.hotreview.org/articles/realignedpresence.htm

Cohn, Ellen. "Pina collage", *The Village Voice* (1 September, 1992), 96.

Constanti, Sophie. "Experimental madness from the dressing-up box", *The Evening Standard* (28 January, 1999).

———. "Pina Bausch: Tanzabend II at the Theatre de la Ville, Paris", *Dance Theatre Journal* 10(1), (Autumn, 1992), 8–10.

———. "Pina Bausch was staying at the Hotel Jolly. The hotel angst must have been full", *The Independent* (4 September, 1995).

Cook, Mark. "Essential performance: Tanztheater Wuppertal Pina Bausch", *The Big Issue* (25 January, 1999), 41.

Craine, Debra. "The big dance: Pina Bausch presents – Victor", *The Times* (23 January, 1999): The Directory Metro 40.

——. "Cabaret of the insane", *The Times* (29 January, 1999).

——. "Life after Pina Bausch, queen of European Dance Theatre", *The Times* (20 March, 2010).

Crisp, Clement. "A theatrical rattatouille", *Financial Times* (29 January, 1999).

Croce, Arlene. "Bad Smells", *The New Yorker* (16 July, 1984), 81–84.

Crompton, Sarah. "Pina Baush: a bold and committed pioneer", *The Telegraph* (1 July, 2009), http://www.telegraph.co.uk/culture/culturecritics/sarahcrompton/5707888/Pina-Bausch-a-bold-and-committed-pioneer.html.

——. "Pina Bausch: the visionary who stripped dance bare", *The Telegraph* (19 October, 2010), http://www.telegraph.co.uk/culture/theatre/dance/8074154/Pina-Bausch-the-visionary-who-stripped-dance-bare.html.

Crow, Susan. "News from Madrid", *The Dancing Times* (February, 1992), 437–38.

Cruickshank, Judith. "Pina Bausch: dancer and choreographer whose seminal work gave an unsettling view of the human condition", *The Independent* (3 July, 2009), http://www.independent.co.uk/news/obituaries/pina-bausch-dancer-and-choreographer-whose-seminal-work-gave-an-unsettling-view-of-the-human-condition-1729387.html.

"Curtain up: talking about Pina", *Dance and Dancers* (December, 1982), 10.

Davis, Dawn. "Waves coming to shore: Pina Bausch and the ineffable beauty of dance/theatre", *The Austin Chronicle* (October 22, 1999).

Dieutre, Vincent. "The death of the German choreographer Pina Bausch", *L'Humanité in English*, trans. Henry Crapo (1 July, 2009), http://humanitein english.com/spip.php?article1265.

Donkin, Ellen and Rhonda Blair. "The Seven Deadly Sins", *Women and Performance* 3(1), (1986), 116–17.

Dougill, David. "Blooming marvelous", *The Sunday Times* (10 September, 1995), 20.

Dover, Julia. "Pina Bausch: dancing the times", *Open Democracy* (7 March, 2009), http://www.opendemocracy.net/article/pina-bausch-dancing-the-times.

Dromgoole, Nicholas. "Queen of the barefoot leads the way", *Sunday Telegraph* (13 September, 1992), 14.

DuPont, Joan. "Making theatre out of life", *New York Times* (26 June, 1988), 10 and 13.

Esterházy, Péter, and Christian Lacroix. "Let's Bauschalise", *Ballett International/ Tanz Aktuell* (October, 1998), 24–25.

Feliciano, Rita. "Berkeley's International Season", *Dance Magazine* (September, 1999).

——. "Pina and beyond", *Dance Magazine* (September, 2010), 36.

——. "Pina Bausch's postcards of the West", *Los Angeles Times* (15 May, 1996), F1 and 11.

Finkel, Anita. "New York dance", *Vandance* (18 October, 1985), 10.

Forster, Emily. "Eccentric artist given free reign in tribute to L.A", *The Daily Bruin* (15 February, 1996), 8.

Gale, Joseph. "Life in '1980' according to Pina Bausch", *The Independent Press* (27 June, 1984), 15.

"German dance legend Pina Bausch dies at 68", *Deutsche Welle* (30 June, 2009), http://www.dw-world.de/dw/article/0,4444691,00.html.

Gilbert, Andrew. "Imaginative dancing", *Contra Costa Times* (14 October, 1999), D1–2.

——. "Kick-butt ballet", *San Jose Mercury News* (15 October, 1999), 29–30.

Gilbert, Jenny. "A legend in her own company", *The Globe* (29 January, 1999), 6.

——. "Tanztheater Wuppertal, Barbican Theatre, London", *The Independent* (10 April, 2010), http://www.independent.co.uk/arts-entertainment/theatre-dance/reviews/tanztheater-wuppertal-barbican-theatre-london-1941111.html.

——. "Tanztheater Wuppertal/Pina Bausch, Merce Cunningham Dance Company", *The Independent* (31 October, 2010), http://www.independent.co.uk/arts-entertainment/theatre-dance/reviews/tanztheater-wuppertal–pina-bausch-sadlers-wells-londonbrmerce-cunningham-dance-company-barbican-theatre-london-2121093.html#.

——. "Tanztheater Wuppertal/Pina Bausch, Sadler's Wells, London", *The Independent* (17 February, 2008).

Giordano, Kevin. "Bausch brings two works to US", *Dance Magazine* (October, 1999), 17.

Gold, Sylvia. "A window on the world", *Newsday* (6 October, 1997), 38.

Goldberg, Marianne. "Pina Bausch Tanztheater Wuppertal", *Artforum* 30(4), (December, 1991), 105–6.

Goodwin, Noel. "Curtain up: Pina's Saturday morning", *Dance and Dancers* (May, 1978), 4–5.

Greskovic, Robert. "Brooklyn", *Ballet News* 6(4), (October 1984), 35–36.

——. "Pina Bausch, visionary", *The Wall Street Journal* (7 July, 2009), http://online.wsj.com/article/ SB124692272148702723.html.

——. "Smoke got in her eyes", *Dance Magazine* (May 1995), 88.

Griffin, Annie. "A passion for Pina", *The Guardian* (31 August, 1995).

Gustin, Marene. "Dance as theatre", *Austin American Statesman* (9 May, 1996), 4.

Haithman, Diane. "Pina Bausch dies at 68; innovative German choreographer", *LA Times* (1 July, 2009), http://www.latimes.com/entertainment/news/arts/la-me-bausch1–2009jul01,0,6610100.story.

Hajari, Nisid. "Picture a city in motion", *Time* (10 March, 1997), 78.

Harmetz, Aljean. "Olympic Arts Festival opens in L.A", *New York Times* (2 June, 1984), A15.

Harris, Dale. "Bausch's battle of the sexes", *Wall Street Journal* (18 October, 1985), 34.

——. "Challenging the definition of dance", *Wall Street Journal* (27 June, 1984), 38.

Hewison, Robert. "A victory for the faithful", *The Sunday Times* (31 January, 1999).

Higgins, Charlotte. "Pina Bausch, 1940–2009", *Guardian* (30 June, 2009), http://www.guardian.co.uk/culture/charlottehigginsblog/2009/jun/30/dance-pinabausch.

Hoffman, Eva. "Pina Bausch: catching intuitions on the wing", *New York Times* (11 September, 1994), H, Section 2, 12.

Hohenadel, Kristin. "A flowering collaboration", *Los Angeles Times* (5 October, 1999), D1, 6.

Holland, Bernard. "The battle of the sexes, to the beat of Bartok", *The New York Times* (28 July, 1998).

James, Jamie. "Pina collider", *Vanity Fair* 57(12), (December, 1994), 57.

Jays, David. "Pina Bausch: a life less ordinary", *The Sunday Times* (5 July, 2009), http://entertainment.timesonline.co.uk/tol/arts_and_entertainment/stage/dance/article6626561.ece.

——. "Steps unseen", *New Statesman and Society* (22 January, 1999), 40.

JCP. "Slap dashing", *Gay Times* (January, 1999).

Jennings, Luke. "Pina Bausch", *Guardian* (1 July, 2009), http://www.guardian.co.uk/stage/2009/jul/01/ pina-bausch-obituary-dance.

——. "Tanztheater Wuppertal Pina Bausch", *The Observer* (28 March, 2010).

Jowitt, Deborah. "Art about art", *Village Voice* (5 November, 1991), 113–14.

——. "Bauschprints", *Village Voice* (15 October, 1991), 105.

——. "Dreams and nightmares", *Village Voice* (17 November, 1987), 101–2.

——. "In Memoriam: Pina Bausch (1940–2009)", *Village Voice* (1 July, 2009).

——. "Laundering anxiety", *Village Voice* (15 October, 1985), 101.

——. "Man as the measure", *Village Voice* (22 October, 1985), 105.

——. "Pinaville", *Village Voice* (6 December, 1994), 83–84.

——. "Pina Bausch's Moon Rivers", *Village Voice* (6 October, 2010),

——. "Rites for the moribund", *Village Voice* (12 July, 1988), 67–68.

Kahn, Judy. "The Paul Sanasardo Dance Company", *Dance Magazine* (October, 1972), 82.

Kaufman, David. "Pina Bausch: The coming of the second comer", *Downtown* (20 July, 1988), 16A.

Kirchner, Birgit. "Varying degrees of maturity", *Ballett International* 16(4), (April, 1993), 28–29.

Kisselgoff, Anna. "Bauch as choreographer of social trauma", *New York Times* (27 October, 1985), H14.

——. "The Bausch imagination still bedazzles", *New York Times* (20 October, 1991), H10.

——. "Dance: Bausch troupe makes New York debut", *New York Times* (13 June, 1984), C18.

——. "Dance: a Bluebeard by Pina Bausch troupe", *New York Times* (16 June, 1984), C14.

——. "Dance: Pina Bausch looks at human nature", *New York Times* (3 October, 1985), C19.

——. "Dance: Pina Bausch's 'Kontakthof' in Montreal", *New York Times* (25 September, 1985), C26.

——. "Dance: Pina Bausch presents 'Mountain'", *New York Times* (10 October, 1985), C22.

——. "Dance: premier of '1980, a piece by Pina Bausch'", *New York Times* (22 June, 1984), C17.

——. "Is Bausch's vision true to life?", *New York Times* (8 July, 1984), H12.

——. "Man as a window washer and a metaphor for futility", *New York Times* (6 October, 1997), C1 and 4.

——. "Pina Bausch adds humor to her palette", *New York Times* (17 July, 1988), H9.

——. "Pina Bausch, but not so sure this time", *New York Times* (11 December, 1994), H36.

——. "Pina Bausch dance: key is emotion", *New York Times* (4 October, 1985), C1 and 4.

——. "Pina Bausch's 'Carnations' in U.S. premiere", *New York Times* (7 July, 1988), C17.

——. "Pina Bausch's 'Palermo, Palermo' explores a world beyond logic", *New York Times* (30 September, 1991), C13–14.

——. "Sun, surf and sexuality in a Pina Bausch romp", *New York Times* (8 November, 2001), E5.

——. "Tanztheater Wuppertal: a bittersweet farewell as time goes by", *New York Times* (4 November, 1999).

——. "The wide universe of Pina Bausch", *New York Times* (19 November, 1994), A13.

Koegler, Hörst. "Pina Bausch: cigarettes smolder in Brooklyn", *Dance Magazine* (November, 1994), 17.

——. "Pina Bausch Tanztheater Wuppertal", *Dance Magazine* (October, 1991), 88.

——. "Sisyphus digs Dance Theatre a grave", *Ballett International* (July/August, 1986), 80.

——. "Sub-Pina", *Dance Now* (Summer, 1999), 45–47.

——. "Tanztheater Wuppertal", *Dance Magazine* (February, 1979), 51–58.

Kothari, Sunil. "Pina Bausch: a legendary dancer, choreographer passes away", *Narthaki* (9 July, 2009), http://www.narthaki.com/info/profiles/profl107.html.

Kourlas, Gia. "Clean fun", *Time Out, New York* (2–9 October, 1997), 34.

——. "Petal pusher", *Mirabella* (October, 1999) 48.

La Rocco, Claudia. "Swimmng through Bausch's world", *New York Times* (30 September, 2010).

Lawson, Valerie. "Pina, queen of the deep", *Sydney Morning Herald* (17 July, 2000), 18–19.

Leaske, Josephine. "Pictures from childhood", *Dance Now* 4(3), (Autumn, 1995), 82–83.

Levene, Louise. "Carrying on like Turks in November", *London Mail* (29 January, 1999).

Lin Ya-tin. "Mo(u)rning Pina", *Taiwan Culture Portal* (14 July, 2009), http://210.69.23.212/index.php?option=com_content&task=view&id=1294& Itemid=157.

Lomax, Sondra. "Austin inspires world-famous choreographer", *Austin American Statesman* (22 October, 1996), E1, 8.

Looseleaf, Victoria. "Germany's 'Tragic Joker'", *Los Angeles Downtown News* 25(41), (7 October, 1996), 1, 17.

Love Hodges, Mary. "The Brooklyn Rail remembers Pina Bausch", *The Brooklyn Rail* (September, 2009), http://brooklynrail.org/2009/09/dance/the-brooklyn-rail-remembers-pina-bausch.

Lundin, Diana. "A city alive with movement", *Daily News* (1 February, 1996), 3.

Lustig, Jessica. "Dance", *Time Out, New York* (2–9 October, 1997), 2.

Mackrell, Judith. "The agony and the ecstasy", *The Guardian* (21 January, 1999), C1.

——. "Chaos theory", *The Guardian* (7 February, 2008), http://www.guardian. co.uk/stage/2008/ feb/07/dance1.

——. "Farewell to Pina Bausch, the dangerous magician of modern dance", *Guardian* (30 June, 2009), http://www.guardian.co.uk/stage/2009/jun/30/pina-bausch-modern-dance.

——. "Hello dance fans", *The Guardian* (30 January, 1999).

——. "Pina Bausch for ever", *Guardian* (9 August, 2010), http://www.guardian. co.uk/stage/ 2010/aug/09/pina-bausch-edinburgh.

——. "Pina Bausch's Tanztheater Wuppertal: Agua", *Guardian* (29 August, 2010), http://www.guardian.co.uk/culture/2010/aug/29/pina-bausch-agua-edinburgh.

——. "Who will protect the legacies of Pina Bausch and Merce Cunningham?" *Guardian* (5 August, 2009), http://www.guardian.co.uk/stage/2009/aug/05/pina-bausch-merce-cunningham-legacies.

Macaulay, Alistair. "A stage for social ego to battle anguished id", *New York Times* (1 July, 2009), C1 and 5.

Manning, Emma. "World with no limits", *Dance Review* (29 January, 1999).

Manning, Susan. "Pina Bausch 1940–2009", *TDR* 54(1), (Spring, 2010), (T 205), 10–13.

Marigny, Chris de. "Theatre of despair and survival", *Dance Theatre Journal* (November, 1991), 14–15.

Marsh, Sarah. "Avant-garde German choreographer Pina Bausch dies", *Reuters* (30 June, 2009). http://www.reuters.com/article/2009/06/30/us-germany-bausch-idUSTRE55T5J620090630.

Martin, Julia. "Festival notes", *Ballett International* 14(11), (November, 1991), 52.

Mazo, Joseph H. "Valhalla with a pool", *Women's Wear Daily* (3 October, 1985), 20.

Meisner, Nadine "Overseas Reviews: Wuppertal Dance Theatre", *Dance and Dancers* (September/October, 1992), 25–26.

——. "Pina Bausch", *The Independent* (23 January, 1999), 24.

——. "Tanztheater Wuppertal", *Dance and Dancers* (December, 1995), 25–27.

Milder, Patricia. "A full moon to mark the end: Pina Bausch", *The Brooklyn Rail* (30 September, 2010), http://brooklynrail.org/2010/11/dance/a-full-moon-to-mark-the-end-pina-bausch-brooklyn-academy-of-music-sept-29-oct-9-2010.

Morris, Michael. "Appreciation: Pina Bausch 1940–2009", Interview by Vanessa Thorpe, *The Observer* (5 July, 2009), http://www.guardian.co.uk/stage/2009/jul/05/pina-bausch-michael-morris-dance.

Munk, Erika. "A lake of tears", *Village Voice* (3 July, 1984), 94.

——. "The victim as executioner", *Village Voice* (5 November, 1985), 105.

Murphy, Ann. "Bausch goes West", *The Oakland Tribune* (2 October, 1996), CUE-1, and 5.

O'Connor, Sara. "End of the world", *New York Native* (18 October, 1984), 18.

"Of mice and men", *The Observer* (26 May, 1996), 28.

O'Mahony, John. "Dancing in the dark", *Guardian* (26 January, 2002).

Pappenheim, Mark. "Viktor", *The Express* (30 January, 1999), 51.

Parish, Paul. "Dancing on a cliff's edge", *Bay Area Reporter* (8 December, 2011), http://www.ebar.com/arts/art_article.php?sec=dance&article=193.

Parry, Jann. "Did the earth move for you?" *The Observer Review* (31 January, 1999).

Peattie, Antony. "Edinburgh Festival: Pina Bausch, Playhouse", *The Independent* (5 September, 1995), 7.

Pepper, Kaija. "Pina Bausch's Bluebeard", *New Dance* N. 33, (Summer, 1985), 26.

Percival, John. "Café Müller", *Dance and Dancers* (November, 1992), 19.

——. "An exhilarating ballet by the possessed", *The Independent* (28 January, 1999), Late edition.

——. "Wuppertal Dance Theatre at the Royal Lyceum Theatre", *Dance and Dancers* (November, 1978), 33–34.

Perlmutter, Donna. "Los Angeles", *Dance Magazine* (September, 1984), 34–35.

Perret, Michel. "Bauschian revels", *Dance Magazine*, trans. Norma McLain Stoop (September, 1982), 86–87.

Perron, Wendy. "Bausch, Brecht and sex", *New York Native* (28 March, 1983), 8.

"Pina Bausch", *The Telegraph* (1 July, 2009), http://www.telegraph.co.uk/news/obituaries/culture-obituaries/dance-obituaries/5713208/Pina-Bausch.html.

Pitt, Freda. "Rome, Paris, Milan", *The Dancing Times* (September, 1986), 1051–52.

Poesio, Giannandrea. "The mighty Bausch", *Spectator* (6 November, 2010), http://www.spectator.co.uk/arts-and-culture/featured/6439398/the-mighty-bausch.thtml.

Purkert, Christina-Maria. "A feast for Wuppertalers", *Ballett International/Tanz Aktuell* (May, 2000), 20–22.

Ramsay, Burt. "Pina Bausch Wuppertal Dance Theatre", *New Dance* 36, (Spring, 1986), 29–30.

Regitz, Hartmut. "Masurca Fogo: the latest Pina Bausch in Wuppertal", *Ballett International/Tanz Aktuel* (May, 1998), 55.

——. "Pina's new piece: an opera", *Ballett International/Tanz Aktuell* (October, 1998), 26.

——. "Theme: Hong Kong", *Ballett International/Tanz Aktuell* (April, 1997), 36–37.

——. "They don't hit each other, they kiss: Untitled by Pina Bausch in Wuppertal", *Ballett International/Tanz Aktuell* (June, 1999), 54.

Rich, Alan. "Stretching the boundaries", *Newsweek* (18 June, 1984), 103.

Riding, Alan. "At the Edinburgh Festival, theatre seizes the day", *New York Times* (19 August, 1996), B1, 4.

——. "Even amid abundance, Edinburgh looks back, instead of forward", *New York Times* (4 September, 1996), C11–12.

——. "Using muscles classical ballet has no need for", *New York Times* (15 June, 1997), H32–33.

Roca, Octavio. "Big dance coup for Cal – premiere by Pina Bausch", *San Francisco Chronicle, Datebook* (29 January, 1996), 1.

——. "Pina Bausch leaves West unwon", *San Francisco Chronicle* (5 October, 1996), E1, 4.

Rockwell, John. "Mixed-media 'Bluebeard' draws on operatic past", *New York Times* (12 July, 1984), C18.

——. "Pina Bausch and the definition of dance", *ArtsJournal* (5 July, 2009), http://www.artsjournal.com/rockwell/2009/07/pina-bausch-and-the-definition.html.

——. "Pina Bausch extends Weimar expressionism", *New York Times* (31 October, 1985), C18.

Rosen, Lillie. "Pina Bausch Wuppertaler Tanztheater", *Dance News* (November, 1984), 12–13.

Rosenfeld, Marina. "My dinner with Pina", *LA Weekly* (11–17 October), 37–38.

Rosenthal, Judy C. "Bluebeard", *Women and Performance* 12(1), (1984), 97–98.

Rosiny, Claudia. "Film Review: Pina Bausch 'The Lament of the Empress'", *Ballett International* 13(6/7), (June/July, 1990), 74.

Roy, Sanjoy. "Step-by-step guide to dance: Pina Bausch/Tanztheater Wuppertal", *Guardian* (30 March, 2010), http://www.guardian.co.uk/stage/2010/mar/29/dance-pina-bausch-tanztheater-wuppertal.

Sandla, Robert. "The world according to Bausch", *New York Native* (25 July, 1988), 29.

Schmidt, Jochen. "A completely normal year", *Ballett International* 14(7/8), (July/August, 1991), 30–31.

——. "Pina Geht Nach Hollywood", *Frankfurter Allgemeine Zeitung* (14 May, 1996), 45.

——. "Return to Wuppertal eleven years later … Pina Bausch's 'He takes her by the hand'", *Ballett International* 12(6), (June, 1989), 44.

——. "Theatre of paradise: Wuppertal Dance Theatre's retrospect on Pina Bausch", *Ballett International* 10(1), (January, 1987), 28–29.

Scott, Trudy. "Café Müller", *Women and Performance* 12(1), (1984), 97.

Segal, Lewis. "Bausch to return with epic new work", *Los Angeles Times* (1 February, 1996), F1, 12.

Servos, Norbert. "And then Pina said … " *Ballett International* 5(8/9), (August/September, 1982), 20.

——. "Becoming a classic? The Wuppertal Dance Theatre and its new production 'Ahnen'", *Ballett International* 10(6), (June, 1987), 26.

——. "Hunters in the fog: a new work by Pina Bausch opens the Dance Festival 'New York and Back'", *Ballett International* 7(6/7), (June/July, 1984), 68.

——. "Longing for sleep and lust for life: Pina Bausch's new, as yet untitled piece in Wuppertal", *Ballett International/Tanz Aktuell* (June, 2000), 50–51.

——. "Love is strong as death", *Ballett International* 6(2), (February, 1983), 19.

——. "Painful clarity: a new look at old works by Pina Bausch", *Ballett International* 7(2), (February, 1984), 38.

——. "Pina Bausch: talking about people through dance", pina-bausch.de Trans. Steph Morris, http://www.pina-bausch.de/en/pina_bausch/index.php? text=lang.

——. "Sad beautiful parties", *Ballett International* 8(6/7), (June/July, 1985), 34.

——. "Über allen Gipfel ist Ruh", *Ballett International/Tanz Aktuell* (July, 1995), 18–19.

——. "Warum Verlieben Sich Die Menschen?" *Ballett International/Tanz Aktuell* (July, 1996), 14–15.

Shaw, Fiona. "'She made you feel thrilled to be human': Fiona Shaw on Pina Bausch", *Guardian* (6 July, 2009), http://www.guardian.co.uk/stage/2009/jul/06/pina-bausch.

Smith, Amanda. "New York City", *Dance Magazine* (September, 1984), 35–37.

Solomons, Gus Jr. "Ups and downs: Next Wave", *Ballet News* (March, 1986), 28–30.

Steinmetz, Muriel. "Pina Bausch, she who made dance speak", *L'Humanité in English*, trans. Henry Capo (2 July, 2009). http://humaniteinenglish.com/spip.php?article1270.

Sterritt, David. "Bausch's cold splash at Next Wave series", *Christian Science Monitor* (9 October, 1985), 23.

——. "Pina Bausch – A sometimes bleak, but always powerful vision", *Christian Science Monitor* (27 June, 1984), 24.

Stuart, Otis. "To flee or not to flee: Pina Bausch and the Wuppertal Dance Theatre", *New York Native* (25 November, 1985), 17.

Sublett, Scott. "Pina Bausch's take on American West", *San Francisco Chronicle* (20 February, 1996), D1, 4.

Sulcas, Roslyn. "Guarding a bright flame's afterglow", *New York Times* (16 September, 2010).

——. "Tanztheater Wuppertal, Edinburgh Playhouse", *Financial Times* (4 September, 2004), http://www.ft.com/cms/s/2/971ace9e-b6e9–11df-b3dd-00144feabdc0.html#axzz1jSijvIjH.

Supree, Burt. "Hit me with your best shot", *Village Voice* (7 October, 1984), 92.

Swed, Mark. " Culture monster: Pina Bausch remembered", *Los Angeles Times* (1 July, 2009), http://latimesblogs.latimes.com/culturemonster/2009/07/pina-bausch-remembered.htm.

——. "Tanztheater Wuppertal Pina Bausch is in the moment", *LA Times* (7 December, 2011), http://articles.latimes.com/2011/dec/07/entertainment/la-et-pina-bausch-critics-notebook-20111207.

Tobias, Tobi. "Cheering up", *Arts Journal* (21 November, 2004), http://www.artsjournal.com/tobias /2004/11/cheering_up.html.

——. "Pina Bausch trades wounded willow for sunny maidens in 'Nefes'", *Arts Journal* (11 December, 2006), http://www.artsjournal.com/tobias/2006/12/pina_bausch_trades_wounded_wil.html.

——. "What they did for love", *New York* (5 December, 1994), 135–36.

Vita, Kati. "Montreal", *Ballet News* 7(7), (January, 1986), 30–32.

Wachunas, Tom. "Next Wave Festival: Pina Bausch Tanztheater Wuppertal", *Dance Magazine* (April 1992), 100–101.

Wakin, Daniel J. "Pina Bausch, a German iconoclast who reshaped dance, dies at 68", *New York Times* (1 July, 2009), A31.

"Wuppertal in London", *Dance and Dancers* (October, 1987), 20–21.

Ward, Nathan. "Dance: hippo crit", *Village Voice* (7 October, 1997), 89.

Watts, Graham. "Pina Bausch 1940–2009", *Ballet Magazine* (July, 2009), http://www.ballet.co.uk/magazines/yr_09/jul09/obituary_pina_bausch_0609.htm.

——. "Tanztheater Wuppertal Pina Bausch: 'Kontakthof'", *Ballet Magazine* (May, 2010), http://www.ballet.co.uk/magazines/yr_10/may10/gw_rev_tanz theater_wuppertal_pina_bausch_0410.htm.

Welsh, Anne Marie. "Festival 'Bluebeard' taxes imagination", *San Diego Union* (8 June, 1984), A30.

——. "Olympic Festival opens to boos, bravos", *San Diego Union* (2 June, 1984), A24.

"What the critics say", *TDR* (Spring, 1986), 80–84.

Whitaker, Rick. "Paris", *Ballet Review* (Spring, 1994), 13–14.

Wiegand, Chris. "Pina Bausch, German choreographer and dancer, dies", *Guardian* (30 June, 2009), http://www.guardian.co.uk/stage/2009/jun/30/pina-bausch-dies-dancer.

——. "Pina Bausch tributes: 'She got the keys to your soul'", *Guardian* (3 July, 2009), http://www.guardian.co.uk/stage/2009/jul/03/pina-bausch-tributes.

Wilson, George Buckley Laird. "Edinburgh 1978", *The Dancing Times* (November, 1978), 90.

Yablonskaya, Linda. "Pina Bausch Tanztheater Wuppertal: Palermo, Palermo and Bandoneon", *High Performance* (Spring, 1992), 50.

Zinn, Radolyn. "Somebody nailed my dress to the wall", *3 Quarks Daily* (25 January, 2010), http://www.3quarksdaily.com/3quarksdaily/2010/01/somebody-nailed-my-dress-to-the-wall-a-glimpse-into-the-work-of-pina-bausch-by-randolyn-zinn.html.

V. Critical perspectives

Birringer, Johannes. "Pina Bausch: dancing across borders", *TDR* (Spring, 1986), 85–97.

Bowman, Michael, and Della Pollock. "'This spectacular body': politics and postmodernism in Pina Bausch's Tanztheater", *TPQ* 9(2), (1989), 113–18.

Brandstätter, Gabrielle. "The crisis of representation", *Ballett International/ Tanz Aktuell* (8 September 1994), 44–49.

Carter, Kathryn. "Response: residing on the line in between, or how not to resolve performative tensions", *TPQ* 9(2), (1989), 119–24.

Coates, Emily. "Beyond the visible legacies of Merce Cunningham and Pina Bausch", *PAJ: A Journal of Performance and Art*, PAJ 95, 32(2), (May, 2010), 1–7.

Cody, Gabrielle. "Woman, man, dog, tree: two decades of intimate and monumental bodies in Pina Bausch's Tanztheater", *TDR* (August, 1999), 115–31.

Daly, Ann (ed.). "Tanztheater: the thrill of the lynch mob or the rage of woman?" *TDR* (Spring, 1986), 46–56.

Fischer, Eva-Elisabeth. "Aesthetic Norms and Today's Social Taboos: The Effect on Innovation and Creativity." *Ballett International* 13(1), (January, 1990), 49–52.

Ferguson, Paul H. "Perspectives on the aesthetics of Pina Bausch's Tanztheater", *TPQ* 9(2), (1989), 99–106.

Fernandes, Ciane. *Pina Bausch and the Wuppertal Dance Theatre: the aesthetics of repetition and transformation*, New York: Peter Lang Publishing, 2001.

Finkel, Anita. "My model, my self", *New Dance Review* 3(3), (March, 1991), 3–6.

Goldberg, Marianne. "Artifice and authenticity: gender scenarios in Pina Bausch's Dance Theatre", *Women and Performance* 4(2), (1989), 104–17.

——. "Pina Bausch", *Women and Performance* 12(1), (1984), 98–101.

Hamera, Judith. "A post-Jungian perspective on repetition and violence in the Tanztheater of Pina Bausch", *TPQ* 9(2), (1989), 107–12.

Honegger, Gitta. "Form as torture: found meanings between Bausch and Kantor", *Theatre* 17(2), (Spring, 1986), 56–60.

Kerkhoven, Marianne van. "The weight of time", *Ballett International* 14(2), (February, 1991), 63–68.

Kirchman, Kay. "Room for the whole world: Pina Bausch and the architecture of her world view", *Ballett International/Tanz Aktuell* (October, 1998), 22–23.

——. "The totality of the body: an essay on Pina Bausch's aesthetic", *Ballett International/Tanz Aktuell* (May, 1994), 37–43.

Klemola, Timo. "Dance and embodiment", *Ballett International* 14(1), (January, 1991), 71–80.

Kozel, Susan. "Bausch and phenomenology", *Dance Now* 2(4), (Winter 93/94), 49–54.

Latham, Daniel. "Dancing Pina Bausch", *TDR* 54(1), (Spring, 2010), (T 205), 150–60.

Mumford, Meg. "Pina Bausch choreographs Blaubart: a transgressive or regressive act?" *German Life and Letters* 57(1), (2004), 44–57.

Nugent, Ann. "Altered states", *Dance Theatre Journal* 12(2), (Autumn, 1995), 16–20.

Pollock, Della. "The aesthetics and anti-aesthetics of postmodern performance: Pina Bausch's Tanztheater", *TPQ* 9(2), (1989), 97–98.

Price, David W. "The politics of the body: Pina Bausch's Tanztheater", *Theatre Journal* (October, 1990), 322–31.

Sanchez-Colberg, Ana. "'You put your left foot in, then you shake it all about … ' Excursions and incursions into feminism and Bausch's Tanztheater", Helen Thomas (ed.), *Dance, Gender and Culture*, New York: Macmillan, 1993, pp. 151–63.

Servos, Norbert: "About Bausch: Pina Bausch explores the existential through movement", *Dance International* 31(2), (Summer, 2003), 8–12.

——. "On the seduction of angels", *Ballett International* 8(12), (December, 1985), 72–76.

Wehle, Philippa. "Pina Bausch's Tanztheater – a place of difficult encounter", *Women and Performance* 1(2), (Winter, 1984), 25–36.

Winnacker, Susanne. "The body as art work: faithfullness in dance", *Ballett International/Tanz Aktuell* (November, 2000), 18–23.

Index